UnSafe

Forensic G
Firearms Acci

A tutorial on firearms design and function with an emphasis on safety, using past investigations of failures to better understand why some guns are safer than others, *by design.*

UnSafe by Design

Foreword

"UnSafe by Design" is a book that takes into account the truism that "knowledge is power" and in this case turns that knowledge to the advantage of anyone who owns, uses or is exposed to firearms by minimizing or avoiding the danger of unintentional or accidental discharges. It has been over half a century in the making. That's how long it has taken its author to develop his unusual and encyclopedic knowledge of this subject.

Part of the extended gestation period of the compilation of these chapters has been the reticence of the shooting sports media to address the subject of dangerous defects in firearms design and manufacture. To publicize those defects would have resulted in the quick ostracism of the firearms industry who jealously defend their market position. There would be no more perks and privileges awarded for favorable press. Additionally those critics would likely be labeled "anti-gun" by a public conditioned to a high level of trust.

Another factor has been the diligence with which the legal representatives of the industry have pursued "non-disclosure" rulings and agreements mandating that adverse trial results and discovery findings are kept secret. Sealed court records are the general rule. Settlements are reached on a regular basis predicated upon the preservation of "trade secrets," but which actually hide the presence of dangerous defects. The shooting public deserves better treatment. Firearms manufacturers are rightfully protected against crippling governmental edicts and regulations concerning gun design and manufacture, but the public should have access to the facts that would enable an informed decision as whether or not to acquire and use any particular make and model, and to decide how it may within reason be safely used.

It is this state of affairs that the author addresses in an unusually personal and informative format using the give and take of an instructional seminar, whose attendees and participants have a wide range of individual knowledge and viewpoints. By so doing he turns what could easily be a dry exercise in technological analysis into a lively forum for examination of hitherto largely unavailable data. He combines a sense of the practical design genius of John M. Browning with a down to earth explanation and application of his own extensive knowledge in the field. I share his passion and highly recommend "UnSafe by Design" to gun owners and users at any stage or level of their involvement with firearms.

John T. "Tom" Butters, P.E.

Acknowledgments

This work is a combination of actual experiences that could have been written by others present at the time but they either forgot, died, or haven't gotten around to it yet. I appreciate y'all holding back and letting me have a chance.

Without editors this work would be still in bits and pieces. Bill Rogers in the piney woods of Alabama worked for weeks prying readable English from disjointed gun-speak loose ideas and arranging too much information into one bundle. His job was much tougher than mine and I really don't know how he got it done. I'm in awe and really appreciate it.

Andy White is an editor without the Southern heritage and I finally talked him into just lightly pecking around the loose edges so the Yankees can read it instead of attacking with axes and matches. Thank you.

My sincere thanks to the late lawyers Rich Miller and Brandon Clark. Early on, they trained my passion for firearms and the truth into usable skills as an expert witness. My thanks also go out for the living attorneys and their able assistants that allowed me to share their passion for justice in offices and court rooms across the country. To E.C Gilbreath, Tim Monseese, Steven Drinnon, Todd Riff, Tom Guelzow, Matt Placzek and Jeff Hightower from whom I have borrowed portions of their cases and hopefully I've told the stories well enough to show my intentions are good even if the results aren't.

I really appreciate my 'audience' of old acquaintances, former students, fellow ex-deputies and very good friends. They asked great questions. Ron and Glenn Koenig, Paul Sannes, Chuck Pensyl, Adam Schultz, Mark Stokeld and Reid Coffield who all suffered through early drafts and offered valuable input. I thank you.

To old friends like Jimmy Dollar, Page Spracher, Kenny Stagmeyer and Les Nicholson who have suffered with my verbal frustrations at trying to get the truth to the right people, thank y'all, too.

To Tom Butters I lift a dewy, cool amber glass and salute a true
warrior. Without your guidance, encouragement, and wise council
I would have gotten myself in trouble even earlier.

I gratefully acknowledge the defense attorneys and their part in our
justice system and my growth as an expert. It is their job to defend
their client. I guess somebody has to do it. Without their
penetrating questions, many of the more important questions
would never be asked. It is only when we must explain that we
learn. That's why being a teacher is a great learning experience.

I want to thank the 'back row' for being my teaching aid. I would
like to hear from you. Emails are preferred over bombs or bullets.

The US Constitution deserves a mention too. Without it, I would
have grown up a crook because guns are my passion. I can't help
it.

About the Author

I started shooting when still in training pants and by the time I was in the third grade I knew what I was going to be when I grew up. Actually it swung back and forth between herpetology, veterinary medicine, and something to do with guns and hunting. By the time I was in the ninth grade, I hated school and everything about it *so* bad, I had stricken the professions requiring further class room work off my list forever.

The author in 1995 with a fine Sako Riihimaki chambered in 6mm CheapShot, a wildcat cartridge developed by Jack and his business partner Brian Shanks.

At fourteen I remodeled an old Short Magazine Lee-Enfield (SMLE) Jungle Carbine and by the following year had killed my first two whitetail bucks with it. I took apart guns I'd traded for at gunshows in the back of the building and traded them for others once I understood how such a thing could work. I got *serious*

©H.J. (Jack) Belk 2014

about studying guns and ammunition and handloading and ballistics and bench rest shooting and building my own shooting irons. Books, magazines, and patent documents centered on guns were my passion.

High school was just hourly imprisonment and I resented it even more. In the summer of '64 I guided fisherman and went barefooted for three months and then joined the Army when my classmates started the senior year. I graduated from high school six months before they did while serving in Korea as a small arms specialist. I was surrounded by hundreds of guns from .45 automatics to M-110, 8 inch howitzers... and had access to the ammo locker.

The Army sent me back to ATC-Ft. Benning in early 1966. There were 260 M-14s under my care and control and a lot of my duty was on the TrainFire ranges teaching others to shoot. By that time I was thankful I didn't strive to be assigned to the Marksmanship Training Unit over on main post. I knew some of those guys... they called it "making donuts." Same stuff every day. No challenge and little hope of it changing.

Duty was great for about six months and then my company commander was replaced by a lieutenant who really didn't like me. We had a 'history' together in Korea and he was not in a good mood. He sent me off to the infiltration course and grenade range, anywhere I was out of his sight. The Army had finally focused my attention, but then they left the ammo and explosives just lying around to focus the attention of others on *me*. That's not good but it can sure be entertaining.

I don't like repetition, but the Army is full of it. The Infiltration Course was the fake combat situation with trainees crawling under barbed wire, while me and three other NCOs shot locked-down1919 Browning machine guns over their heads. Simulators blew mud all over them and the red tracers streaking overhead made it all pretty realistic, but very boring to the guys sitting behind the guns and pushing buttons.

Each burst of five was followed by a burst of three, then another five. Then the guy next in line shot his the same way. The guns were fixed and the impact area totally 'broken in' so every tracer arced out to about 800 yards and ricocheted to the right because the 1919 barrels, as are most American barrels, were right hand twist. It was very pretty to see for about five minutes. We had six hours a night, six nights a week, rain or shine, hot or cold, and three thousand rounds a night for each gun. We switched barrels twice a week. I knew the guy in supply that delivered the barrels to the range and for a trade of mess hall coffee, he brought me a genuine BSA 30 USA '06, 1919 barrel made in England just after WW-I. It had left hand twist, and I had a hundred rounds of NATO green tracers.

Sandhills of Nebraska in 2000 with Rufus the Lab and 12 ga. Merkel 201ET.

The next night the boredom was broken for the first time since six artillery simulators went off all at once in the water filled bunker. I was on the number three gun in the moonless dark at midnight when we switched barrels, re-headspaced and timed each gun. The cadence of shooting became second nature and the right hand ricochets were normal. So were the steady streams of WW-II red tracers. My lime green Italian NATO tracers shot from a Brit barrel that zinged the ricochets hard left were an entertaining novelty that didn't even get anybody wet. Unfortunately (maybe), it was done in too close of proximity to a serious officer and I found myself assigned to the grenade range. Practical jokes are harder there, but not impossible.

By the time I entered the Colorado School of Trades (CST) in Denver, just two weeks after an honorable discharge in South Georgia, I knew a lot about guns but nothing much about how to work on them. I needed Machine Shop and Welding/soldering and Metallurgy training. CST supplied all a student could ask for. The information was there, but it had to be asked for. I learn very fast in a Q&A setting, and CST was an interesting and very educational time.

Jim Johnson was my Design and Functions instructor and he had a great talent for asking very good questions in response to my dumb ones. By answering his pointed questions about mechanics and constantly reminding me to "Remember Newton!" I grasped the 'modality' of firearms and was able to better recognize what makes some work and others fail. I also learned a very valuable lesson in accident investigations that has served me well in the forty-odd years since. Jim said, "Know what to look for *before* you take anything apart."

"D&F" class usually started with the student showing up with nothing pressing for him to do that day. All students worked on projects for the customers of the school, or their own gun projects, and some days you'd be assigned a lathe and some days you needed to blue something and other days Jim Johnson knew you could be tortured with his knowledge. He soon found out that I looked forward to the days when I 'had his ear' and he had my attention.

The school has a big rack of old guns that have been cut away in parts and pieces so the inner workings can be taught in a classroom or in one-on-one demonstrations. There're guns still complete but obviously accustomed to being in pieces as training aids, too. Jim would meet you at your bench just as you opened your locker and toolbox and say, "See me before lunch to go over this gun."

"Go over" to Jim Johnson was to listen to you recite the name, location, job and connecting parts to each and every part of the subject gun given that morning. He wanted the cycle of operation from fired to ready to fire again and then would come the 'what if' quiz. What if this part breaks or that pivot comes out?

The gun parts were in cigar boxes or baking tins, and the big parts like barrels and stocks were in longer boxes. All morning long those parts would be transformed in your memory from the page of a parts book to 3D understanding of actually what made the things work. Nomenclature, terms, and odd names of parts common to all guns suddenly started making more sense. The 'firing pin retractor return spring' and 'action bar lock take-down pin retaining spring' suddenly made sense in the Model 12 Winchester, and a 'map' of names and places and actions began to complete my gun design education.

One of Jim's favorite teaching methods was to drop a part not belonging to the gun you were studying in your parts box... and take one out. He tested students by dropping in a part you'd already studied. He'd grin like a possum if you could catch his switch and name the parts involved. "All right Jim, give me back my A-5 carrier pivot lock screw, and you can have back the Python crane cap screw." would get you a beer after school. He'd talk guns with anybody.

Almost immediately upon graduating and taking a job as a general gunsmith back in my home town of Tallahassee, Florida, I was asked to investigate an accidental discharge of a rifle that blew apart the victim's knee when it 'fired on safety release'. I remembered what Jim Johnson had just recently told me: "Know what you're looking for before messing with it."

That Remington Model 722 in .222 Remington caliber started a quest for the truth that continues to this day. Little did I know how that first investigation would open a Pandora's Box of information that has come at a very high cost to many people. As with any subject, the further a person delves into it, the more of it becomes visible.

After nearly fifty years of study of a wide variety of firearms, turn-bolt rifles are my passion, and the study of the nuances of the designs is, to me, a fascinating subject. In that study have come some surprising discoveries that leave a sour taste in one that wants future generations to have the same freedoms I enjoy.

It's time to tell the stories and the secrets. They are not well known.

Oakley, Idaho in 2010 with a custom made turn-bolt in 6x51BS, another of the author's wildcats. The receiver and bolt came from a Remington Model 722. The scope came from Leupold and the scope rings from Conetrol, but the rest of the gun started out as blanks or raw steel. It could almost qualify as a 'Hunter Class Benchrest Rifle', but it's a bit heavy.

Introduction

"It just went off!"

Those are the most dreaded words ever spoken by a shooter and many times they're too true. An 'accidental shooting' can occur several different ways and bullets don't have brakes. The seconds after that loudest of noises are filled with the most deeply seated dread and most serious of questions: *Who might I have killed? What might I have hit? Where in the world did that land? When will I know for sure?*

How in the world did that just happen?

Whether by human error committed at the gun, or a human error at the factory, an explanation needs to be forthcoming. Guns don't 'just shoot'. There is a reason, and it can be deduced using tried and true mechanical facts as a basis.

Mechanical things obey several laws: One is of their make and origin. They can't help it, they were made that way. Another set of important laws are those of physics as described by Sir Isaac Newton. The last 'law' is Murphy's: If something can go wrong it will, and at the worst time.

Firearms are mechanical things that initiate a chemical reaction by committing an impact on the primer of whatever ammunition it shoots. All sporting guns we'll be discussing supply that impact by way of stored energy in simple springs. There are no hidden wires or tubes or power sources, only springs that have received their initial charge of energy from a human being, the 'shooter'.

Guns are, by definition, only useful and safe when loaded but controlled by a person. Gravity has to be guarded against, and misuse by humans is always bad, but otherwise guns are instruments of power projection to a distant place at the time of the shooter's choosing, but at no other. To protect against shooting without command of a person, guns are designed with certain features and details that make them 'safe'.

The shooter chooses to shoot by way of a *trigger.* The shooter

-11-   ©H.J. (Jack) Belk 2014

chooses to wait to shoot by way of the *safety*.

Over more than twenty years of intense study of some of the mechanisms that have failed in their duty of staying quiet until told to bark, it's easier to take some of the sentiment out of firearms and examine each for specific features of design to determine how the gun was supposed to behave, and more importantly how it failed, simply by *looking* at it really *close*.

So close at times it takes a scanning electron microscope to see the 'tracks' of the energy gone astray, but at the heart of it all we must know exactly where to look for those energy tracks and what they mean. 'Following the energy' from input by a person or gravity to the cartridge primer is the trail we'll follow using Newton's predictions of behavior and the best witnesses we have: the shooter, or the survivors... and the guns themselves.

Sometimes there are no survivors but the guns.

I've enlisted some help in this effort primarily because I'm not organized enough to do it on my own. In addition to editors that remind me why I had to forge English teacher's signatures to have good enough grades in school to go hunting on the weekends, I have incorporated an audience of two groups into the body of this work. Several I've invited here have asked why they were selected for this punishment. My reply is so that others (hopefully) won't have to suffer in order to get the important information. All it'll cost them is money.

One group wants to know the unvarnished truth... or just hear me talk about guns because they love them like I do. They are active students of things gun-related because they're interested in the guns themselves, how they work and how they fail. Some are here because they're interested in the people affected by the guns blamed. Some are victims themselves, maybe not of a gunshot wound, but of the uncertainty that comes from not knowing how such a powerful and mysterious tool could suddenly go so wrong.

Many of this group are new to the mechanics of firearms and need background and history and context. I count on them to ask for clarity.

Their comments and questions are in plain italics.

The group on the back row is varied and mostly real. The doubters, the naysayers, the experts and the uninformed many times take on the same characteristics. Their questions are often cynical, sarcastic, rhetorical, personal and very tough. I want it that way, so I invited them here. Please excuse their passion while appreciating their position.

Most in the back row are now or want to be in 'the gun business'. They are the ones that most need this information but the least likely to listen to it. I will answer all their questions and invite debate.

They'll speak in bold italics.

This is written as a lecture.

<Sometimes I think to myself or make side comments between these arrows.>

The world of guns in America is a political minefield about three-deep in mines. I'm pro-gun, pro-Second Ammendment, and a champion of responsibility. But, I view that responsibility as a two-way business deal. No matter if I'm the customer or the seller I should know without a doubt what I'm buying and exactly what I'm selling because by any definition, guns are dangerous just like airplanes are 'dangerous' no matter how 'safe' they are. It is my view they should not be even more dangerous *by design*. Some are, and it's time to tell their story.

Guns don't come from pet stores. The manufacturers can't claim environment and lack of love made their product bite the owner or others without actual evidence of it. Guns are not puppies; they are the slaves of their designer and their makers. Some are specialists at certain duties. We'll talk about what those purposes and duties are and most of all what are their limitations.

My goal is the perpetuation of the shooting sports through education of its fans and proponents. I strive for greater safety in the shooting sports through better understanding of the basic principals of firearms design.

This book introduces the field of "Forensic Gunsmithing." Through a tutorial on firearms design and function, I'll be using past investigations of failures in a wide variety of guns to better understand how and why the guns hurt or killed someone and how that relates to the gun business today.

What follows is half a century of insider information, observations, facts, evidence, opinion and commentary, but to make it portable by one person I cut out a lot.

1. Setting the Stage

We never know when something learned will be useful. Lessons learned as a kid about hot things and high places, and a thousand other lessons of how best to live our lives without pain and regrets form our existence. Many successful people knew at an early age what their place in life was going to be and a pretty good idea of how to get there.

Dick Cabela, who went on to build a tremendous series of outdoor stores, drew pictures of what those stores would look like when he was twelve years old. Many people have a good map of the way ahead by the early teens. That was the case with me. Guns would be my life in some way or other because they were fascinating to me then. It took many years to find out why and by that time it was lawyers asking hours of very specific questions that finally gelled my life with guns into a form that's finally easier to explain because I've had to do it so many times.

I knew I was going to be a gunsmith before puberty. It was just going to happen, and as soon as possible. 'As soon as possible' was right after three years in the Army, in Denver, at the Colorado School of Trades, sitting on a metal stool and working on some gun in the center of the D&F, or Design and Function section, and near graduation. My good shooting and fishing buddy, Will, came toddling over in my direction, but veered off to retrieve a shotgun from another student's locker. I watched him pick up the Model 1897 and, being left-handed, he had the whole right side to me as he pushed the action bar lock button to open the slide. It blew pieces of glass and 20 years of thick dust in all directions but the load of goose shot went up through the light shade and safely into the ceiling.

The memory of an unintended discharge is deeply burned and long remembered.

There was an investigation and I was a witness. Little did I know it would shape my life. From that investigation to the several open files on my desk now, I've learned things that should be passed along. They need to be passed along. They *have* to be passed along. Otherwise, we shooters are being painted into a corner of our own making.

My first love is and always has been firearms. I wish everybody enjoyed them as I do and I wish there wan't pain involved with them, but it's too late for that. Now, how can that pain be lessened without killing the guns that I love? I'll let the class ask the questions that might provide the answers we all need to hear.

In the meantime, *respect* firearms because they're made by mankind and all men are fallible, especially where money is involved.

We'll jump into some pretty complicated subjects early on and then circle back to fill in the details about them. The subject of safe firearms design is not well known, but with just a few rules to go by, can be understood by the layman as well as the mechanics that work with guns. There will be some very specific examinations into the very hearts of several firing mechanisms that are of particular interest.

It might disappoint some that we don't go into blow up failures much at all. They're lumped into two categories: Obstructions and Metallurgy. If you see a barrel split from end to end, it was a 'long' obstruction, usually either ice or grease. 'Short' failures are from stuck patches, bullets or cleaning rods. Chambers fail by high pressure or poor metallurgy. Cases fail by lack of support. I'll answer specific questions if you like.

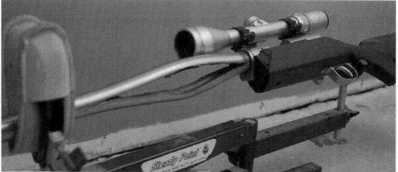

Savage 10ML-II muzzleloader. The barrel obstruction that caused this wreck was the bullet itself. It wasn't properly seated on a smokeless powder charge.

We'll be talking about guns primarily made for the civilian, sporting and home/self defense markets. The basic designs go back at least a hundred years and many times even older. We define a 'firearm' as a mechanical device that initiates a chemical reaction that projects one or more 'bullets' to a distant place at a specific time. A person holds it and it doesn't have batteries, pneumatics, hydraulics, plasma power sources or electronics. Guns operate by *springs.*

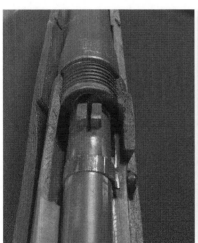

Springfield '03-A3 blowup. The case is still in the chamber and the bullet is still in the barrel. That's an indication of a very fast pistol powder used by mistake. Note the safety lever is completely gone.

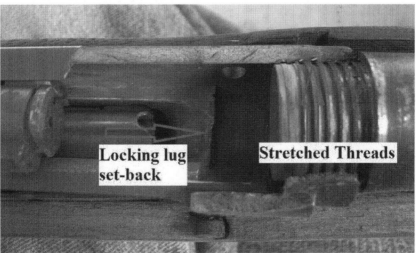

Springfield '03-A3 showing locking lug and thread damage

Guns are a hot button issue for most people and anything said critical of any of them tends to bring an immediate negative reaction from those that truly love them. Some of this reaction is ill-informed and counter productive. The goal here is to explain how guns sometimes fail by using tried and true techniques of investigations that work in other products and mechanisms, and equally well in firearms. We will 'follow the energy' from where it came from and track it to the primer.

First, the foundations…

Some guns *do* fail. That one statement has probably raised the blood pressure of many in attendance and I already hear the silent screams of denial. Please bear with me, I can prove it.

The second question is almost always, "Is mine one of them?"

We will be concentrating on post WW-II guns because that's when guns changed from durable goods to consumer goods, but nobody bothered to tell the customers. As in all consumer goods, price plays a larger part in the decision to buy. This has become a real problem and it will be addressed all through this course. My goal is to teach each of you how to determine the inherent safety of your specific firearm. I don't know them all and they change almost overnight in everything but model number.

Most are very surprised to learn the Consumer Products Safety Commission has no role in firearms design, manufacture or sale. The Second Amendment assures the rights of Americans to defend ourselves and our neighbors. "Shall Not Be Infringed" means exactly what it says and that precludes some bureaucracy dictating how guns will be made. It is perfectly legal to design, manufacture, market and sell a firearm that is *not* safe in any manner and is so made as to nearly guarantee failure. There are such guns on the market today and we'll be talking about some of them later on.

We will sort out guns by how they operate and how big they are and what kinds of ammo they shoot, but to keep it as simple as possible, the first division discussed is between the *un-cocked* guns and the *cocked* guns. I prefer 'inert' to describe the guns that are exactly that, but the words may not mean much until you know what operates a firearm.

'Lock, Stock and Barrel' describes a couple hundred years worth of firearms history. The 'lock' is the firing mechanism, the stock the wooden handle and the barrel contains both the chamber and the barrel. Modern guns use an 'action' or 'receiver' that serves as a foundation to support the barrel, the feed mechanism and the fire control group. There are few real differences in many different guns.

Winchester M70 post-'64 in .300 Win Mag. This was caused by a light charge of very slow burning powder. Note the front bolt lugs are sheared off and a piece is stuck to the casing. The shooter lost an eye from this wreck.

All the guns we'll be talking about operate on two very basic principals...

1) **Energy** has to be fed to the gun by a human being

2) Energy is stored in the gun until needed by way of **springs**.

The guns we're studying are collections of cams, plungers, levers, springs and pivots. Cams and levers change directions and can multiply forces, springs store energy, plungers deliver energy, and the pivots and screws hold it all together. A 'housing' or 'receiver' is the box the parts go in. That could be the shortest gunsmithing course on earth.

Energy by a human is what compresses or deflects springs which in turn will eventually drive the firing pin into the primer. For that very reason, guns are fairly easy to figure out. There are no phantom power sources. Only human energy input and our ever-present gravity have any effect on a firearm. If we can figure out where the power came from to compress the mainspring, we should be able to figure out how that power was released and how it got to the primer. By design, that energy should never be released except by the actions of the shooter.

Winchester M70 blowup. It takes a lot of force to do that kind of damage.

We'll talk about the family of inert guns, but for our immediate purposes, the family of guns that are somehow cocked, and a period of time goes by until they're fired, will be the focus. The 'kinetic' guns have parts that are under tension and they fail most often and with the most mystery about them.

Kinetic guns fire by one of two means: a swinging hammer or a plunging striker. It is the firing pin that hits the primer and it's the primer that we never want to hit by mistake. The firing pin can be part of the hammer or striker or a separate part, but the firing pin is impacted by one or the other to fire. To prevent a gun from firing takes some sort of 'safety'. There are many kinds and many variables in performance in myriad mechanical safeties. We'll be discussing some that don't work *as designed.*

Ah sir, let's cut to the chase. There are no unsafe guns, only unsafe people.

Thanks for that comment. You are correct. People are unsafe, some more so than others. That's why gun *design* is so cotton pickin' *important!*

What I hope to address here is: If people are basically unsafe, why in the world would a gun manufacturer double the chances of death by designing an unsafe gun for them to use? Some guns are safe by the way they are designed to operate. Some are not. We're here to find out how to tell them apart.

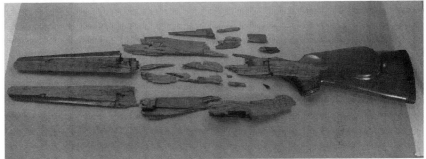

Winchester M70 blowup. The stock literally exploded in the shooter's hands.

Aren't all guns safe because they.....I guess it's against the law to make one that isn't... isn't it?

There are no laws against guns with *design flaws*. Some of those flaws *will* kill the shooter and can kill anybody within a mile or two. Many of these defects and mistakes and flaws are not well known. They're only known because somebody got sued and a lawyer hired investigators that *really* looked hard to find what must have happened, to a degree of mechanical certainty. A witness then put his entire life on the line by swearing under oath that's how it must have happened. Gun accidents in general are rare and to trace them to a mechanical failure is much more so. Those failures are very important because of the deadly *nature* of firearms.

Sir, you said springs made the guns work. Can you expand on that?

Sure can. Springs are the very foundation of all guns and it's important to know how they act and react. Springs are like gravity, but they operate in any direction. All we have to do is point it in the right direction and figure out a way to keep it compressed until it's needed. Springs are what return gun parts to their proper position. I use 'gravity' as a comparable force because it's so dependable. Springs can 'wear out' but that takes a lot of wearing. Consider a compressed spring just like a weight held off the ground. If given a chance, it *will* fall. That is its natural job.

Firearms use springs of every type in a wide variety of places doing different jobs, but the one that makes the firing pin hit the primer is the one we're going to be worrying about. The rest of the springs in the gun usually just return a part that's been moved by another part back to its original position. It is that particular *main* spring that transfers the energy the shooter put into the gun to the chemical pellet that's going to shoot something. If that one spring is not controlled reliably, what gets shot might not be the target intended. How that one spring is operated tells us a lot about the gun's *design*, too.

1) Hammer fired
2) Striker fired.

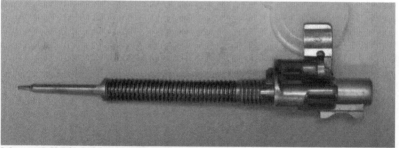

Mauser M98 bolt interior. Firing pin and striker are made into a single piece.

These terms refer to what hits or is connected to the firing pin. Hammers can be internal or external, but strikers are all internal.

Hammers swing through an arc around a pivot, strikers move linearly. In some designs the striker and firing pin are a single part, in others they're separate pieces.

Hammers look and work much like the tool they're named after. The fancy flintlock hammers looked like rooster heads and so gained the name 'cock'. That's where 'cocked the gun' comes from; pulling back the rooster's head. I guess his backbone is the mainspring.

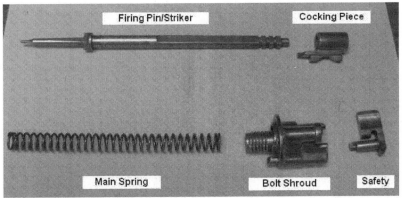

Mauser M98 bolt interior exploded view

No matter if hammer fired or striker fired, the strongest and most important spring in the entire gun drives them. It's called the 'mainspring' or 'hammer spring' or 'striker spring'. It can be a coil spring that's compressed or a leaf spring that's deflected. Both are storing the energy the primer needs to fire.

The control of that strong mainspring is the job of the 'fire control group' or 'trigger group'. In that assembly will also be the means of preventing the gun from firing unless the trigger is pulled. That is called the 'safety'. The safety should *never* fail, but some do... *by design*.

2. Accident Investigation

A gunsmith is called on once in a while to answer a question for the cops or game wardens or a reporter doing background work. Once in a great while a customer wants to know how his gun hurt somebody.

My first one came just months after starting work at a big gunshop in Tallahassee. A local college student hung out at the gunshop between classes. One day he brought in a Remington Model 722 in .222 Remington caliber and asked me to figure out how it had shot his father-in-law in the left knee. Just the thought of such a wound made me cringe.

Remington M722 in .222 Remington. Made 1950, first year of production.

I thought of Jim Johnson and his rather pointed instructions for such cases and I also thought of his comment in class one day that, "Remington triggers are 'good' but they're a collection of parts flying in loose formation. Don't trust them." I had adjusted some and cleaned a bunch of them and had no idea how it fired unexpectedly, but I was sure curious enough to try to find out. The customer made arrangements for me to meet the victim and ask all the questions I wanted about how it happened.

The house was small, close and hot and that big ball of bandages kept my attention as he told me of idling through the piney woods in search of a turkey. His rifle rode resting on the front seat with the muzzle on the floorboard. He said the scope made it swing down and ride upside down most of the time.

He saw turkeys running from a field through the scattered trees and hurried up to try for a shot before they crossed the road in front of him. He turned the truck to the right while stopping it and reaching for the rifle, all at the same time, while watching one hen get uncertain and start to turn back. She would be his soon. He had the rifle by the grip and had just grabbed the forend with the left hand to swing it left and out the window when he flipped the safety switch to OFF and the rifle fired a 50 grain hollow point into the top right of his left knee just under the knee cap. He kept talking even though I had had plenty of details for one case. That big wad of bandage and the smell of medicine in an overly warm house had my claustrophobia tuned up and I was ready to go!

Back at the shop, I took two old Remington triggers apart and studied everything about them (I thought at the time) and finally figured out how to test what I called the Turkey rifle to see if it failed the only way I could figure it could have. It did! I could see movement inside the trigger as the 'connector' got displaced when I tapped on the rifle action to duplicate riding upside down on a washboard dirt road. I gave my report to the customer and his father-in-law and devised a way to repair the trigger by attaching the connector to the trigger body with epoxy and then regrinding the rear to take a *design flaw* out of the trigger.

Why grind on it?

That question is ahead of it's time, but you'll soon see the epoxy will fail if you don't.

The information was passed on to Remington at the next NRA show because the shop I worked in had no direct dealings with them. We bought Remington's from a jobber but our main supplier was Browning. As a brand new gunsmith, maybe I'd found a solution to my customer's problem rifle, but I had no way of knowing that nearly 50 years later I'd be answering questions under oath about it!

Why didn't they just recall them then when you could see the way it shot the guy?

It's so easy to wonder that now. The Model 722 was a very early gun and I'd already noticed the later Remington triggers had a [-

shaped connector that should solve the problem I saw in the Turkey rifle.

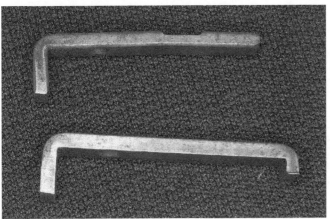

Remington-Walker trigger Connectors. Early design on top.

I didn't know any better and had plenty else on my mind rather than find out. The truth is truly scary, but it's certainly not well known. I'm trying to fix that.

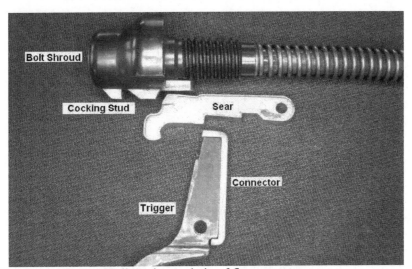

M700 Remington-Walker trigger, chain-of-fire components.

Let me give just a little history and context as to how a high-school drop-out became an 'engineer' in the eyes of the Court.

Becoming a 'commercial' gunsmith with a shingle hanging outside and regular business hours is like any other job as a mechanic....or doctor. Information has to be gathered in a meaningful fashion and a 'picture' of the failure formulated and the possible and probable causes pretty much figured out from the description given by the customer. Guns are a 'group' of mechanisms tied together in the middle to make them all work together. If the customer says the gun isn't feeding or extracting or ejecting or firing, it's clear the problem lies in the feeding group, extractor, ejector or 'something' in the trigger group.

Of course, it's common for the customer to say something like this, "H'it ain't rejectin' jus' right but it shore do hurt when it finally shoots!" It took me totally by surprise to hear my customer's version of proper gun nomenclature and it took a while to figure out a 'splunge' was usually a spring and plunger working together...or not. I had been a total gun nut since single digits of age and had no idea gun *owners* can be so oblivious to the simplest of gun facts. Many of them insist on proving their ignorance by preaching total BS to whoever is standing around at the time.

"My daddy brought back his GI .45 automatic from the big war and filed on the sear to make it full automatic. I learned how to shoot with that gun. It would strike a kitchen match at 50 yards every time, if you held it just right." All you can do is roll your eyes and hope the moron leaves before you have to run him off. It could be that's why so many good gunsmiths are known as total asses. I just ask you to consider the source, please.

We think they have a point.

Y'all could be right. As Justin Wilson the great Cajun cook and humorist used to say, "Maybe a little story will help."

Brian Shanks and I started Belk and Shanks Gunworks in Carbondale, Colorado on a combined sixty five dollars in cash in a bank bag and a desire to combine his existing gun trading and pawn shop with my extensive collection of machine tools in a new location. We would specialize in custom gun work, used gun sales and hopefully we'd be able to pay the monthly bills with 'commercial gunsmithing' work from walk-in and shipped-in traffic.

We signed a $60K lease when we still had $40 in the bag but Brian traded for an M-19 S&W at lunch, sold it before we got back to the shop and we made a tidy $200. Astute gun trading bought wiring and used stuff from a recycle place and we turned a restaurant into a gunshop.

The gun repair business exploded once the shop was wired and ready to work because there was no one else in the valley that could do quality work. We were in the heart of Colorado's big game area and out of state hunters took word back home of an old fashioned gunshop with a guy that could fix or build most anything you brought in the door *but*, he didn't work on junk and wasn't shy about passing judgment on it, either. We had a 'reputation' in about a year. The shooting editor of Guns and Ammo wrote several complimentary articles about our work and the UPS guy had to work hard bringing guns from all over to be rechambered or tuned according to the latest Seyfried article.

Brian Shanks (left) and the author in the late 1990s. Those are albino Rockchucks, possibly from the same litter.

A very good friend and fellow deputy sheriff once said, "To inventory the nuts in any area, first stake out the gunshop." He had a point.

There seems to be a steady stream of talkative people with nothing to do but share wasted time with somebody else. They occupy a gunshop about two to one compared to paying customers. Some lasting friendships can be made that way, and have, but some are a real pain in the ass! One such hanger-rounder at BSGW was Hunter S. Thompson. He lived about 30 miles up the valley and Brian had at one time been a (bad) neighbor to him when he ran the race track at Woody Creek, but they'd come to an uneasy truce in later years.

Hunter would nod at Brian, usually firmly ensconced in an easy chair and unwilling to be bothered by a customer anyway, and make a straight line for my service window to holler loudly, "What are you doing today!?" One time I was engraving when he did that and I broke him of it.

He would stand at the window and tell me of every gun he ever owned, wanted to own, nearly owned, sold by mistake or was going to soon buy. He would ramble on about impossible shots and impossible guns and then say, "I happen to have one with me." and go out to get another ugly, black piece of stamped metal and plastic crap I'd rather not have around and I sure wasn't going to work on it. I have no idea how he functioned as well as he did, but we never saw him before late afternoon.

There are times when two gears come together with slightly different geometry. They work OK, but there's a hum that eventually gets louder and then they solve the problem by coming apart in a semi-explosion. I had a Fiat that did that one time. Hunter Thompson and I were that way, too. I'd had enough of his company.

One afternoon Brian gave me a warning that Hunter was on the way in the door. I made sure I had something to do on the lathe so my back was to him at the window and he knew damn good and well not to holler, so I let him cool his heels a few minutes before turning off and around to 'finally see him there.' He bitched about the wait and the traffic and how bad he felt and then said he had a gun for me to see. He brought in a German MP-40 machine gun in a black case. I asked him for the tax papers and he said, "didn't think to bring them." I used the opportunity to '86' him from the store forever and told him if he ever came back inside I would whip his ass and then call the cops. He was so out of it he nearly started crying. Our gears had shed their teeth.

He had the gall to have the Pitkin County (Aspen) sheriff call me and try to tell me I was wrong and that he was really harmless enough. I told him I was very tired of a doped up idiot hanging around the shop and I considered H.S. Thompson a danger to the public and would not have him around and to please pass along he was to never come in again. It worked. I never saw him again.

We also had many 'celebrities' that did business with us and some fun times were had when Buddy Hackett came by to talk about his extra fine Colt single-action collection and check out the latest projects in progress in the shop. He always had a long, drawn out joke to tell. Race car drivers, sports personalities and all sorts of actors and actresses occasionally came 'down valley' to be seen by the natives and many would come in to buy or talk. My wife was the bookkeeper and nearly fainted when she saw I'd sold a gun to Kurt Russell. I'm not a movie guy and didn't know him, but the gun was for his son and he shot sporting clays with us. It is a small world sometimes.

We also had a guy that was there daily for a couple of months in a pick-up camper truck. He'd park outside while wasting a lot of Brian's time with questions with no purchases in mind and even stay there while Brian and I went to lunch....a ritual reserved for us and very few close friends. When we returned, 'Max', or whatever his name was, would be there waiting to come back in and tell of his Vietnam war injuries and disabilities and his great life as a rancher somewhere about 30 miles east but a whole mountain range and ski town away.

One day he asked me very quietly to do a little machine work on the QT. My BS antenna went to full attention as he described having the drawing of the parts pocket of an AR-15 to accept the full auto parts, and he just needed me to work about an hour on my milling machine to do it....no parts in the shop, just the drawings. I drew a slow breath before answering because that question always comes from one of two kinds of people and I don't especially like either one. Such a conversation is either a trap or a conspiracy. Either way it puts a gunsmith out of business forever and never worth the gamble.

I've been around machine guns since about age sixteen when I saw my first M-2 Carbine at a gunshow. Once I saw how the full auto sear operated, my curiosity was pretty much satisfied. Not so satisfied I didn't make a few just to 'make sure I fully understood the principal', you understand. I shudder to think of some of the very foolish 'just so I fully understand' experiments I survived.

In the Army in Korea, I had M-60s and M-14s in my arms room. I learned before I left highschool that somebody else needs to be paying the ammo bill if you're really into the full auto stuff. In that case, they're great fun.

After what I considered a significant and ponderous pause, I told 'Max' that my milling machine was for good guns for good purposes, and I didn't want to hear anymore about it. I gave my standard advice to "buy the two hundred dollar stamp, go about it legally and then you can laugh at the deputy that answers the call of full auto fire because you're legal. Compared with your ammunition bill, the tax stamp is chicken feed."

I told Brian to watch out for Max.

A week later, Max said he had a steer that needed shot and he'd do that if we'd clean up the bandsaw enough to cut meat one night after work, and he'd halve the steer with us. I hired my son to spend several hours cleaning the bandsaw of wood and metal chips and we bought rolls of wrapping paper and tape and set up folding tables. We were ready to cut up a beef in the back room of the gunshop.

Max never showed up. Not that night with a beef, or ever again. I was curious enough to try to find out who he was and went looking south of Vail at the ranch he supposedly ran and found another rancher there instead. Nobody had heard of him. The driver's license he gave to buy a gun from Brian was bogus as was the license plate on his truck. It's really good to know the right people in law enforcement that can give a good guy that good information. It's illegal to do so, I think, but it told us he was somehow 'officially' bad and not just a phony.

A month went by with no sign of Max but right at quitting time, with Brian already gone, another guy came in and told me quietly he had a TRW National Match M-14 for sale....cheap. My BS antenna did a victory lap. The gun was one of the National Match guns with a gloss finished stock done for state rifle teams competing at Camp Perry. That was the last bait of an elaborate scheme to entrap Brian and me into something illegal. I'll talk guns with anybody and anybody that pays attention soon learns the TRW M-14 is the only gun I want and can't own. Max had sent an assistant to see if I'd rise to that most delicious of bait. We had talked about M-14s many times. That sure was a beauty!!!

It was about two years later, when I was in another job and in another state that I saw Max again. He was chatting with a clerk in a big shop in a big town with a shady reputation, just like he'd chatted with me and Brian. He saw me looking at him and next thing I knew he was close by me and whispering to please keep the peace. I did and the shop went down not long after that for some very bad stuff. At least I knew for sure who 'Max' was. Brian was furious at the confirmation even though we'd agreed to call Max an undercover guy long before we knew for sure.

What was the point of all that?

<...asked the lady on row two>

Thank you, ma'am, like I said, I'll talk guns with anybody! I'll try to stick to things that actually teach something but to do that I have to tell you how I learned to investigate firearms functions by 'following the energy' in my own way.

Ah, what does Max look like?

Max looks like any guy that asks you to break the law.

I'm convinced that understanding mechanics must be a 'talent' much like music. From the time I was about eight years old, I could read patent drawings and figure out parts movements by staring long enough at the Stoeger's Shooter's Bible parts drawings.

At twelve, I designed a palm-fired, two shot pistol. By fifteen I'd remodeled a military rifle into a deer rifle and killed my first two bucks with it. But, I've tried for 35 years to play the guitar and still can't tell one note from another.

Asking 'why' something works as it does or looks as it does is natural to me. So much so that it surprises me when somebody hasn't considered the geology of where they live or how their hunting rifle works. 'Mechanics' is the key to my interest. Maybe it's because the 'talent' makes them easy to understand.

Just last month I asked a teenager to really examine a common locking blade folding knife to figure out what parts he needed to make to duplicate it. He couldn't properly analyze any aspect of how those two simple levers worked and where the spring had to be located but was hidden from his view. That's also the worst case of purely limited anecdotal evidence ever presented, but it's the latest personal experience I have with those that look at pliers as a mechanical mystery.

It is said that 40% of college students don't know how to change a tire. Think of what a rare occurrence it is to get twelve people on a jury that can learn what needs to be learned in about three hours of stilted, lawyer language questions.

"Why does it not work?" is a question I can usually answer IF the energy flow is caused by a human or gravity. If a controller tripped a relay that energized a cylinder that applied the force...somebody else needs to figure it out. Wires are for pulling in my world, not for transmitting an invisible energy.

Showing a talent for something will many times grease the skids in otherwise tough duty. In Korea I got lucky and missed the gun battery assignments and instead got into a job that got me in contact with the guy that had the key to the Arms Room, and through him and some serious politicking for an E-2 private, got assigned there. Once in the arms room with hundreds of guns to study and maintain, I made contact with the Battalion officer that had the keys to the ammo dump. He liked to shoot too, so we got along and through him I was assigned Battalion pre-IG inspector and even gave oral arguments before all the Battalion officers as to readiness, cleanliness and proper inventories of all the small arms.

Back in the states at Fort Benning in the Army Training Center there, the job of firearms study, use, maintenance and operation, and teaching it to others became a natural part of where ever I was assigned. One of the duties most unit armorers hated was the four hours of classroom time spent teaching the M-14 service rifle. I rather enjoyed it so was assigned to teach it to six training companies every two months. I've often thought of how much easier it would be to teach a jury about a gun if I could use the same techniques.

Ft. Benning at Sand Hill in the mid '60s was a newly reactivated batch of WW-II barracks that had coal heat and no air conditioning. Coats of paint and barrels of Johnson's Wax held them together. In summer time, the mess hall would be stifling hot while 240 troops with their rifles learned what they were shooting, how it worked, how it came apart, what needed cleaning and how often, and how to get it all back together again and how to test it without shooting it. In summer it was miserable. In wintertime the coal fumes and soldier sweat was sometimes worse. We resorted to firecrackers to keep troops awake in some places and the sound of a Zippo lighter was enough to wake up a bunch of them after just a few easy applications. The class was four hours long with the first one being theory and history and why it's so important to know what you're doing. Up to that point, their rifle had only been a handle for their bayonet.

M1A National Match

About half way through the first hour and just before it came time to explain their M-14 rifle was 'gas operated', I lit a very long firecracker fuse. The important lesson was in how the energy flowed in their rifle. The fuse was to keep them awake long enough to see the fuse burn into a jar-lid of black powder which would erupt in a vast, sulfury white cloud of billowing smoke, which I could then point to and say THAT is the gas that operates your rifle.

With just a little leeway, I could make Federal Court more entertaining.

Investigation of firearms incidents and accidents took a strange turn when I became a deputy sheriff in Leon County, Florida in 1970. The classes taught by the FBI, at that time in forensics investigations and preservation and marking of evidence not only came in handy as crime fighting tools but also in understanding how to explain things clearly to a jury much later.

As a deputy and a gunsmith that had set up his first shop on rented land way out in the country, I still had my 'civilian' friendships and customers, but suddenly a whole new group of lawmen *and the cases they were called on to work* came into play. I love a good mystery and to step into a crime scene and try to nearly instantaneously figure out what happened because the guy with the gun could be in a closet, or is that him dead on the bed, was considerably more interesting than anything I'd done before.

Knowing how guns operate solved quite a few 'mysteries' and I like to think maybe I also taught a few deputies something about what they depend on for their very lives. It seems common sense to think a cop would know how his duty gun operated and how to maintain it, but I'll guarantee it's not true and two (short) stories will prove it.

I hear the unrest in the back row, but this is something important.

In our sheriff's office of the early '70s, before bullet proof vests, SWAT teams, laser sights, stun guns, walkie-talkies and sap gloves were the costume of choice, a deputy could carry any gun he wanted as long as it was a double-action revolver of .38 special or larger and he could shoot at least 70% on the old PPC course twice a year with THAT gun. That sorted out a few guys with big flinches that wanted to carry a .44 magnum. The sheriff allowed no cowboys, but he insisted on a hat. He allowed deputies to continue in the job that couldn't shoot well because they had better attributes than shooting at people. In fact, we had a couple deputies that never did hit a target when I was looking. One of them worked for five sheriffs and retired and probably had never qualified and never had to use his gun, anyway. We never had an 'us against them' attitude because we always dealt with our boss' voters. That makes a difference.

Many of the deputies shot quite a lot and hunted every chance they got (innumerable chances when you have all night to prowl around looking for the feral among us.) Some of our deputies shot fifty rounds twice a year and their service revolver got cleaned when somebody noticed green goo running from it. Many of the guys prided themselves on their side-arm and maintained fresh ammo and never used WD-40 and were good to have behind you when a citizen went crazy. Others not so much so, but every one of us expected our service revolver to work when we wanted it to.

One of the shift captains had a Python he was really proud of. Four inch, nickeled with uncommonly dark grips on it. I can't help but mentally note and name every gun I see (which causes strife around inaccurate movies) and I'd noticed several times that the captain's Python grips had a big dent on the very back corner. He was overweight and long on the job and the grips were nearly smooth where his arm and uniform shirt had worn off the checkering, but the dent was something new. It took me a month to notice it at a time I could ask him about it. He said he'd put the gun on the top shelf of a closet because a youngster was going to be in the house on his days off. He'd wrapped the gun belt around the holster and stuffed it in a spare space. When he went to get it, the whole wad of leather came unwrapped at once and the gun had smacked the hardwood floor hard enough to dent the walnut grips, but not to break them. I marveled at that and asked to see the gun for a minute in a closed office. Sometimes DA Colts are sensitive to grip impacts and the bind in the rebound lever makes them hard to cock. I'd seen an old New Service that way one time and bought it really cheap because it had to be refitted to work right.

His first generation Python was locked up *solid*. It would not open or rotate. The trigger would not pull but about an eighth of an inch. It was a shiny club with the handle on the wrong end. The captain went pale. He'd carried that gun for about two months not knowing it couldn't shoot.

Ah, could you tell me what caused that?

The old Colts have a rebound lever that is anchored deep down in the grip frame. If the grip frame bends it binds up the trigger, hammer and bolt. It takes judicious use of a lead hammer to fix them. I think we could use that as an example of a gun that is 'safe' because it won't shoot, but *un*safe because it won't shoot on command, either.

Some guns are safe and they do shoot on command, too.

One night about three in the morning when everything in the universe should be asleep instead of driving back roads, checking doors on rural businesses and answering the inevitable 'he's too drunk to sleep' calls, I got a call to go to the radio room of the Court House. That was the nerve center of an overcrowded half floor that never slept and was rarely swept unless we weren't busy when the maids showed up about eight at night. I don't remember that ever happening. It was usually the civilian telephone operator that made sure nobody tripped on teletype paper the next morning. The coffee pot was never empty or washed.

As soon as I stepped inside, the bits of white something was visible on the teletype machine and a table. I knew the three deputies but they were from another shift working a special duty. I was told one had been on the radio, one on the phone and the third came in "to show him a gun." About then, I noticed the gouge out of the hospital-grade asphalt tile floor with concrete showing beneath it with the tell-tale gray-silver smear at the bottom. That of course accounted for the debris scattered around the room and the big hole in the acoustic tile ceiling, too.

My question was who shot what and why? The one that shot wanted to know *how*! He handed me his now un-loaded Model 19 S&W with four inch barrel. It was in original condition and none of the side plate screws had been visibly touched. In a Smith and Wesson, the screws are important. If a guy hasn't got the skill to work on it without damage, he's not qualified to go inside it, either. If it looks 'virginal' it's easy to show what is "wrong" with it and I was anxious to show "Bill" how he had screwed up.

Part of my uniform was a S&W screwdriver in my handcuff case. We spread out a newspaper on the warrant counter and I took the grips off, then the sideplate and carefully rearranged the safety bar to its at-rest position on the rebound slide peg.

M65 S&W with trigger at rest. Hammer is blocked by 2 parts, the safety bar and the rebound slide.

Then I explained to Bill the bar is held in the slot in the sideplate, and that makes it run up and down as the rebound slide goes back and forth as the trigger is pulled and released. Then I showed him the lump on top of the rebound slide and the corresponding flat on the bottom of the hammer.

I cocked the revolver, repositioned the safety bar and showed him how the hammer has to fall with two parts pulled out of the way by the trigger in order to hit the primer with its fixed firing pin. I demonstrated how the parts clash and the gun *cannot* fire unless *he* pulled the trigger and held it back.

He was duly convinced that he must have done it and the radio room got the best cleaning I saw in five years of working there.

So what's the point? Why bring it up now?

Well, I only mention it because the defense lawyers love to ask questions about that in front of a jury to demonstrate even a deputy sheriff will try to lie his way out of a discharge that was actually his fault. I can 'see' the jury (invisibly) nodding in agreement until I answer by pointing out the S&W revolver has specific parts and *design* to prevent it from firing, absolutely, unless the trigger is pulled.

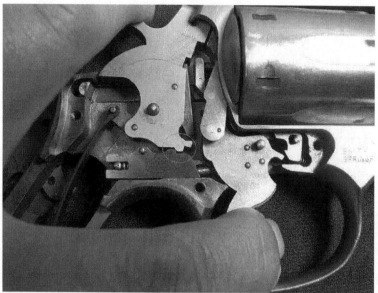

M65 S&W with trigger pulled. Trigger movement pushes rebound slide to the rear unblocking hammer. Safety bar has been removed for clarity.

The triggers that happen to be under trial are *not certain* in their operation, *by design*. If the defendant triggers were as reliable as S&W there would be no lawsuits filed against them. That usually draws an objection, but that bell won't be un-rung, either.

What kind of gun cases did you work as a deputy?

There were quite a few gun cases but every time it was a human that malfunctioned and not the gun. Gun *function* errors are not at all common. Human error (or purpose) is almost an everyday occurrence somewhere in every jurisdiction.

It's always good to know how guns work, and I used my knowledge to disarm a guy with a revolver in his pocket. It was a small DA revolver and I could see the hammer was down as he jammed his hand in to get it, but I grabbed it and held on tight. It can't shoot unless it can revolve. His name was Hatfield and he tried to pull the trigger several times before I could bring a left-handed flashlight lick to his noggin that made him relax enough to get the gun away from him. His soon to be ex-wife took time out of packing up her stuff to chew me out for not killing him. I'm glad I didn't have to sort through stun guns, blackjacks, and pepper spray to figure out how to handle him, though. By today's standards, we traveled very light.

I got a call one night of a possible problem at a closed business with a light in the back. There was a guy and a wife and a boyfriend looking pretty tensely over a table with a case of empty beer bottles on it. The one I judged to be the husband showed the butt of a Blackhawk he had balanced on his leg. I had to draw on him in case he wanted to use it, but he only wanted to show me he had a gun. Which was his right, but the circumstances were pretty tense. Had it been a Glock, and just that half a heart-beat faster to shoot because it didn't take cocking first, would I have had to shoot him? I don't want to think about that. My decision was made by the knowledge of single-action revolvers and how much time I knew it would take him to get off a shot.

I was called to the hospital one night just to look at the X-rays of a murder victim that had little flying saucers stuck in his body. I told the detective they were most likely the gas checks from W-W .357, 158 grain Lubaloy ammunition and they would have land and groove information that would tell make and usually the model of the gun that shot them. That turned out to be true so I got called as a witness.

Then there was the case of a murdered college student and her dog left in the piney woods in the locked trunk of her car for a week or more. She and the dog were shot with a .22 rimfire many times. There was a clue stuck in the left rear door jamb worthy of a crime novel. It was a tuft of odd vegetation. It looked to be some kind of clover. The University said it was a very special kind of clover only grown in our area on another university's dairy farm. We went there and found the clover and the victim's tire tracks and eventually, 14 fired .22 Long Rifle cases with the distinctive conical mark of a certain 14 shot .22 rifle that was owned by a professor with a recently deceased, pregnant student girlfriend.

Even after being gone from the sheriff's office more than five years, I was asked about an odd firing pin mark that led to and eventually convicted one of my old high school chums of murder in the first degree.

Experience in real cases also showed me that the law enforcement 'experts' depend on classes to be certified to testify to various specialties. It really means nothing unless the class he took taught something useful. When a fellow deputy was involved in a gun battle up in the edge of Georgia while off duty, the GBI said the wound in the dead man was reversed from reality, because their 'expert' had never seen a contact wound. That ignorance meant a Florida deputy spent time in a Georgia jail accused of shooting a man in the back, when the truth was the gun was brought out when the fight was hand to hand and belly to belly wrestling for the bad guy's gun. .44s DO that!

Ignorance of the facts is no excuse for a law man, just like ignorance of the law is no excuse for a citizen. I'll describe multiple cases of utter incompetence in firearms examiners nation wide later on. I hope truth and justice will prevail.

Sir, I am a firearms examiner and you can bet I'll be listening very closely.

I'm counting on you to do exactly that. You are in the target audience, if you'll pardon the gun-ism.

In the sheriff's office was a bunch of Class III machine guns either signed out to criminal shift deputies or in the arms room at the jail. It was easy to pick out a sub of some kind and use it enough to know you could, and shoot up just enough of *your* ammo to know the gun was ok and to see how it's best used. Most everybody had a sub or a shotgun, usually in the trunk for 'special occasions'. We could also buy anything that would be useful in the department and have that gun issued on a permanent basis. When a deputy left the department the gun stayed.

One of my first submachine guns was one I bought brand new from a police supply house. It was the S&W Model 76. It was just a modern 9mm version of the M-3 Grease gun and I'd already owned a couple of those as a kid.

The first time I shot the M-76 was at feral cats at a popular but remote sinkhole picnic ground. One cat had succumbed to a small burst but the other ran up a tall pine tree. I re-aimed the spot light and squeezed off a burst.....but it only shot once. I tried again; same thing. The magazine catch was the wrong size and shape. A sub-machine gun made by one of the finest gunmakers on earth would not shoot uphill, *by design.*

S&W M76 submachine gun, 9x19 Parabellum with 36 round magazine.

There was a time I tore open a screaming man's shirt expecting to see a .25 auto bullet hole but instead found a bruise. The bullet stopped in a new pack of Camels. Just about time the evidence became convincing of the inadequacies of the .25 auto, I worked the murder of a woman where the .25 auto bullet penetrated the top of the skull, the entire head and part of the spine. I also saw the path of a .38 special bullet that ran around the outside of a young man's skull to exit the back side without penetrating at all and a tire iron through the aorta and the man lived. One of our deputies was shot with his own .357 down through the chest and out the back and he drove himself to the hospital and lived through it.

I learned my temperament is better suited to investigating gun accidents involving people rather than people accidents involving guns. I have unlimited patience with mechanical objects but very little patience with stubborn people.

<I hear muttering on the back row.>

Do you remember what you came here to talk about?

Good question!

I never realized how important it is to have a good memory until lawyers started trying to download all of it in multiple depositions.

About 1970, on a skeet range near Coonbottom Crossroads, a man on my squad complained of a trigger pull on his Remington shotgun that had suddenly gone extremely light. It turned into a 'hair-trigger' while shooting a round of skeet. Sudden changes in mechanics are always interesting so I pulled a nail out of the trap house as a 'Remington disassembly tool' and drifted the pins from the Model 1100 and found a sliver of lead stuck to the back of the hammer in the sear notch. The sear was slipping almost completely off the hammer on lead instead of steel. I used my pocket knife to scrape away the piece of lead shot and put the gun back together so we could finish our round. Twenty five years later I found out it was surprisingly common for those triggers to fail and one guy had lost his arm to one. I testified in his behalf and introduced a design to repair the defect.

Who knew they killed people?

Who says they do?

Answered in due time. Your patience is admirable.

Ten years or so after the Model 722 that shot a knee instead of a turkey, I was still repairing Remington triggers by attaching the connectors and precision grinding away the angle at the rear of it as a matter of course in my shop in Colorado. The triggers of the 80s were especially rough, hard, gritty and nearly unusable as they came from the factory. I adjusted dozens of the so-called 'lawyer triggers' not having any clue as to the back story and how closely I would become tied to it.

You just hit a nerve back here on the gunsmith's row. Are you going to talk about that some more?

Oh yes! You'll get your fill of triggers before long. I'm still painting backdrops for the stage.

I almost testified in a murder case about 1980. The local sheriff asked me to do some measurements on a rifle that had the rear sight obviously knocked way off center. I calculated how much off center the shot would be if the sight were used without correction and came up with the trajectory of the bullet that missed a neighbor's dog and killed the neighbor instead. I was told many years later by a lady that had been a court reporter at the time it was my graph and explanation of measurements and formulas had played a large role in a plea arrangement in that case.

In 1993, the nations leading plaintiff's lawyer involving firearms cases hired me to investigate a case involving a Remington Model 700 that had shot a boy through the knee while elk hunting with his brother in Montana. Without knowing it at the time, my knowledge of the design and function of a wide variety of firearms and the ability to tell a judge and jury about them would change not only my career and my life, but how I looked at firearms for ever more.

It made me wonder what I'd become a part of, too.

At the time of my being hired to examine the testimony in a case in Montana that had so far defied a reasonable explanation, I was very active as a charter member of the American Custom Gunmaker's Guild and held high offices there. Rich Miller, from Springfield, MO had been invited as a guest of the exhibition and guest speaker to tell us gunmakers what kind of legal problems we could face if we did things wrong. He was the head of the firearms litigation group of high powered law firms.

I'd met Tom Butters the year before at the same event and found we were brothers from a different mother and became fast friends. Tom was a battle-hardened veteran Professional Engineer that had answered many questions in many gun cases that I had no clue had ever happened. He also helped guide me through the minefields of working for the law. It is very different from anything I'd done before. His advice was some of the best I've ever had, too. Tom Butters told me more than twenty years ago: *You're obligated by what you say, but you are a slave to what you write .*

I was anxious to get started educating a whole new group of people that seemed anxious to know what I knew about guns.

I had no idea how much the lawyers already knew! Rich Miller sent me several boxes of highly confidential documents to 'get up to speed on the Remington thing' and I immediately saw why they were confidential. For that information to be released to be public would forever change the perception of guns and shooters. It was very easy to see why what the lawyers call 'the secrets' had to remain that way.

At least it was easy to see then.

3. Safety by Design

When I say one word out loud it will bring a multitude of images to the minds of many people just because it has so many meanings depending entirely on the subject matter. As a small boy, I was fascinated by my dad's big office safe with the combination lock. When grandmother told me to get dishes out of the safe for supper the confusion lasted quite a while. We had cabinets at our house.

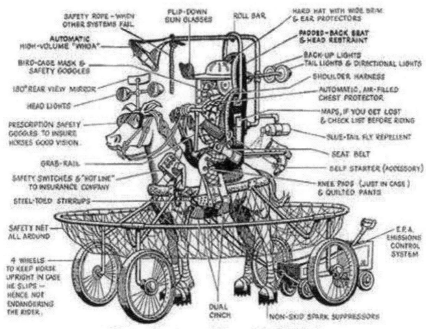

Cowboy after O.S.H.A.

"Safety" in any product or object is subject to definitions and expectations. Is there a safe way to walk a tight rope? Sure. Just don't raise it above ground level. Is there a safe way to fly? Given the fact that humans are likely to get killed if they travel faster than they can run, flying above about 30 feet can't, by the usual definitions, ever be entirely "safe."

But, we humans are a crafty bunch and for more than a hundred years every effort has been made to make flying 'safe' enough for most of us to do often and without worry. Traveling faster than we can run is done by many modes of transportation and 'safety' again is at the forefront. Motorcycles, bicycles, skate boards, skis and hang gliders remind us that too many safety items make the whole thing unworkable, so compromises are made. The 'safe' bicycle would be too heavy to pedal and hang gliders couldn't fly.

We all know mistakes made with such contraptions can be fatal. It still happens of course, but the point is that when conditions of danger are present we humans become more careful. We compare risk with rewards and usually decide to take the great chance of driving somewhere or flying somewhere and assume everything is designed and manufactured to give you the best chance of arriving safely. The same guy that's proud of his expedient repair of his bicycle with zip ties and duct tape would probably not try to get his ultra-light aircraft back home by the same creative means. The risk is much higher when you're off the ground far enough to add 'mash' to the road rash.

Anything that has enough energy to disrupt the human body is 'dangerous'. When primitive man figured out penetration worked better and with less effort than blunt force, the entire universe of 'deadly weapons' was invented. As soon as it was discovered that a sharp object could be *thrown,* instead of jabbed, it caused a race to see who could throw it farther, faster and with more accuracy. Sharp points made of wood, bone, stone, bronze, iron and steel all work exactly the same way but with varying degrees of efficiency and durability.

When firearms came on the scene somewhere in feudal China as bamboo hand cannons, "safety" took on a whole new aspect that suddenly and with great force reminded those early shooters that danger now existed in a form never seen before. First was the matter of an explosion taking place just in front of the shooter's face. Early firearms were about as dangerous to the shooter as the target. Since the performance of the firearm depends mainly on how much energy that 'explosion' has in it, the chance of failure is high at the outer edges of the design envelope.

The problem of trying to overcome Newtonian physics with gun powder exploding close to tender body parts is a continuing battle of metallurgy and design features.... and added shields and responsibilities of the shooter. Speaking of that, when did 'safety glasses' become a part of the shooting sports? Did anybody bother to ask why? The answer lies in economy. Cheap guns leak gas *by design*. The shooter needs to protect against what the gunmaker didn't.

That is a pet peeve of mine that dates back to middleschool. Almost all gun injuries involve the eyes or fingers. With the sudden surge in cheap pistols blowing the sides out of their chambers, maybe chain-mail gloves and a full face mask will be the next 'safety gear' recommended by the factories and their compliant propaganda ministers, the gun writers in the popular press. By all prior evidence, all it takes to change the paradigm in the gun world is some English major that wants to write outdoor stories to do a 'test report' on the latest cheap piece of miss-designed hardware that would fit right into the toy section by mistake, and suddenly he's a 'gun writer'... .

I think that little rant scared a few in the seats up close. Sorry.

Ah, sir. We haven't had 'trigger' yet, why all this safety stuff?

Well, there's another good question. "Safety" means more than a part to make it safe, it means a *design* that makes it safe. Part of that design is to make the gun safe independent of the trigger. There are parts that keep the gun from firing out of battery, and to keep it from firing while being improperly held and to keep it from firing when dropped. Many of these features are not part of 'the safety' but are parts of what makes the gun safe.

Stick to teaching about guns. You suck at English.

Thanks. Many of my teachers said exactly the same thing.

Let me start over---

"The Safety" on any firearm is assumed to keep it from firing until it's released. I say 'assumed' because the name is there...it should mean *something* shouldn't it? Yes, but it doesn't. Some 'safeties' are that in name only.

So, what is a safety?

In the most painfully simple terms, the **springs** make a gun fire and the **safety** prevents it from firing. The springs either drive a hammer or a striker to make a gun fire, and there is either a locker, a blocker, an interceptor or an interrupter to prevent it.

A what'?

Blockers, lockers, interceptors and interrupters are all safety devices.

Winchester M94 in .30 WCF.

A hammer or striker can be **locked** into the safe position by a wedge or cam like a Colt 1911, or the hammer/striker/firing pin can be **blocked** from moving by a safety like the Walther PPK. Either part can be **intercepted** in its motion if conditions are right, like the double-action (DA) sear does in a S&W revolver. An **interrupter** prevents firing when parts are not properly in position or aligned, like the two piece firing pin and lock block actuator on the Marlin Model 336 and Winchester Model 94. All of these safety features, and the disconnectors that also interrupt operation, make guns NOT fire unless commanded.

Marlin 336 in .30-30.

What causes them to fire without command?

Now, we're getting to the crux of the matter and that's a great question that sometimes takes on some surprising answers. There are many cases to analyze and find that out.

Two rules first:

No gun should fire without the trigger being pulled.
No gun should be capable of firing with the safety engaged.

Hey, haven't you heard. Safeties are not to be trusted. They're just mechanical and of course they sometimes fail. The Ten Commandments says so.

I'm sure glad you brought that up!! Let's discuss it some.

Have y'all noticed those long black, parallel skid marks headed towards the shoulder of the highway? Those are 'failed brakes' on a big truck. You notice he's not piled up at the bottom of the hill with dead folks under him. The brakes 'failed safe' *by design.* When the air supply was lost from a broken hose, the brakes automatically applied and stopped the truck and kept him stopped until the brakes got repaired.

Why does a gun shoot when it breaks? Why doesn't it fail safe and NOT shoot?

Springs are one reason why guns don't follow Mr. Westinghouse and his brake idea. Springs are like gravity to the semi truck. Safeties are like the brakes on that truck. Mr. Westinghouse added a source of energy in compressed air. Nobody wants an air tank or a battery in their firearm, so we're stuck with using mechanics to block, lock or intercept the hammer or striker to keep them from firing.

Why don't they make guns that fail safe?

That is an important question that has several answers, but for now just understand one concept- *energy.* The speeding semi has a LOT of energy, but all the driver had to do was mash the accelerator to produce it. A shooter pulls the trigger and it's too late to call that energy back. There are no brakes on a bullet.

Can we still use the semi in the analogy, then?

Yes, but a bowling ball would be easier.

Should we leave now or wait until they come haul you away?

Give this a try: Guns have to have energy to fire. Gravity can supply that, but a gun is designed to shoot by energy stored in its springs and also designed to block, lock or intercept energy from gravity AND the release of the energy stored in the spring if it's released by anything other than a trigger pull.

It better get clearer than that or I'm forever lost.

Forget the guy driving the semi. I've found through many years of trying, that to better understand something, take it to extremes. Blow it up so large you can walk around it or slow it down so slow you can see what is actually happening, or simplify it to the lowest number of variables. Ignore what's not important but always wonder why it's there. Understanding the fire control system is easy if you can… Follow the energy!

Assume for a minute you have cocked a rifle. It makes no difference what kind, but whatever it is, it has a manual safety that is OFF, or disengaged, and as far as you know it's ready to make a very loud noise. You also have a bowling ball being held up on a steep ramp. It has gathered energy by being rolled up there and it's still under tension being held there until a little shelf pops out and it balances there. Whew! You can turn loose of the weight just like cocking the hammer on a gun. Suddenly it's 'cocked' and you don't have to hold it anymore.

Now, what keeps the rifle from firing and the ball from falling off the shelf?

The trigger, of course!

Well, not really. The trigger is the hangy-down part that's handy for a forfinger to snag and if you pull it just right I'll bet it 'sure nuff' shoots, so how can the trigger not control the firing of the gun? It does 'control' the firing of the gun, but it's not preventing it from firing. The **sear** is the part that actually engages with the hammer or striker and keeps them from moving until the trigger says it's time. The sear is the part that takes the most explaining to lawyers and a jury, but it's important to the entire process to really understand **sears** and how they operate and how triggers interact with them to control the firing and the safety of any firearm.

Triggers, sears and safeties usually work in close association with each other. How certain, simple, strong, positive and solid that interaction is determines how reliable the system is. An example of a very simple system that has caused a lot of painful injuries might be in order.

You're not going to leave that bowling ball up there are you? I have a vivid imagination and it makes me nervous.

I understand that! Try this: Very carefully point that fully loaded rifle we cocked while ago at the bowling ball and then back away from them. Hopefully nothing will go wrong, but the tension is good when we're talking about gun safety. The gun and the bowling ball are in a 'kinetic' condition.

As a deputy, I worked the case of a traveling salesman that dropped a fully loaded Ruger old style .41 Mag on a tile floor while searching his bag for a clean shirt.

Old model Ruger. Note 3 pivot screws on side. New models have 2 pins.

I met him in the emergency room, lying on a gurney with the largest sweat beads I've ever seen on a human being clinging to his face. He was pale and hurting from a 210 grain hollow point bullet that centered the left testicle and then went on to break the ball of his hip where a large fragment split off and penetrated a kidney. I wiped what seemed a pint of hanging sweat from his brow and got his story as the morphine kicked in. He asked how it could have happened but for once I was brief when I told him it was a *weak design* that shot him.

After getting the particulars from the victim at the hospital, I went with two detectives to look at the gun and the scene. The motel room was preserved as the EMTs had found it and secured. The gun was still wrapped in a now shredded towel on the terrazzo floor under the luggage rack in the motel room, next to a big puddle of now blackened blood. The soft-sided, multi-pocketed suitcase was on the bed but two compartments were open. His story made sense that he'd gone in the bag for a shirt but opened the wrong one. When he flipped the bag over, the Ruger Blackhawk, wrapped in a towel, shot him very badly, but he would recover.

Old model Ruger Blackhawk with sear-end of trigger in half-cock notch. Impact with hammer can cause the trigger end to break off and gun to fire.

I told the detectives that according to what I knew about the guns combined with what he had just told me at the hospital, the gun should be hammer down and safe with a fired case under the hammer.....and a broken trigger tip probably still inside the gun. It was exactly that way. It has been that way since about the year

1650.....

You're nuts! They didn't have Ruger Blackhawks in 1650!

They had hammer-fired guns with half cock notches and thin trigger tips. That was the weak part that got the salesman shot. It fails on old Rugers just like a stirrup falling off a saddle horn as the cowboy hunches the girth up tight and his Colt shoots him in the leg. The stirrup hits the hammer on the six shooter hard enough to break the sear end of the trigger off, and the hammer hits the firing pin and primer in much the same way as it did when the old model Ruger hit the hard floor on the hammer and the sear end of the trigger broke. Such guns are said to have a 'weak' safety because they can fire with the safety engaged. It breaks the sear surface from the trigger and it's easy to explain how that system failed to a jury. The evidence speaks for itself.

Old model Ruger Blackhawk at full cock.

That occurred in 1971 and just about the time a lawyer grabbed a similar case and proved by way of convincing a jury that an old, out of date design should not have been put on an affordable and very popular new revolver. He established again by trial and jury that a gun that can fire without a trigger pull is unsafe and defective and a gun that is able to fire while the safety is engaged is unduly defective and dangerous. Let me say that again because it is the beating heart of the whole argument for SAFE guns.

NO GUN SHOULD FIRE WITHOUT A PULL OF THE TRIGGER.

NO GUN SHOULD BE CAPABLE OF FIRING WITH THE SAFETY ENGAGED.

In the case of old model Rugers and the Colt and all their copies, the gun could fire on 'safe' because the sear was weak. It could fire without the trigger being pulled by impact on the hammer.

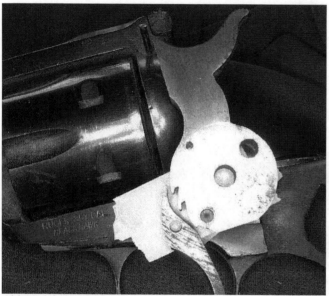

Old model Ruger Blackhawk shown in fired position.

The only good news about that is, it was very easy to see the weakness and to understand it. The old time cowboys knew to only load five chambers of a six shooter revolver but those lessons had been lost over time. Bill Ruger was certainly a genius of gun design and economical manufacturing. He didn't appreciate how important education was and how much knowledge had been lost.

The broken sear tip on single-action revolvers is an example of an 'interceptor' safety.

I would have called it a blocker and a locker. The hammer is blocked by the trigger and sear and the trigger is locked into the deep notch. Why not?

In the above example, you are exactly right. The shooter put it in that position thinking it was safe, too. He didn't know the 'safety' was weak.

So, why did you call it an 'interceptor' safety?

Because there is another safety that's extremely important to the single-action revolver and other guns of that simple, rotating hammer type. It is another 'spring' but one of organic origin:

<The man in the second row with the neat beard and professor's jacket calls BS.>

Mr. Belk, do you mean to assert there are organic parts within gun designs?

Finger Springs

I'm talking of the connection between human flesh and the gun.

The 'finger spring' is the pad of skin and flesh between the trigger portion of the gun and the finger bone. The trigger is pulled with a 'springy' finger because it has some meat on it. Some guns won't shoot easily without it. That small portion of soft flesh acts as a 'spring' on the trigger piece that maintains pressure on the trigger long enough to allow the hammer to completely fall and fire the gun. A S&W will fire with a screwdriver handle if you hold it down on the trigger, but not if you tap the trigger with it. That's why even the very fragile Colt SA's don't usually fire if dropped. They also have to have the 'finger spring' to hold the trigger back long enough to dodge the loading and half cock notches.

One of the ways to mess up a perfectly good S&W is to shorten the rebound slide spring to lighten the DA pull. That makes it doubtful the trigger is fast enough to intercept the hammer in case of a dropped gun.

What part does the trigger play in all this?

Triggers

I've left the word 'trigger' out of a lot of conversation so far because it is a 'muddy' word. It means so many different things to so many different people that it takes a lot of explaining. There will be whole discussions of just one trigger design, but for now, lets just say the trigger is the part that hangs down in a place really handy for pulling. It is the part that connects the person with the machine. It should only obey orders from the shooter. The trigger's role in safety is paramount. Its job is so important that most guns have a guard around the trigger to make sure nothing but a finger can activate it. The trigger is what tells the gun to fire. Nothing else should.

In reality, the trigger acts through the sear to the hammer or striker, but as already noted, some triggers have the sear as one end of the trigger piece itself. For right now, let's divide triggers into two parts:

1) Direct-acting
2) Over-ride type.

Where do these strange names and phrases come from?

The names usually come from what they do or how they act. Some are carry-overs from older times. Colt calls the part that pushes against the cylinder ratchet a 'pawl', just like a millwright or a clockmaker would. S&W calls it a 'hand' like a weaver would. They do the same thing. It really gets confusing when you see that a Colt revolver has a 'bolt' in it, and that part does lock the cylinder into battery, much like a 'bolt-action' rifle does. I'll try to describe them as I go along so you see the name and activity (usually) match. 'Safety' is a glaring exception.

Direct-acting triggers pull the sear out of engagement with the hammer or striker. When the shooter pulls the trigger, the sear moves with it even though there can be multiple linkage parts in between. They all move together on command of the trigger.

'Over-ride' types use part of the energy of the mainspring to set up a geometric 'trap' that allows a trigger pull considerably better than the older direct action systems because much of the energy it takes to pull the trigger is actually done by the mainspring. The gun 'helps' the shooter shoot it by 'leaning' on the sear which is being propped up by a trigger.

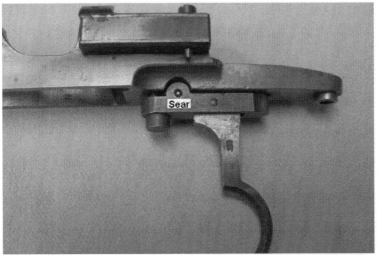

M98 direct acting trigger. Trigger is hinged to sear. Trigger movement levers the tail end of the sear down, pulling it out of the way of the cocking piece.

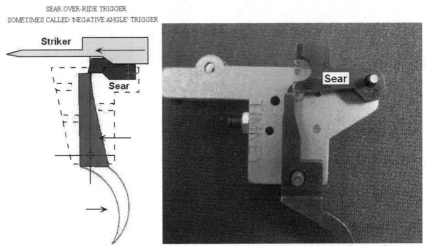

Simple Sear Override Trigger. Trigger props up Sear. Sear blocks forward motion of Striker and Cocking Piece (or Cocking Stud)

Override type triggers are only used in bolt action rifles except for some really odd guns, and one uncommonly dangerous one. Override type trigger systems aren't needed on most other firearms types. There will be plenty to study about them later on. The problems of positively blocking or locking the firing pin on an override trigger becomes more difficult, as we will see in a later chapter devoted entirely to over-ride triggers. Most of the hullabaloo has been about a certain over-ride trigger and we'll dissect it, examine it, analyze it, study it and figure out where its design mistakes are.

Where is that and I'll skip ahead.

Be patient. Later. We still have hammer-fired systems and simple safeties to talk about.

He's still got this bowling ball over here with a loaded rifle pointed at it too!

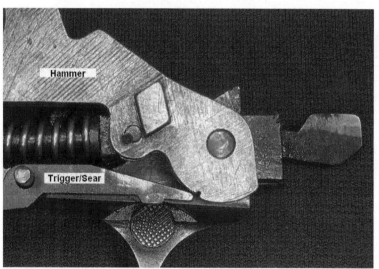

Winchester M12, simple hammer/sear trigger system. Note rounded edges at sear-hammer interface. This one is worn out

As a good example of a simple trigger-sear, hammer and safety system, the Winchester Model 12 offers an easy one to see.

The forward tip of the trigger is the sear. The safety slides under the trigger so the sear end is locked into the hammer notch. The hammer is **locked** by the sear which is **blocked** by the safety and nothing moves until the safety gets out of the way. All three parts make a solid whole and none can move until the safety does. That is a positive, mechanical safety that has locked and blocked the energy of the mainspring from escaping. There are other safety 'features' too.

Winchester M12, in fired position

The safety button is located at the forward end of the trigger guard
which means the trigger finger (instead of the thumb up on top) is
used to push the safety OFF safe. That means the trigger finger is
busy and can't pull the trigger until it's finished with the safety.
The safety also travels cross-ways to the trigger in operation.
There is less chance of pulling the trigger if you're busy
somewhere else pushing on a safety the other direction. The
trigger is balanced in weight on both sides of its pivot so dropping
it won't dislodge the sear from inertia, either.

All these features and attributes add up to a 'safe' gun that cannot
fire without the trigger being pulled and is incapable of firing with
the safety engaged. Thousands of other guns use similar systems.

So what's the big deal?

The big deal is there're something over 30 million guns that use
different systems, different materials and most of all, different
designs that have one or more problems that can make even a
simple system fail. Worse than that is the fact they can fail very
intermittently.

Just to clarify what we just went over, we just saw a firing mechanism that seems the ultimate in 'safe'. The sear is part of the trigger and the safety locks everything together and nothing moves until the safety does, and the safety button is away from the trigger so the safety and trigger can't be operated together by the same finger.

Winchester M12, full cock position, safety OFF. Safety button in ON position holds sear firmly against hammer, nothing can move.

<I see enough nods to continue>

If such a gun fires, it is because of one of two things *only.*

    1) The trigger was pulled while the safety was OFF,
    2) Something broke.

The Ruger revolver broke the sear end off the trigger and shot the salesman. A golfing partner's Model '97 shotgun fell on a door sill and broke the half cock notch of the hammer and blew his thumb off.

A 'safety' that will not withstand the impact of a dropped gun is not sufficiently safe to be called such on a firearm.

We've all had a car that made a funny noise until we got to the mechanic's place. Guns are worse about that than cars. A gun that 'sometimes' messes up is a hard one for a gunsmith to figure out unless he extracts some detailed observations from the shooter.

We sometimes don't have that information because the shooter is dead. We have to rely on analysis of the *design* to determine what *must* have happened.

Is that what makes the back row so mad?

I'll not speak for them, but I suspect the agony is caused by a lack of understanding. The trick is keeping everyone here long enough to explain it.

To sum up, the trigger connects the shooter to the gun, the sear connects the trigger to the hammer or striker. The safety can be any number of different lockers, blockers or interceptors that prevent the gun from firing unless a person pulls the trigger and keeps it pulled until the hammer or striker fires the gun. Even a cocked gun should not fire if dropped, bumped or thrown, but never tempt Murphy.

Why not tempt Murphy? Soldiers drop, throw, bump and abuse their guns all the time. Why can't I?

The overall security of any firearm depends entirely on its design, materials and workmanship. They don't grow on trees. There was a person that made a decision that affects the overall safety of any firearm by how it was designed and built. Somebody's signature is on a blueprint and somebody decided it was right enough to build. There is a human behind every gun ever 'born'. Nobody is watching how it's designed or built except engineers and accountants. Who do you trust?

It's a gun! Don't they make them as good as they can, like airplanes? Everybody trusts a gun!

I'm afraid not. Guns are made for economy. It is rare to find any gun that is made to be as good as it can be, only as good as is price competitive. There have always been cheap guns just like there were iron swords and inferior stone arrow heads, and somebody probably tried to peddle light weight rocks, too. Economy is always a factor....until a government gets involved. Since governments invent their own money and defense is a primary duty of all governments, military designs are almost always better than the civilian guns that sell on price alone. We usually can't afford a 'perfect' gun, so surplus military arms are always of great interest and usually affordable.

Gun models undergo near constant changes and minor tweaks to either make them better or cheaper. Sometimes a gun manufacturer really screws up and it costs them a bunch of money.

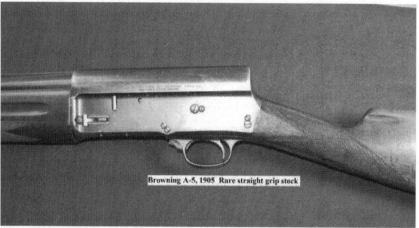

Browning A-5 with rare straight grip stock.

One of the best (short) books on American guns is "John M. Browning, America's Gunmaker." In it is chronicled his absolutely amazing mastery of gun design and told at length of his decades long association with Winchester. They bought everything he invented and their patent lawyers made sure nobody could steal it.

Then, when Browning set his genius to an auto-loading shotgun and came up with the great A-5 in 1898, Winchester decided they'd take a pass on such a radical idea. They figured nobody would want such a thing because four kinds of shotgun shell propellants meant it couldn't be reliable, but a double gun would shoot them all, mix or match......but the market sages at Winchester were wrong.

By the time the marketplace told Winchester they were missing the auto-loading shotgun boat, Remington had snapped up the Browning A-5 'humpback' patent and introduced the Model 11

Sportsman that looked like a Browning and worked like a Browning but was considerably cheapened to make it more affordable. (Pay close attention to that creed.) Shooters loved shotguns that (sometimes) shot five times by only pulling the trigger and Winchester had no auto shotgun to market. Winchester soon learned how hard it was to steal a patent, and from their own lawyers, too.

Remington M11

The shotgun they built to compete with the FN-made Browning A-5 and the Remington M11 was the Model 11 Winchester. Browning already had the patents that made an auto-loading shotgun comfortable and safe to shoot. FN, in Belgium had been manufacturing the A-5 since 1905. Remington had announced the 'American Browning' was coming soon. Winchester tried to catch up (too) quickly with a long-recoil shotgun of their own.

Winchester M11

The Model 11 Winchester has several unusual features, one is there is no operating handle. Instead, there is a section of barrel that's knurled so the barrel can be pulled or pushed back into the receiver, just as the Browning 'long recoil' design does when it fires. But the Winchester had no friction ring recoil brake on it so the barrel was relatively easy to operate for most shooters. Others had to put the butt on the ground and use both hands to push the barrel back to load the first of five shells.

Another annoying feature of the Winchester Model 11 was the propensity for it to break the sear link pivot pin and fire every time the bolt closed. It took very few cases of some poor shooter riding his shotgun like a very messy and deadly pogo stick, and

Winchester decided to dump the model entirely about ten years after introduction and offered to trade a brand new Model 12 pump gun for any Model 11 returned, no matter the condition.

Salesmen were said to be given permission to pay up to full value of the gun in boot to get them back if possible. They're still occasionally seen at gun shows and pawnshops and some people still shoot them, too, but they are truly a beast because each shot kicks you twice. Remember that lack of a friction brake? One gun writer of the day said he was most thankful when his Winchester Model 11 didn't shoot at all.

The Winchester Model 11 was an unsafe gun by design in three ways. It required some shooters to get in front of it to operate it, it had a design flaw that allowed it to shoot if a part broke, and it made that part weak during operation. Seldom do we see such an example.

Example of what?

An example of a firearms company taking responsibility for something done wrong and then paying for it. But, that was before WW-I!

4. Follow the Energy

Sir, I'm here to learn more about real cases and less about theory. Can you do that?

Sure, as long as I can reserve the right to back-up and fill-in, because details are very important.

Product liability cases that are generated by firearms are few and far between. They're based on the same laws as other products and must jump through the same hoops. There are defects in design, defects in material or workmanship and there's failure to notify the customer of a defect. Some states have smaller, more difficult hoops, but most cases go to Federal Court because guns are sold across state lines.

I'm not a lawyer and certainly not qualified to give legal advice, but I can say without qualification of any kind, when you enter the legal system in any way, it's much like being put through a meat grinder. You will be different on the other side even though still made of the same material.

The one thing that really stands out in the legal world is the preciseness of the language used. I thought I knew how the Walker-designed Remington 700 series trigger worked until I read the engineering study done by Tom T. Butters in Texas, in response to several suits he worked on. There, in black and white was the description of that mechanism that went beyond the patent in describing it. It took very little time to realize *details* are extremely important. Sometimes millions of dollars depend on the smallest of details.

It took me two cases to figure out there were some rich and powerful people that wanted to shut me up. No threats of any kind, just an attempt to impeach what I was saying in testimony so I'd no longer be a factor. I don't mind really tough questions and rather enjoy the sparring that goes on between a lawyer and his expert adversary, but I'm a Southerner by the grace of God and sometimes I say things that if taken literally in a courtroom would really mess things up. There's no doubt it's stressful trying to be entirely accurate at all times, but so is getting shot! Giving testimony is always hard work.

I'm a mechanical witness, and guns are entirely mechanical outside the cartridge case. Inside the cartridge case is where the chemical magic happens. The field of mechanics is all about reality. I'm a firm believer in there being a specific reason for every mechanical action and reaction and usually there's a trace left behind when a gun fails. I pride myself in figuring out how a gun did that. I also dearly love guns!! I want them to be safe and if it takes me to tell a company how they messed up, so be it.

My first civil case in which I was a designated expert that actually went to testimony was in Springfield, MO. It came just a month after being hired on a Remington Model 700 case in Montana, but the lawyer for the Montana case was located in Springfield, MO. These guys skip around a lot because cases are usually tried where they happened.

H&R M58 'Topper'

The K-Mart case was the perfect platform for a brand new expert witness. It was easy for me to see the defect and even easier to explain it and demonstrate it. The opposition had made terrible errors of the most rudimentary analysis of the 'crime scene' photographs supplied by law enforcement, and a very basic error in testing had been made by them, too. I was hired way late and had to catch up quickly, but I was mainly in the dark because this was my first dive into the murky depths of the law.

In the first half hour of examining the gun in Missouri, I told the lawyer the gun was defective and demonstrably so. The simplest of gunsmithing tests showed the gun certainly could fire without the trigger being pulled because the most rudimentary of safeties was made incorrectly by the factory. They installed the wrong length firing pin.

Sir, aren't you skipping around a lot? What you just said doesn't match anything you've said before.

There seems to be a consensus in the room.

Yes, I am, mainly because the subject matter is rather complicated and what is a 'sear' in one gun might be different in others. I'm covering this case because it introduces the simplest of all firearms mechanisms, that has been around since the late 1880s, that was done wrong by the maker, sold wrongly by a major discount chain store and the defense was so inept as to be downright funny. It will also introduce the simplest of passive safety systems that is subject to failure. One of the guns later shot a man dead center of his chest because of that failure. Besides that, I'm unorganized. Please try to deal with it.

<I'm the one that better bear down and pay attention!>

Here's the story as I heard it from the lawyer and then read in their depositions taken a month previous. The family was rural poor and seemed to be stuck there for good. Multiple generations occupied a 'compound' of old mobile homes and sheds and chicken pens and what they bought came from the cheapest sources available. One of those things was a Model 58 H&R single-shot shotgun bought from K-Mart to shoot varmints. It was 12 gauge and had certainly been used some, but was in good overall mechanical condition. It was stored with a shell in the chamber but with the action broken open and laid under a double bed in the corner of a small bedroom.

A 15 year old girl was in the process of changing that bed for another one and had stripped the covers and saw the barrel of the shotgun under the bed. She knelt down and reached with her right hand and grabbed the barrel to pull the gun out. She noticed it was 'broken' in the middle before starting to move the gun towards her. It snagged something once, then again because there was a night stand in the way, but one more tug and BOOM! The load of 7 ½ shot hit her just left of the navel. Roughly 350 lead balls traveling right at the speed of sound, with the plastic wad behind them, blew a large hole in her belly. Modern medicine saved her life but she lost an ovary and suffered greatly.

Yeah, it was her fault too! Nobody should drag a gun towards themselves. That's just stupid!

The law doesn't separate out the stupid from the smart. The law says a product should be suitable for its intended use. A gun has two ends and both of them fit a human hand. If the gun is *safe*, it really makes little difference, but nobody smart enough to eat regular looks down a muzzle if they can help it.

There is no safe direction to point an unsafe gun.

The law, in this case, was not about the defective gun except that the retailer knew the gun they were selling as a new product had been replaced by a newer model that incorporated a much better safety system. That new safety on the Model 158 would have prevented the accident and I could easily prove the old model was made wrong to begin with and that *caused* the accident. The case was against the retailer for selling an old design and it was near air tight because the causation was so plain even I, the beginner, could explain it to twelve people who might know how pliers work when they were chosen to serve on the jury.

Why did they fight it if it was so plain to see?

Nothing is plain to see if you're not looking for it.

The defense had already examined the gun and their hired expert had found nothing wrong with it and they even tried to fire a live shell from the gun by duplicating the accident. The hammer spur on the subject gun had been scarred up with a screwdriver in their test and it was easy to see why, too. The spur was sharply serrated and the hammer spring was strong and the test was to pull the hammer back just short of the full cock notch and turn it loose to see if it fired the shell. Thumbprints lasted for very few tests so a screwdriver was used to pull the hammer back. It did not fire in the defense team's test. They had the video tape to prove it and they used the same Federal ammunition, too. That was important because Federal primers are known to be more sensitive than others.

His report also noted the shot pattern and blood-tissue splatter pattern on a door that had been removed from the bedroom after the accident. The report was professionally done by a guy that had testified in many cases and wrote for national publications and had published several books on gunsmithing subjects. He was the real deal but boy was he ever WRONG!

Mechanism similar to H&R's with sear-end of trigger resting on safety shelf

I showed the lawyers how the gun was defective by removing the barrel and forearm, standing the gun on its butt on the table and placing a penny over the firing pin hole. Then the hammer was pulled back to as close to the cocking notch as possible without going into it and then letting the hammer slip off. On the very first try, the penny bounced more than the magical 12 inches high that shows a gun *can* fire with that much firing pin energy. It was clear the safety step on the hammer was not doing its job. Later in the case, I cut the sides away on the same make and model shotgun to show the jury how the gun worked, was supposed to work, and how it had failed.

Look at the photo above. The mechanism shown is similar to the H&R M58, and the basic design is the same as the single action revolver we looked at awhile ago. The hammer rotates back against the mainspring and the sear end of the trigger catches in the full cock notch. What was the half cock notch in the revolver is just a stop shelf in this much larger gun. Remember the finger spring. Both guns use it to get the hammer past the sear end of the trigger.

On the H&R shotgun that had fired without the trigger being pulled it was clear that the hammer hit the end of the firing pin *before* it hit the safety step and that was enough to drive it into the primer and fire the gun.

Hold on right there, please. I see the hammer hitting the firing pin but it's nowhere close to the primer. You have to be wrong on this one!

Thank you. It must be time to talk about inertial firing pins.

Intertial firing pin, Colt M1911. Firing pin will not touch primer in hammer-down condition.

We talked awhile ago about safeties and safety features. One of the safety features that John M. Browning came up with is used in a vast multitude of guns today. The inertial firing pin is shorter than the space in which it sits. They're used in hammer fired and striker-fired mechanisms, especially in handguns. It just means that with the firing pin depressed as far as it'll go into the frame, it still doesn't touch the primer.

How in the world does it do that!?

Thank you, ma'am.

Sir Isaac Newton describes it better than I can in his First Law of Motion but I'll sum it up this way: An object at rest stays at rest and one in motion stays in motion (until something stops it.)

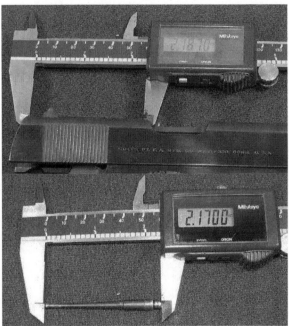

This M1911 firing pin has to move .017" before it touches the primer.

The firing pin is a plunger that is put in motion by the hammer hitting it. The firing pin return spring is not very strong and it allows the hammer to drive the pin forward with quite some force, but once the firing pin has gone as far as it can against the spring, the spring will push it back to the rear position again.

The motion of the firing pin is a sharp 'peck'. It only takes about 40 inch-ounces of force to fire a shotgun shell and that's just about what it takes to throw a penny a foot high.

For reliable ignition, a penny is usually thrown six to eight feet high and it's common to bounce them off the ceiling, but the foot high bounce, which was recorded by video camera against a graph paper background, is known throughout the gunsmithing world as 'barely enough' to fire a gun.

Didn't you say the defense team video taped it NOT shooting?

Yes they did. I watched the video very carefully, frame by frame and detected no effort to sway the results. The hammer was withdrawn all the way back to where it should have fired but it didn't. The gun was held on a stool in the middle of the indoor pistol range at Bass Pro Shop in Springfield and the attempt was made several times to fire it and it did not. In fact, the very slight mark left on the primer was so light and insignificant to show the jury it could not have fired in that manner. Their expert's report said so. Their demonstration was all very convincing. Even 'my' lawyers believed it.

The defense expert also said, and drew diagrams to prove, the gun had not been under the bed. In fact, according to his calculations, it was across the room in the other corner and no way could the girl's sworn testimony be true. Somebody had to have shot her and the tale was just an attempt to get money from a terrible event, not the retailer's fault at all. The lawyers for the defense believed him about that, too.

So, how was it a slam dunk case given their expert's test and report?

First thing was that the analysis of his analysis showed he had the evidence picture of the shot-splattered bedroom door upside down. The door knob hole showed the difference, but his diagram had the whole scene reversed because he didn't notice the upside down photo... or, he decided his way was better to win the case. That one glaring and embarrassing finding pretty much killed their defense, but their video tape was still dangerous to us, too. The defense stayed in the game even after the mistake in bedroom geometry was brought to their attention.

I knew the gun was capable of firing but it didn't fire in their test, so the question is, "why didn't it fire?"

Cheap guns are always suspect, even in the most simple of ways. I had already answered that question for myself in that first thirty minutes of examination but it had to be proven somehow. The gun had about .030" excess 'headspace'. That is the critical 'gap' the shell is held to in the chamber to give it the support needed to make it shoot to the front and not backfire to the rear. In the case of rimmed cases, like a shotgun, it is based on the thickness of the rim of the shell. This gun was very sloppy in that dimension. I was working with two young lawyers that were reporting back to their boss and it was my first case. I didn't know the rules or how best to demonstrate my findings but I was very confident the gun would fire IF we duplicated the actual event (without the injury!)

The question in my mind that I didn't dare share was *How much friction was there between shell and chamber when the accident happened?* Friction from dirt, rust, goo or just ordinary dust bunnies under the bed could gum up the shell enough to make it fire, but would it also fire with a cleaner chamber as in our test? I was counting on the inertia of the shot shell to allow the primer to fire but I could visualize it only bouncing the shell without being enough to fire it, too. A dirty chamber could become very important but there was no way to 're-dirty' it before the test.

The lawyer rented the pistol range for an hour and hired the same professional videographer used by the defense lawyers to video tape our live fire test the next morning at Bass Pro Shops. Just before quitting time the day before the test, the boss lawyer came in to check on progress and asked me several very pointed questions that seemed designed to scare me to death with what a failure of that video test would mean to the case. My first reaction was to say, "Fine, let's go out back and try it in the parking lot, first." City people have very little humor when six figures are on the line.

His reasoning was simple, though, and I agreed with his decision not to do a prior test once he told me why. He said it would be much more powerful testimony if I could refute the other side every step of the way. The photograph was upside down, that part of the defense is gone. The gun was defective by looking at it and the tests they conducted were not meaningful. That kills their defense. And, we were so confident in the results of the gun reenactment examination there was no need for a pre-test. We just did it. If that sequence could be gotten into the record during my deposition it would strengthen our position. The bouncing penny pictures should be enough to win, but their video of an un-firing gun was a trump card still in their hands.

The defense's tests on the firing line had been a full thirty minutes long. Their expert gun handler kept misreading the serial number and then he would fully cock the gun and have to safely get it de-cocked to try again. The video was many minutes of boredom with several dry 'clicks' when the gun failed to fire. I was determined to do better than that, so I memorized the make, model, gauge and serial number and a little statement of what I was going to do, how it would be done, and then just did it. My intention was to do one test and be done in a dramatic one minute or less.

The videographer was a girl of about 25 years that usually shot advertisements for car lots and beauty parlors and had not quite gotten used to the fact we were in the middle of a shooting range mid-way between the firing points and the backstop, because that's where the light was best and it was less crowded. She was still spooked by being around loaded guns but said several times, "At least it only clicks instead of shoots!"

I loaded the gun with the barrel pointing upward and rotated it around to close it just as it would have been under the bed. The videographer had been told to get in close and catch the different angles and she was right there. I'd also marked the receiver with a small ink spot to tell me exactly where to release the hammer.

I went through the evidence spiel of date, time, location, subject gun and the test to be performed for the record, and then just did it. BOOM! The camera hit the floor and its operator hit the door at about the same time. It was hilarious to see. She was hyperventilating and apologizing and examining her (still running) camera all at the same time. It made a great tape for the jury. We did three more tests with three more shots just to show it consistently failed and then we had a beer for lunch. Their trump card was proven to be a joker, but they still didn't fold their hand.

The entire case was fast-tracked as far as I was concerned. The plaintiff's lawyer had been looking for an expert and I was last on the list because I was brand new. But the trial was to be in the hometown of the largest Remington plaintiff's lawyers in the country, and they had just hired me on a Remington case in Montana and the present case would give them a chance to see me in the courtroom. They got me hired on the K-Mart case so they could see me work and get a preview of testimony to come in their Montana Remington Model 700 case.

The examination, the various tests, my written report and testimony, first by deposition and then in federal court, would take place before my first Remington deposition testimony in Great Falls, MT.

The K-Mart case was so far along by the time I was brought on board, that when I mentioned a firing pin spring rate calculation I'd done, the lawyers turned a little pale and told me an engineer would have to testify to that and it was too late to hire one. What to do? The lead lawyer mentioned that I'd already done the calculations so maybe I'd qualify and asked me directly how much math I'd had in school. I told him I'd had three years of algebra. He could see it was a simple algebraic formula that was easy to do. He was ecstatic and said that would certainly qualify me as enough of an engineer to get it in the record. Then I told him he should know that all three years of my algebra were Algebra One. He went a little pale again but he gambled the judge wouldn't ask too many detailed questions about what that algebra had consisted of, and he was right.

My written report was short and to the point and followed a format I'd read in one of Tom Butter's reports. I was confident in my conclusions, and I knew lawyers could really bore in and get tough, but I'd never been 'over the wall' to do battle with them before. I had read enough depositions in the few short months as a new expert to know more or less about what to expect though. I didn't fully realize the depositions I'd been reading were mostly of the victims and the defense treated them gingerly and with respect. That was not necessarily so with an adversarial expert.

Deposition day came in Missouri about two months before the trial. The lawyers and paralegals told me to always listen very closely to the entire question before starting to formulate an answer. That's tough to do, but it's the best advice I've ever gotten from a lawyer. They also told me to expect every question of real importance to be asked at least three times in at least three different ways. It was a short course on how to testify and what to be wary of. I was told that once a statement is 'on the record' it's hard to ever wipe it out. The deposition was to be videotaped and I was reminded that I was talking to the jury during a deposition.

As it turned out, the deposition went great. I'm always comfortable talking about guns and it was pretty clear the defense knew very little about them. The difficult part was making the spoken word easily readable. I needed practice there!

The trial was three days of intense work on my part. I got on the stand in my first Federal Court case in early afternoon and was examined by 'my guy' to establish who I was, what my qualifications were and what I was going to testify to. The defense asked the judge to let them cross-examine me on my qualifications before admitting me as an expert. They didn't tell me about that part, but it went well and I was certified as a Firearms Expert.....and even a mechanical engineer later when the firing pin return spring rate was brought up.

In response from my attorney's direct questioning, I showed the jury how the gun was lying under the bed and how it was removed and how the hammer spur snagged on the nightstand leg that we had in the court room. I demonstrated the penny test and stood for an hour or more at the Elmo machine with a laser pointer showing the path of energy inside the gun. I showed how the hammer was drawn back to store energy in the mainspring and what happened when that energy was released in a gun that had a firing pin just a smidgeon too long. In the back of the courtroom were three lawyers from across town making notes. Rich Miller, the only one of them I'd met, nodded slightly and smiled as he left. I thought that was a good sign.

The next day was cross examination day by a tall, thin lawyer from St. Louis with a stiff neck and a habit of letting his arms flop outward when he turned around fast. The arm motion was almost distracting, but he was boring in hard on every word I'd said or written and basically went back over the deposition, reports, and yesterday's testimony again and again. He was getting to be very redundant but the judge had leaned back in his monstrous black chair and seemed to be asleep. The jury had quit paying much attention as the lawyer asked yet another question that was not quite redundant enough to object to but just obnoxiously inconsequential to the trial.

Then, the defense lawyer started in a direction I'd been told was 'off limits' because it made no difference to the case. I'd been sent a couple of shotgun shells to look at to determine if they'd been shot in the same gun. I'm not a tool marks examiner, have limited training in that job, and certainly couldn't be called an 'expert' so why bring it up? It looked like he was trying to justify his fees to the big company bean counters perched in the courtroom behind the defense table. He wasn't helping his case, but he was ticking off hours with question after redundant question and then he veered off into the field of the tool examiner. I glanced at my attorney and he shrugged.

I took a drink of water (to speed up the time to recess) and we went through about ten minutes of testimony about how I'd looked at both primers through my microscope with an oblique light source and I could tell that both had been hit by the same firing pin, but one had been hit more than once by "a" firing pin, but the last impact had been by 'the' firing pin. I fully expected to be called a non-expert and why would I say such a thing without having one or more degrees to qualify me as a tool mark examiner.

No doubt there was a trick coming but I didn't know what. I recognized the danger sign of trying to analyze one strategic puzzle while answering another question about a different subject, so tried to concentrate hard on what he was asking and not where he was going with the line of questioning. Then he took a different and surprising direction again! He asked if the gun had also been sent to me to examine under my 'non-professional' microscope. He'd been snide and condescending all day but he was now down right venomously arrogant like he could make me go away with a tough question and the jury would laugh at such an imposter in the witness chair, and maybe I'd disappear in a puff of smoke.

I said, "No sir."

He wheeled around to the jury so fast he nearly backhanded the court reporter and started into a high-sounding, semi-rhetorical question directed to the rafters as his grand summation of that line of questioning:

"Mr. Belk, do you mean to tell the jury here today, under OATH, that you can tell a mark made by a piece of steel without also having that piece of steel?! How do you propose to do that?" I thought he'd strained something there at the end. The double question was improper, but he probably thought he'd killed my credibility with that one bluster.

I said, "The same way the FBI identifies your fingerprints without having your finger."

The first sound I heard through the giggles of the jury was the judge's chair flopping forwards and the judge asked, "Are you finished with this witness *now*?" His neck was even stiffer walking back to his chair....and red. That was my first time of 'Poking the Dragon'. It can be costly.

My lawyer's re-direct cleared up a few things that might still be lingering as a misconception in the jury's mind and we ate a good steak that night rather comfortable in our position. I was asked to stay at the office and field questions during the defense portion of the trial that started the next day. "Sure!"

I sat in the conference room and reread the oppositions (ridiculous) report and depositions to be prepared for how he might testify, while in the courtroom the defense expert was wowing the jury with his education and experience and his books and articles and expertise as proven by his many cases. After lunch the cross-exam began with questions I'd helped formulate the night before and during the lunch recess.

By the first break the jury had laughed at his upside down door pictures and he'd had to testify he'd not accounted for excess headspace in the test firing demonstration and then that he'd actually testified for the plaintiff in a case involving the same model shotgun and his testimony was at odds. Then, for another hour, my guy bored in with every misinterpretation, misstatement, wrong analysis, and conflicting testimony already given, and nailed him to the wall again and again with the details.... and then the second break.

During the second break, the 'expert' witness was seen by the grandmother of the victim going into the woman's restroom. Then the grandmother warned ladies of the jury of that fact and that got the bailiff involved because a plaintiff's family member had spoken to a juror, and then the judge got involved by word of the bailiff that a violation had been noted. The judge told the bailiff to go in and get the gun expert out of the stall.

The expert said he wasn't feeling well and asked to be excused.

Their case had been smoke and mirrors all along and the jury gave the victim what was asked. The girl with the terrible scars got enough money to go to college... and the lawyer's kid did too.

Didn't you get paid, too? How much?

Not enough to share with my kids, but I made about $5k on that case. That is part of the lawyer's expenses and is paid no matter the outcome. I have no skin in the game, only my expertise is considered.

So, what happens when one of your gun buddies gets sued? What then?

Interesting question that has never come up, but I testify to mechanical facts as seen in a specific place. *Who* made it wrong is not something I consider. I don't testify against anybody or any company. I testify for one side as to the mechanical facts and let the rest of the case happen as it will. I have no part in it but the technical. I don't 'keep score'.

But, it is illegal to build a faulty gun, right?

Not really. There is no law saying what gun can or cannot be made or how they're made. Some guns are *so* bad as to invite accidents.

Some are so good by design and manufacture that they cannot fail. It's the ones that 'can' fail that need to be well documented. There is a reason you don't see recognized unsafe products in **any** store in America. The above case used the "Ozark's Law" against a major discount chain. It all came about with toasters on sale in the Ozark Mountains. They were really cheap toasters, too.

It only took six house fires that were traced back to a bad toaster to find a major discount house had bought a container load of the toasters *after* they were found to have defective wiring. The Ozark's Law says you can't sell to po' folks inferior goods that are dangerous, no matter how cheap they might be.

Hey! I have an H&R shotgun like that. Is it also dangerous?

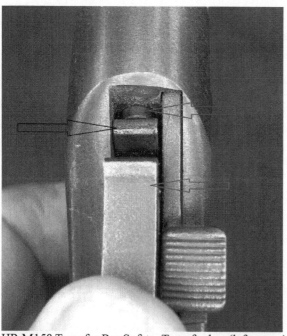

HR M158 Transfer Bar Safety. Transfer bar (left arrow) rises to cover firing pin as the hammer is cocked, but must be held there by finger pressure against the trigger for the gun to fire.

The H&R M58 had been around for several generations, and there's no way of telling how many long firing pins were put in them. Sometimes small screw machine parts are bought by the steel drum full so many thousands of bad firing pins could be in place yet today. Guns don't heal themselves of a defect just because the factory fixed the problem in subsequent models.

You can tell if an M58 is an early model if it does not have a rising trigger transfer bar system. Slowly pull the hammer back and see if a part rises to cover the firing pin. That is the transfer bar (left arrow) that allows the hammer to hit the firing pin. If the transfer bar is *not* there, it is certainly susceptible to failure like was found in the Missouri shotgun.

That simple safety system can also fail by the safety notch being misshaped. That was seen in the case of a death by the same type shotgun in a neighboring state many years later. That was a single shot shotgun, under a bed that was pulled just a short way before the lamp cord wrapped around the hammer pulled it far enough back and then let it go which killed the guy. That firing pin was NOT too long, but the safety shelf of the hammer had been rounded off to where it did no good as a safety. When the hammer went forward the trigger rode over the safety shelf and the gun killed him.

Rule--- The firing pin cannot be impacted in any way except by the hammer and by action of the shooter.

Why the qualification, 'by the shooter'?

Because if the hammer is impacted by something else, like the ground or a falling saddle stirrup, the gun can fire if the firing pin is affected. There has to be a way of preventing a falling gun from hitting the hammer and firing. That is what takes gravity out of the operation of the gun. Only springs should fire the gun, and springs should be controlled by the shooter.

Let me review just a minute what we're trying to learn here. The first case I mentioned about the Ruger Blackhawk .41 that shot the traveling salesman failed in its safety by breaking the fragile sear portion of the trigger. That is a *defect in design* because there isn't any steel available that can take that much impact on that small a part and survive. For the trigger to be light enough to use, the safety portion has to be too weak to be safe, *by design*.

The second case, of the single barreled shotgun shooting the girl in the belly, was a *defect in workmanship*. The wrong length firing pin was installed. The blueprint called for the proper, shorter length pin. A shorter firing pin would not have allowed the gun to fire because the trigger would have banged into the safety ledge before the hammer hit the firing pin. The major retailer also *failed to warn* their customers they were selling guns already deemed 'not state of the art'.

So far, everything has had a visible and explainable cause to it and reason for it. Where's the big mystery?

Thanks for the question.

I'm skipping around some trying to get everybody familiar with following the energy before getting too complicated...

Complicated my butt! Don't pull the trigger and don't cock the hammer and don't point at what you're not going to shoot. That's it!

< It could be a long road with this bunch.>

The object lesson here is how the trigger and its sear end engage with the hammer. Here is another picture of the system used by H&R and made famous by Hopkins and Allen in the 1800s, and how the simplest of the passive safety systems work using a hammer **block** that uses the sear end of the trigger to block it.

Notice how the hammer spring rests against the hammer and causes the hammer to come to rest *behind* the tip of the trigger? The trigger return spring pushes the sear end up against the hammer any chance it gets. The hammer rotates so that the sear end of the trigger just barely misses the safety shelf if the trigger is held back. That's where the 'finger spring' comes into play and keeps the trigger pulled long enough for the two parts to skim past each other without touching.

If the gun is dropped or jarred so hard that the trigger and hammer were disengaged, the trigger return spring makes sure the trigger end impacts the safety shelf and blocks the hammer from hitting the end of the firing pin, if the firing pin is the right length.

Mechanism similar to H&R's in cocked position. The trigger must be held back for the sear-end to clear the hammer-block safety shelf as the hammer rotates.

In the subject gun, the hammer hit the firing pin about .018" before the sear contacted the safety shelf. That critical eighteen thousandths of an inch, about a match book cover of thickness, of too much length, ruined a little girl's life.

As seen in the example of the salesman's Ruger .41 mag, safety depends on the toughness of the weakest part. That weakest part is the sear tip of the trigger, and impact can crush it and cause the gun to fire if dropped.

Why don't they make the trigger bigger and tougher so it won't break?

To make rotating hammer triggers useful to the shooter, they have to be thin and very hard and that means brittle. John M. Browning solved some of that problem by making an independent sear with its own pivot that the trigger pushes or pulls on and that is what disengages from the hammer. That divides the impact of a drop of the gun between two cross pins instead of one and it allows the sear to be much tougher than the tip of the trigger would be by using a leverage advantage to thicken the hammer-sear engagement surface. The chance of crushing a sear tip in a Winchester Model 94 is much less than in a Colt single action revolver. The 'safety' works exactly the same, but the Winchester is much tougher, but not tough enough to prevent an accident involving a falling gun with enough energy applied to the hammer to break the sear and fire the gun and badly injure somebody. That's why they now have a cross button, additional manual safety, that positively blocks the hammer.

The Old Model Ruger Blackhawks, any single action Colt or Colt clone, all the hammer fired lever actions and many more are dependent on the simple 'block the hammer with the sear in a safety notch' system with varying amounts of safety involved.

Browning Superposed, full cock position, safety ON

One of the finest guns in the affordable realm is the Browning Superposed. Note the extremely simple safety system that does nothing but pull the trigger bar back away from the sear. The top thumb safety is nothing but a disconnector! The real safety features are passive and operate without instructions from the shooter.

That bottom notch in the hammer (big shiny thing in middle) is the safety notch. If the sear (directly above) becomes displaced from the hammer, the sear will *intercept* and *block* the hammer before it hits the primer. If the impact should break a sear pivot pin, the sear is jammed into a socket in the upper tang. The hammer still doesn't fall far enough to risk hitting the primer. The right big shiny thing is an inertia block that swings sharply back when the butt hits your shoulder in recoil and switches the trigger bar to the unfired barrel.

What about pistols? My brother in law just shot himself in the leg and the cops said it was 'common'! That seems an odd way to describe a gun accident.

There is a clear line between 'common' accidents and 'rare' accidents. The dividing line stands at about 15 pounds of applied force in handguns. A gun that fired with less than 15 pounds of force would have been called defective until a new generation of pistols showed up in the last few decades.

<I sense a ripple of discontent and angst in the back row.>

5. Glocks and Glockenclones

What about double-action autos? Do you claim they're unsafe too?

It depends on another definition. They are 'inert'. They don't have any compressed springs except the magazine spring. Most are by design, safe, but not *as* safe as a good quality DA revolver.

Glock 19 compact model

<Muttering in the back row is higher than normal, like a bee hive that's just smelled a skunk.>

Why not?

Yeah, why not?

Remember the big family of perfectly safe, so-called 'inert' guns I mentioned but we never talked much about in chapter 1? It's time to run back and make sure they're understood.

There's an entire group of guns that are 'inert' in that no springs are compressed, even with the guns fully loaded. Those guns will eventually rust away into a wad of geologic goo if nobody messes with them. They *cannot* fire if dropped, beat on, squashed, thrown or drowned. They will fire if exposed to enough heat, but otherwise they're just a lump of assorted metals with a lot of potential, but a certain amount of force has to be exerted and held on a very specific part to make it fire. That force not only compresses the 'mainspring' that will cause the firing pin to hit the primer, but it also unlocks several 'passive safeties' that are in place until removed by the shooter by simply pulling the trigger. These designs started in 1898 and by about 1905 had been adopted in one way or other by most all the pocket pistol makers. Up until that time, the 'inert' guns were 'single-action'. They were cocked by something other than the trigger.

The new pocket guns are 'double-action' revolvers. There are no safer guns on the planet *by design*. I have recovered hidden guns for people after a death in the family that were loaded with ammunition not available in the same century we are in. The guns are always ready, but are totally inert until needed.

The family of 'safe/inert' guns has been divided and seriously degraded *by design*, and that genie will not be put back in the bottle. Some so-called 'inert-safe guns' can now be fired by toddlers and dogs, and even by trying to catch them to keep them from falling. This is the result of simply lightening the amount of pressure needed to 'operate' the gun. Sure, they're more accurate to fire with a seven pound pull, but your cat can supply that by jumping off of it (Yes, I know of the case.). The fifteen pound dividing line is real.

Double-action revolvers since 1903 and single-actions since 1973 have mostly been of a 'safe' design that demands the 'main' spring be compressed *and* the trigger pulled, *and* held to the rear to fire. That is no longer the case today, and in many instances it's not even the norm.

I will always be critical of guns that operate in DA mode on less than fifteen pounds of trigger pull. I'll also always be critical of a gun that does not use a secondary 'finger spring' safety to assure the gun does not 'jar off' by being dropped or snag on something if thrown. Limit firearms firing to a human activity and the accidents are fewer and easier to understand. A gun should shoot only by direction of the shooter in pursuit of sport, defense, or to use as a weapon offensively. There should never be a *'the gun did it'* discharge.

I agree guns shouldn't fire until we want them to, but why fifteen pounds?

Fifteen pounds of double-action pull is the approximate point where a kid can't shoot it.

What size kid? MY kid can!

Maybe your kid can fire your run of the mill DA revolver, but it's because you taught him and urged him through the pain of tender fingers on a sharp-edged trigger. Toddlers don't usually shoot revolvers but they sure do the new 'plastic' autos with the light DA pulls. The news is full of them. There is a YouTube video that shows a Middle Eastern wedding party dancing and partying pretty hard for folks without liquor. In the middle of it a portly guy in uniform pulls a CZ-75 pistol and shoots a couple rounds into the ballroom ceiling. Then he allows a very small boy to have the pistol while he dances around with the arms up and obviously in some kind of bliss. In the mean time, we see the kid fumbling with the pistol but can't quite get it right until he gets two fingers inside the guard, then shoots the prancing officer right under the ribs. Of course that's a stupid-cubed example, but it's one that has a lesson in it (besides avoiding people that don't know pistols from firecrackers.).

That's a CZ with a heavy pull, too.

I suggest you see the video yourself to see how the kid could not pull the trigger with one finger. Had anyone been paying attention that particular shooting would not have happened. I still wonder about the photographer that filmed it without warning anybody.

Fifteen pounds of DA pull is also about the point the gun becomes immune from falling from six feet high. You can work out the energy of weight and acceleration for your gun if you like. Sir Isaac wrote out that law, too. It involves the weight of the gun and the speed at impact. The formula applies to impact on the hammer or snagging the trigger on something like a stub of some kind. Will the trigger be pulled if it falls from a closet shelf six feet high and snags on a high heel shoe? It will if the trigger pull is only seven pounds and it doesn't need the 'finger spring'. All it takes is impact on the trigger of sufficient force and the gun can fire. I know of that case, too. At least they usually shoot downward. Tender toes should not be targets, either.

Fifteen pounds of steady pressure will usually dislodge the gun from its position instead of pulling the trigger if, for instance, the cat jumps from the couch to the chair with his hind foot on the trigger. There are multiple cases similar to that.

Fifteen pounds of DA pull is heavy enough to catch your falling gun without it shooting you. The instinctive grab of something valuable about to be lost forever can kill you if the trigger only takes seven pounds of DA pull. Catching a revolver will unlock the cylinder many times, but it won't fire without fifteen pounds of DA pull.

It requires about fifteen pounds to seat the gun in an old fashioned leather holster. Many cops have been shot in the leg while holstering a gun that takes less than 'normal' DA pull to fire it. All it took was a holster strap run through the trigger guard as the gun was holstered (common occurrence) and the gun fired as the cop seated the gun. That was a wake up call that less than fifteen pounds of DA pull is unduly dangerous *by design.*

We all know the answer from the industry; redesign holsters and train cops to shoot entirely differently than they do with heavier DA revolver pulls. To an old-timer, the 'finger outside the guard until XX time' is patently ridiculous and stupid. With fifteen pounds of pull, there can be no 'mistaking' the pulling of the trigger. Pulling a trigger should be a very conscious act. Of course, if we cock a revolver single action and take careful aim, we're doing exactly what we intend to do. Pulling the trigger double-action should be hard enough to not misunderstand what you're doing.

It used to be said, and I believe it's true of revolvers in a gun fight: a third of the DA pull is nerves, a third is on purpose and the last third is in panic that it won't be quick enough. That one third of an old DA pull is now more than it takes to fire the gun. How many (honestly) have fired without real intention?

Every known accidental shooting of the 'safe' and inert guns has been with a trigger pull of less than fifteen pounds. Last week it was yet another police firearms instructor that had the ultimate failure of training and blush control when his service pistol shot him as he preached to the class how smart and attentive you have to be to operate a Glockenclone pistol. Let me correct that. He shot himself... with a gun that *by design* is not as safe as guns were previously known to be.

I'm not here to argue Glocks and clones versus S&W etc. I just give information.

<...loud jeers from the rear end of the room>

I'd much rather talk of specific cases that better illustrate the point. The similarities in Glocks and their clones to the traditional, century old S&W and Colt designs are striking, of course. Both are in a totally un-compressed, un-cocked, but fully loaded condition until the trigger is pulled. Both have positive blocks or locks that prevent the firing pin from touching the primer *unless* the trigger is pulled.... but, then they diverge in a cluster of systems to actually fire the gun.

Hold on just a second, please. Let's go back to that magic fifteen pounds of force. Are you saying anything below that is unsafe?

That is an absolute that I won't commit to. There are guns that are using creative leverages and linkages to get a light pull but over a longer distance. The main difference is in how the mainspring is compressed. More leverage means less force. That means less DA pull is needed to fire the gun. Both guns have internal 'passive' safety devices that are designed to block or prevent firing unless pressure is applied and held on the trigger. The force *and* the length of the trigger pull needed to fire the gun constitutes the safety. If you pull the trigger hard enough and far enough, it WILL fire! The operational phrase common to all of them is 'pull the trigger to fire'. Passive, inert, totally safe revolvers and autos many times are just that simple. The force the shooter has to introduce into the trigger pull and the length of the trigger pull determines the safety of the gun.

In an effort to get under the fifteen pound 'rule' some makers are allowing a lighter pull (usually ten pounds or so) but with a longer than normal trigger motion. The Ruger LCP is a good example of that. I'm sure there are others. The advantages are obvious. They're usually small, light and easy enough for a lady to shoot. A lady fumbling for lipstick is unlikely to pull the trigger *far* enough to fire it, even if she did pull it *hard* enough.

Ruger LCP. Trigger is light like a Glock but it has to be pulled through a much greater distance.

I'm sure the guy in Arizona that was peacefully sitting in the barber chair with both arms outside the shroud, when his brand new light pull, short-pull, plastic 9mm pistol removed a most valuable body part as he shifted position slightly. He thought his brand new, big name pistol was safe. He never thought a little belly roll could apply eight pounds of pressure and nearly a half inch of motion, but it sure did. The gun was otherwise perfectly inert and safe. A virtual multitude of law enforcement officers can testify (if they wanted to) how surprising a short, light trigger pull can be. Many have the scars to prove it.

When nerves alone are worth six pounds, seven is unsafe.

I call the cases 'Glockenclones' and I've had several. In every case the gun operated *as designed* and shot somebody. That, by my definition, is NOT a firearms accident except for the variance in known safe design parameters. Too light and/or short DA trigger

pull is said to have resulted in an 'inadvertent discharge'.
Sometimes it resulted in death or injury.

I hear the ones yammering in the back about training and practice
and range time and proficiency in operation of your pistol, but you
are missing a big point. Let me try it another way.

Guns are by nature meant to be comfortable and semi-instinctive to
shoot. That's why the trigger is not out of place or the grip on the
wrong end. They're meant to be natural to point and easy to pull
the trigger. Hand an **empty** pistol to a toddler and he'll show you
how. Let him have an easy enough time of it and he'll find one
laying around and kill you with it, too. Do we rate such a killing
as an 'accident'? Not of the gun. It performed exactly as **designed.**
It was (a preventable) accidental use of a deadly weapon by one
too young to understand the ramifications of pulling the trigger,
"just a little bit."

The light trigger 'plastic pistols' (hey, it's my book) are popular for
many reasons. I don't think movie placements can be overlooked.
It worked for Dirty Harry and the Model 29 S&W. Newer movies
featured 'cool' guns that became a must have by those that follow
the herd. As said before, the light pull DA auto will not be put
back in the genie's bottle, but it would be nice for that particular
deadly genie to at least be understood.

It is a given that a seven pound pull in a DA pistol is more accurate
than a fifteen, or more commonly, eighteen pound pull on a
revolver. Yes, there's no doubt about it. The question becomes *Is
it more important that the shot be accurate, or is it the need for
shooting that is more important?* The citizen suffers when cop
guns shoot too soon.

If a DA auto pistol with a light pull fires by surprise (read the
hundreds of reports) it means the gun is deficient in safe design
just like the Colt single action that breaks the tip of the trigger and
shoots the cowboy down his hind leg without warning. But in the
case of a Glockenclone, it could be a dead citizen and a cop that
had *reason* to shoot, but not the *intention* of shooting a threatening
guy. I believe that makes them both a victim of *poor gun design.*

What are the specifications that must be met? You can't have a really light accelerator on a sports car, why then an unsafe trigger on a pistol?

There are no such specifications. What was learned through trial and error and military wish lists became 'standard' over the last hundred years, but nobody enforces anything. Some Glock kits will give the (unwise) shooter carrying it a three pound trigger pull. That is not an inert pistol if its weight will fire it, no more than a rifle would be safe to carry around with a set trigger only. Light trigger pulls are advantageous on the range and downright dangerous in the field. Such light pull kits should be considered 'specialty' conversions.

When defense is the job, we all want something dependable and instinctive to use.

If there's any action more than simply pulling the trigger to shoot a defense gun, especially in guns meant to be carried, it does take training and practice and experience and dedication to get good at it in tight situations. The Army figured that out when they adopted the 1911 Colt (single-action) auto. It was carried cocked and the hammer locked back by the safety, so it took two motions to shoot it. You had to remove the safety and then pull the trigger. It takes a *lot* of training for those actions to become natural when the adrenalin starts squirting. Then, some autos were made in which the safety lever works in the opposite direction of the 1911. Officers have been killed that reverted to 1911 training but were carrying a newer, European pistol.

The vast majority of the 'inert' guns are kept in night stands and closet tops waiting for that thump in the night just before your heart tries to escape and your mouth goes bone dry and the silhouette has a weapon! Training be damned, grab the gun and pull the trigger! With revolvers, at least if it doesn't shoot the first time, just keep pulling until ammo shows up. You can do it one handed, too. That is a great tactical advantage regardless of the experience level.

Can you name a time a Glock has malfunctioned.

'Malfunctioned' is a very specific word when it comes to firearms. The guns 'performed as designed'. My point is the design, by being different that the historical norm means more accidents from one group of guns than others. I personally know three cops with bullet scars caused by their own Glockenclones. There has never been an instance of S&W or Colt DA revolvers shooting cops by accident no matter the millions of man hours they've been carried. They have at least fifteen pounds of resistance to being fired. Maybe that's a better way to put it.

Even anecdotal evidence has weight when piled up that high.

It gets even more significant when the testimony of a fourteen year old boy is read. He and his best buddy were going to sleep in the pasture that night and went to get the sleeping bags stored in his parent's room. A Glock M19 was hanging in a holster on the bed post. He only showed his buddy and pulled the trigger "just a little bit!" That little bit was measured to be 8.3 pounds. About half of the K-38 S&W his dad let him shoot sometimes. Half the K-38's trigger pull was deadly, but the pistol operated exactly *as designed.*

I would welcome an ergonomic study of firearms operational forces and how they compare across the industry. Some such studies have been done and some generalizations can be made. Trigger pulls are easy to understand, but how about other operational forces needed to operate other parts of the gun? I saw a rifle being shown to a lady one time that cut her finger trying to apply the safety. Obviously it can't be that hard because people would quit using them. But they can't be too easy, either. A safety should be taken off on purpose, but not so a deer can hear it!

Whoa! What happened to the revolvers versus automatics and what made them dangerous. Why suddenly the shift to rifle safeties?

Guns, by design, are different but with many commonalities. One of the things in common is they're used by human beings and if people can't operate a gun as it was designed to be used, a country could be lost.

I've told you forty million times to quit exaggerating.

Well, our government found out most women could only operate the safety on a 1911 service pistol about five times before they *automatically* turned the gun on the side and pushed the safety with the other thumb. There's not enough surface to apply that much pressure to a tender-thumbed shooter over the long haul. Of course a pistol turned sideways is pointing to the recruit next to the recruit with the sore thumb and sometimes it's that person that gets shot. Surely it's never good to shoot your own troops.

Mausers made for the Peruvian and Turkish governments had high-sided clip guides because the soldiers' thumbs weren't long enough to load the clip German style. The high sides offered more support and allowed faster loading by those short of thumb. There were a batch of made-in-Brazil Winchester Model 92 clones that had such sharp serrations on the top of the hammer spur that several people got shot when their buddy went to let the hammer down to the safety notch and turned loose of it when it cheese-gratered his thumb. (That might not have been a word...'til now.)

Let's just agree that the forces to operate a gun are known well enough to recognize when something is 'different'. Watch someone try to shoot a gun that's on SAFE to see how much pressure he puts on the trigger before (finally) figuring out something is wrong.

I submit that force applied is less than fifteen pounds.

Hand a brand new shooter a brand new S&W revolver and tell him to shoot it double-action. You'll have to talk him through the heavy pull every time. Hand an old time revolver shooter a brand new Glockenclone and he'll be mightily surprised when it fires 'early'. That is not *proof* but it is an *indication* of why so many people, and so many young kids, are getting shot with inadvertent discharges by guns that still operate *as designed*. And the basic design is *safe,* but it causes unsafe results.

To gain market share, one company changed a design parameter that had stood the test of safety and time through several wars and a couple of centuries. When those easy to shoot guns became popular and nobody complained, other manufacturers had to follow suit or die. That's not the first time that's happened to the gun industry. Competition for quality drives up quality. Prices have to rise with quality. Competition on the basis of price drives prices down. Quality has to go down with prices.

Guns have to have a certain amount of precision to be safe. Precision costs money.

6. Durable Goods to Consumer Goods

I was passed a note during the break that asked a background question that might as well be answered now. It's a good 'un!

If guns are hundreds of years old, how come they still make some that don't work right?

To answer that takes a short history lesson.

Guns were first made for only one reason, to kill people and break things. Mistakes in design meant people getting hurt that are on the good side of the war. It is a fascinating study of efficiency to see the evolution of battle rifles and the pains taken to protect the soldier shooting them. It took only two failures of the new Springfield model 1903 to tell the arsenal something was wrong with their heat-treating, and banned the use of all rifles below certain serial numbers in the two arsenals affected shortly thereafter.

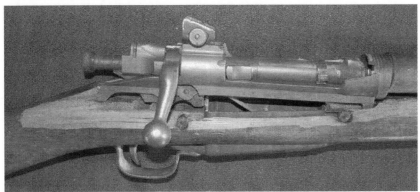

Springfield 1903A3. Pistol powder used by mistake (49 grains H-110.) The safety drilled a divot in the bridge of the shooter's nose.

Mechanical devices to make guns safer to carry and use by civilians were started in the flint-lock days when some loser in a duel shot the winner with a dropped pistol. After that 'injustice', dueling pistols had a grip safety or 'fly' in them to prevent a dropped gun from firing. By 1898, pocket pistols were being made that would not fire if dropped or even thrown. Military rifles, by the late 1890s were much safer than the brand new Remchester you're likely to buy off the shelf right now. It is a matter of

©H.J. (Jack) Belk 2014

economics.

I submit guns were much safer before process engineers got involved with them. The pained look on a guy in the front tells me maybe I hit a nerve and a puzzled look tells me one lady doesn't know what a process engineer is. They make products affordable.

I will offer as evidence guns made after WW-II in the good old USA. I think we can trace, by following design changes, the decline of safety in firearms dating back to just after the war with one company and then, like a domino falling in line, the others followed. Everybody had to get cheap or go broke.

At the end of WW-II the whole gun industry changed. There was a big intake of breath in the manufacturing industries. As in all wars, technology had run all over itself in advancement.

Machines ran faster because of better tooling, steel cut cleaner because of better alloys and heat-treating had gone from art to science. New methods, more choices, new steels and new machine tools meant complicated parts that had been milled and fitted could now be stamped, cast, formed or made on machines that ran until they broke or were shut off.

At some point just after the war, the decision was made to switch one company's marketing and manufacturing strategy from 'durable goods' to 'consumer goods'. That decision meant they would compete solely on price and availability, rather than on quality and durability in the rifle and shotgun market. Of course they tried for the best product possible because they were competing against traditional designs, but the selling price was what determined what was manufactured.....and how.

Remington Arms Company decided to scrap the forging shops over a period of a very few years and develop new models of firearms based on new and less expensive manufacturing tools, materials, techniques, and methods. The Browning designs would be phased out.

By 1948, a brand new long recoil operated shotgun, copied directly from the vastly more intricate and complicated Browning Auto 5 patent, was introduced. Even though it was short-lived by a vast jump in shotgun technology with the gas-operated gun introduced soon after, it did set the stage for the use of large blocks of intricate parts being adapted to a wide variety of guns.

The Remington Common Fire Control (RCFC) was born with the Model 11-48 shotgun. Eleven refers to the original Model 11 Remington made from the Browning A-5 patent in 1911, and [nineteen] forty-eight is the year the new shotgun was introduced.

The new design shotgun was less than a year old when the complaints started. Sometimes it would shoot twice or even three times with one pull of the trigger. That is especially disconcerting in a close duck blind or goose pit. The failure was traced down to debris gathering in a dead-end pit in the trigger group that gradually decreased sear engagement until the vibration of the bolt closing would jar the hammer loose and shoot another round.

The factory 'repair' of that recognized defect was to drill a hole in that pit so the trash could drop on through. The hole is still there but few realize why.

Drain or "Gunk" Hole, M1100

The RCFC is recognized by the two cross pins through a slab-sided receiver. They're found in rifles, shotguns, and rimfires. There are an estimated 26 million of them in use today. Once in a great while, they fail. There's more to come about that later, of course.

During the same heady times just after the war, the design of what was a pretty nice rifle, the Model 720, was being cheapened in every way possible into the Model 721. To reduce time and expense, the excellent tang mounted safety, patterned after the Enfield of 1914/1917 that Remington had been building and using in sporting firearms for decades, was changed to a stamping from sheet metal and mounted to a trigger housing. The solid trigger and sear were replaced by two sears and a die-cast 'pot metal' trigger with a hardened stamped steel part called the... *Connector*. You'll hear about that part a lot should you hang around here long enough.

Remington Common Fire Control cutaway, M7400

Instead of milling and finish grinding of hardened steel parts and then pinning them to a milled steel receiver (a la Winchester), the Remington-Walker trigger had stamped metal parts inside a folded metal box pinned to the receiver. A patent was prepared. The Walker-Haskel trigger was born in 1950 by patent, but it was already on the market and was already in bad trouble by then. It had been in rifles for three years and even the very first ones failed. Fire on Safety Release (FSR) was the primary complaint.

The Walker trigger was still in diapers when its inventor, a fine shooter and gentleman, was told there were failures from his target shooting friends and there were reports of uncontrolled firings from even the few advance triggers distributed to the trade. He wrote a memo in 1947 telling of those failures and suggesting by a hand drawn diagram in the margin, a simple fix for the most common of the reports: FIRE on SAFETY RELEASE. Walker recognized the displacement of the connector and suggested a manual re-set for it before it went into full production. He recommended what became the X-Mark Pro of 2007, but a full sixty years earlier.

That important design change had been suggested many times in the sixty years between the first complaints of FSR and the final introduction of the XMP... and Remington was essentially free to do so at any time. They made safe Browning designs for more than forty years, but suddenly had failures with their own replacement designs; failures that they denied when customers complained about them.

Sir, could I interrupt there just a minute? How can they deny it happened? The customer said it did.

They say they can't duplicate the complaint. By inference that means the trigger must have been pulled. One of my primary complaints with Remington is their unwillingness to listen to the best 'testers' in the world on the best rifle ranges in the world. Those are the places their customers use their guns and then take the time and trouble to report back to them and warn them in no uncertain terms of a very dangerous and scary condition.

A fine gun from Remington's durable goods era, the M30. Built around a modified P17 Enfield action, it has a Mauser 2-stage direct acting trigger.

The old Model 721 and its slightly later little brother, the M-722, had the shooting world abuzz. The first American post-war center-fire rifle to be offered to the public was not only less expensive than the foreign guns being snapped up by serious shooters and beginners alike at high cost, but also was more accurate, had a great, crisp, fully adjustable trigger, and didn't waste time on the finer points of stockmaking and milled parts just to look pretty. Walker also designed the great .222 Remington cartridge for the M722 and for the first time Americans had an accurate rifle that was affordable, too. The War had made rifles and rifle shooting even more popular and the gun business expanded to satisfy the market.

The great American firearms decline had begun with its oldest member taking a dive into the 'cheaper means more profits' business model. And, nobody was looking.

Between the designs of Mr. Walker and Mr. Crittenden and an engineer named Leek that designed the truly wretched Nylon 66 .22 rifle, Remington has manufactured over thirty million guns that...

CAN FIRE without the trigger being pulled

And more than 25 million of them will also...

FIRE WITH THE MANUAL SAFETY engaged.

Mine never did and I've shot Remington's until they were wore out!

I wonder how many airplanes I've ridden in have crashed? Your objection is invalid. Some do fail and if you'll be patient, I'll do my best to show you how and why.

Several times I've testified to the so-called 'Remington Rule', a phrase coined by me in testimony, in fact. The Remington Rule says that anytime five good shooters get together, somebody has a story about a Remington gun messing up and shooting when it wasn't supposed to. Many times it's the cousin of a friend of a business partner or something equally remote to the actual reporter, but somebody will have a story.

<I think the whole back row just accepted that!>

I was in a cab headed to the airport from a deposition in a Winchester 1300 case in Phoenix about 1998. The cheap Winchester shotgun had broken an incredibly flimsy piece of plastic that was supposed to serve as support for the torsion hammer spring, but instead it broke and made the hammer lean way to one side and just barely catch on the corner of the sear when it cocked. The jar of the kid jumping a drainage ditch made the sear become disconnected from the hammer and the gun fired while on safe and without a trigger pull. It killed his buddy. They were on the same dove hunt.

The cab driver asked why I was in town and when I told him of the circumstance he nearly ran off the road. He got all excited and said he'd been shot through the hips by his uncle when he was only seven years old. Just a few questions of him determined the gun in that case was a Remington Model 11-48. I explained to him how it had become obvious to me over just a few years that the accidents were more common than thought. We would all be well advised to ask *why* is that?

Don't gunsmiths share information and the companies issue re-calls and warnings and updates just like with cars and planes and dish washers and vacuum cleaners?

Not really. The internet is changing that some but for decades it was a factory rep or gunsmiths that passed information on to customers. I well remember when Winchester decided the Model 100 semi-auto rifles should not be used at all due to breakage of firing pins that turned them into machine guns that pierced the primer on every shot so the gun suddenly shot everything in the magazine and smoked like a pile of burning leaves doing it. That news came to me by way of Brownell's newsletter. Several large supply houses have email lists of customers and newsletters of one sort or another. The reality is that no one has the authority to *force* any gun company to admit anything....and some don't.

The word from Remington during the late '70s was that they were being harassed by a group of greedy lawyers that wanted to impugn the reputation of America's oldest gunmaker by making outrageous claims. I heard through customers who were lawyers in Texas of a Texas lawyer shot through the back by a Remington Model 600 rifle being unloaded by his son in the back seat. I'm sure we shared 'Remington stories', but the case in Texas really didn't affect me. I was adjusting triggers for every sport shop in the region and accepted the guns for what they were.....dangerous objects by design.

The M720, another excellent Remington from the pre-war era. Only 2427 were made from 1941 to 1944.

Several magazine articles came out that praised the Remington Model 700 trigger and even gave it an award. Nobody associated with any of those had any clue how the trigger actually worked. The only reason I did is because I'd seen one fail!

The very first reaction to the unexpected discharge of a firearm is utter disbelief and dread. By long training, most humans automatically run through a list of possible causes. "I must have touched the trigger." is almost always first on the list. Some stop there, even though in their hearts they know the trigger was not pulled. Thankfully, and due to intense safety programs all across the country, the vast majority of inadvertent discharges fire bullets or shot, up and away, and somehow miss everything important. The unlucky few blow up a transmission or a tire or a favorite hunting dog. The true victims are the people hurt by the guns and forevermore hurt by what the gun did.

Is this where you bad mouth Remington and make everybody on the back row even madder?

That happens sometimes, but facts are pesky things to ignore. I'd rather drag them out and look at them real close, but the problem is that there's probably not many here that know enough about bolt action rifle triggers to understand the significance of what I'm saying, yet. The Remington-Walker trigger is a study all unto itself and we still haven't established what a *'trigger'* is. Let's get started.

We've covered the inert guns that have no compressed springs; they are a family of firearms *more likely* to be safe to carry, store and maintain in a fully loaded condition. Let's talk about those guns that are 'cocked' and ready to shoot as soon as it gets a signal. This family includes all bolt action rifles, both rimfire and centerfire. These guns are *kinetic* guns that have enough stored energy in them to fire them.

Energy stored in the spring that drives the striker forward to hit the firing pin is energy that MUST be controlled by the shooter. A gun that can fire at any time is a hazard unlike most we have around the home. It is far more dangerous than most realize. What maintains control of that spring and how that is accomplished determines the *inherent* safety of the firearm.

The history of bolt action rifles is about a hundred and sixty years old with very rapid advances taking place concurrent with ammunition development. The secret to 'power' in a cartridge is making sure all the energy goes forward instead of leaking out the sides or back. Until the brass cartridge case became the gas seal that allowed very high pressures to build inside the gun without leakage, most guns were comparatively low-powered. By 1893, Paul Mauser was well on his way to perfecting the centerfire bolt action rifle. He chose as the triggering mechanism a tried and true, direct acting, truly simple system that allowed the soldier plenty of warning and very near the ultimate in a safe to shoot and easy to use rifle.

The simple, direct-acting trigger system blocks the cocking piece back with a sear that has a staggering .020 sq. inches of engagement with the cocking piece. This is roughly ten times more overlap, or engagement, than a modern day 'sporting' trigger.

What do you mean by 'overlap' and 'engagement'?

That refers to the amount of conflict between parts. One part, the cocking piece and attached firing pin, is being urged forward about twenty pounds worth. The sear is holding it back by interfering with that motion. The sear 'blocks' the firing pin. The trigger moves the sear.

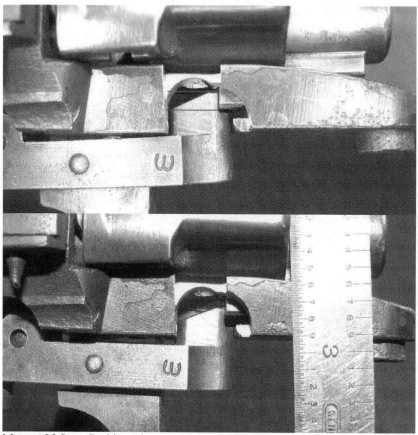

Mauser 98 Sear-Cocking Piece engagement. Top: At rest. Lines show engagement overlap. Bottom: At transfer of leverage point between 1st and 2nd stage.

With any type of triggering device, there is severe stress and abrasion. As the sear and the cocking piece separate, more pressure or 'weight' is supported by less and less material. As the sear moves, the amount of overlap decreases, but the 'weight' of the mainspring remains constant at about twenty pounds of force. The decreasing amount of surface area holding back that weight takes more and more pressure until the two parts finally separate and the firing pin is driven forward. The increased pressure right at the point of disengagement is what wears out soft triggers and breaks those that are too hard and brittle. Heat treating must be right or a trigger will fail with use.

The photos above show the sear-striker engagement in a Mauser with a standard, direct-acting trigger and sear.

I hate to be a bother, but could you tell me what a 'trigger' is again?

Trigger is a confusing term that means several different things. As a verb it means to trip or to release a source of energy. The very first triggers were in dead-fall traps. By using levers, a very heavy rock or log could be suspended over a bait or trail and allowed to fall on the quarry. That's why I have so much faith in this group understanding triggers....if Neanderthals could build and use them, surely we can understand them too!

When do we talk about adjustable triggers?

Real soon. First we need to understand there are TWO trigger systems.

Excuse me, but I don't understand one of them yet.

Let me try to cut a bunch of details out now and then try to refill the gaps with the details later.

The first trigger is 'direct-acting'. The motion of the trigger by the shooter is directly passed to the sear which disengages from the cocking piece which allows the gun to fire.

The photos that follow show sear movement in a 'two-stage, direct-acting trigger'.

The first stage is an easy pull because of the tremendous mechanical advantage of the trigger leverage. It's roughly 8 to 1, so two pounds applied to the trigger with your finger exerts about sixteen pounds of energy to the sear to displace it from the cocking piece by about 75%, but then notice the second leverage point on the trigger. By moving that leverage point back, the leverage advantage is cut down to about 4 to 1. The first stage has already moved the sear well over half way to the disengagement distance with a bare 2 to 3 pounds of force.

The remaining distance will be harder to move because the leverage was cut nearly in half. It'll take about 8 pounds of pull on the second stage to make the gun fire by pulling the sear down the last .050" or so. The inherent 'safety' portion of that is in the amount of engagement between cocking piece and the sear.

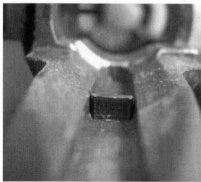

M98 Sear. Left: At rest. Right: At transfer of leverage point between 1st and 2nd stages. Only about 3 lb trigger pull up to this point.

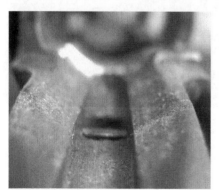

M98 Sear in fire position

With twenty thousandths of a square inch of engagement, they certainly aren't going to disconnect by accident. The sear is overlapping the cocking piece by nearly .100". The first stage trigger pull reduces that engagement considerably which makes the gun 'less safe' but at that point the rifle is being aimed and in the process of being fired. Of course it's less safe. The shooter applies the extra force needed to separate the parts in the second stage of the pull.

The security of the rifle, with the manual safety OFF, is surprisingly high. The trigger pull is long and as stated above, gets harder at the second stage. Even with no manual safety, the rifle is unlikely to fire unless something snags the trigger and pulls it a long way.

So, why aren't all triggers like that?

Because they're hard to shoot accurately. When Frenchmen were the targets, accuracy standards were pretty low. The target is large. When shooters try to do their very best, a long, hard trigger pull is very hard to manage and sport shooters demanded something better. The Germans came up with a great solution in set triggers, but they have all sorts of dangers associated with them. Winchester came up with a better solution in 1937.

Excuse me please. Way while ago you talked about sears and triggers and now you're doing it again. Could you review that part a little?

It is confusing, isn't it?

The *trigger* hangs down so your finger can pull it back to fire the gun. The *sear* is the portion of the trigger, or a separate part, that actually takes the 'weight' of the hammer or striker. A 'trigger' also refers to the entire group of parts that controls the firing of the gun. Now let me throw a big rock in your puddle of understanding.

A direct-acting trigger, as drawn and described above, is the normal trigger found in military rifles, most rimfire rifles, and all shotguns. Handguns also use some variation of a direct-acting trigger. When the trigger moves, so does the sear and it is the sear movement that allows it to disengage from the hammer or striker, and allow those firing parts to obey their spring and rush forward to thump the primer and fire the gun. Following the energy for such a trigger is as simple as pulling the trigger and seeing what moves and where and how far. Sometimes there are pivots and levers and extended bars with a hook on the end that snag the sear and fire the gun. Sometimes the trigger connects to a part that actually cocks the gun before firing it. That's the 'double-action' part of revolvers and autos.

If we look at the Neanderthal trap trigger again, a direct acting trigger is one the animal pulls on. Since early man couldn't count on his supper pulling the rock off a ledge that was going to mash him, he figured how to *prop up* that rock with a trigger that took very little force to dislodge it. That trapper ate better, had more kids and eventually invented the *over-ride trigger systems* for centerfire rifles. They're next.

Override triggers are lighter to pull and have much, much less total motion than direct acting triggers *by design.*

7. The Override Triggers

I don't know of any sporting centerfire bolt-action rifle made today without an override trigger in it, so maybe we better figure out what these things are and how they work. How they fail will come naturally. These triggers are scary-fragile yet surprisingly reliable. They are so reliable, when one fails it sometimes makes the news.

Is that the same as a 'hair trigger'?

That term is used a lot by those who have heard the term but don't understand what it is. Most think of a 'hair trigger' as an overly light weight trigger pull and the term is used as an adjective that way. Its actual root is in the springs that operate it. A true 'hair trigger' works by thumping the sear with a small hammer that has its own very light trigger. In use, the shooter 'sets' the trigger by cocking the little hammer contained in it. Then the front trigger releases the hammer with very little pressure to thump the sear and disengage it from the cocking piece. Stuart Otteson has already covered those in his excellent books and his wheel is plenty round enough. I don't need to reinvent it.

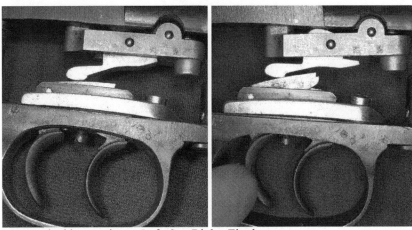

Mauser double-set trigger. Left: Set. Right: Fired.

The above described 'double-set trigger' works on a direct-acting sear.

A 'single-set' trigger operates with override designs.

CZ single-set trigger. Left: Set. Right: Un-set.

When the sear is *pulled* out of engagement, the trigger is said to be 'direct-acting'. When the sear is *propped up* by the trigger, it is said to be an 'override' trigger. The sear is the intermediary between the striker, which is storing a major bunch of energy in its compressed spring, and the trigger which is preventing the sear from falling and releasing the striker. Every sporting rifle you're likely to pick up has this type of trigger in it.

Let's just for a minute examine how this 'prop' works, because the first one to be mass marketed is upside down and backwards, and that makes all the others 'seem' backwards. Since the problems have never been with the first one made, but with the second, I'll spend very little time on the Model 70 Winchester.

In 1937, Winchester took a tremendous gamble. They installed a 'target' trigger in a hunting gun. They designed the trigger to be the simplest, safest, most dependable trigger in the world and they succeeded spectacularly. The M70 trigger is called by Winchester the 'negative angle' trigger. This refers to the angularity of the sear surface and mating surface on the cocking piece. On direct-acting triggers these surfaces MUST be square with the bore line or be extremely dangerous.

The M70 cocking piece and sear have a steep angle that makes the powerful striker spring push DOWN on the sear. The trigger is pivoted in such a way that a portion of the trigger stops the sear from going down. That is the engagement point where the trigger PROPS UP the sear. When the trigger is moved just a small amount, about .030", the sear is suddenly allowed to pivot down and the cocking piece goes forward to fire the rifle.

BASIC MODEL 70 TRIGGER

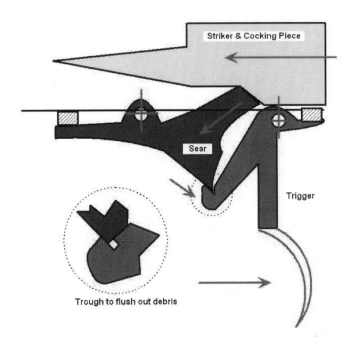

Trough to flush out debris

Notice the sear and trigger are part of a geometric intersecting of circle segments.

By *design*, the M70 trigger is self cleaning, and there is clearance for whatever gunk is cleaned from the engagement surfaces to be flushed away. There is no housing to catch debris and very limited friction points anywhere. It has two major parts and two springs and the simplicity of the design has made it famous the world over. Never mind the fact it's been discontinued for reasons still not clear. The replacement is a poor substitute, but the cheap manufacturing methods tried on the old trigger were a total disaster, too.

A certain amount of precision is necessary for a good and safe trigger. Precision costs money. There is a point at which safety is sacrificed for economy. Nobody is watching for that critical safety versus price point, either.

1953 M70 Trigger. Lines show sear engagement overlap.

The Model 70 was America's big game rifle for only ten years before it had serious competition. Four of those years were the WW-II years when sports and leisure were at their low ebb.

M70 triggers. Left: Pre-64 bottom, newer investment cast on top. Right: Sear edge on newer trigger is prematurely worn.

Very shortly after the war ended, the gun business went through a tremendous change. Some companies switched military production back to civilian models almost immediately and some had to gear up. The Model 70 override 'target' trigger had proven itself in the field as reliable and safe. No doubt there would be copies of it used in other guns. The first was Sako in Finland. FN in Belgium also made some rifles with M70 triggers installed. They're seen sometimes in the J.C. Higgins Model 51. Winchester objected as infringement and both were very soon discontinued.

Sako came up with another way to make the same trigger. But, the Sako trigger was contained inside a housing that was then attached to the rifle's receiver. The 'modular override' was born. It became the most popular trigger in the world. Sako was smart enough to design their large rifle actions to use the same modular trigger that could be retro-fitted into a military Mauser. *SHAZAM!* That threw a big rock in the sporting rifle pond. There was competition to the M70 using the *same idea* but just different enough to dodge the patent lawyers.

The modular override trigger is the same the world over in function and basic design, but varies considerably in details.

I've heard about all I can listen to without pictures. Please show me.

The diagram shows the SAKO trigger in a simplified form.

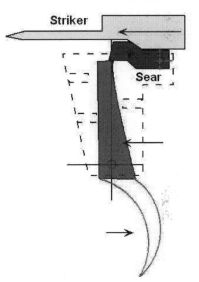

SEAR OVER-RIDE TRIGGER
SOMETIMES CALLED 'NEGATIVE ANGLE' TRIGGER

Arrows show direction of movement. The top arrow has about twenty pounds of force trying to fire the gun. The bottom, trigger arrow needs about four pounds to trip it. There are springs that return all the parts back into position ready for the next pull. It is simply two levers arranged so that the top one is being pushed *downward* and out of the way of the striker. The trigger is a lever standing vertically and propping up the sear. Pull the bottom and the top is pulled out from under the sear and the striker goes forward and fires the gun.

As can be seen here, there is a *tiny* area of overlap of the sear onto the 'shelf' of the trigger. That is the 'contact patch' of the trigger and sear. The amount of overlap is the 'sear engagement'. So the surfaces of that area are sometimes called the 'engagement surface' of the trigger and sear. That is the mechanical link between 'cocked' and 'fired' condition. When the sear falls off the trigger, which is moving forward and has tension on it from a trigger pull, it unblocks the cocking piece. That allows the firing pin to fall very quickly to 'fire' the rifle. *SNAP!*

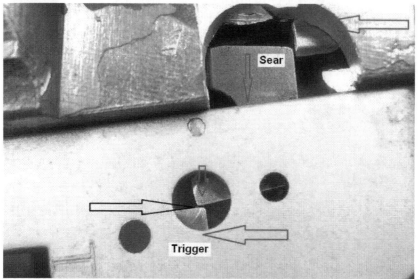

Override trigger on M98 showing lines of movement.

Obviously, the engagement surfaces of the direct-acting Mauser-type trigger has been reduced by a factor of about five. In the highest quality after market triggers the contact patch between sear and trigger can be as small as .010" deep and .125" wide......that is *one and a quarter* thousandths of a square inch. (.00125") To put that in perspective, the 'load' on that contact patch equals about sixteen *thousand* pounds per square inch! Those are 'specialist' triggers, don't try it at home.

You keep throwing out these numbers and I don't know if that's smaller than an acre or larger...

Let me get that clarified right now because we're using big words to describe very small things.

Hook thumbnails like the over-ride trigger diagram above. Left thumb up with thumbnail to the right, then hook the right thumbnail on it at right angles. If they overlap about .020", which is less than half the diameter of a paper clip, it means there's right at two thousandths of a square inch overlap. Now push down twenty pounds worth. You can't do that. The toughest of oyster-shucking thumbnails might hold half that. It takes very good steel to last the life of a rifle.

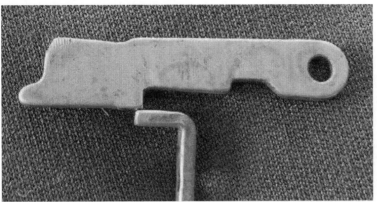

Walker Sear-Connector overlap. Holds about 20# of force.

Normal factory engagements of hunting rifle triggers are about .020" by .190" which is the width of the trigger. That adds up to three point eight thousandths of a square inch. (.0038") The 'load' placed on the contact patch is just over fifty-two hundred PSI.

So, the amount of overlap determines the security of the trigger?

Not really. Geometry, alignment, and materials suitability are the main reasons for additional security, but other issues such as lubrication, tolerance stacking, and contamination can affect performance and the safety of any trigger.

Don't you agree a dirty trigger can mess up?

No doubt about it. A dirty trigger is always a bad idea, but it is the geometry in an over-ride trigger system that is about as important as it gets. The contact patch between the trigger and the sear is the *most* important contact point in the entire mechanism and if it's not 'right' the trigger is 'wrong'. There are few 'in between' triggers. The geometry of the mating parts that is incorrect in one direction will render the trigger useless to the shooter as being too heavy or too rough of a pull from having a 'hook angle'. If the geometry is 'off' by just a small amount the other way, it can be *very* unsafe from a 'skid angle'.

Remember, the trigger is a 'prop'. Vibrations, impacts and jars are very dangerous to the prop if it's not securely positioned with flat engagement surfaces, well mated.

Skid Angles!

That picture scares me!

Me too!

The following diagram shows three examples of skid angles in override triggers.

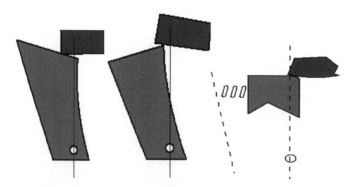

Those with critical thinking skills will immediately notice there are a whole lot of ways to screw up a precision trigger.

The illustration on the left is fragile and as dangerous as a stepped on rattlesnake. Not only is there a skid angle, but the force is applied to the trigger ahead of the pivot center. That means the sear is *pushing* the trigger forward against the trigger spring (and looking for the slightest chance to shoot somebody.)

The center illustration represents an old and common form of override trigger. Most are recognized by a hard, grating pull much like pulling a fingernail over concrete block. They then 'wear themselves in' by burnishing the top of the trigger through use because they're made of cheap material. Most of those triggers 'speak Spanish' and were mounted on Santa Barbara actions and then sold to several outfits 'sporterizing' M98 actions over the last thirty years. I've encountered them on many cheap rifles with some kind of Mauser action.

The illustration on the right is as dangerous as slapping that rattler you just stepped on in #1. This is a poorly gunsmithed trigger that was 'honed' or 'stoned' or 'polished' or 'buffed' by hand. The human hand doesn't work that well. Check out the fixtures and jigs and attachments used to maintain geometry in sharpening gravers and chisels and knives. Trigger and sear surfaces are hardened and then ground and then the good ones are lapped. ALL that work is done in a solid working environment, not by hand.

My uncle's best buddy was a gunsmith and he stoned them so fine it's unbelievable and...

He was probably very skilled at what he did. Did you notice how many times he stoned and then tried the trigger to get the very best pull?

Sure did! He worked over my dad's rifle and got the pull down to two pounds! But it took a lot of trying to get it just perfect.

There are many ways to answer your observations and I'd like to really delve into this and explain exactly what is happening. Thank you for your comment.

Take a look at the lock work below just a minute...

That's a drop-lock Westley-Richards from Birmingham, England. I've labeled the important parts. I used this illustration to put 'gunmaking' into perspective and what kind of skill it takes to fit the sear-hammer connection, which equates to our sear-trigger relationship in an override trigger.

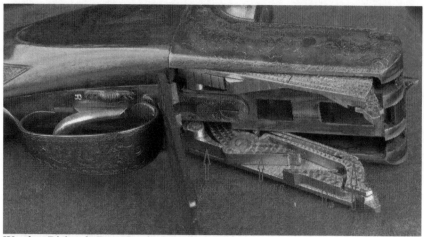

Westley-Richards Drop-Lock. Supplied with extra set of locks in the case.

The Westley-Richards drop-locks were supplied with an extra set of locks in the case. To say they're 'smooth' and 'fine' is an understatement. This is a good example of 'hand-fitted' gun making that's visible to us without too much trouble. The floorplate is hinged on both sides of the trigger plate. The little checked tab at the front of the floorplate at bottom foreground is the latch. The locks are attached to their own plate that simply slips into slots in the receiver. The tail end of the sear extends back over the triggers so that when a trigger is pulled, the sear is pushed up at the tail which forces down the sear end that is in the notch on the cocked hammer.

When the sear slips off the hammer, the hammer rotates clockwise, in this picture. The firing pin is contained in the standing breech above, and the upper end of the hammer hits the firing pin to fire the gun. The tail end of the hammer rotates downward and closes the gap we see between the hammer and the cocking bar. The tail of the cocking bar can be seen under the mainspring. It engages in the forend iron and the gun is recocked when the barrels are forced downward to reload.

Hey! Even I can see that!

Well, the point is actually this: As fine a firearm as this is, the sear surfaces were done by machine. Just take a look at a cut diamond and think about doing that holding it by hand. That can't be done. Our 'finger springs' don't allow it.

What has actually happened is that surfaces that should be flat in order to offer the most security are rounded. That reduces the friction between the parts by reducing the surface area. When done to a trigger and sear, it's like sections of ball bearings being forced together. You are right! Some very 'good' trigger pulls are attained by hand stoning or lapping, but the surfaces that make up most of the 'safety' of the trigger are seriously degraded. When somebody advertises an 'action job' on a handgun or 'trigger tuned by' on a rifle, I automatically reduce the value to *me* by the amount of replacement parts that will have to be bought. The 'action job' actually ruins the parts in most guns. At the very least, the part's usable life is cut considerably. In most guns that makes little difference, but I'd rather wear out a gun by shooting it rather than pre-rounding parts.

Why not just put the messed up parts on your machine and make them flat again?

I wish! Actually, if a trigger or sear is not too badly rounded, that can be done, but if it's more than about .002 inch it changes the geometry between sear and trigger too much. Those surfaces have to be square with the lines of force to make the two levers interact just right for maximum security.

Wait a minute. I want my trigger light and crisp and you keep talking about security. How can you have both?

All override triggers are a fine balance between 'too heavy' in pull and 'too fragile' to use. The *engagement* of parts is NOT the only factor involved. Remember geometry and proper heat treatment?

The goal is to build a trigger that releases *only* if the trigger is PULLED by the shooter, not displaced by vibration, bumps, drops, or falls.

I don't see how two little parts hanging onto each other like two fingernails can last.

As I said before, the pressures put on trigger and sear parts by a bolt action rifle are considerable. The M.H. Canjar Co. used to make some of the finest triggers in the world. They had a display showing a test trigger with no heat treating done to the parts and then one properly heat treated and both 'shot' on a test machine. The heat treated trigger was 'fired' ten thousand times and was still sharp and square. Hardened steel has very little friction, but soft steel is 'sticky' and it wears out very quickly. The un-heat-treated trigger was a rounded mess with no security at all in less that 200 pulls. By the same token, if the trigger parts were too hard and brittle, micro-fractures would begin on the sharp corners and eventually wear the trigger out by pieces flaking off the contact surfaces. Triggers and sears have to be hard and tough at the same time to withstand wear. The closest steel and heat-treat to trigger and sear specifications is a power saw blade. Saw blades and good triggers are almost identical in composition and heat-treat.

Triggers are seldom 'worn out'. Most 'bad' triggers are either bad by their very nature, or have been 'adjusted' into a dangerous condition. The important thing is to know what trigger you're using and what its limitations are. There is no magic adjustment in most triggers to make them still safe at two pounds and we'll learn why soon. The material has to match the *design*.

8. Override Trigger Design Issues

Thankfully, the national campaign for safer hunting has brought up a couple of generations of *safer* hunters and when a cheap trigger breaks or malfunctions it scares somebody enough to take it to the gun shop for a replacement. Many good aftermarket triggers are sold. Precision parts must have precision machinery and very good materials, but they both cost money and so does advertising. You can calculate a fair price from there.

The danger in all override triggers is in their fragility, unless done exactly right.

Consider how two pieces of hardened steel can possibly be overlapped and see how easy it is to make a serious mistake. The sear is on top and the trigger is on bottom and both are pivoted in the housing.

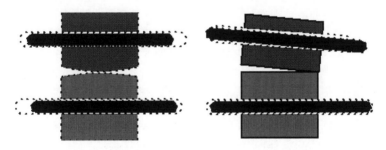

The left unit is square in the pivot holes but the parts are rounded, or they could be angled so just a corner actually connects. Either way, the amount of steel on steel friction is a tiny fraction of what it should be *by design.*

The right unit has a part mounted wrong. It can be as simple as any hole, in any direction that is not absolutely square with the housing and the other parts, and the trigger is not 'right'. Consider the pressures involved if the parts are absolutely flat, then think of all that pressure on one tiny corner. Even good steels will deform or break if misaligned. In the highest quality triggers, the holes are drilled, reamed and then lapped. Precision work costs money.

I notice you keep bringing up money? Nobody is going to buy those multi-thousand dollar rifles when you don't have to.

©H.J. (Jack) Belk 2014

We are free to buy whatever we like and can afford. But the lack of knowledge can hurt people and I've seen enough hurt people, both living and dead, to try very hard to explain how these fairly simple mechanisms fail to operate.

Let's take a break from trigger geometry and tiny overlaps and talk of a couple ways guns can fail and try to tie some mechanics to legalities and....too much blood.

Rules to go by, again…

No gun should shoot without the trigger being pulled.
No gun should be capable of shooting with the safety engaged.

The first case of the .41 Mag Ruger Blackhawk involved *no* trigger pull and the *manual safety*, the so called half-cock notch, was not sufficiently safe for the product involved, but it was engaged.

The Turkey M722 Remington fired *without* a pull of the trigger, but the safety was *being* disengaged when it fired.

The H&R Model 58 shotgun that shot the girl, fired without the trigger being pulled and the safety system did not work as designed due to bad parts installed at the factory. It was a less than currently produced safe design with a defect in manufacture.

The S&W M19 that Bill shot in the radio room worked exactly as designed. So did the Glock that killed the 14 year old boy. A lawyer asked me to review a domestic shooting case where one was paralyzed, one was killed and the ex boyfriend survived two 12 gauge slugs through the gut in a suicide attempt. He wanted to know if we could blame the gun? It was a Remington. No, it operated five times in a row exactly as designed.

How about carelessness with a safe gun?

That's a sneakily great question. I'm going to answer it, too.

Is everybody comfortable getting a case story instead of geometry?

<...lot of smiles with that one>

You feel like I did about algebra.

A young man lived with a girlfriend that worked at a pizza place that had been robbed before. It was a bad part of a rough and tumble town in Alaska. He carried as protection a tiny North American revolver in .22 LR. The first ones could be had in a belt buckle and several of my SO buddies carried them as backup guns. The sheriff would fire anybody he found without a gun within reach. He didn't say how big it had to be.

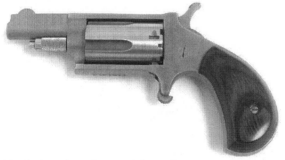

North American Arms mini-revolver.

Anyhow, the guy and his girl had gotten back to the apartment safe and sound and he watched the news while she went to bed. He reached for his pack of smokes and the gun was in a little leather slip holster lying on top of the pack. He picked them both up at the same time and reached up to pull the chain on the reading light. The gun came out of the holster and the hammer hit the corner of the lamp. The bullet hit him in the bridge of the nose and took out one eye. The lights went out for a while, but he lived.

That gun IS safe, by 1836 standards.

I thought you said there were no standards.

Correct. The lawyers call it 'state of the art'. Cars no longer have hand brakes mounted on the fender because Oldsmobile found out few people used them because they were hard to reach. To be useful, they have to be handy. If you gave Uncle Sam regulation of safety, he'd have you take the safety off with a key.

He did? Oh! For storage, I can see that.

Where were we? Oh, the NA mini-revolver. That gun has the same safety as the early Colt revolvers, before the *Civil* War.

What's wrong with that?

Nothing is wrong with it, but it takes two hands and good eyesight to put the gun 'on safety'. The cylinder is rotated by hand into the 'safe' position and then the hammer rests in a notch cut between the chambers. The hammer and its firing pin are not touching the cartridge so the gun is inert and safe at that point. It has to be cocked then the trigger pulled to fire it.

So, the gun wasn't on safe?

That's correct.

So, it was not the guns fault, then?

The gun is still defective because it fired without a pull of the trigger, but the safety is the issue. Is it also defective to not have a modern hammer block or firing pin transfer bar safety system because it can be made that way and we know that's safer? It has been done that way for a hundred years....but it costs more. Should it be required or is education enough?

He bought it! Didn't he read the manual?

Yes he did on both counts.

What happened?

The jury thought he should have been more careful.

So, you lost the case?

I told you, I'm not a lawyer. I'm not subject to wins and losses. I just give the information the best way I know how.

But, if you had of convinced the jury of the need for the new

safety, he'd have won the case, right?

It wasn't my job to convince them of anything. I showed a hammer block safety that could have been incorporated and answered questions from both lawyers while under oath. Besides, we have the freedom to buy what we want and some people like nostalgic guns that work just like the original. I'm glad I wasn't on the jury, but I didn't hear the judge's instructions and don't even know the laws in that state. I just answered questions about guns from both sides in front of people that have that important civil duty and job to decide.

Just so I get this right. The only cases are ones with a bad trigger or safety?

Firearms design and function is my specialty, but I've also given testimony in a case involving the design of a rifle range in Wisconsin and helped acquit a man accused of a shooting because he himself had been shot from a certain direction. I'll talk guns with anybody for free and the lawyers know that, so they call and ask me about interviews with clients they've had that involve guns. There are some extremely interesting cases that I wish I had the expertise to work, but instead I refer the lawyer to someone that can better help.

Yeah, Right! You pass up a chance to make a buck off of it?

I'm not in it for money, even though the opposition lawyers can't get their heads around that at all. I'm in it for *gun safety*.

Don't you have to go to school to be an expert? Aren't they all doctors and engineers and professors and things?

The American court system is very lenient when it comes to information. An 'expert' can be called that for a number of reasons. Education, experience and being a peer reviewed author, are the major ones. Both sides get a shot at knocking you off the stand, if you'll pardon the deer hunting analogy where the deer have guns.

Many times, an opposition lawyer saves his most determined attack on credibility just before you're going to answer the same questions he asked you three times before. If that fails, he'll ask the important questions three more times, three more ways and then figure out how to hang you with the intertwining answers. That's why absolutes are not used unless it's such solid, well known, common, and accepted as fact knowledge, you better include a qualifier.

Sounds interesting, what's an example?

Consider these…

Did the gun shoot?
Or, was the gun shot?

If you answer his question, you accept his premise. The only right answer is, "It shot." The argument can go on for quite a while about who or what shot it.

How do you know if the gun shot by itself or not?

Evidence is given in several forms. The shot is documented by law enforcement, emergency medical staff, hunting partners, and witness statements. There have usually been depositions of the victims, shooter, witnesses and sometimes the opposition's experts. Reading depositions is a lot like I imagine reading the lines of computer code looking for a virus. I know how the gun is supposed to work. I know how it can fail, usually. If not then, I will soon. I also know human nature and reactions to gunshots that were unplanned.

How do you know if it was the gun's fault or not?

I answer how the gun *must* have fired, to a degree of mechanical certainty. One of the reasons it *could have* fired is somebody pulled the trigger with the safety OFF. That's usually going to be the defense position of the case involving any gun accident. "Isn't it likely the gun performed exactly as designed?" is an often asked question.

I'll bet you have to answer yes to that one every time, don't you?

No, I don't. If the rifle could *not* have fired by having the trigger pulled with the safety off, but did, I have to answer "No."

Hold on just a second now. You say a gun fired but the trigger could not have been pulled?

I want to hear this one!

Here's the evidence. Figure out how it *could* have happened and you'll have how it *did* happen. It led to a safety advisory and free repair.

The rifle was a Howa .300 Win. Mag. also marketed as the Weatherby Vanguard. It is essentially a Sako copy made in Japan with new tools and very high quality. It was stored with the bolt removed in a hard gun carrying case. The victim was the shooter. He loaded three cartridges in the box magazine and inserted the bolt for the first time that year but didn't immediately close it. The rifle was now loaded with three in the magazine and the bolt is open. He pushed the bolt forward to chamber the first round and the bolt pushed back in a big way. It tore the right thumb nearly off and then broke his arm just above the elbow. The bolt was recovered more than fifty feet behind where the incident occurred.

Howa M1500 in .300 Win. Mag.

Rifles don't fire with the bolt open. They can't.

The evidence and the witnesses said it did. My job, with another expert hired in Arizona, was to find out how it fired with the bolt open. It took almost two minutes to see the defect in the *design* of the rifle. The factory mistake was very obvious and easy to repair. I think they still are repairing them for free. How many engineers didn't see the mistake? How many bean counters told them to overlook it because 'it's cheaper that way?' I don't know. We didn't get that far along.

Are you going to tell us how it happened or not?

Sorry.

The bolt was stored outside the gun in the case. As is the case with all cheapened bolt action rifles, there is no bolt shroud lock. The nose of the cocking piece in the back of the bolt serves that purpose.

Cheapened? My Remington works like that.

Paul Mauser went to great lengths to lock the bolt shroud when the bolt was open so it could not be displaced.

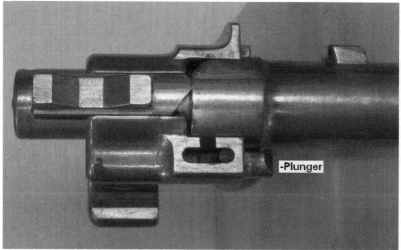

M98 Shroud Lock. Spring loaded plunger locks shroud when bolt is open. Since the shroud can't rotate, the cocking piece stays put.

The 1903 Springfield has a shroud lock as does the Model 70, but the P-17 Enfield rifle had already eliminated a separate lock in favor of using the nose of the cocking piece resting in a small notch in the rear of the bolt body. Remington copied it in the 720 and carried it on into all the 600 and 700 series rifles. They're much cheaper to build that way.

Anyhow, the bolt shrouds pictured here are all typical of bolt action rifles. Every one of them is eccentric to the bore which means they will only go in the gun if turned the right way. It's much cheaper to have just a round bolt shroud that can be turned on a screw machine. It certainly saves much time and money and materials to make them round as did Howa Machine in the early rifles.

Left: M700 cocking stud shroud lock. Right: M600 displaced shroud

What happened was this: The shroud became dislodged from its perch on the edge of the cocking notch and the cocking piece fell into the notch. That displaced the shroud and cocking piece 90 degrees counter clockwise. That turned the cocking piece stud, the piece that normally contacts the sear in the override trigger in the six O'clock position, to the *right* side of the tang to the three O'clock position.

Since the safety lever is also on the right side of the tang, like a M700, the stem of the safety lever is 'within striking range' of the cocking stud. The shroud being concentric with the bolt slides right into the tang without hitting anything until the cocking stud hits the safety lever. That pushes the safety OFF (if it was ON) and the stud hangs on the back edge of the safety just long enough to push the bolt forward against the mainspring pressure. It feels just like a cock-on-closing bolt action.

But then the pressure gets to be too much for the safety lever and the cocking stud slips off of it. The shooter has supplied the energy to compress the mainspring by simply pushing the bolt forward. The mainspring is only held captive by the cocking stud's tenuous interference with the safety lever. The locking lugs at the front of the bolt are still entirely unlocked, but the bolt is so far forward that the extractor has snapped over the cartridge rim and the cartridge is seated fully in the chamber. The bolt is only supported by the shooter's hand. That hand was not tough enough to take the approximate 10kpsi applied to the face of the bolt.

I have one of those!! Is it one of the bad ones?

The simple test is to feel the bottom of the bolt shroud. Has it got flats milled on both sides of the slot so it can't go in the rifle displaced? If it has the flats, it's a good one. *Don't* use a bad one until the shroud has been replaced. It's a bad way to nearly lose an arm. Thankfully, the scope was in the way of the hot brass fragments that could have blinded him, too.

So, was that rifle'defective in design or manufacture?

That is a classic case of *design defect*. The workmanship is top notch as is the materials used in the Howa rifles. Their mistake was designing a gun with a cost to manufacture figure firmly established before hand. It's unconscionable to allow rifle design to be determined solely by engineers and accountants. Without historical context of safety features and designs they're very likely to leave something out of extreme importance.

I heard from a magazine writer that those were the best rifles on earth! I bought four of 'em! (And I believe him more than you.)

Thank you, that's common and I'm used to it.

When the popular 'gun rag' magazines are read by the shooting public the information received is many times geared to the glossy advertising pages.

Are you accusing the gun writers of taking pay-o-la from the manufacturers?

No, never! I think there's a good case to be made they were misled by the gun companies as part of misleading the public. Marketing is like that. Howa is not going to advertise they saved almost nine cents a gun in material so it can tear your hand up. Somebody has to look at the product and recognize the presence or absence of features *needed* to make a gun safe. It's obvious the ad writers for the major gun companies are experts at language, but totally clueless about firearms.

Are you saying the gun companies are making bad guns on purpose!?

If we look objectively and pragmatically at any firearm ever made, the design, the material and how they are assembled immediately tells the knowledgeable shooter the approximate *quality* of the gun. It tells no one how *safe* it is.

My gun has a place on it that says in plain English: SAFE

Here's where definitions play a part.

The Howa, for instance, has a thumb safety much like a Remington M700. It blocks the trigger from moving while applied. That is *the* safety but that played no part in the above accident except it was *acting* as a sear. What I'm trying to get at here is one gun part can malfunction in such a way as to change the flow of energy in the gun. The quality of the rifle makes little difference if the basic *design* is not sound. That is a very important point to really get your head around. Very well made parts that are unsafely designed are just as unsafe as chintzy, cheaply made parts.

Howa 1500. Thumb safety works much like the M700

Most shooters (and drivers and golfers and every consumer) are very protective of what they have or what they trust. It's normal to want to have the best and many have trouble accepting that cost has very little bearing on safety. For that reason, it's important to know what you're paying for.

So, you think that gives you a license to be critical of everything that's not perfect?

Only with guns. I don't know enough about another product to be qualified to say. I have to take the word of the people that write reviews about them to know. Most people follow more or less that rule with buying anything. Some like Fords and some like Chevy's. Some don't care. Some like Winchester and some like Remington... why, because they don't know?

I know you're full of it!

Yep, and trying my best to dump as many true facts on you as possible. Just hold still and keep asking questions, please.

I assume, sir, your protracted and pointless ramblings have some sort of target, if you'll forgive the pun?

That's a good one.

The target is gun safety for everyone. The point is to show that we really need to be aware of the problems because we already have many millions in circulation. My purpose is to show how the industry has led us *way* astray in safety, quality, and responsibility. The very first, kneejerk, instinctively defensive action taken by the denizens of the dark back row is to holler "Personal responsibility means if you're holding the gun, it's *your fault* if it shoots something."

Damn right!

See.

Well, if you follow the rules of safe gun handling you can't shoot something you don't want to.

Listen carefully, please. There is no safe direction to point an unsafe gun.

I'll bite. What does that mean?

It means the Ten Commandments, as well intentioned as they may (or may not) be, set an unattainable goal for shooters. I think that is unfair. A shooter can *not* be at fault for handling an unsafe gun if he doesn't know how unsafe that gun might be. Would the guy that stepped in the badger hole holding a Model 1100 Remington around the receiver with the safety on, blame himself for killing his pointer puppy when the gun fired? It also tore up his right hand when the bolt handle tried to break it. There was nothing to pull the trigger and the trigger was solidly locked by the safety anyway. Whose fault is it? The hunter stepped in the hole and jarred the gun. He was carrying it as any hunter is likely to when he knows the birds went around the mountain and he's trying to get his pup back in a position to learn something. Or, was it his fault for buying a gun that contained an unpublicized defect?

Are you saying it does or does not take a broken part for a gun to shoot? Mine quit working and I took it in to be fixed. Now, I'm confused.

Up until now, everything we've discussed can be seen. There is clearly seen evidence of how the failure happened. In some instances, like the Ruger old model Blackhawk, a known problem has gotten a lot of people shot for more than a hundred years. It wasn't a secret, it was just forgotten. I see plain evidence of a much more widespread problem in the gun world that not only is not well known, it has been purposefully hidden from public view. It's time to talk of the intermittent failures in triggers.

Don't you want to finish how the triggers are made first?

For right now, every one of them is made perfectly out of perfect materials and everything about it is within factory specifications. There are no alterations, improper adjustments or aftermarket fiddling.

Then, that means there's no way it can fire improperly, right?

Going in for the early KO? But, you're wrong.

It means the *design* must be somehow *wrong*. If the rifle *still* fails, when the materials and the workmanship are perfect, it means it was *designed* wrong.

9. Override Trigger Safety

Mike Walker, as an engineer and a 'gun guy', knew there were failures in 1947 when the first batch of 200 brand new Model 721 rifles were distributed to civilian testers. They reported an especially sinister, dangerous, and insidious failure in the brand new trigger design that still carries Walker's name.

Here we go guys!

To identify what is wrong, many times its first necessary to figure out what's different.

For more than twenty years, I've been paid by attorneys to examine, explain and testify to the Walker trigger and how it fails. In addition, I'm curious and want to know for my own comfort. Some of these discussions involve the actual part named *the safety.* Some shooters are defensive about that, too.

For the record, I do not use *any* safety on *any* bolt action rifle but for a raised bolt handle.

Author's preferred bolt gun safety: Bolt open, but closed just enough for the cocking stud to be resting lightly on sear, the 'Hunter Safety'.

I have no dog in this fight, but I can explain why one is better than the other and give examples. I will also show why and how a company set a 'standard' that's been copied millions of times and makes a gun *unduly dangerous*.

Unduly what?

That is a step above *defective*. It means a design feature makes the object more dangerous to operate than it need be. Why put the gas pedal higher than the brake and too close together. It introduces an *uncertainty* into the mechanism for no good reason. I guess if somebody wanted to get around a gear shifter patent they could just move the gear shift to the left side of the steering wheel. Why not?

Let's revisit the post war rush to produce a competition-grade trigger tough enough to use away from the rifle range just a moment. Winchester had an override design that only had two major parts and no housing. It was simple, strong, very light weight, self cleaning, and field tested rugged. Sako copied it and their lawyers got letters from Winchester, so they redesigned (using several existing target triggers as models) the override trigger into a vertical trigger, pivoted in a housing, with a sear that pushed down on the trigger by action of the cocking piece. The first ones used a plunger instead of a lever as a sear.

In the diagram, the cocking piece is not shown at the top, but it would be pushing down on the sear (top) by way of the angularity on the right upper corner. These were very good triggers, but dirt sensitive. Sako changed to a horizontal lever sear and that is still the most commonly seen.

Note in the picture below the channel on the bottom of the receiver that forms the parallel mounting slot for the trigger and sear. The only adjustments are in the overtravel screw and the spring tension under the lock nuts.

Is that trigger safe?

The trigger *is* as safe as any trigger of its type.

How do you know that?

Sako with M70 trigger

I tested mine, and they have to pass the test or be changed to one that will. "What kind of test?" you're probably wondering.

Mauser Werkes-DWM was the biggest of the German small arms arsenals and made rifles for any country that wanted to pay the money. Mauser also had a sporting rifle division. Many of those fine, 'commercial Mauser' actions and rifles were going to the major makers of the time, and all over the globe to shoot exotic critters.

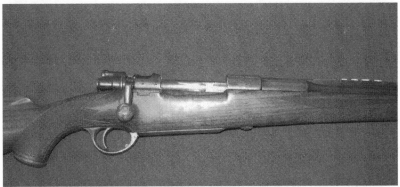

Hoffman .375 H&H Magnum. M98 action with 'dangerous game' trigger

An English sporting man that went to Africa in search of dangerous game most likely carried an English made rifle with a pure German heart. The triggers in the sporting rifles were different than the military but they're made from the same trigger. Both are direct-acting, pull the sear down from the cocking piece trigger systems, but sportsmen wanted a lighter, crisper, more target-like trigger pull. Mauser did it by reducing the amount of sear-cocking piece overlap by nearly 70%.

Didn't you say (about a year ago it seems) that reducing that connection makes the gun less safe and secure?

Great memory! I'm impressed. Now who else got the significance of the question?

<...a few nods>

All trigger systems have a sear that holds back the striker, somehow. Direct-acting pulls the sear, override pushes the sear out of the way. The amount and the quality of the overlap between those two parts that take all the mainspring pressure determine the *friction* between them. Two parts that overlap more usually have more *friction*. The geometry of the two parts determines if there's also a reduction of friction as the trigger moves by a skid angle, or an increase in friction by a hook angle. One is dangerous and the other is advantageous on a near microscopic level.

If the two hardened steel, ground and maybe even lapped surfaces travel parallel to each other as shown, a trigger pull would start out with a slight jerk and then it would slide and creep until the top part fell off the corner of the bottom part. It would be called a 'terrible trigger', but it sure would be safe.

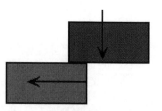

The Mauser trigger works a lot like that. Here it is 'shooting' to the right. The sear, bottom, is being pulled down by the trigger and the cocking piece on top is headed for the primer to make a big noise. Mauser decided if friction was equal to the trigger return spring pressure so that half the pull the shooter feels is interference and half is

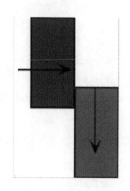

spring tension, the trigger would be *safe* to carry in the hunting fields. It was less safe than the combat trigger because he reduced that sear engagement by more than half!

How would you know if the trigger is half friction and half spring pressure?

The test is simple. It will tell you immediately if your rifle is as safe as designed. It demonstrates the ruination of many 'tuned triggers', too. I can nearly hear the howls of the trigger tuners now. Sorry guys. Our sport depends on the truth and this is it.

To test any trigger for the 'Mauser standard' which was used also by our military rifle match programs, just remove the return spring and reset the trigger and sear by pushing the trigger forward while closing the bolt on an *empty* chamber or fired/dummy case, please! (I test triggers with a fired case to catch the firing pin. Dry firing can break most.) First, take five good measurements of the trigger pull as it is now. Then, measure the trigger pull with the trigger reset by hand and the return spring removed.

Do it five times to see what the average is. If they're more than 10% different, you have a problem somewhere anyhow. The pull amounts should be very close to the same. How does the last series compare with the first?

Let's just say for instance your trigger is a factory original Model 721 made in 1955 or so. If the trigger pull is 5 lbs. with the spring, it'll be about 1.8 pounds without it. A new Model 700 of about 1980 would have a second measurement closer to 3 lbs. Some even have 5 lbs of friction. Friction was increased by doubling the amount of sear-trigger engagement surface, first by the change to the one piece sear in 1966.

That automatically doubled the sear engagement of the M700. Then, in response to law suits nobody knew much about, they increased sear engagement again about 1979... the so called 'lawyer triggers'. The lesson is this: If you have a very nice 3 lb. pull but only have one pound of friction pull, the trigger *is* unsafe. You're now in the territory of a drop or bump firing the rifle.

The test is used best in setting sear engagements before adjusting the spring. Make sure you have two pounds of friction and then make sure you push the trigger back against the sear adjustment screw by about the same amount as supplied by the return spring. Don't cheat!

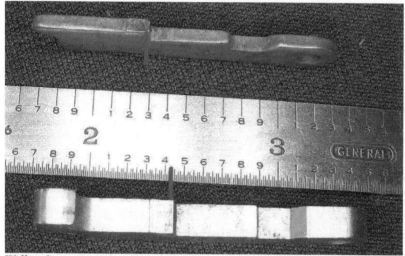

Walker Sear comparison. Top is from early 2-sear design. Engagement area doubled in 1966 when a single wide sear replaced 2 narrow ones. Lines show trigger contact patches.

Wait up there! That makes a four pound trigger pull and me and my sniper buddies will never accept that. We want two pounds and glass rod crisp!

There are ways to accomplish that. It calls for an extra, or 'two lever' lever to reduce pressures so smaller overlaps can be used. All you have to do is be willing to pay for such a trigger. If you go with cheap triggers and two pound pulls, accidents will happen, by *design*.

There have been several discharges of 'sniper rifles' in SWAT situations, but I don't know of a citizen being killed, yet. It is certainly coming. Aimed towards a citizen is definitely not a safe direction to point an unsafe gun.

Most of us know we can reduce any override trigger pull into the scary range just by reducing the sear engagement. Really fine, target grade triggers have very small trigger-sear overlaps, and triggers made from the right material and mounted exactly right can attain two pound pulls that are safer than four pound pulls on cheaper triggers. They can maintain their shape and sharpness for many thousands of rounds. There are no factory-made triggers unless you count the real target triggers that are safe to reduce the sear overlap onto the trigger by less than about .015 inch. Overlaps below that measurement are *uncertain* unless the trigger maker designed the trigger for that much stress. That's why the best triggers have the maker's name on it. Who do you trust?

That's different from how our factory trained armorers do it!

It sure is, I am one! Sometimes we have to adjust the sear way down to get a good pull. I think ten thou or so.

I don't trust a sniper rifle with a trigger that has been adjusted improperly for the materials used therein. Unless an armorer can demonstrate his mastery of the metallurgy and physical properties needed for the trigger he's adjusting, and can swear the materials in that trigger meets those specifications in every detail, your department insurance company should be extremely nervous.

Well, I don't think your 50/50 friction/spring idea is valid and I'm not going to use it.

See? I just told you what Paul Mauser said was safe in the 1890s and you want to lynch me for the information! But, I do think it's a good idea and have adjusted triggers that way for many years. Hopefully we don't meet in court with a claim pending and the case boils down to an improperly adjusted police rifle. The scanning electron microscope will show how the material failed and somebody will testify it was predictable it would fail when subjected to more forces than it was designed for. If you want a two pound trigger pull, buy a trigger designed to give it.

I think a trigger would have too much creep in it with two pounds of friction in it.

Thank you, Mr. Engineer.

What does he mean 'creep'?

'Creep' is the motion the shooter feels between the time he puts pressure on the trigger and when the trigger 'trips' and the gun goes off. It is the most distracting of all things about a trigger and one hard to eliminate.

Two sliding surfaces, like we saw in the illustrations above, have a 'differential trigger pull' that equates trigger travel with trigger pull weight. They creep naturally and can be plotted on a strain gauge coupled with a measuring recorder. The trigger moves and the strain gauge keeps track of the pull by the thousandth of an inch movement. Let's call the overlap between sear and trigger twenty thousandth of an inch (.020").

In such a measuring device, a direct acting trigger with flat surfaces sliding on the same plane, the strain line would rise on the graph very steeply at first, then peak and then decrease in peaks and valleys until the end of the pull at .020 inch. You can feel much the same as the graph by sliding a book on the floor with your fingertips. Newton was right, it takes more to get it going that it does to keep it going. Armorers figured out (about 1700) a very slight hook angle would build the trigger pull higher than a simple sliding surface and it would very suddenly override the hook angle to create a very crisp pull with a much sharper peak to the trigger graph.

I thought you said these surfaces had to be flat!

Guilty, I did that.

To make a very good trigger (that is also safe) takes some creative geometry.

Aw man! Could we talk guns instead of math?

No. I don't want you to accidentally shoot somebody with a bad trigger.

<Ooo! That stirred the hornet's nest with a stick.>

Now that everybody's back in their seats, where were we? Ah yes, trying to push the security envelope to make safer but lighter triggers by using creative geometry.

A trigger pull should act like some earthquakes do "All at once in a bunch" to quote the Cajun. The shooter should not feel the trigger move or 'give' in any way until the shot surprises him. The rifle fires as the pressure on the trigger builds to exactly the desired amount.

Canjar trigger showing sear (bottom) in un-cocked (left) and cocked condition. Sear engagement is .010"

The slight 'hook angle' works with override triggers too, but it's done differently. The trigger contact with the sear should occur slightly *behind* the pivot point of the trigger. That means the trigger, since it's actually traveling in an arc instead of straight line at the top, rises behind that pivot line when the trigger is moved. That lifts the very rear edge of the trigger as it moves from under the sear.

Do you see the need for accurate surfaces, considering the forces involved? How about really good steel that is the correct blend of strong and hard? The diagram illustrates the theoretical idea with the light colored circles showing places of energy. The upper one is the sear-trigger contact patch. Assuming the surfaces are true and flat, there's about 20 pounds of compression on that surface. That is transferred to the trigger pivot below it,

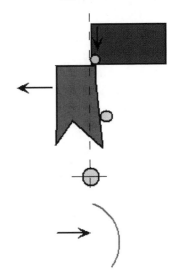

but a small amount is transferred to the rear, much like leaning against a table edge during a long conversation. Just a little bit of support takes a load off your feet. The sear is actually helping the trigger stay in position by pushing down on it behind the line of the pivot.

It seems to me, you couldn't pull the trigger if the overlap is too much.

The distance from the pivot point up to the top is far enough that the lift is very, very small, but enough to allow the buildup of trigger pull before suddenly disconnecting. But you're right, a strain gauge shows the more overlap the more mechanical 'pull' without the return spring in place, but the forces needed to pull the trigger go up geometrically, like a reversed bullet path chart. That's why it takes some skill and understanding to correctly adjust a trigger and to see why one doesn't act right. It could be out of whack *by design.*

How do you adjust a trigger to operate this way?

It's not adjusted that way. It's made that way *by design.* Part of that design is fit, finish and metallurgy. The entire design depends on a certain amount of precision and....

<...in unison>

Precision costs money.

We have some common ground!

Before we leave this diagram, let's fill in a blank left early in the class. Remember my Walker fix of epoxying the connector to the trigger and then precision grinding off the angularity?

The concept of keeping the pressure on the top of the trigger *behind* the line of the pivot is extremely important to the security of the trigger. At first, I ground them with a mounted stone in a drill press and the trigger held in a heavy fixture, and ground so the angularity is removed but *none* off the top of the trigger, just the angle. Of course the rear corner *has* to be square, too. It's an easier job with a Landis precision grinder and a microscope to look at the corner with. Yes, precision does cost money.

Grinding connector angle to square. That relieves the camming load and preserves the epoxy attachment system.

Yes ma'am, you have a question? I've noticed you taking copious notes. Thank you.

I'm a reporter and was wondering when you're going to talk about the Barber case in Montana?

<I hear grumbling in the back row.>

Yes ma'am. That and its ramifications will be covered in detail later on. I'm still trying to describe an elephant to people that have never seen one.

Doesn't the Remington trigger work just like you've been describing?

The Remington Walker trigger is NOT like I've been talking about. It has an extra part in it... *by design.*

10. The Remington-Walker Trigger

Remington had no hunting rifle to sell at the end of WW-II in sufficient quantities to capture a significant part of Winchester's Model 70 dominance. Telescopic sights were just coming into use and it was easy to mount one on a Model 70, but tough on the others. Remington designed the Model 721 to be a lower cost alternative to the Model 70 with a price point closer to the recently cheapened Model 99 Savage lever-action rifle. The Model 721was designed to undercut the competition with innovative concepts in firearms manufacturing.

Remington M721 in .30-06

The DuPont family of industries swapped engineers and manufacturing capability to prop up some companies and kill off others. Remington was propped up in a very large way. They were out of business if they couldn't find a product to manufacture and show a profit, and soon.

The M721 development was in parallel with the new auto shotgun that became the Model 11-48. When put side by side, the similarities are striking in manufacturing processes and techniques. It is clear to see that Remington Arms Co. changed direction after the war. Many companies did. War is the ultimate in destruction but great strides in creativity accompany it.

Winchester's simple trigger had two parts pinned directly to the receiver and they weren't going to share it. Sako had two parts in a housing, but it wasn't easily adaptable to a round bottomed receiver. Remington had quit forging receivers and started machining 'pipe', or chrome-moly tubing. It's not only much cheaper to make a receiver that way, it's more accurate too. It was the genius of Walker and his crew of GM engineers that (accurately) calculated the 'three rings of steel' breeching system

©H.J. (Jack) Belk 2014

was strong enough to market.

Yeah! No more weak Mauser's!

You may want to check when safety glasses got so popular. It wasn't because of Mausers. The push-feed versus controlled-round feeding debate is worthy of another class. Now, let's get back to triggers.

It is my *opinion* that Remington was directed to patent new guns so they would no longer have to pay licensing fees to Browning and his successors. They patented guns, gun ideas, gun looks, gun furniture, gun trademarks and two very popular trigger mechanisms, both demonstrably defective in design and unduly dangerous in use. There are more than 30 million of them.

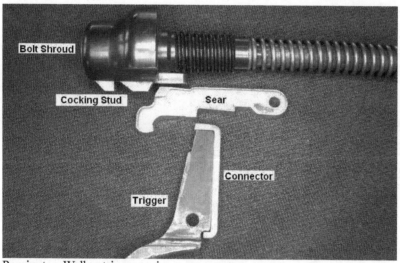

Remington-Walker trigger major components

The rumble and midscale Richter you just felt was the back row seats falling over backwards. I've been meaning to fix that.

The Model 11-48 shotgun was just a Model 11 Remington made to the new, much cheaper standards of the company. Some shortcuts were taken with that too. That will be covered later in the Common Fire Controls chapter.

The Model 721 program needed a trigger. Mike Walker was the head of the program and was a match shooter of some note even then. He certainly knew of override trigger designs. Remington even had one in a rimfire match rifle. He saw that the Sako modular trigger could be adapted by turning the sear around, but there was no patentable advantage to that change. There had to be something else or another way to have a 'target trigger' tough enough for a hunting rifle.

It had to be *really* cheap, too.

The postwar Remington designs were dependent upon stamped metal parts. Gone were the massive straddle mills and pocket mills doing small parts the old fashioned way. Instead were stamping dies making parts to be riveted together or folded into any number of complicated shapes previously made from forgings or slugs. It was a daunting engineering task that broke new ground in firearms manufacturing. The engineers assigned to work the Remington factory were bright, competent and in some cases downright brilliant. Only Walker seems to have known one end of a gun from another though. They were DuPont paid, General Motors engineers.

The first Walker triggers were made of folded sheet metal with inserts or tabs to thread the three adjustment screws into. Some of these folded housings were made for the later Model 600 series, too.

M600 Trigger with folded housing. Note sealed adjustment screws

So, that's how they cheapened them by folding the housing?

That's one way the costs were cut for sure. Remington was determined to not do any more forging. It would be stock-removal machining, casting, formed 'pot' metals and stampings attached by rivets or silver brazed together.

Well, you can't make a bolt-action rifle bolt without forging it!

Remington has been doing it for more than 60 years. Look closely about a quarter inch behind the locking lugs for a very fine line around the bolt. That's where the locking lug and bolt face section is silver brazed into the body. The handle is brazed to the body, too. Sometimes the handles come off.

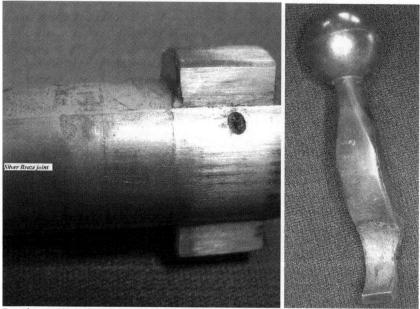

Silver Braze joint

Remington bolt face section and handle are silver brazed to body

One way of cheapening any assembly is to make it adjustable. Of course that could be advertised as a tremendous attribute to the avid shooter, and once a gun writer or two says how wonderful it is, everybody that wants to have a 'real' rifle has to have adjustable triggers.

Of course it is! It's pretty stupid to say otherwise, too.

Well, consider this:

Adjustable triggers are much like adjustable headlights and adjusted for the same reason and on about the same schedule, which is to say never to maybe once.

Sometimes they need adjusting the first day or two when you load the welder, compressor, pipe vise and tool boxes in the back and realize those red sparkles are possum eyes above the road. I've seen factory triggers like that, too; unusable.

M600 Sear-Connector engagement adjustment screw.

It's good to be able to adjust them, but it's better to figure out why they came out of the box that way.

Lawyers made them that way. Any fool knows that!

I've been around a lot of lawyers. Some have guns but none of them make guns. Want to try again?

Well, the lawyers made Remington change their triggers. I had some of them.

Remington Model 700 triggers were changed several times, quite dramatically and for good reason. People were getting shot with them! The lawyers have pointed that out many times. It was the company that changed them.

So, they fixed them then?

Not really.

There you go! Y'all start recording, he's going to step in it!

If I do step in it (by accident) it'll be because my eyes are on a higher goal.

I was asked under oath one time the difference in my analysis of how a now forgotten firearms failure happened and the company engineer's findings. I said, "I look for answers and he looks for excuses." That pretty well sums it up. Now let's look at factual observations. Many of the conclusions are my own, but the evidence is there for anybody to look at. Everybody is invited to do that looking. It might be complicated at first until we peel away the excess and understand how these things work. Then, it's pretty easy to see how they fail, too.

You're still stuck on stupid. It was the human that failed.

You're right, but Mark Twain said it best about the automobile about two years after they hit the road:

The Court to the Machine... Prisoner, it is charged and proven than you are poorly contrived and badly constructed. What have you to say to this?

The Machine... I did not contrive myself, I did not construct myself. I am a machine. I am slave to the law of my make. I do nothing for myself. My parts and pieces are set in motion by outside influences, I never set them in motion myself.

In the Animals Court,
Letters from the Earth
Mark Twain

Amen to that!

There are a whole bunch of humans at fault, but the last one to handle what became a gun from bare metal, wood and plastic was a victim, a victim of *poor gun design*.

Enough of the theorizing and pontificating! Put up or shut up. I have six adjustable triggers at home and all of them are the same. Same adjustment screws and everything. The only difference in the Walker is that a big company uses it and the lawyers go after

the big guys with a vengeance.

First let me guess which triggers you have. Weatherby MkV? Tikka? Browning? Ruger 77? Savage 110 series? Parker Hale? BSA? FN? CZ? Remington M700? All of the above? If you have them all, you see roughly the same configuration, but there's one that's different enough to kill you, a member of your family, a neighbor, or even the guy in El Paso who was shot while mowing his lawn more than a mile away. The Walker is THAT much different.

OK, prove it. But first, how can anybody be so careless as to point a gun at something and pull the trigger hoping the safety would hold?

Dog-ear this page. Here is the common misconception that has been torturous for those that experience it. It was first described in 1947 by the designer of the trigger.

What misconception?

That the safety failed and that the trigger was pulled. Neither is strictly true.

Well, hold on right there. I've heard for years these triggers fail because of a bad safety. That's one reason I came here.

And that is exactly why this is written. It is a complicated subject that is hard to illuminate without working models that are blown up so you can see what happens inside the trigger.

It's your job to simplify it, so get with it.

OK, the Walker trigger has an extra part in it.

What? Why? What do you mean 'extra'?

That takes some study and I'm going to use an actual case as an illustration. Nobody witnessed the shooting, but the post-event investigation of the circumstances and the rifle that killed him showed the way it *had* to have happened. How do we know it happened that way? It's the only way that fills in all the questions and likelihoods, using the evidence and the design of the rifle itself to reconstruct the accident.

The Houston M660

It was early on Sunday morning that the businessman loaded his SUV to go to the deer lease with his grandson for his first hunt. It was a suburban Texas neighborhood of nice houses and attached garages. About 8 am, a neighbor went outside and saw the body of the businessman next to his Jeep.

He was shot diagonally through the chest with the entry at the bottom right of the right hand shirt pocket. A .243 Winchester, Model 660 Remington carbine was lying with the butt on the threshold of the left rear door of the SUV. The barrel was resting on the ground. A fired round was in the chamber and two loaded rounds were in the magazine.

The background of the gun came to light through statements of friends, neighbors and kin. The gun was bought new in the late '70s for the victim's son. The son stated he used the gun as a young man, but one time it fired when he flipped the safety while sitting in a tree stand and he became scared of it and bought another rifle.

The rifle had been loaned to a neighbor about 25 years prior to this accident and had been returned just the day before. It could not be stated with certainty if the gun was loaded when it was returned or not, but examination of the fired case and ammo showed long term storage in the gun and no sign of recent movement of the cartridge that killed the man. It was probably stored for more than twenty years, loaded and ON safe.

The SUV was parked out of its normal place. No effort was made to determine when the change took place, but it was assumed, the victim had pulled out of the driveway and then thought of the Remington rifle for his grandson still in the garage, so he pulled back in temporarily to retrieve the rifle.

The police had custody of the rifle for about six months, but no 'tests' had been run and no conclusions made. No nitrate residue tests were done on the victim or clothing but a 'scorch' was noted on his right inner shirt sleeve near the elbow. It was clear from the evidence the gun was being held by the right hand with the butt away from the man. It seems he was placing the rifle, butt down, in the rear seat floor board.

So, you're going to try to tell us it was the gun's fault?

Not only tell you, but also show you. It is rare an intermittent failure can be identified by actual evidence, but modern technology helped explain, without any doubt, how the man was killed by a defective rifle. It needs some history to it, of course.

<...groans in the back seats>

In the late 1970s, a lawyer and his son were deer hunting and changing stands in a hunting partner's SUV. The son was young and had gotten in the back seat. His dad was in the passenger seat ahead of him. His dad reminded him (too late, of course) to be sure his Remington Model 600 carbine was unloaded. In testimony, the boy said he tried to open the bolt, but it wouldn't open with the safety still on, so he had to push the safety OFF. When he did, the rifle fired through the truck seat and hit his dad in the back. This was one of the very first occasions a lawyer decided to find out why. The boy was absolutely, positively SURE he did NOT touch the trigger.

It was found in investigations by Remington that more than half the brand new rifles in just one wholesaler's warehouse could be 'tricked' into firing by way of the safety lever instead of the trigger.

How in the world can it do that?

It's easy to see how it **can**. The better question is "why make it that way," if it can fail?

The Walker trigger has an extra part inside it that the shooter doesn't see and has no control over it. It's called the *connector*. It is a nonsensical name in the world of override triggers, because it's the only part that does what it does. There are connectors in other mechanisms but the Walker connector is quite a bit different.

Here's the patent drawing of the Walker trigger:

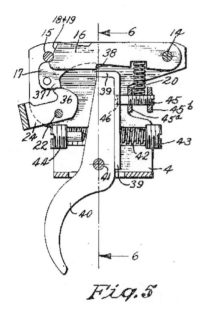

Fig. 5

This is the very first generation and the trigger that has proven most dangerous. There are many ways this one can mess up.

WHAT killed the Texas man? The rifle, the trigger, the safety or his own carelessness?

<Asked a practical man in the third row.>

Could I suggest that it was the design of the trigger? Or maybe the continued use of a design known to be defective and dangerous? Or could it be the man died because nobody *warned* him that particular rifle was unduly dangerous and defective in its very *design*?

Who cares? I'm careful and I'm not going to shoot anybody.

What about the guy that's not? How many of them live within two miles of you? What about those people? Help me educate everybody so everyone won't be so cocksure of himself. Pardon the gun talk, again. It's part of the language.

Why not just say the triggers are bad or safeties don't hold or whatever it is and be done with it?

There are many more questions than there have ever been answers. Incorrect, incomplete and downright subversive knowledge has been passed on to perpetuate the defect by factory employees. Documents have been destroyed, evidence hidden, and information that should have been made public more than six decades ago has been purposefully hidden, obfuscated, and put under protection of the federal courts to further hide it from the very people most at risk, information that could have saved their lives.

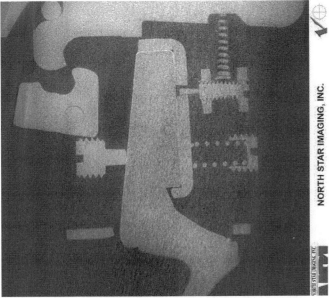

CT scan of the actual Remington Houston M660

<The back row erupts and several in the front rows go pale.>

To answer the general groundswell of inquiry as to whether I've lost my mind: No. I am risking a lot because to tell the story there's likely to be some information that's technically protected by one or more orders from a multitude of courts. It is not my desire or intention to draw the wrath of lawyers, judges or expose my freedom to risk, but the pure mechanical and economic facts can be seen as clear evidence in the formed and machined triggers of Walker design and the very patent from which they were born.

That's fine and dandy, but I still want to know what's wrong with the Remington Walker trigger.

<…says the same guy on the third row>

Refer to the patent drawing part #39 the connector. The upside down L-shaped early connector is clearly seen as a more [-shaped part in the CT scan. The bracket-shaped part is a change done to prevent the fault I'd seen in the Turkey rifle where the connector was able to slip up the trigger and by-pass the corner of the sear which resulted in the blowing up of a turkey hunter's knee.

BINGO, there you go. You admit they repaired the problem!

You're a little premature, again.

The connector is an *extraneous* part that does not perform the duties assigned it in the patent that applies.

Who cares? If it works it must be performing something. Why else is it there? Mine works just fine.

That is the heart of the matter and exactly what should have been asked by a multitude of people at the time of its introduction. WHY is the connector in the Walker trigger?

Well, are you going to answer or just ramble some more?

I've been asked that question under oath several times. My answer has been 'inconsistent' because my knowledge has increased.

In 1994, in the Aleksich case, I testified that I thought the connector was a money saving part that allowed Remington to use a very cheap to produce, formed metal 'trigger' instead of a hardened steel, accurately ground trigger. Instead of one trigger, made from good material, Remington had used two parts of different material that in total was less expensive than a well made, one piece trigger.

I've seen bimetal parts done a lot! Look at industrial saw blades.

<…comments a skeptic suspiciously in the front row>

Correct. Laminated or joined parts are common but they're attached. The connector is "flexibly attached" to the trigger. Not only that, the connector is designed to *separate* from the trigger every time it's pulled.

Now, you've got my attention. I'm a gunsmith that later became an engineer and separating parts inside a trigger doesn't seem like a good idea to me.

I thought I recognized you from 35 years ago! Welcome to another class. To understand the connector it's necessary to study the patent to see why it was not made to be an integral part of the trigger. Instead, the connector is a separate 'trigger' that the shooter knows nothing about.

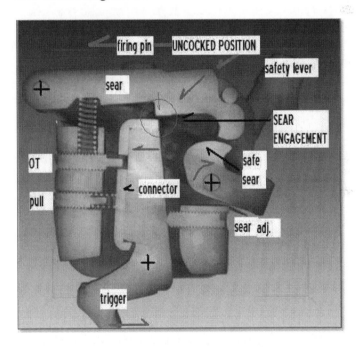

I'm still lost as to what all those parts are and what they do.

Look at the annotated CT scan that shows the parts and which way they go.

Isn't that backwards?

This picture is the innards as seen from the left side. Get used to it. The military has a protocol as to what orientation small arms are viewed from, but the civilian makers switch them around. The CT process creates a 3D image so the trigger can be seen from any direction or angle.

This is a very clear picture of the trigger and controls and adjustments for it. The sear is up and away from the trigger and the safety because the bolt has been removed. The sear spring at the far left is pushing the sear upwards until stopped by the rear mounting pin at the right end of the sear.

When the bolt is closed in the gun, the cocking stud, not shown, will be pushing forward and downwardly on the sear. That pushes the sear down onto the top of the rear corner of the connector. That patch of contact is about .018" deep and .190" wide. The pressure on that patch is about 20 lbs.

Think of the hooked thumbnails we discussed before. Does everybody see the vertical trigger prop under the horizontal sear? I see lots of nods and a couple of frowns. Let's go back over it using the diagram above.

The trigger is pivoted at the black **+**. The bottom portion off the picture is the finger piece. When it's pulled back, the top of the trigger goes forward. That allows the sear to drop downward and allows the cocking piece, not seen, to rush forward, to the left in the picture, and fire the gun.

The safety cams the sear up and off the trigger/connector. That blocks the cocking piece from moving forward and constitutes a *blocker* and *locker* type safety.

I thought you said the safety failed? In fact, you've said that for years!! 'Fire on safety release' is what you call it.

I'm sure glad you're paying attention but this time, try to hear what I actually say instead of filling in the blanks with incorrectness. Is that a word?

The *safety* is safe, but the safety is only part of the chain of energy we have to follow inside the trigger assembly. Are you ready?

<…mumbles>

Try the 'follow the energy' exercise that shows the sear pressing down on the top of the connector, which is pressing down on the top of the trigger, and the trigger is pressing down on the trigger pivot pin which divides the energy in half as it is pressing down on both sides of the trigger housing.

Go slow!

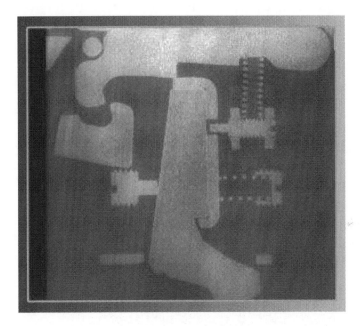

Ok. The energy is coming from the cocking piece which is attached to the firing pin, and we know the cocking piece is driven by a mainspring of about 26 lbs force when compressed into firing position. That 26 lbs is straight ahead towards the primer. Some of it is divided at the angled surfaces of the sear and cocking stud. The actual force downward on the sear has been measured to be right around 20 lbs, depending on lubrication and surface finishes. The 20 lbs is transferred straight down to the connector in its entirety. The 20 lbs force is also transferred to the top of the trigger through the connector.

Have we got that much?

No, what does the safety do?

The safety lifts the 20 lbs off the top of the connector and trigger when it's rotated back.

I have four of the rifles and it sure doesn't take 20 lbs to put the safety on!

You're right. It only takes about 5 to 7 lbs force on the safety lever to lift the 20lbs off the connector. It's done by leverage. Just measure the distance from the pivot point to the safety cam, and the pivot point to the thumb piece of the safety. That is a four to one ratio, so five pounds on the safety thumb piece lifts 20lbs at the sear tail. It works just like a claw hammer. You can go even further and see the slight leverage advantage in lifting the tail like a wheel barrow, because the load is between the pivot and the lift point.

Ok, so the sear is lifted and the gun can't fire. What's wrong with that?

Nothing is wrong with that. Blocking the motion of the firing pin and locking it to the rear is as safe as that part gets. It is the connector that fails, not the safety.

Then, how does the connector fail?

Great question. Notice the slight angle on the rear of the connector? That angle is not only the heart of the connector defect, it is also at the heart of a patent that is patently false in its claims.

THAT is a serious charge!

<Says the attorney in the front row. Wonder who he works for?>

It is serious because not only was patent obtained under clear and demonstrably false claims, the Remington engineers STILL don't understand why it is because they, judging by their latest trigger design, have continued to design around something that does not and *can not* happen inside the trigger.

You better start giving me some really good examples.

\<At least I know now who he works for.\>

Let's start looking at the actual patent and parsing some of the language, shall we?

> letoff if it were not for the flexible mounting of the connector, for it is not practicably possible to produce and maintain absolutely sharp square corners on the engaging surfaces of a sear and conventional trigger. Invariably after normal wear these corners will be rounded on a small radius which will permit the movement of the sear to start before the trigger has fully disengaged therefrom. If the sear is to completely release the striker a conventional trigger must have an overtravel or slap and the release will not be clean and crisp. If we examine the

The underlined portion explains how a sear and trigger disconnect when the gun fires. The patent argues any rounding of surfaces of the trigger and sear to somehow be a detriment, which it is, if taken to extremes, but sears and triggers have been made with sharp *enough* corners for many hundreds of years. Why bring it up now? It also brings up the overtravel or 'slap' in a trigger. That is the clearance between parts and is measured in just a few thousandths of an inch. All triggers have to have a clearance.

The angle on the rear of the connector was Walker's answer to this overtravel. I think Walker was smart enough to know it was a bad claim. So, then why did he make it?

You ask more questions than you answer.

Do you wonder why nobody has asked them of you before?

Look at the patent extract below. I've never seen a Walker with "radii existing on the points" on purpose and they just told us it was bad for triggers to have radii, but notice they claim the connector is cammed forward when the sear falls. That is because the corner of the sear contacts the angle on the connector.

> tively light trigger spring **42** and, as the sear is
> cammed down, the radii existing on the points
> of the connector and sear cause the connector
> to be cammed forwardly and completely clear
> 50 the sear step. This allows a clean crisp let-off

How do you know?

Well, the trigger parts can be installed with indicators like smoke or common marker pen that show movement. A small wad of modeling clay will show the imprint of the connector is it flies forward on firing. It's an easy thing to see and understand. Think of something very heavy with a corner falling on the angled leg of a stepladder. What's going to happen? Ask any carpenter that's pulled the ladder out from under the scaffold board. He can tell you for sure! The angled portion is propelled away from the falling object. The heavier the object is, the more energy the 'stepladder leg' has in it. That angle is a 'cam'.

Well, so what?

When the connector moves forward and away from the trigger body, (not 'if', it moves by design) what puts it back in place?

I heard that one enough in gunsmith's school to know it forever more! What puts it back is a SPRING!

Yeah, that was hammered into our heads every hour or two.

The trigger pull or return spring pushes on the front of the connector and pushes it and the trigger back against the sear adjustment screw....and before more remarks from the back row...Yes, that's just the way every other override trigger works, too. The trigger pull spring pushes the trigger back under the sear. Every trigger has a 'return spring' and the system depends on it returning reliably. That's why triggers many times have a 'boss' around the pivot hole so there is nothing to hang up on the sides as the trigger positively returns to it's proper place. That is a very important spring.

I like a light trigger pull so I back mine WAY off.

Then please pay attention to why that's a bad idea.

What happens if the connector doesn't quite go back exactly right? Yes, I'm asking the entire class that question. We know there's a very small amount of overlap to start with. What happens if it's reduced by a connector that didn't quite seat right? What happens if a very small piece of debris hangs up between the trigger and connector?

Who says it didn't seat right? Mine's never failed me and I've worn out two barrels and shot a hundred pounds of powder through it! It's the same with my shooting buddies, too. It sounds like a bunch of lawyers just trying to hold somebody up, legally.

First question first. Evidence shows the connector doesn't always seat right. Tests run by Remington show the connector doesn't always seat right. Fire on safety release proves the connector doesn't always seat right. Fire on Bolt Close proves it, too.

As for your second question, that's called anecdotal evidence. I've never been in a plane crash, either. I've never even had a friend in a plane crash and two are retired pilots! You're not suggesting I conclude planes don't crash, do you?

You think greedy lawyers are driving the suits? Actually plaintiff's lawyers, by training and profession, and in my experience, have actual personal empathy for the 'little guy'. They represent someone that is injured through no fault of his own and are trying to cure the damages caused by the defendant. You might want to ask, who else does that for a living?

Yeah, but they take big companies for millions and rake off a portion so they'll say anything to get paid, and it looks like will also hire whatever 'expert' it takes to say what it takes to win.

What they actually do is take the facts as presented by their client and determine if there is a rule of law that's been violated.

Americans are protected against willfully bad products or actions. If a car fails to obey a traffic law and wrecks you, it is his insurance company that your insurance company sues, if necessary to get you relief.

Right....how do you relieve someone for the loss of a child?

Under our law, adopted from English Common Law, the only penalty that can be levied is *money*. Those are the facts. In some cases, a judge has ordered a company to cease doing business or to be shut down, but the ultimate penalty is money. There is no 'payment' for loss of a child, or a leg or loss of the pleasures of life except for money. Nobody has the right to shoot the engineer that designed a faulty gun.

The lawyer that hears how you've been damaged might have a very good idea of a law that has been violated. Maybe a truck driver ran over somebody in his 13th hour behind the wheel. Did he violate company policy? Or was he following company policy? Sometimes millions of dollars rest on the answer.

It is the lawyer's job to look at the facts and determine if recovery can be made. Lawyers tell me many cases only require a letter from someone that has the clout to back it up, to get a check in the mail.

Sometimes it takes filing a suit to find all the answers. Many times, a gun case has been settled after depositions are taken on both sides. Then the lawyers can see what will be said at trial and what exhibits will be shown.

But, the lawyer always gets paid.

Not at all. The lawyer puts up his own money. That's why paralegals that don't pay attention to minute details leave law firms. The lawyer has his money on the line and nothing less than perfection will get it back. Sometimes these cases last for years and the stacks of paperwork that change hands is staggering. There are times a small law firm is not up to the task and have to put on extra help to sort through important documentation, but the nuggets are buried in pounds of paper.

I still don't quite understand your job!

Many don't. I'll try to be brief.

Fat chance of that!

An 'expert' is one that through training, education, research or practical experience is judged by the court, after examination by the defense, to be qualified to tell the jury of the facts presented to him, facts observed by him, and *opinions* given to subject at hand. The opinion part is what the entire case usually hinges on. The defense has experts, too. Their opinions are almost always different than mine. It's the lawyer's job to ask pertinent questions of the witnesses and let the jury decide who is most credible in the case.

I see! You get a case and the more money you can get out of the company the more you make. Neat job if you can get it.

<This guy has a corner on snark!>

Not even close! I consult with a lawyer first, sometimes in four phone calls, and hear what his client has relayed. Sometimes the client is in on a conference call so I can ask the questions that really need answering. I tell the lawyer that I'm the gun guy, but I'm also an investigator, so let me know the facts and I'll tell him if I'm qualified or not. I was involved in a police shooting of a guy with a Glock pistol... Thank you. Some in the back row were nodding. That woke you right up.

Anyhow, a cop shot a guy with a Glock and got fired for it. I determined the gun had operated as it was meant to, but found out the cop had only had a 20 minute orientation when it was issued. I have a good friend that trains cops. He said that's not enough. I put him in touch with the lawyer and they got the guy's job back. Remember the 15 pound minimum 'rule'? It worked in that case, but I never gave testimony and never charged a dime for my part in it.

My job first is to save lawyers time, money and bother, but I don't ask the shooter how many beers he had that morning or how much dope he smoked before going shooting. That's the lawyer's job and sometimes it catches them unaware. It never catches the gun companies, though. They hire a PI first thing. That drug test you thought was confidential will likely find its way into a file folder before trial. I've seen information by mistake that's scary.

So, what's a 'good' case, then?

A 'good' case to me is one that the shooter's bright flash of deeply seated memory is consistent with mechanical facts. Beyond that is lawyer territory. I've interviewed enough crooks as a deputy and heard thousands of 'gun stories' from customers, friends and people off the street. The truth is pretty easy to see. The 'less than truths' are much easier to see for one who knows guns. Those cases are politely declined, sometimes over the strong protestations of the lawyer that asked me. It could be a 'perfect case' from his perspective, but I'm constrained by physical facts and motions.

Does that mean every case you take is a 'good' one?

Not really. I've worked cases that were 'bad' from my perspective, but I had to be designated immediately to fulfill the paperwork requirements. They turned out to be cases that couldn't be explained to the jury as the shooter had explained his own accident to the defense lawyer in deposition.

Why did you take it then?

I hadn't seen the shooter's deposition until the day before my deposition was already scheduled by subpoena. I testified how the gun works and how it most likely failed as an FSR, but there was 'energy' missing in one place that *precluded* an FSR. At trial, I answered every question from the defense knowing he knew how energy flows in that trigger and he knew there was a gap in that train of energy, and he knew I knew there was a gap.

He also knew that I wasn't going to 'dance' like an engineer in my answers. I still think he drew out the cross exam to make me sweat, but why sweat it when you know where he's going?

That case was rightly lost, but the lawyer I was working for showed me a side of his profession that affected me profoundly. He worked harder than I've ever seen a lawyer work, without secretarial help or a big office behind him, too. He worked night and day and all through the weekend until he was bedraggled at trial but still digging for a few dollars for his client. It was a display of dedication to his calling much more than the cannon of ethics requires. He should have at least gotten a medal for it. Instead he got bills and more bills for hotels, laundries, experts and taxi cabs. When a good friend was injured on a job in Texas, I told him to give this lawyer in Dallas a call. Sometimes all it takes is a strong letter with the weight to back it up and that's all it took to get his medical bills and lost time paid for, and since the lawyer found out the super had lied to another supervisor about the case, he got some extra to PUNISH the company that did wrong. That is what lawyers do.

I don't believe a word of it.

I guess that means I have to keep going, then.

You keep talking about fire on safety release. Isn't it about time to explain it?

As long as everyone understands that the connector moves at every shot *by design*. The claim in the patent is bogus and we'll get back to that, but for now just see that the angularity on the rear of the connector was designed to move the connector forward as the sear falls. That one thing sets up failures that kill people and the maker of the trigger denies it.

Is this going to explain the man in Houston shot with the Model 660?

Yes it will.

I want to know what the demonstrably false claim is in the patent before you go any further.

<...says the lawyer in the green suit>

I'm glad you asked that because maybe you can pass along a design mistake in Remington's latest trigger, the X Mark Pro.

Says who?

Just hold on a minute, let's look at U. S. Patent number 2,514,981. This is on page four in section four of claims:

> mounting, this screw may conveniently be
> 20 mounted in threaded holes in brackets **45a** and
> **45b** turned inwardly from the side walls of the
> trigger housing **4**. This stop screw provides an
> adjustment to positively stop trigger movement
> just as the sear is released and makes possible
> 25 the complete elimination of undesirable trigger
> slap or overtravel. This complete elimination
> of trigger slap could not, however, be accomp-
> lished without endangering the crispness of the
> letoff if it were not for the flexible mounting of
> 30 the connector, for it is not practicably possible
> to produce and maintain absolutely sharp square
> corners on the engaging surfaces of a sear and
> conventional trigger. Invariably after normal
> wear these corners will be rounded on a small
> 35 radius which will permit the movement of the
> sear to start before the trigger has fully disen-
> gaged therefrom. If the sear is to completely
> release the striker a conventional trigger must
> have an overtravel or slap and the release will
> 40 not be clean and crisp. If we examine the
> functioning of the unit, we will observe that the
> trigger and connector move as a unit until the
> instant the connector starts to clear the edge of
> the sear step. At this point the trigger stops
> 45 but the connector is restrained only by the rela-
> tively light trigger spring **42** and, as the sear is
> cammed down, the radii existing on the points
> of the connector and sear cause the connector
> to be cammed forwardly and completely clear
> 50 the sear step. This allows a clean crisp let-off
> closely approaching the target shooter's ideal

There as 45a and 45b on lines 20-23 are the tabs that proved deadly in Houston, but more on that later. Those tabs are what hold the overtravel (OT) screw and stops forward motion of the trigger.

Now please, if no other dozen or so lines of text are deemed important enough to really read and understand, it is mid-line #23 at 4. At the very end is the patented basis of the Walker trigger. It assumes poor quality and workmanship in all other triggers and then states a physical impossibility has to occur in the Walker trigger to make it different.

> **"This stop screw provides an adjustment to positively stop trigger movement just as the sear is released and makes possible the complete elimination of undesirable trigger slap or overtravel. This complete elimination of trigger slap or overtranel, however, could not be accomplished without endangering the crispness of the the letoff if it were not for the flexible mounting of the connector."**

There will be a quiz shortly, because if you don't 'get' the operation of the trigger *as designed*, the failures will be much harder to show you, and you might even remain unconvinced of the *defect* in the basic *design*.

11. The Walker-Haskel Patent

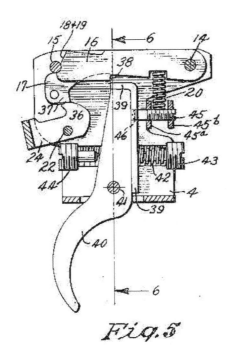

Fig. 5

Parsing the Patent

At line 23, the patent explains that the overtravel (OT) screw (45) is:

"to positively stop trigger movement just as the sear is released and makes possible the complete elimination of undesirable trigger slap or overtravel."

BS! There has to be enough clearance for the moving sear and trigger and connector to reset. That is generally considered .008 to .010" and the Walker also has it, but the real clincher starts in line 40:

"If we examine the functioning of the unit, we will observe that the trigger and connector move as a unit until the instant the connector starts to clear the edge of the sear step. At this point the trigger stops...."

NO! It absolutely does NOT stop at that point and it's very easy to verify it. But, to continue with their lie:

"...but the connector is restrained only by the relatively light trigger spring and, as the sear is cammed down, the radii existing on the points of the connector and sear cause the connector to be cammed forwardly and completely clear the sear step."

This entire section is a straw man argument that assumes mechanical actions that we know can't happen.

Why not? I guess I don't see where they're wrong in that statement .

Here are the facts of an override trigger, no matter who makes it. Twenty thousandths of sear overlap is about maximum for most triggers. Past that, creep and too heavy a pull result. So, let's say our trigger has .020" sear engagement and needs .010" clearance between the parts so they don't rub and interfere with each other. That means the trigger has to move .020" to disengage from the sear. As we've already established, a trigger has to build stresses before the frictional overlap can fail all at once, with no 'creep' to the trigger. Does anyone think your 'finger spring' won't pull that last .010 inch of overtravel?

I watched a guy drill the fender of a car for an antenna one time. He had his free hand underneath, but any fool can stop a drill after it goes through a car fender, can't they? He didn't. It drilled through the fender and the backlash of the energy-loaded drill drilled his hand, too. The point is, the trigger is going to move the amount it *can* move after the sear falls, up to about an eighth of an inch of overtravel or 'slap'.

So, what does that mean besides they told a falsehood in applying for a patent. So what?

It means that automotive engineers don't know the forces within a trigger mechanism and the patent office doesn't either. The language of the patent tells a person that knows how triggers operate that Remington set up a straw man of bad parts and bad workmanship and then said they could fix it really cheap.

Alright, I read and reread the patent. Why is the connector in there? It's obvious it has no benefit.

I testified the first several times that it was a cost cutting measure so Remington could form a trigger out of inferior material and use the connector as the heat treated section of that trigger. I also qualified it in several ways because I'm not a gun parts production expert that can testify to what it costs to make something. I do know that Remington is cost conscience to a fault.

So, why is the connector in the trigger, then?

I have an alternative opinion that I think is as valid as the cost considerations. The patent is the key, I think. Mike Walker knew the problems posed by that design. He got reports of failures when there were only 200 rifles with Walker triggers in existence. Walker understood the failure of the connector to fully reposition and proposed at least two fixes for it in 1947; one at no cost to Remington beyond a new stamp die and the other at a cost of less than a nickel each.

Why weren't those fixes adopted and saved all this headache and money?

I'll add heartache to that and tell you flat out, I have no clue why Remington didn't fix an *obvious* problem at the very beginning, except they were pressed for time to introduce a new rifle and pressed for money so had to keep it cheap. They instead tell people they can't reproduce the complaints and there's nothing wrong with the trigger system... even in court.

I don't think you ever said why the connector design was so important to them.

At the end of the war, it is my *opinion* that Remington Arms was told by their 100% owner, DuPont, they would not pay licensing fees or use the designs that had to be licensed from another designer, most notably, John M. Browning. Those firearms designs had been Remington's primary product since about 1910. Everything post war was to be done in-house using their own engineers. The result is that the post war Remington's were cheap copies of guns they used to make using much more economical manufacturing methods. The recent influx of GM engineers meant Remington could design their own guns using their newer, much cheaper manufacturing methods already used in the car industry.

Shortcuts were taken that a knowledgeable gun person would have immediately pointed out were dangerous. Nobody did. Or, if they pointed it out they were ignored, like Walker was.

Doesn't that mean they didn't fail in their testing?

Not at all. We know the guns failed before they went on the open market. So did the 11-48 using the Common Fire Control. It also failed and they had to have figured out why, but refused to make a meaningful repair. If the design of a firearm is faulty, the firearm is defective even if it's never shot a single round. Mechanical facts are very durable.

Well it didn't fail often or they would have done something about it!

I would certainly want to believe that is true. I know different and you will too soon. The focus was getting a cheap rifle to market, right *now!*

How many uncontrolled discharges would you think is 'too many'? Are we talking about guns or ICBMs? To the families of the victims it makes little difference. And both should be safe.

If the failures are so common, why can't you show us how it does it with a rifle?

Because it is extremely rare to have a failure unless the trigger has been misadjusted. They *can* be adjusted to fail nearly every time. Of course, that means it is out of factory specifications and therefore the factory denies responsibility for it. What is hard to get across to the jury is that this particular trigger, The Remington Walker, by having an extra part internally that's made to move during violent recoil, *can adjust itself!...* and then revert to normal without leaving a trace.

When any mechanism, not just an override trigger, works in a way described as 'uncertain' we have to carefully examine *why* that makes a difference. If an air rifle occasionally fails to load another BB (mine did as a kid) it's no big thing. If a riot gun fails to feed, it could cost a life. But if a trigger fails, everyone and everything within a couple miles is in danger.

Most gunsmiths know that some Browning A-5 shotguns will shoot the shell in the chamber, reload one from the magazine, and throw a loaded round on the ground, but it might not do it every time. Car mechanics know the funny noise heard by the driver yesterday may not be there today, but he knows where to look if the customer can adequately describe the noise. Intermittent failure in electrical gear can be a daunting task to track down. All these trouble shooting tips have something in common, though. The mechanic, by deduction, determines what caused the failure by observing and analyzing what is right, what is wrong, what is different and what the possibilities are for failure.

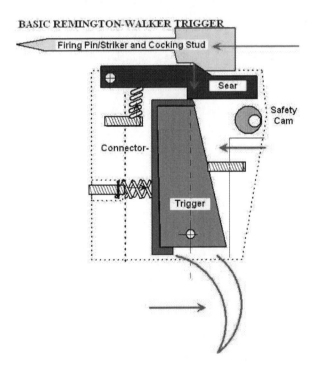

The moving connector in the Walker trigger is the key to the failures because it's not always where it's supposed to be.

How do you know that?

Because if it was in its proper position, the sear would be supported and the rifle wouldn't fire on safety release.

So, are you claiming the rifle only fires when the connector is out of place?

That is technically true, but the connector doesn't have to be 'dislodged' to cause a failure of *geometry*. Remember we talked about how the surfaces have to be flat and engage as a flat so there is no 'skid angle' to the connector. The possibilities for Walker trigger failures are numerous. They all involve the connector and its most important position, firmly against the trigger and completely under the sear, but the connector also has to maintain the same flat orientation to the sear as designed. Otherwise, the trigger becomes 'fragile' to handle due to the skid angle.

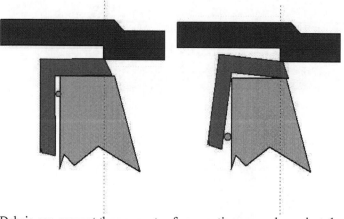

Debris can prevent the connector from seating properly against the trigger body. The connector bounces away from the trigger each time the gun is fired, creating a gap that can trap debris.

Even I can see that! Surely there's something to make sure the space between the connector and trigger remains clean, isn't there?

No, there's not. In fact, the design of the Walker, with the long sear totally exposed to the elements at the bottom of a trough in the action tang, tends to gather debris and 'pump' it into the trigger every time the sear falls by firing.

So, it's trash that causes the trigger to fail? Easy man, clean your #*&%@ rifle every once in a while!

Still premature, I'm afraid.

What else could make the connector not return?

The possibilities for interference of the connector to prevent full reposition include debris or congealed lubricants that cause a gummy interface with the sides of the trigger housing. The one definite interference that is well documented is the survey by Remington of Model 600 rifles in one Texas warehouse. It was found that more than half the brand new rifles could be 'tricked' into firing.

In 2011 a Walker trigger was examined by CT scan and found to have multiple pieces of debris in places critical to the safety of the trigger. I'll show you that one later.

I heard that way while ago. You're going in circles.

Only in an attempt to explain the failures, but you're right. We're back to what is called the 'trick test'. We see the sear lifted up by the safety cam so that the cocking piece is locked back and the gun is safe, but what keeps the trigger and connector from moving while on safe?

Nothing, ya ditz. Just like the rest of the triggers on the market, even your precious Model 70.

Thanks, Mr. Personality.

The trigger and connector are free to move when the rifle is on safe, just like the others. Is that better? The trigger return spring makes sure they're pushed back into position, too. Just like the others, right?

What happens if the trigger is pushed back, but the connector hangs up on something?

Like what?

Like the corner of the sear for one. Many, many years ago it was seen that the safety cam would wear enough that the sear would still block the striker, but the trigger would drag just a little as the connector slid out from underneath the sear. Then, the trigger return spring wasn't strong enough to push the connector back.

I don't believe it. I don't think a company would allow that.

Thank you. Me neither, but they not only allowed it, but they have spent millions to keep it secret. That's why we're here.

So, the guy was killed by a gun that was worn out, then?

Patience just isn't part of your makeup is it?

Worn out safeties can cause it. So can safeties not made to specifications, or manufacturing errors that were poorly repaired but did not, in any way, make the trigger safe. The safety is not the problem, but in some cases it demonstrates the problem.

The Trick Test

Make sure the rifle is unloaded, of course. Place the rifle in the cocked and ON safe position. Now carefully pull the trigger and try to hear or feel the slightest click or drag. Pull the trigger slowly and release slowly several times. Now, push the safety to OFF. Did it fire? How about if the safety is between FIRE and SAFE? The 'null position' is supposed to be precluded by the use of a detent ball and spring, but sometimes a trigger will hang up half way. Try it.

Did it fire?

Of course not!

Many have. Let's go through another simple test while the gun is safe and test for a known problem that has caused death and misery.

The Screw Driver Test

The screwdriver test determines if the connector is a loose fit on the trigger body. While ON safe, pull the trigger and keep it pulled while the bottom of the connector, visible just ahead of the bolt release, is pressed with the tip of a small punch or screwdriver. Try to displace the connector 'upward' in relation to the trigger body. Now, slowly release the trigger and then push the safety to OFF.

Did it fire?

Of course not, again. I call BS.

The turkey hunter in Florida blew his left knee apart just after his rattling pickup supplied the screw-driver test.

Is this what killed the businessman in Texas, too?

No, in fact it was found that trigger would pass the screwdriver test every time.

<A man down front has been quiet until now. He speaks loud enough for all to hear.>

Sir, I've been a hunter and a shooter for more than thirty years and I own several Model 700 rifles. Every accident with these guns seems to involve pushing the safety OFF while the gun is loaded. Why not unload the gun with the safety ON or have it pointed downrange if you're going to shoot. That's what I do and it just seems like too much common sense to do otherwise.

I join in the applause.

Thank you, Sir. Well said and very much to the point. Let me address unloading while ON safe first because it's had the most tragic results in the Remington rifles. Before 1982, a Model 600 or 700 rifle had to be taken OFF safe to unload it.

<...a ripple of disbelief>

I hope that you see now, the failure of the connector to fully reestablish its proper position on the trigger body actually takes the 'trigger' from beneath the sear. The safety is supporting the sear until the safety cam rotates out from under it. The so-called 'safety' becomes the 'trigger'.

That's why you always point in a safe direction, isn't it?

That's the theory, but remember there is no safe direction to point an unsafe gun. Up and down and sideways have all produced life altering injuries and death.

So, this is the Fire on Safety Release you've been referring to?

Yes it is. As we've seen, it can take on many initial forms as to how the connector is dislocated, but in the end the failure is said to be FSR, or Fire on Safety Release. Remington changed the design by simply cutting off the end of the safety lever where it extends through the receiver and into the slot under the bolt handle of the bolt. Grind that off and the bolt is no longer 'locked' closed.

My Model 70 has a position to unload while on safety, why not Remington's?

Remington rifles had a 'three position' safety for many years, but it was dropped as a cost cutting measure.

That leaves the second part of the question and that is, why not have the rifle pointed 'down range' when taking the safety OFF. That is part of the "Ten Commandments of Gun Safety" (TCGS) and just makes sense. Most of us were trained to remove the manual safety as the gun comes up to shoot and not before.

Let's see the patent language and then look at the reality we must all live with.

"...have been achieved in a construction which is absolutely safe in the hands of the hunter or target shooter and rugged enough to remain so in spite of the abuse and neglect which are often heaped upon sporting

arms."

It is obvious that any gun with an internal trigger that can be displaced on a dirt road riding in a pickup truck is not "absolutely safe".

Nobody should point at anything they don't intend to shoot.

Please tell me how you get the barrel to where it's 'pointed' without it 'pointing' somewhere else. We humans 'point at' a target, but the gun *always* has muzzle 'pointed' somewhere. The gun has no clue. We are the ones that determine the 'target'. The real 'trigger' should be the human in charge of the trigger, don't you all agree with that?

<...lots of nodding heads, that's encouraging.>

The TCGS says not to load a gun until you're going to shoot it. That would solve that problem, wouldn't it?

Yes, it would. Let's look at reality again:

When would a target shooter load his gun? When it's pointed down range and the shooter is ready, right? How about a pheasant hunter? Do we have different rules for people with and without dogs? Should we have different rules for pointing dogs and flushing dogs? How about those without a dog but with a boy along? When is it safe to load a hunting gun? Not at home, and not in the car or truck. It should be loaded in the field and away from other people.

How about a cop? Should the Barney Fife rule be in effect because their guns might be unsafe? The fact is, a gun without ammo is a poor club. Of course you don't load a trap or skeet gun or bench-rest rifle before you're on the firing line, especially a BR rifle because that trigger has to be very light by design.

How about the guy in Houston?

It's easy to get sidetracked, isn't it?

You seem to have a talent.

Yeah, it's good to have at least one.

For several decades, a gun that was said to have failed was examined according to a written protocol developed by plaintiff's engineers and the representatives of the manufacturer to measure and quantify every measurement possible of the Walker trigger. Several cases were pursued that had a rifle at issue that would occasionally show the same failure in the same manner as described, but the nature of the trigger and the fact that shooting a rifle is many times a violent exercise in forces induced into the gun through recoil, means any debris large enough to cause a failure can be immediately released by the gun to fall where it may.

The evidence of the failure is not always there. Such a failure is said to have been caused by 'transit debris'.

It was plain to see for many, many years that the connector was the common denominator in all the injuries and deaths attributed to the Walker trigger. Legal maneuvers and the general lack of mechanical understanding by the lawyers and the jury in many cases inadequately explained how such an ordinarily reliable mechanism could suddenly be deadly. Only people are supposed to kill people.

Houston?

Soon, I promise.

Debris can hang up anywhere it gets a chance to in the Walker trigger. The connector squirts away from the trigger body like a water melon seed as the sear falls, then the sear remains behind the connector as the rifle recoils which causes the connector to 'bounce' away from the trigger body as many as four times.

The oil, dust, lint, soot and other fine materials that are flying around inside the trigger during recoil and settles there in storage are all suspect. The slivers of brass from a rough extractor are common to find inside the tang and magazine box. Check the trash that catches on the underside of the bolt stop tab that has drained through the trigger already.

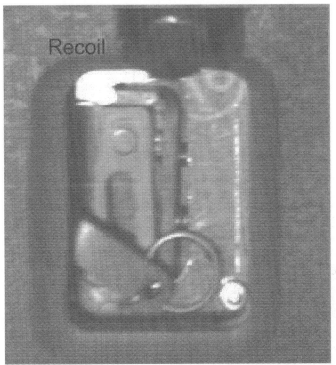

High speed capture of connector bouncing away from trigger body on recoil.

We know the triggers fail from this debris. I've got great pictures of cartridge brass scraps in a Walker trigger. But, the Houston trigger was clean and had never been altered from the factory trigger adjustments and it operated perfectly every time it was tried.

A new tool in firearms examination became available about 2006. Remington found North Star Imaging in Rogers, Minnesota. NSI builds and operates very strong CT/x-ray machines and wrote the software that makes the product as detailed as a medical CT/MRI with the same 3D and sorting features for all things mechanical or natural. Their internet demonstrations of a duck egg and Rolex watch and fishing reel are just fascinating, more so in person I might add.

For the first time, a gun said to be faulty could be looked at in detail without first taking it apart. The deliverable files from NSI are stacks of X, Y and Z axis x-rays that are of just a small slice of the mechanism. These stacks of photos comprise the total trigger in all three axes in layers about .005 inch thick. Each axis file contains approximately 1800 large digital pictures that must be examined in detail to make sure the internals are correct. A trigger out of adjustment or cluttered with metallic debris is easy and plain to see. The 3D images are invaluable as jury demonstrations to show relationships of parts. It *is* rather cluttered in there!

The Model 660 in the Houston case went into the machine and as usual, all the legal parties involved were standing calmly trying to spot an obvious defect. None were seen. Nearly a week later, while scrolling through the X axis of that CT scan, I saw this:

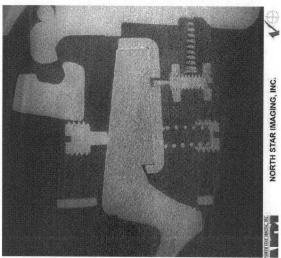

CT scan, bolt open

This view is with the muzzle pointed right and the trigger is pointing down. The bolt is open as seen by the sear being raised above the connector.

Several important points are on this photo. First noticed is that the connector is not tight to the trigger at the very bottom. There is a gap there of about .008". That means the connector should displace upward by that .008 with the screwdriver test, but that wasn't detected during the physical examination. Why not?

Look high-center of the photograph where the overtravel (OT) screw goes though the connector. The amount of space between the face of the trigger and the overtravel screw is about .028 which makes sense. OT is the amount the trigger moves after the sear falls. The total trigger movement is equal to the sear-trigger overlap, plus about .008 clearance. But why is the unthreaded nose of that OT screw shaped like that?

I saw that. It's not in the hole on center, either.

Good call. That's why the connector didn't rise when the screwdriver was applied. The connector can't move any higher.

Isn't that a good thing, though? Seems like if the connector was held downwardly towards the trigger, it would be better that way.

It would seem so, but what about the angle on the back of the connector? When the sear falls it cams the connector forward with considerable force. Think about pinching a watermelon seed with 20 lbs of force on it. If the connector is being thrown into a 'corner' of some kind where it becomes stuck, it's dangerous. The sear spring is also out of true flat, but in another plane. I was curious which was right, so I switched to the Y view....

Sir, before we leave that picture could I ask a question about it? Thanks. What is that bright line between the trigger body and the connector?

You have mighty sharp eyes. The Remington Model 660 was a 'dressed up' version of other carbines in short calibers using the Model 600 action. It has a gold plated trigger. Since the picture is of a thin 'slice' of the mechanism, we only see that thickness of gold around the trigger body.

Wouldn't that keep it cleaner?

The same amount of 'gunk' will be there, it's just easier to see with a gold background.

At this point, the OT screw was a suspect in a failure and another axis slice was located that showed where the screw was in another plane. In the scan below, the OT screw is that bright dot sitting at about 6:30 to the hole in the connector. That is really wrong!

Where is that in relation to a rifle? I sure can't tell heads or tails from that one!

CT scan of off-center overtravel (OT) screw. Viewed from front, trigger to the left.

Some landmarks will help. The view is from the front of the rifle with the barrel pointed over your right shoulder. The trigger is on the left side. So, the OT screw is pointed left of the bore line somehow. Let's look at another axis:

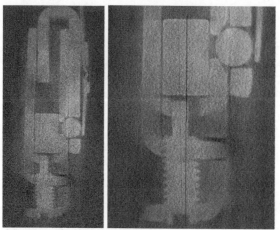

CT scans of off-center OT screw, viewed from bottom

Yikes! That's pretty clear!

In this view, the barrel is pointed downward and the trigger is pointed straight at you so we're looking at the trigger unit from below. The square notch in the OT screw is the adjustment slot. The threads can be seen clearly. That is the safety detent ball on the right side of the picture. Notice the hole in the connector is also off center. That makes the angled holes that the OT screw goes through even more pronounced....and dangerous.

How could it be that wrong?

The housing is stamped metal and folded. If the drill goes through crooked, the tap will follow it. Tooling costs had to have been high in that operation with those small taps running at such an angle, but nobody knows how many housings were mismade before the error was discovered.

I'm not sure I see how that hole being wrong caused the guy to die.

Every time the trigger is pulled, the sear dropping off the angled corner of the connector pushes the connector forward with great force. The trigger return spring pushes them back into proper position against the sear engagement screw in the rear. The total movement of the trigger is less than the thickness of a dime. The connector can and does travel further than that because the OT screw goes through that hole. The OT screw acts on the trigger body, not the connector.

What happens if the connector is rubbing on the OT screw AND the OT screw is set at an angle? It sets up a trap for the connector! The connector is pushed by the sear forward, along the OT screw, and it hangs up there because the screw is crooked and so is the hole in the connector so it can wedge forward against the side of the trigger housing, and the spring isn't strong enough to push it back in place. If the connector is forward and then the man going hunting with his grandson brushes the safety lever on the edge of the back seat on the way into the SUV, the safety goes OFF and the sear drops and the man does too. FSR has killed another person. The trigger has failed without the trigger being pulled, but by action of the safety. The trigger has done that by *design*.

Whoa now! For the connector to be displaced didn't the trigger have to be pulled?

Yes you are right. For the connector to be displaced, it had to get the energy from somewhere. That's usually traced to a trigger pull.

In the case of the Houston rifle the trigger was pulled but it was pulled before the accident with the safety ON. Very possibly 20 years ago. Some hunter safety instructors teach kids to 'test their safety'. It is a dangerous practice and my first failure to have control of my own gun happened just that way. I was 'testing the safety' while pointing at a squirrel nest and the gun fired when I was about nine years old. That made a lasting impression!

Then it's pretty simple. DON'T pull the trigger with the safety on.

That's like not sticking your tongue in the hole left by a pulled tooth. Even the promise of it growing back gold will never keep down the exploration. Triggers and safeties are the same way. It's human nature.

How do you propose to get around human nature?

You don't 'get around' it. You account for it and make it harmless. I saw a schoolmate of mine keep time with the radio with the brake pedal because there was an indicator light on the dash that came on when the brake lights did. There's no telling how much money he cost his dad in brake shoes. That is human nature of the barely sane kind, but common in the high schools I went to. 'Testing' of something called a 'safety' satisfies young curious minds. I hunted with a guy that enjoyed getting his dog's attention with his shotgun safety, but at least it was broken open at the time.

In guns, there are certain 'rules', but enough exceptions to make many guns 'backwards'. The factories started putting red paint on the safety when it was OFF a hundred years ago so people could tell what was what. Right now, the best for the dollar bolt action rifle has a safety that is OFF if it's pulled *back*. It is opposite any rifle safety I've seen in a long time. I have three of the excellent CZ rifles and simply lift the bolt handle as the 'safe' position. Why wonder how it works when you know how one surefire way works anyhow? Notice that gun-ism? Open the bolt to make any gun safe.

The military small arms always have the very best safeties due to the abuse they're subjected to, but I've seen literally *dozens* of 'Fire on safety application' on the M-14 rifle on the ranges of Fort

Benning. We taught trainees how to apply the safety for hours, but there were always a couple that pulled the trigger instead.

That shows the forethought of some military minds when the M-1 Garand was adopted in the late 1930s.

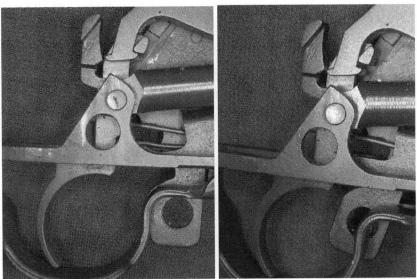

M-1 Garand Safety. Left: Off, ready to fire. Right: ON safe. Applying the safety is similar to pulling the trigger.

It was roundly criticized by the old guard for having a safety that operated in the same direction as the trigger, and close to it. It was adopted anyway and thirty years later I was watching the successor to the Garand, with the same general trigger group, fail in exactly the same way, as predicted.

Does anyone want to contemplate the friendly fire incidents in war time by simply trying to make your battle rifle safe?

How about locking the trigger so it can't move? My rifles have a 'solid' feeling trigger when it's on safe.

Walker suggested that in 1947 but it wasn't done. One of the best things a designer can do is lock all the parts he can together. Motion is the danger time in any gun and it's better if nothing moves but the safety. You notice the Xmark Pro trigger locks the trigger and the sear and the cocking piece together in a unit much like the simple Model 12 Winchester pump gun.

One of the most positive safeties in the world is that same M1 Garand trigger that troops confuse with the safety. The M1 safety pulls the hammer back away from the sear, which is a double-hook style that is also blocked by the safety. It is secure enough to use as a bayonet handle or club in times of need. Patton called the Garand the single finest tool of war ever invented.

That seems like just common sense to me to lock everything together somehow.

<The pale lady in the front row is beginning to bother me. Now she speaks in a tenuous voice.>

Years ago near my home town a little boy was killed on a hunting trip with his family. It divided our town and some mean things were said... and I'm afraid many things were just ignorant. From what you've said so far, I know they were....can you tell me the truth?

<...and she sat down>

It's hard to swallow just right when the Gus Barber case is brought up. Let's take a break and tackle that just after we come back.

12. The Barber Rifle

At this point, in what is supposed to be a lesson in firearms design, there is an intersection of goals and objectives. The very best to be hoped for in a book of this type is for someone to learn something not otherwise known. Experience is said to be the very best teacher and the very best teachers have a lot of experience. Oscar Wilde must have had that in mind when he said, "Education is an admirable thing, but it is well to remember from time to time that nothing that is worth knowing can be taught."

Gunsmithing used to be passed down father to sons; Manton, Purdey, Holland, Greener, and Browning. The great names in great guns learned how guns worked at their dad's bench. Mechanics of any genre are almost always of a family lineage heavy in practical knowledge. When we look at the lives of the great inventors we see people that dedicated a large portion of their lives to figuring out how to make things work. By 'things' I mean real, touchable mechanisms whether it's a way to make windows lighter with cast iron counter-weights or creating a first time piece worthy of navigation with a chronometer.

The fact is levers and cams and pivots were discovered (not invented) before the wheel. The simple act of bending a twig to better snag lunch has been mastered by many animals and some can figure out more complicated methods of getting fed than many of so-called 'smarter' humans on the planet. Managing money is a totally different skill set. It's no body's 'fault'. It's just human nature. Some call it 'talent', some instinct, I prefer to call such things 'human nature' and allow for it in my thinking as much as possible and accept it as fact instead of being envious of someone who can tell what key a song is in or remember numbers for months or names of people introduced after about twelve seconds. They all escaped me but I do know guns and my dad was an accountant. Go figure.

In the world of guns and gunsmithing of 1999 it was my great fortune to be several steps ahead of every other gunsmith in the United States. I not only had a innate curiosity about guns and a memory for things mechanical that allowed one disassembly and certain amount of 'thousand yard stare' time to re-assemble the gun in my mind so I knew where the paths of energy and how those paths were blocked and intercepted, diverted, reversed and altered. I could, with good certainty, trace how about four pounds of trigger finger pressure after about twenty pounds of initial effort could be turned into many thousands of foot pounds of penetrative energy projected over many multitudes of time and distance more than my long arms could throw a rock. I also had inside information that was very seldom shared. In 1999 I knew guns and I also had the benefit of their maker's records. I knew how they were made as well as how they turned out. I knew why they turned out how they did, too. It is much cheaper to build unsafe guns.

When I was sixteen years old, there were two events that forever more impressed on my memory the power of an accurate firearm. The first was in the mid summer when north Florida weather forecast says, "Possible heavy thunderstorm to hit at 2PM plus or minus a minute or two." I was down in the Apalachicola National Forest with near new Remington M700 in .222 Remington. Mike Walker had just won a bunch of bench rest matches with one and I had mowed a lot of grass and guided Texas bass fishermen to stringers of ten pounders for mounting (informal 'tip/bounty' for ten, ten pound bass was a $100 bill) to earn the money for that rifle and 10X Lyman scope with Redfield mounts. I had enough for reloading gear and Sisk bullets and a fifty pound drum of Hogdens surplus IMR-4891 and a case of small rifle primers.

Factory ammunition will now out shoot the best I could do with that rifle then, but I was well within 'minute of crow' at 300 yards with that rifle and the little Sisk Hornet bullets that were hotrodded in the Deuce would seem to come apart on a heavy feather. The 'splatter factor' was phenomenal and it made clouds of black feathers as a result of a center hit. That afternoon, the thunderstorm had already lashed the piney woods with at least an inch of very hard rain with wind, lightning and thunder that flooded the woods and wet the crows to their very hide.

The sun had come out from under the purple wall cloud late and was yellowish green with every pine needle pointed with a sparkle. The eastern sky was as black and ominous as it gets. The crows were in a gaggle of maybe a dozen sitting in the very tops of thick long-leaf pines about fifty feet tall with the dark sky behind and bright sun shining in their eyes. I'm convinced crows and coyotes can hear brake lights come on so I coasted the '59 Olds to a stop while trying to pick an opening to shoot through. One big crow was a little further along than the rest and the sun was full on him at about 225 yards. Through the luck of lighting and setting and a center mass hit, the crow virtually exploded in a cloud of black feathers... and a big circular rainbow that perfectly framed it.

Years later, while attending gunsmithing school in Colorado, I shot buy-in matches at sticks of dynamite at the maximum range of 610 yards out at Frank Pike's Ranch on what is now Interstate 470. A dollar a shot got the pot if you hit the target, and hitting the 'bulls eye' was never as exciting as that one very wet Florida crow.

To 'project power' is an inherited instinct of the majority of human males. Some don't have that particular gene or instinct, and some even ridicule those that have an over abundance of it. That group of 'inert' people supply the world with anti-gunners. Can we all agree that that particular group will not understand this effort to educate shooters? Can we explain it to them? Can we somehow de-fuse their natural instinct to levitate, squeal like a fresh-cut pig and immediately demand the entire universe bend to their inflated sense of worth and bow down to their brand of insanity? I doubt it considerably and I see everybody here indicating a certain cynicism. I call that having a grip on reality. We know they'll pitch a hissy fit and if history has any weight, the compliant and mostly ignorant media will see their hissy fit, magnify it, totally misdiagnose the reason for it, and saturate the air waves with opaque stupidity.

I saw it first with the JFK assassination. I owned four of those rifle-scope combinations at the time. The reporting by the press was absolutely laughable and when I got the complete Warren Report in Korea, I found it laughable, too. I have never trusted a federal law enforcement agency since then even though I worked with some. I know what they are capable of because I know how clueless they are about some things... or just plain crooked. The results are the same either way.

I address this to everyone here, especially those in the back row reserved for the naysayers, doubters and the hard-headed. The reason we're here and the reason you know so much and so little at the same time of the 'Remington problem' is directly traced to one man and his search for the truth.

On October 23, 2000, when Gus Barber was shot and killed by a pre-'82 Model 700 Remington containing the Walker trigger, that particular mechanism had been in Federal court many times. Remington had run their own surveys on new guns and found failures. Letters complaining of a rifle firing as it was being unloaded numbered in the thousands. I was privy to mountains of information, but I'd never thought about what I'd do 'next time it happens'. My job was to look at history and not predict the future. What I'd seen as protected documents answered a lot of questions I naturally had about the way guns are made. That's my business and I'm curious, but the documents also showed a massive, ongoing, purposeful cover-up that was so hard to believe, so outrageous to see in black and white, and so plainly anti-gun that it seemed impossible such a corporate decision would have ever been made... but those decisions were made nonetheless.

No one wants to believe an American institution with millions of loyal customers would knowingly lie to them and defend a mechanism that is demonstrably and dangerously defective, but I knew for a fact they most certainly did that and they did it daily. All you have to is call and tell them your story. The answer seems to be the same every time.

As a deputy I was taught to give everybody the benefit of the doubt. Maybe there's some fright involved and somebody could come out with a lie by accident. We always gave them a chance to clarify their statements and ask the question again. The chances of a mistaken lie are much smaller the second time. They've had a chance to think about the situation and figure out the risk and rewards of telling the truth. Sometimes the second clarification wasn't quite enough and a third time is needed. That third time is when you know it is safe to believe what the interviewee is saying. He's either finally telling the truth or it's safe to say he's telling a purposeful lie. With crooks the results are usually the same: he has to make bail before he goes home. In corporate America, they change company directors on the second question so the process has to start over. If things get too hot, they just give the company to another set of directors and start again with *Who, me? What records?* It has worked pretty well for Remington Arms for more than sixty years. The end result of such company secrecy is that the people that know the truth can't say it and those that need the truth won't believe it.

Besides that, the entire basis for the case of an intermittent discharge being hard to prove to a jury because it can't be repeated without artificially altering the natural position of the connector and of course artificial 'evidence' is an arguing point that cost lawyers thousands of dollars and months of time. The job of the expert is to show the jury how the displacement of the connector *has* to happen but without being able to actually show them a displaced connector. The odds of twelve people understanding how a nutcracker works is pretty slim, and much less so with a firearm.

And then there are the Ten Commandments of Gun Safety which have become so ingrained through hunter safety programs, scouts, boy's clubs, and instruction manuals, that any guilt to be assigned to any gun accident is automatically put on the holder of the gun. Even those people that should know better than to assume anything will assume that the company did not build an unsafe gun by design. But I knew they did and I knew they built them that way on purpose and I knew they lied about it when caught. I knew a lot of 'the secrets' but I told the Court those secrets were safe with me.

In early December, I got a call from Rich Barber in Montana. I had heard of a kid being killed in Montana and somebody said it was a Remington. I knew I'd hear the details sooner or later. Usually the gory details are communicated to me by way of a lawyer. This time it was a father. He told me the story without breaking down which truly impressed me. I can tear-up by telling someone else's story. He told his own details and it was heartbreaking in every aspect. Every detailed question I could ask him he answered with certainty. He was certainly a 'good witness' from my mechanical viewpoint. When he asked me why it happened, I told him the truth. I told him there were many dark secrets to be known but I couldn't say what they were, but I told him who to call. Rich and family were also given my word that I'd help them anyway I could.

Barber had posted some of his questions on an internet discussion board that caused a lot of pain. Our own back-row helped to re-hurt a very badly hurt family and then refused to be educated through stubbornness.

<The grumbles in the back row are sweet music to my ears.>

I agreed to help explain the defect in the Walker trigger on the gunsmithing forum of HuntAmerica.com. That was the first criticism of the Walker in public and it caused a storm that later spread to AccurateReloading.com and several other internet discussion boards.

Let me remind those I see coming in late that sometimes the back row speaks up in **bold italics.** It might seem hard to believe but the back row is very useful and is my 'target audience'. Everybody has a voice here. The front rows talk normally in *plain italics.*

'Nothing but the facts' isn't enough to convince some people, and personal attacks and dirty tricks soon tire anyone of fighting a battle of wits against the unarmed. When the shills showed up to attack any statement I might have made and then I read the emails they sent to Remington attorneys bragging about how they had diverted the conversation and tried to trash the messenger, I decided I'd had enough of the internet boards. I'd saved enough gunsmith advice for a book or two and learned some valuable lessons while being disabled by a neck traction sentence that lasted months.

The most valuable lesson is a hard one to accept: **Those that most need to know are the least likely to listen.**

One Remington lawyer had stated during my first deposition he would spend all summer in his motor home deposing acquaintances of mine to find out what I'd said in various speeches and classes in schools and seminars. That threat to my friends was enough that I resigned from the American Custom Gunmaker's Guild where I'd held many offices including two terms as president. It wasn't worth the hassle for me or the pure aggravation to my friends that don't understand the job I'd taken on. Politically, of course, any statement judged to be somehow against guns can cause an uproar from shooters. A couple generations of fighting against the Kennedys and Dodds of the country has set everyone on a hair trigger, if you'll pardon another gun-ism.

Of course you have to be anti-gun to do what you do!

Actually you have to be pro gun and pro-truth enough to risk everything to warn those that most need to know. I explained the mechanisms and gave gunsmithing advice more than 5,000 times on two discussion boards and took quite a bit of abuse as a result. Looking back about 14 years and reading many of those posts now, the ignorance of the gun community then was just astounding. The word has finally leaked out some. Some of the thousands of victims of discharges from Remington guns have computers, too. They know what happened to them without any doubt. Their voices are finally being heard. Again, thanks to one very determined man.

Rich Barber had immediately seen the weakness in the design and was justifiably furious to find out what had been covered up. Barber kept his case in the news and he started finding out that federal judges had allowed even the losing cases to be kept secret from the public. Indeed, one of the standard settlement requirements was a gag order. All the evidence and discovery documents are sealed. There had been one in Montana just a few years earlier. Why wasn't it in the news? That rifle fired without the trigger being pulled. Isn't that news? Rich Barber rightly asked "Shouldn't I know if a rifle has a 'history' when buying one?"

Knowledge is power and Rich Barber started gathering information. He started his archive of documents and made his first trip in an airplane to go see a judge in South Texas. That judge had seen a Model 700 fire without a trigger pull in open court with a Remington expert holding it. The judge had seen many millions of dollars paid for a man's foot in that case. (No, down is not a safe direction to point a gun, either.) Rich knew that the judge knew the gun was bad, yet he had sealed the case. Rich wanted to change that. He did it with a dramatic appeal. Instead of shaking hands, he handed a picture of Gus to the judge and introduced him as the nine year old boy killed by the judge's bad decision. The judge was so moved that he gave him everything he asked for, and soon, many more judges did, too. Lawyers who were no longer active had file drawers full of discovery material from cases that had settled out of court and the records were sealed. Rich Barber became Remington's historian whether they liked it or not. They most certainly did not like what he was doing. They had met a man that money couldn't buy and their lies would never appease. Barber got us on Montana Public TV one Sunday morning in 2002 and we put several blurbs in papers, and then NBC called. A reporter that knew the story was promoted to a national spot and the story went with him.

Rich Barber also became an advocate of a consumer protection law. He lobbied the Montana legislature for Gus' Law that makes it illegal for a judge to protect an unsafe gun or other product in Montana. The first time Gus' Law came up for a vote it failed, but two years later when they met again it passed unanimously. Every single Montana congressman voted for Gus' Law. Rich Barber might get delayed but he's never defeated.

There had been magazine articles suggesting Remington had a 'liability problem' but nobody knew any details. Besides that, the Ten Commandments of Gun Safety tells us safeties are mechanical devices and can break so don't trust them. Why name it a 'safety' then?

NBC was pitching a program about the 'Remington problem'. The Barber story anchored the program but by this time, many cases were known of, and thanks to the vocal but ignorant people that had caused such a stink nearly ten years earlier when the failures of the trigger was first publicized, more and more victims had come forward. CNBC, the business end of NBC, produced "Remington Under Fire."

On October 23rd, 2010 Remington Under Fire was shown for the first time on CNBC. It aired two times that first night and then three or four times a week for months afterward. Many people, for the very first time, heard that there might be something 'not right' about some Remington triggers. It also caused a storm in the lawyer's offices ofnboth sides. It kept me very busy for a while.

Some of that was bogus! I saw it and don't believe it.

Good for you! Always be skeptical. There were cases mentioned that I'd already decided were not a defect I could describe to a jury, so I declined to get involved, but there were many cases that are true, too. If you listen real close you'll be able to tell which are which, but you might want to really pay attention to how the trigger works, first.

Well, Remington made a rebuttal to it that shows you the fool.

I've heard of it but never watched it. My friends that know of my testimony says they took quite a bit out of context, but I'm not interested enough to watch it to find out. I testify to the mechanical facts of the trigger and I've not yet been wrong. Remington's people want to play school yard political games with reputations instead of explaining why they can't see a defect even after thousands of shooters have explained to them in letters exactly how it happened to them. Some of them go into great detail. The flash of an unexpected gunshot burns deep and vivid memories. It's easy to see the truth in them, too. Remington does not believe their own customer's complaints. Not even thousands of them that witnessed, very scarily, exactly the same thing. When someone brings up Remington's internet rebuttal, I ask if they discussed the fault in their triggers in their program. If not, I have no need to watch it.

You mean there have been complaints about these accidents you're talking about?

I first saw complaint letters in 1994. One in particular struck a cord because I recognized the person and the story. It was part of a 'Remington story' among customers and cowboys in Elko, Nevada in 1989. Five years later, there were his letters as part of the discovery production from Remington in a law suit involving the same rifle and same circumstances, so it stuck with me even though I read a couple of thousand such letters during three or four cases. I knew of that one!

Did you say thousands?

Yes ma'am, but those are only about seven years of complaints at a time when there were some 'safer' Walkers being made. Complaints from the decades-long folded housing, double sear era were said to have been destroyed.

And Rich Barber found this out?

That and much more. He became an expert at corporate dodging and shell games where one company becomes another and the new company has a document destruction policy in place that destroys documents deemed too old to keep... and way too dangerous to produce in a law suit.

What's the point in Barber collecting stacks of papers?

Well, first it proves someone with a purpose can wade through and eventually understand a very complex subject. He systematically sorted and re-sorted and read and re-read many thousands of Remington's own documents to find that not only did they know the Walker trigger was bad, he knew how many times they'd refused to fix it, too. He found out that Remington Arms Co. had never written a paycheck. In fact, they never even had a bank account! He found the drawings of a replacement trigger dated 1949 that would have saved his son's life, too. It cost less than five cents extra to build at that time.

So, he became a millionaire working for predatory lawyers?

Not at all! Rich Barber became the greatest resource a lawyer could ever hope for, but he wouldn't risk his documents or his single-minded search for the pure truth by signing any gag orders. There'd be no confidentiality agreements and no money for silence, either. They had no way to shut him up, no way to pay him to shut up and no way to prove him wrong, either. Rich Barber had a major gun company treed way up a rotten snag. He still does, and his ax is sharp.

Did you work his case, or not?

I never knew if there ever was a case. I know it was an event and I agreed to help anyway I could. Part of that was an inspection of the gun and the trailer but by that time the rifle had been caught in a flash flood in a Texas gunshop and it was no longer in the condition when it killed Gus. It did fail the screwdriver test and had the normal amount of 'gunk' but the surface rust was new from bad storage in a plastic case that got wet. Remington claimed the rifle was rusty and dirty when it shot Gus, but that's not so.

I followed that case. Remington says the trigger "had been adjusted."

Thank you for bring up that most illustrative example of Remington's campaign of denial and innuendo. Let me ask you sir, what does that "been adjusted" mean to you?

I'm a gunsmith and it means somebody was tinkering with the trigger and got it too light. That's common sense!

Thank you again. Let me suggest you made a common assumption but an incorrect one. The most valuable lessons are the ones you learn hard. I know the truth of that and even have the written report from Remington's examination of the Barber rifle trigger. The Barber trigger *had* been adjusted, but only in one way. The sear engagement screw had been adjusted to *increase* engagement to *more* than factory specifications.

That makes no sense at all. Nobody makes a trigger harder to pull. They bring them to us to have us reduce them.

How about if your customer said it fired and scared him? What would you do to make sure it didn't do it again? Would you simply give it more security if you didn't know what else to do? Isn't that exactly what Remington did in 1978 that created the 'lawyer triggers'? Didn't Remington 'fix' the Walker by doing what somebody did to the Barber rifle?

In the Barber rifle, it passed the trick test and would not FSR in that test, but occasionally failed the screwdriver test. The connector was loose on the trigger body but not by enough to account for the failure of the screwdriver test. I never had it apart to measure anything, but Remington did. They found a sear lift while on safety of only .004". That is about half the minimum specified. Does everyone see the danger of a sear that is lifted less than specified? Any debris that lands on top of the connector ahead of the sear step can act as a door stop if the trigger and connector move forward while the sear is held up by the safety cam. The debris prevents return of the connector and that leaves the safety cam as the only 'trigger'.

Does that explain how Gus was shot?

It certainly points to the most likely cause of failure. We know the connector was not in place to catch the sear. A lack of safety lift clearance and the looseness of the connector on the trigger as shown by the failed screwdriver test both signify the failure occurred due to the well known design fault contained within the Walker fire control.

That's not the 'rest of the story'. The most heartbreaking post-event investigations involve kids. It was so as a deputy and it's still so today. Gus was one very unlucky boy. The bullet passed through two aluminum panels and ricocheted off another one. There was one small deflection in the first panel and a major deflection in the second, then a ricochet from the third. The rifle's muzzle was pointed away from the invisible Gus but the largest bullet fragment found him. Had the bullet gone straight, it would have missed him by several feet.

Doesn't that just prove what the TCGS says about always point in a safe direction?

What is a safe direction for a rifle that could shoot at any instant? How about the guy that tried to unload his elk rifle and had a Fire on Safety Release? When the gun fired his horse spooked and nearly stomped him to death. Was that one pointed in a safe direction?

I never thought of a firearms accident that didn't involve shooting something or somebody.

All guns have to be pointed somewhere all the time. If it's going to shoot without a trigger pull, luck plays a very large part in the results. The reports are in the thousands of such accidents... in writing, sometimes in a very shaky hand. I recognize that from the sheriff's office reports that had to be written after a fight. Your heart tells you how scary it was.

Sir, I'm one of the ones that wrote to Remington about a rifle that went off on a hunting trip. They were very nice and had me send it back so they could inspect it, but they said it didn't mess up with them and sent it back. It fired again and destroyed my brother's ATV, but I raised enough hell they paid for it!

Part of the 'secrets' is the slush fund that pays for transmissions and pack horses and bird dogs. Only the really squeaky wheels get greased with cash, though. Did they also replace your trigger?

Yes, they did. Twice!

We have to ask of Remington, why replace a trigger that failed with one that's also likely to fail again *by design*? Is that practice in the best interest of shooters and sportsmen?

There's no way you can convince me that Remington went 60 years without changing the trigger.

That seems to be a case of you hearing something I've never said. There have been a dozen or more *changes*, just no *repairs*. A major change was the switch to a solid sear instead of the dual sears of the first triggers. That one move doubled the amount of sear engagement and made the sear and connector interact all across the width of the connector instead of half the width of the original. That was a 1966 change. The second major change came in 1982 when the bolt lock feature was removed. FSR became much less frequent when people could unload while the sear was positively blocked from firing the rifle. Remington finally recognized the danger of the bolt lock feature and agreed to cut the end off of customer's safety levers. Or they install a new safety lever. I've seen both.

In the case of FSR, the special circumstance of a bolt lock became too evident and costly to ignore. Remington changed to a non-bolt lock safety lever and then told the public they would change the guns already sold in direct response to outright demands by Rich

Barber and his legal champion, Rich Miller. There are company documents that say the bolt lock was better off gone but it was still there many years (and lives) later. Finally, about 2002, Remington acknowledged they were at least paying some attention.

Rich Miller in Kansas City, an experienced attorney in Remington cases had channeled Barber's passion for research into productive investigations and document productions. Miller answered the questions a former building contractor would have in order to understand corporate structuring and how to best decide which ones are the truly meaningful documents. Miller worked tirelessly between cases going through the hundreds of pertinent documents being uncovered by Barber. Many discovery productions were compared and he found several possible fraudulent document productions. Some cases were missing pertinent documents that were known of from previous cases. Some memos were found that filled in many blanks. Discovery abuse by the defense was plain enough to see in many cases. That is an ax hanging over lawyer's heads they have to be worried about as long as they live.

Rich Miller told me on the way to an inspection in Texas that he had the particularly snide and arrogant expert engineer, who had been a pain and a fixture in Remington cases for many years, pretty much toasted on the case we were just beginning. He said he had the goods on many of his conflicts in testimony and he'd be blown out of the water in the upcoming trial in Dallas. It was great news to hear. The Remington engineer had been as slimy as Bill Clinton in answering very plain questions and I was anxious to see him gutted on the stand.

Rich Miller drove to Topeka for a tennis tournament but became ill on the way over and then hospitalized on the way back. A brain tumor was growing fast. His heart failed the day after brain surgery. He was only 50 years old.

The Remington cases had to start over. The Barber family had lost a steady and loyal supporter, but Barber kept digging. He drove a thousand miles for a pick-up truck full of documents, all marked as protected by some court or another. He had his finger on the pulse of many levels of the gun industry. He made friends in high places and developed a network of insiders that could shine a light in a particular corner to find the incriminating documents that proved exactly why his son was dead. He petitioned the Federal Court to release documents in a prior Montana case.

Aleksich was my first Remington case, and it had settled the day before trial. I knew a lot of the reasons why and I had read a document that is the 'smoking gun' in all the Walker trigger cases. I'd found and read the memo to Rich Miller at one AM. I saw him read it the next morning at breakfast. The case settled later that day for reasons still not in the public domain, but the memo has not been seen since. I sat in on the settlement meeting at a local attorney's office by invitation of Miller, and learned some of what are called 'the secrets'.

It has been Rich Barber that has driven 100% of the non-money interest in the Remington cases. Lawyers are in business and the cases that won't pay won't be taken. Those are just facts. Another fact that is especially hard for the victims to understand is why the lawyers won't fight for truth and justice after the money shows up.

The lawyer understands full well a company can't be punished except by costing them money. He also knows pretty closely what the case is worth in time and money. Beyond that amount means a court fight and no lawyer will risk a case to twelve people that had rather be somewhere other than jury duty. To do that would risk getting nothing. It happens. So, lawyers are dedicated to an extraordinary degree in getting the best deal. Cases get settled under terms that really frustrate a searcher for the real truth. But Rich Barber was (and still is) the bulldog that won't turn loose until the hog is tied up and ready to do whatever *he* deems suitable for the hog. The hog will not have much say in the matter at all.

You mentioned a while ago that Remington was using improper testing procedures. What do you mean by that?

I was referring to the testing protocols adopted by SAAMI to determine the security of a gun against firing when dropped.

There has to be somebody watching, or ammo wouldn't fit!

You're right. The companies set up SAMMI to administer

standards. That's why new 30-06 ammunition fits my 1906 Sauer rifle the same as old 30-06 ammo fits the latest offering from anybody in the world. The standards maintained by SAMMI and the tolerances maintained by the companies are truly phenomenal. Mistakes are rare (and very interesting!) SAMMI is the primary watch dog for safety testing but the tests are designed to show failures. They don't test the design.

How can they test a gun and not test the design?

They assume the engineers designed it properly. They just test for failures.

Well, isn't that the same thing?

Not at all. It's an indication but not a determination. The SAMMI drop test is what I'm familiar with and have testified they not only don't demonstrate failure in a bad mechanism, but the SAMMI drop test would be counter-intuitive to an investigator that understood firearms features and designs.

Now you've jumped the shark. You say not only is SAMMI incompetent to test firearms safety, but the people that follow their protocol are also wrong? I'm a state firearms examiner and KNOW you're wrong about this.

<Most of the row seems to agree.>

Please consider the case of Kendrick in Tennessee. He was convicted of murdering his wife with a Remington M7400 sporting-auto rifle. The same year, other victims of the Remington Common Fire Control, which is common to almost all pump and auto models, got paid for injuries sustained in uncontrolled discharges.

Unknown to the jury at Kendrick's trial was the fact the rifle was recovered by a police evidence technician from near the scene. The police tech was using standard, very careful handling protocols when the gun had shot him in the foot back at the police station. It was *assumed* by the appointed defense attorney that a gun only fires when the trigger is pulled even though his client said he didn't and the cop certainly knew he didn't.

Kendrick did 19 years before his final appeal was granted based on several technicalities and my demonstrations and testimony before a judge a crowded court room about how the gun could fire even on safe and without the trigger being pulled. It helped that I could also testify I was very easy to find during the time of his trial and would have testified for free had I known he needed help.

The (neighboring) State Firearms Examiner put that rifle through the SAMMI drop test, which is considered destructive to evidence, and then testified at trial that nothing was wrong with the gun. Kendrick always said he was mad and pointed the rifle but did NOT pull the trigger. When I heard his statements made after his arrest, I believed him. That 'flash-bulb' of true memory burns a very deep picture.

Kendrick was granted a new trial based on new evidence and released because he had already served enough time for a lesser charge.

So, what is the SAMMI test and why is it wrong?

The SAMMI test is to simply drop the gun in several orientations and if it doesn't fire, it must be safe. The Remington Common Fire Control has a recapture angle to the sear and hammer. If the sear is restrained in one of four ways, the sear and hammer can meet 'point to point' and be extremely unsafe until a drop either knocks the parts back into engagement or separates them and the gun fires.

Trigger mechanisms set up to fail by adjusting the sear adjustment screw show it more often falls *into* engagement and the gun does not fire. But, if the mechanism is slightly different in orientation on impact, it can fire every time. It is the ultimate in uncertainty *by design.*

I've worked several cases where a firearms examiner tested the gun and came to a totally erroneous conclusion because he has no clue how the gun actually works.

You mean if a gun doesn't fire it's declared safe by SAAMI?

There is no clearing house for safety. If the gun passes the SAMMI test it is assumed to be safe.

What does this have to do with the Barber case?

The point is that testing a gun that is said to have failed could be just destroying whatever evidence might have been present, but it seems testing is one of the prime requirements of the court system. It would help everyone if the examiners knew how the mechanism operated first and did their testing on an exemplar. Once the examiner knows it's possible (or impossible) for the gun to fail, the investigation can focus in the correct direction.

In almost every 'failure of a firearm' case, there is a Firearms Examiner that has already ruined the evidence. I know of two cases where the testimony by the FE is best described as totally clueless. I feel bad for them when they see me point to the possible sites of failure on their own riot guns. Some just won't believe they've been lied to by the factory, but the record is very clear. I don't believe firearms examiners are being deceitful. I think they're just ignorant of how much they don't know. My sincere hope is that they strive to find out!

In the Barber case, the 'must have pulled the trigger' assumption by every investigator and many friends and neighbors was especially hurtful. It has taken many years for some of the truth to come out. The polarization of thought following the publicity of the Barber accident lasted many years. The lack of proper examination for the purpose of explanation by those that should want to know how guns work and fail was truly extraordinary.

In a conversation with Rich Barber just a few days ago, he mentioned the effect on families is these tragedies. He is close with many victims and survivors and has tried to apply his knowledge for their benefit. As in many cases of trauma and loss, the survivors are much more prone to alcohol and drug abuse. In Alaska, the brother that got shot recovered from it partially but became incapacitated by drink and died from self aspiration. It was his older brother who had laid the rifle against the boat seat that had later fired and hit the boy in the neck who committed suicide sitting on his brother's grave. The pain is just too much. How do you give closure to such a thing? How can you possibly help with such a problem? Rich Barber found a way to do both, but it has taken nearly 15 years to do so. What the public knows of the 'Remington problem' is a credit to the Rich Barber family's indomitable spirit and the solemn promise made to Rich's dying son.

Gus Barber

The late Rich Miller and his paralegal Christie. She's still working Remington cases.

From left: Rich Miller, Tom Butters, Mary Patty Butters, Jack Belk, Rich Barber and daughter Chanda.

RICH
YOU OBVIOUSLY
LIKE SHOOTING
AS MUCH AS I DO
mike Walker

Mike Walker and Rich Barber became good friends

13. Assumed to be Safe

<The lady with the trembling lip is staring straight at me. It's time.>

Yes ma'am, you have a question?

<She stood and glanced at a card in her hand to refresh her thoughts.>

Several years ago my son went with some of his friends on a hunting trip. There was a terrible accident and he was shot and killed by his best friend.

<She paused a second for composure and continued. I knew the story.>

The game wardens and deputies and the coroner and his best friend all said it was an accident and the rifle fired when it shouldn't have. His friend said it was ON safe and he did NOT pull the trigger! But, my lawyer said there was nothing he could do so I called two more lawyers in other states and even though they waited almost two years, nobody would do ANYTHING to help. Can you?

<The room was silent as she sat with a tissue and waited. I've combined some stories here to make a point. The facts are true.>

Ma'am, I know your name and I know the circumstances. I've read the reports and studied the drawings, diagrams and photographs. I read and reread the statements made by the boy holding the rifle and the reports of those that heard him answering questions. I've heard his answers in his own voice.

I can understand exactly what he's saying and why he said it, but it was wrong and that 'bell' can't be un-rung. I told three different lawyers that your case was the perfect platform to bring several subjects of defective designs into the court room to be decided, but there is no way to do it with the only living witness caught out on a ledge of his own making.

The event as I remember it was in the southern Big Horn Mountains on a steep ridge. The trail had become muddy as the sun melted fresh snow so they split up going down to pick their own paths. Both had slipped going down and one even slid on a patch of snow in one place to clean some of the mud off the seat of his pants. It was very steep. Your son was slightly ahead and to the left and downhill about 25 feet when his buddy slipped on an Aspen limb hidden under wet leaves and he slid on one boot for several feet before tripping forward and slamming into the ground. It knocked the breath out of him and he lost the rifle at impact. His back pack had flown over his head and he was disoriented for several seconds as he struggled to breath.

The shortcut seemed like a good idea at the time. They could see the truck down below. He said he finally got his breath back and got the backpack off his head and flopped over to rest a minute and he heard your son below saying he was coming up to help, but he waved him off and said he'd be ok, just give him a minute. They laughed at the fall and mentioned how it would have been much different had he landed on a rock or snag sticking up. It was a hard fall.

He said his rifle was lying very near where he ended up after rolling around trying to get out from under the pack and catch his breath. It was lying in the leaves, right side down and he was relieved to see there was no mud around the muzzle as he reached to pick it up with his left hand. He had to reach out full length to hook two fingers between the scope and the receiver to lift the rifle. When he lifted it up and brought it back to where he was sitting, he saw leaves and litter stuck between the bolt handle and the stock and the right side had wet stuff clinging to it and jammed in every crack and crevice.

He **said** he was going to clean the leaves from under the bolt handle when it fired while still on safe. He repeated that many times during the day. He blamed the rifle for firing while ON safe. He wasn't 'pointing' at anything; he was just brushing the wet leaves off the side. He demonstrated it to deputies, but the rifle didn't (dry) fire during the demonstration.

What rifle are we talking about?

<...asks another lady>

Thank you. So many times it's the obvious that become the details. The rifle was a Remington Model 600 carbine made about 1968 in .308 Winchester caliber. At the time it was made, it was the lightest, shortest and most powerful carbine made in America. It was made in calibers from the tiny .222 to the truly painful .350 Remington Mag.

Had the trigger been adjusted?

Yes, it had....

Then, there's the problem, it's not Remington's fault somebody changed their rifle!

Ma'am, please bear with me while I try to tamp down the back row.

The rifle had been very badly adjusted by following the directions in the owner's manual.

<The general murmur is good.>

For many years Remington included in the Model 721 and Model 600 and 700 owner's manuals instructions for adjusting your own trigger. It was even advertised as being a benefit.

Well, any fool can do it.

You are right. And many fools do.

Are you saying any trigger that has been adjusted is automatically 'bad'?

Thank you, sir! You see the trap that was set by Remington and it's used as a defense in every case where a trigger has been adjusted. If we 'assume' any dimension outside what the factory sets when they make it is 'bad' for the trigger's security, we miss a major indication of *bad design.*

Now you've lost me.

Let's go back to the Barber rifle a minute because that's where further confirmation lies.

Fact one: Both rifles were pre-owned. Somebody traded in or sold the rifles. Dealers trade among themselves for guns that sell better in their market area, so a used rifle bought in Montana could have come from Arizona or from across the street. Seldom is it known who owned a gun before you bought it except who you bought it from.

Fact two: Both the victim owners bought their rifles from dealers who represented them to be 'good' rifles. Gunshops have different views and protocols about used guns. It's a risky market that takes trading ability to do well in. It's not your normal 'retail' marketplace but can be compared to car lots that take trade-ins. My dad's advice was never buy a car from a dealer without an attached repair business. The same could be said of guns. Otherwise it'll cost you to repair whatever was wrong with it.

Fact three: Both triggers showed signs of adjustments.

Hold on just a minute, how can you tell?

Remington pioneered the 'sealing' of their triggers from the post war beginning. At first there was a 'stake' mark in the screw slot that prevented the adjustment screws from being turned without some real effort. Later they just put a drop of glue on each screw head. To adjust any screw, the glue has to be scraped or pried off first.

I put LocTite on mine.

<...lots of agreement in the room>

Just understand that LocTite is a thread locker. It works in places air can't get to. Too much of it, and you've got REAL problems inside a Walker trigger. It's much better to stake screws in place and leave LocTite to scope mounts and car mechanics.

Isn't there a recall of Remington triggers right now for 'too much sealant'?

Yes, there is and we'll cover that in some detail in the XMP section. Let me get these Walkers out of the way first and we have an important case before us, now.

The Barber rifle and the 'BigHorn' rifle's triggers had been unsealed by somebody. The Barber rifle had one seal broken and the BigHorn had two. Both were used guns, but clean and dry inside with nothing otherwise altered. Both triggers had *more than* factory specification sear-connector overlap, but much less than factory specified tolerance for 'sear lift on safety'.

Let's go back and look at the diagram.

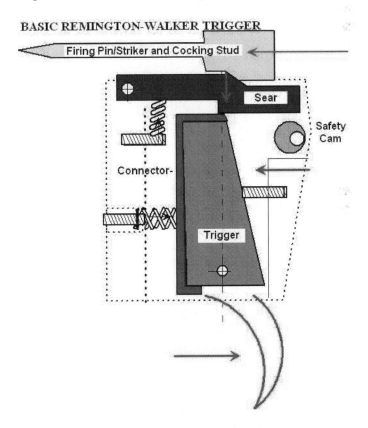

When the safety lever is rotated back towards the 'SAFE' position, the safety cam lifts the tail of the sear and locks the cocking stud and firing pin in the rear position. Notice the gap between the top of the connector and the bottom of the sear. That is the 'sear lift on safe' dimension. It should be .016 to .022". It is roughly the same as the sear-connector overlap.

Sir, could you point out the screws that are 'sealed'?

Sure, here's a picture.

Walker trigger, sealed adjustment screws.

Remember the lesson about two pieces of steel resting one on the other and how 'more is better' when it comes to triggers, but triggers also have to be light enough to be used? We also talked of 'human nature'. It is natural for any mechanic to see a fragile looking overlap and assume any failure in that overlap could be cured by increasing it. That is common mechanical sense and would be the first location to 'repair' a rifle that was said to have failed. Remember! That's exactly what the factory did to 'repair' the defect and 'lawyer triggers' were the result.

I see nods all over the room. Doesn't that explain the adjustment toward *more* security instead of less?

So, why didn't, it work? Both rifles failed anyway!

Yes, they did. Not because the sear-connector overlap was too little, but because the *connector* became displaced while it was ON safety.

Wait a minute now, you said the BigHorn rifle went off while it was ON safety.

If you listened very carefully, I said HE said it did. It did not.

That's why there were no law suits.

You mean he lied about it to the cops?

Let's examine what he did very carefully because it happens a lot. It's human nature and it's very hard to deal with sometimes. Both of these young men were engineering students and very bright. Both were mechanically inclined and loved the outdoors. They were both long time shooters and knew guns.

I read the statements very carefully. I heard the recording made in the cab of the Game Warden's truck. I can understand how he made, and then reinforced, an incorrect statement. Some of you gunsmiths will recognize it, too. I heard it the instant his memory went from true memory to speculation, uncertainty, and creative thinking. Had the game warden asked him how he opened the bolt to clean under the handle, it would have probably been a completely different case. It was a pre-'82 rifle with the bolt lock still in place. He could not have even started to open the bolt without first having taken it OFF safe.

In the flash of noise and dread that is an accidental discharge, the mind races for an explanation. Psychologists and other researchers of such mysterious things say proof of that automatic mental response can be seen in our own dreams. Most here have had a vivid dream of something that culminates in a noise that wakes you up. Where did that dream come from *before* the noise? It all fit together but it hadn't happened yet. That's an example of the human brain sorting through possibilities and throwing one out before true analysis has taken place.

The possible mental flash that takes place in less than a second could be:

The rifle FIRED!

The trigger has to be pulled for that to happen and I DID NOT pull the trigger, therefore the rifle is defective.

A defective rifle fired when it should have been safe.

It must have fired while ON safe.

There is NO WAY I AM TO BLAME!

A mechanically inclined student of engineering is being trained to think critically. Every problem must have a solution. The brain supplies the information it has at the time. Many times that information is incomplete or incorrect. The mistake is in not recognizing it when it happens.

I don't see how anybody could get such a thing wrong.

That's one good thing about our legal system. There are many here that truly believe that there are people who got paid for doing something that was entirely their fault.

<…lots of nods on that one!>

Let me see a show of hands. How many here have been interviewed by a team of detectives investigating a murder and consider you the suspect? Nobody? How about robbery, assault or grand theft? Nobody? How many have sat for six hours under oath answering questions from a lawyer trying to disprove every word you say?

<A man nods up front.>

I'm a doctor.

Yes sir. I understand that one. It is tough, isn't it?

The long and the short of it is this: It takes a really *in*competent lawyer to let a lie get by. Sometimes they do. I don't deny it and I've seen it in the court room. When does the lack of knowledge become a lie instead of ignorance, though? This is part of the firearms examiner's problem that we addressed earlier.

Not to my satisfaction!

Let's agree that ignorance is widespread problem that completely covers both sides of any legal situation. In the Barber case, the rifle fired while it was being stared at. The right thumb was sore from taking most of the recoil. In the earlier Aleksich case, the M700 was taken off safety (very hard) with a pinching motion of the safety lever between thumb and fist. No way could the trigger have been pulled. In both those cases the gun handler knew exactly what happened and there was nothing to invent or excuse. There are literally thousands of 'testimonials' written to Remington, many times in a shaky hand, that perfectly describe Fire on Safety Release, Fire on Bolt Close, Fire on Bolt Opening and other failures due to the bad design.

In the BigHorn case, the gun handler was too smart and too scared to admit he didn't know *how* the gun failed, but he knew it wasn't his fault. Sooner or later, he'd have to take an oath and re-tell the story in much more detail than the cops could ever hope to do; hours of answering, demonstrating and testifying with the unblinking eye of the video camera staring at him as he tries to fill in blanks he's totally ignorant of. At the end of the day some things are obvious.

That doesn't mean some greedy lawyer won't sue anyhow.

I'm not a lawyer and glad of it. It's their job to get their client paid if at all possible. It's well known that some civil cases can cost a million dollars to pursue OR defend. Lawyers seem to have a schedule that allows satisfaction on all sides and we all know for any lawyer to ever be 'satisfied', he has to be paid.

<The chuckle did us all good.>

So, you say the case involving the death of my son was bogus!?

No ma'am, not at all. I'm saying it is an example of what is certainly one of human's strongest inherent desires: to be not at fault. I gave an example of the deputy in the radio room horsing around and shot a .357 Magnum into the floor in front of the teletype machine. He did not want to be at fault, but the certainty of the firearms *design*, showed him to be 100% at fault for that shot. I'm sure he was embarrassed and, as a matter of fact, he didn't last long as a deputy after that.

In your son's case, his buddy couldn't face the fact he was holding the gun when it fired. It *had* to be the gun's fault because he *knew* he did not pull the trigger, but to clean the leaves from under the bolt handle he *had* to take the safety off. Did he forget that part? No. People don't forget, but they do try to excuse things the best way they can. He failed to correct the record on the second telling of the story and to correct it now is just too embarrassing to face. The case failed for the lack of a good witness and it could be said the witness wasn't a good one because the investigating officers knew no more about the gun than he did. They could have asked better questions which would have brought the correct answers. I understand the tragedy didn't stop there.

What do you mean by that? It seems plenty tragic to me, and now he has to live his life knowing he killed his friend and his lie made it worse. How much worse could it get?

The student holding the Model 600 rifle when it fired learned of the outrageous 'repair' done by the factory on his rifle. Here's why some countries consider bad engineering a capital offense: Shortly after the gun survey taken of several hundred new rifles in a Texas warehouse showed hundreds of short safety cams caused the connector to drag on the bottom of the sear and then not recapture reliably, many brand new guns failed the basic tests after just being shipped from the factory. He must have realized the ramifications of his incorrect statements and how his shortcomings under severe pressure made exposure of the company policy in court impossible. He realized his failure to tell *exactly* what happened could very well serve to perpetuate a dangerous defect and get others hurt or killed.

He committed suicide.

Four in the back row whisper among themselves and one then asked:

Could we take a break a minute?

I'd much prefer you sit down and listen for a while, yet. You need to hear it and you've refused to listen before. It's time for you to hear the truth and be exposed to a secret or two. Hopefully by now you've recognized defects in guns you didn't know were defective and that should give you the confidence to keep listening. The so called 'repair' of the M600 safeties in the late '70s should be considered criminally negligent.

The Model 660 Remington was the one that killed the guy in Houston, remember? That rifle had a folded housing with a crooked overtravel screw that captured the connector in the forward position. That was not the first time a trigger had been found to be faulty, but it was the first time the fault was found before a law suit was filed. A bunch of money still changed hands to settle up with the widow and his sons, but not as costly as losing a trial or even going through the expense of litigation to be settled later. That seemed to signal a change in Remington's behavior, for the better. It wasn't always that way.

Remington M660 carbine

In the late '70s the boy accidentally shot his dad through the Jeep seat with a Model 600 Remington. We've talked about that case. It was found during the investigation that the gun would fail the 'trick test'. Remington took a survey of Model 600s, brand new in a warehouse. The numbers were staggering. From hundreds of rifles tested, over 50% failed the Trick Test and/or the Screwdriver Test. And, it was easy to see why, too.

The safety cams that lift the tail of the sears up and off the connector by .012 to .016" were only lifting them .000 to about .008. They were lifting way less than specified. Some of the connectors were loose also and could slip above the level of the sear and fail the Screwdriver Test even though they passed the Trick Test. Something had to be done in a hurry and Remington did. It was cheap, too.

They redesigned the safety cam and sear to give more lift. As seen in the Houston rifle, there was plenty of sear lift. But they salvaged the safety levers already on hand by knurling the top of the safety cam.

Didn't you say that cam lifts about 20 lbs?

Yes, it does. I've seen several of them that have been used enough to just scrub the knurling right off, and were worse than they were before the 'fix'. I've owned two of them.

Are you saying Remington 'repaired' a bad part by just coining the edge of a dry cam?

That's exactly what they did. The part is sheet metal to begin with and is subject to a lot of pressure and wear and there's no way to lubricate it without contaminating the inside of the trigger. Then, to make up for not enough metal, they cast some up with a tool that moves metal around but also leaves it much more susceptible to excess wear.

I just don't believe it.

It's a free country....

Ah, sir, your honor, or whatever, I'm sitting on the same row as he is, but I've got to speak up. We've had half a dozen of those in the shop over the years. One customer said it cost him a big buck when it fired as took the safety off but it wouldn't do it in the shop.

<I see two outright confirmations and several averted looks. A nerve has been hit with a sharp hammer.>

I appreciate your honesty. That has been seen in other shops as well. Now, I'm going to assume for a minute somebody else has also had a customer that said his rifle fired when the safety was flipped off?

<...two more>

Did you, in your heart of hearts, believe he had somehow pulled the trigger and just didn't remember it?

I showed him how easy it was to pull the trigger early when a big buck is in the scope. I didn't believe him.

Do you now?

I can see how it could happen.

That is real progress. Thanks.

I'm really confused about this. I thought you said it wasn't the safety that was bad.

You have a great point and a good memory. In these cases, it was the safety cam portion that was too small and created a condition for failure by not lifting the sear high enough. Let me explain how the connector makes that situation even worse.

In all override triggers, the actual trigger piece movement is very small. If the trigger is in adjustment, the trigger motion is only about .030 of an inch. A thin dime is .052" thick. This small amount of motion makes a trigger 'good' for the shooter and more accurate to shoot. People that don't shoot regularly usually don't believe that a shooter can 'feel' that difference in trigger location, but my test has proven they do. Here's the test. You'll need help.

With your eyes closed, have someone hand you your favorite hunting rifle with it either ready to fire or already been fired but without you knowing which. Now, shoulder the rifle and prepare to shoot. Can you tell if it needs cocking? About 90% of regular rifle shooters can determine that with guns using override triggers.... unless it's a Remington and you pull a simple trick on them. The Walker trigger will return to a 'ready to fire' position even though it's already fired. Remember that 'flexibly mounted connector'? Just push the trigger piece back forward, sometimes it'll flop there by itself. Now the shooter thinks his trigger is properly under the sear, but the connector is actually displaced.

That's a lot of talking for no point.

It explains how even a seasoned shooter with his favorite and most familiar rifle can have an FSR.

<I just witnessed another convert in the back row see a bright light.>

So, the connector is still at fault?

Not entirely. The safety cam is a defect in manufacturing if it differs from the blueprint. If the blueprint is wrong and calls out the wrong measurement for the cam, it is a defect in design. I'm not sure which was the case in 1978, but Remington found a way to cheaply salvage bad parts by making them worse.

Who warned the public?

You ask great questions, sir. I suspect you're a lawyer.

I am now, but I was a clerk in a drug store that sold guns in the '80s and I remember what you call 'Remington triggers' and the 'Remington stories' being told among hunters. What struck me then was how many careless hunters there must be. I'm glad I came today. I had just started working at the sporting goods counter that hunting season and saw a kid my age from somewhere back East that was so embarrassed he was day-glo orange from teasing about shooting his rented horse. I would have hated to ride all the way home with that crew!

There's nothing quite as bad as an accidental discharge, whether the gun was to blame or not. I've seen two discharges in the middle of big gun shows. It goes so quiet so quick you can hear the echo of the shot in the otherwise cavernous show space. The guy holding the smoking gun was always bright, flaming-faced red.

I had a shop in Colorado in the heart of the deer and elk hunting Rockies that saw more than a hundred thousand out of state hunters come in for a month of deer and elk seasons. It got crazy around the license shops and outfitter's stores. I was told it was the lawyers that caused the sudden increase in trigger pulls. Nothing was said about M600 safeties being out of spec, not that I got anyhow. I was not an 'authorized repair' station because I didn't want the hassle, but I was active in gunsmithing and did weekly business with the supply houses, and still heard nothing.

You didn't speak up? I thought you were the over-seer of all things faulty.

<Some people do have a knack.>

Let's put a few things into perspective here. The benefit of hindsight is often overlooked. The Texas lawyer was shot in the back by a faulty Model 600 carbine in 1977. I was the daytime stockmaking instructor at Colorado School of Trades in Denver at the time with about 85 students. I know what the comments were then among the students of gunsmithing: "Stupid kid, should have unloaded somewhere else." I had seen a Walker fail in Florida but that connector didn't have the 'foot' on the bottom to keep it in place. I had no real ground to stand on and no real knowledge of but what I had observed.

In hindsight, after I know what I've learned in the nearly 40 years since, a full investigation should have been done at the Gunsmith's school as a public service and a service to the trade and that knowledge passed to Brownell's and others so word would spread of the failure and how it happened. I didn't think of it. I didn't hear of anybody else suggesting it, either. I heard suggestions about what to do with the lawyers involved, but nothing at all about the guns. Some things never seem to change.

By 1978, when I had a gunshop in western Colorado, Remington trigger pulls were so heavy and grating that all three of the local sports shops had a deal with my shop to have triggers adjusted at no charge to the customer. All it took was a guy coming in and say, AllStar in Rifle sent me to get my new rifle adjusted. I did it and put a hash mark on the work sheet. We called them 'Lawyer Triggers'.

<Nods along the back row have me feeling pretty good.>

Let's get back just a minute to the Big Horn Mountains Model 600.

That rifle was a repaired rifle that had then prematurely worn out the safety cam and that allowed it to fail the trick test about one out of four tries. Not only was it a defective Walker trigger design because of the connector, it also had an out of spec part, the safety cam, which was 'repaired' in a way no engineer could defend. But the best witness didn't believe his own eyes. Guns only fire when you pull the trigger was so ingrained, he couldn't shake it.

Does that answer your questions, ma'am?

<That was the saddest smile I've ever seen and she was given a polite round of applause as she made her way to the door. Even the guys in the back row were respectful. I'm impressed.>

I'm a target shooter and I dearly love my Remington triggers. Are you trying to sell an alternative?

No sir. I have no triggers for sale at this time, but I'm always thinking about it, and I don't have any trigger makers that get my unfettered endorsement. But I do have my favorites. I see no reason to change. Your Remington trigger is just fine. I wouldn't worry about it.

He just went totally insane! Did y'all hear that?

<…a troubling burble of agreement>

Before somebody fetches the big net, let me explain what I just said and try to compare it with what you think you just heard.

The override trigger was proved safe enough for the hunting fields in the Model 70. The Montana action and Dakota Arms use this system now and some fine replacements of that type are available for purchase. They are fine triggers *by design,* but target shooters want something lighter than is perfect for an override trigger. Remember the half friction, half spring rule of Paul Mauser? It applies here in Spades. Four pounds total means two pounds of metal to metal pull with no return spring in place and four pounds of pull with the spring in place and adjusted. The Model 70 is usually 5 to 7lbs when new and will wear into a perfect 4 lbs in about 500 rounds of shooting. Most Model 70 triggers are ruined before then by those too impatient to wait.

The Remington Walker trigger was designed by a target shooter, for target shooters, and he invented a target cartridge to go with it, the 'Triple Deuce', .222 Remington. The Walker trigger is a target trigger designed for more expert shooters. The reason no one was hurt in the very first test of 200 rifles was because they were given out to mostly target shooters. The failures happened on the range. Check the sod in front of any trap club firing line in the world for evidence of target guns failing on the range.

Let's look one more time at the patent, shall we?

"...which is absolutely safe in the hands of the hunter or target shooter and rugged enough to remain so in spite of the abuse and neglect which are often heaped upon sporting arms."

That, ladies and gentlemen is a bigger damned lie than the 'trigger stops the instant the sear falls' statement earlier in the patent, and I believe it has caused more heart ache than any other patent lie in American history. The engineers at Remington knew the Walker trigger was defective a year before they applied for a patent. It wasn't even safe enough for target shooters. The first trials proved that to Walker and he suggested a trigger blocker in 1947 but Remington was in too big a hurry and too damn cheap to repair it right then at about a nickel a gun extra cost.

Is there a part of the Walker design that's not clear, now?

You seem to be making pretty good sense, all of a sudden. But, we have several points to bring up.

With a challenge to your literal thinking, shoot.

How come the bolt lock was still in place on the Big Horn M600 if the factory had 'repaired' it?

That's a great question and sharp listening. It did still have the bolt lock. Remington didn't change the triggers sent back to the factory until forced to by further evidence uncovered by Rich Barber after his young son was killed by a bolt-lock era Model 700. That was the first victory over Remington Arms in their desire to keep everything a secret.

You mean they knew the bolt lock was a bad idea but they continued to use it?

By the documents uncovered and made public by Rich Barber and CNBC and others, Remington knew the bolt lock was a bad idea in 1947. They spent cubic dollars on three position safeties and alternate designs for decades but didn't adopt the non-bolt lock safety until 1982. But they still installed safety levers with the locking 'tail' if it was asked for by the customer. Nobody knew the safeties should be altered for greater safety until they made the halfhearted effort in 2002 that did publicize the defect and offered to remove the bolt lock, but FSR wasn't part of the discussion.

What did Walker do about the failures of the first test triggers?

Walker wrote at least one memo with suggestions for how to repair the identified flaw in his design. He even drew a sketch in a margin of a memo to the engineering department. He also drew blueprints of a design that would have absolutely stopped FSR.

How can you do that as long as the connector is in there?

Just like the Xmark Pro does it now with a solid trigger. All it takes is something that pushes the trigger back into proper position when the safety lever is engaged should the trigger return springs not do the job. That locks the trigger so it's always reliably there when the safety cam lets the sear down on top.

That seems like only common sense to me!

It does to me too but remember, the gun companies set the trends and the writers validate them. If the rifle had a bolt lock, so what? Some people thought their rifle would fly open when running through the woods like an infantryman. Winchester's bolt locked down, but their three position safety in the bolt shroud cost more to make than Remington's complete trigger and safety assembly. That's no way to get market share when you're trying every trick in the book to bring down cost.

Do you still think the connector was done for economy? Why was it there for 60 years?

I have no inside knowledge of why the connector is in the Walker trigger except that it is the heart of the Walker-Haskel patent. Without the connector, the Remington trigger wouldn't be patentable. The connector made it unique mechanically. I believe the parent company insisted on in-house patents and nothing else. What else could they do but invent a bogus trigger claiming supernatural powers and then defend it though millions of dollars of jury findings instead of admit the problem, adopt a more expensive but safe trigger and safety system and actually be 'America's Gunmaker' instead of what they've become.

The Walker was improved at every step of the way, but the primary defect remained until 2006. I think it's also important to point out the rifles that use the Walker design, but are not a true Model 600 or 700 or their many variations, too.

You're not going to pick on my rare Model 788 in 44 Mag are you?

No, I'm not. That trigger is also terribly cheaply made, but it's made right. Some early rifles are bolt-lock guns and have a pin that comes up from beneath. That should be removed unless you're 'leaping the palmettos after wild hog' kind of hunter. The 788 was 'cheap done well'.

Remington M788. Cheap done well. This one is in .308 Win.

What are you talking about then?

Primarily the Model 710 and 770. They're mostly plastic proof of low dollar, low quality concept designs, with a very low production cost numbers in mind. I think that whole generation of rifles is shamefully chintzy and the Walker used in them got even more dangerous with a flimsy mounting system that causes it to fail.

Some people can't afford any more.

Maybe somebody should ask how much of a new gun is materials, labor and marketing. If that question was asked, the jobber price to the warehouse and the wholesaler's cut and the dealer's profit could be estimated and maybe figure out how much of new gun prices are liability insurance premiums.

Of course they have to be high, look what you and the other vultures do to a gun company!

That's a good point and the next topic of discussion unless we have some more Walker questions.

In the back row, yes?

Several times you've said the people that need to hear this stuff are not listening. Most of us back here think you're talking to us, but some of us are just skeptics, especially when there's so much BS about guns. Nobody seems to know anything! Most of us back here love guns in a major way and think we know what we're talking about. To hear some hick saying the guns we've been around for decades are somehow bad is just downright unacceptable, that's all.

I'm counting on you all being skeptics. Please do. Run your own experiments by introducing little sections of wires of different diameters in different places to see how much displacement of the connector it takes to make it fail. Please do study the slow motion stills of a Model 710 Walker connector in recoil to see for yourself how much gap is created between connector and the trigger body. Compare those gaps and obstructions with the scrap that is many times present in any trigger, but downright common in enclosed triggers.

Whoa now, how much scrap have you seen in a Walker trigger that was big enough to make it fail?

Great question again. I'm going to assume there are gun

mechanics here that have never seen a piece of anything inside a Walker trigger that would make it fail. Maybe a few have seen what WD-40 does to them. That stuff is a lint magnet and pretty good dust glue, too. That can cause a serious problem, especially in cold weather. Any excess lubricant or solvent that drizzles down next to the sear is bad, but it's a natural trap for it. Just look at the top side of the bolt release leaf to see some of the stuff that falls through. But, where is that magic sliver of something that made the connector stay away from the trigger body? Where does it come from? Where does it go? Why can't we see it?

I think you read several of our minds.

Look at these CT scans of a Model 700 with a Walker trigger in it.

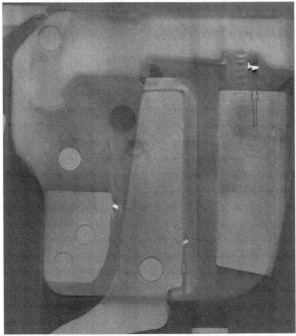

CT scan showing debris in several places.

What in the world is THAT?

That's a good question. This trigger was not taken apart to determine what the material is.

Why not? That seems like such a slam dunk for a lawyer.

Does that mean you're ready to admit it can happen?

It seems pretty clear to me. Why don't we see this in court somewhere so the word could get out?

Actually, there are many such pictures of many such guns, not necessarily this dramatic or as definite in their conclusions as the Houston rifle and this one, but these pictures are from the initial investigation by a plaintiff's lawyer. Many times I'm hired to watch the proceeding so I can testify to what is found at those exams. This is an example of something found three years before this is written and I have no idea what happened in that case. It went away. That's why you don't see this in court as well as the secret nature of the results.

What is that in that trigger and how did it get there? That DOES look dangerous!

That calls for an opinion and I'm willing to give it if you're willing to listen. Rebuttal is welcome.

This rifle had traces of a semisolid, white grease in places where in shouldn't have been. It could be seen through the inspection hole in the trigger, too. That's a no-no, but it's also human nature. When the CT scan started up and the flecks and flakes of dense metal showed up, there was some speculation as to what is was...and still is, as far as I know. A big clue was stuck in the bolt face. The Remington extractor can be too sharp and shear off little bits of brass case as it rotates into place and then scatters it in the magazine box and in the trigger when the bolt is removed.

I suspect the heavy grease formed a trap for debris that usually falls on through. Of course, then we have to ask ourselves what mischievous treachery that scrap might have caused just once, at the very worst time, on its way through. That is an uncertainty that we shouldn't have to worry about. It should have been accounted for *by design*.

You know Remington is going to criticize the grease. That is strictly against any instructions and against good sense, really.

No doubt about it. If I'm asked if the grease is according to normal, accepted and safe practice, I have to say "No." In this particular case I would also point out that the grease proves what Tom Butters has been telling the courts for nearly forty years and I've testified to for more than twenty. In the case of the rifle pictured above, 'transit debris' has been caught long enough to see it. The transit debris theory has just gained a tremendous amount of creditability and the reaction here to actually seeing it as opposed to imagining it does make a difference. Juries are people just like you.

Remington bolt face with brass debris caused by sharp extractor.

A lawyer once told me a trial was like an old fashioned flipbook cartoon. When the pages are flipped just right the entire thing takes on motion and tells a story. Evidence and testimony and more evidence taken together are like that. For nearly twenty years, I answered the question of, "Have you seen debris that could cause the type of failure you describe?" in the negative, beyond a hard black 'varnish' that forms between the trigger and sear over many years of use and (probably) spray lubrication. The last time I was asked that question, the answer was a resounding *yes*. But there were no follow up questions at all.

Telling the story of a firearms failure is often telling how something failed *by design*. Accumulated experience can never be overlooked.

In that X-ray above, none of that scrap is in a critical place is it?

Two of the three scraps shown are. There are others in the mechanism that are not in very critical places. The two lower particles are in a position to reposition into a place that would potentially cause the rifle to fire uncontrolled by the trigger. The upper piece is stuck between the sear and the housing and will eventually migrate out probably without harm.

The left lower particle is laying on top of the sear engagement screw. Here's a better view in 3D.

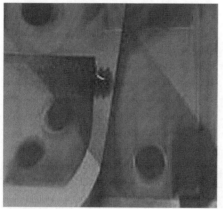

CT scan, 3D view, showing debris on sear engagement screw.

Obviously the trigger moves every time it's pulled and remains pulled until recoil or a relaxed finger un-pulls it. The trigger pull event is a violent time inside the gun. Should that bit of debris fall between the sear engagement screw and the trigger body, the sear engagement is reduced just like the screw had been (unsafely) adjusted to reduce the amount of sear overlap. Let me also point out all triggers can suffer from debris in that particular place. Adjustment screws are usually pointed to reduce that possibility.

The debris to the right in the CT scan is lying in the seam between the trigger body and the connector.

We know the connector separates from the trigger body on every trigger pull and bounces several times due to recoil. The odds are very much in favor of that scrap falling on through without ever causing a problem, but there is no way of accurately knowing.

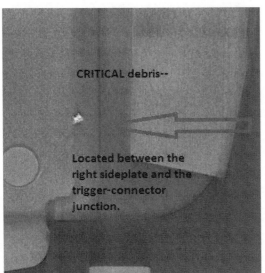

CT scan showing debris at the trigger-connector junction.

That debris probably came from the bolt face and has migrated through the trigger to the position it's in now over how many shots? We don't know. How many times had that particle been caught between the connector and trigger face and had come back out again? How many particles that size have been there but now gone? If the pieces of presumed scrap metal seen in the trigger now did not cause an uncontrolled discharge that injured someone, what did?

Real gun designers don't allow such a weakness to exist in a trigger assembly. Triggers must be dependable *by design.*

14. Safeties and the Indian Creek Nylon 66

<A guy in the front row asks for attention.>

Could I suggest now that you've taught us a separate trigger deep inside the trigger housing is a very bad idea, would you care to tell us what is a good idea? How do you make a kinetic gun safe?

If we're talking only of bolt action rifles with override triggers, suitable for 'the abuse heaped upon them', that is a tall order. Just about everything thought of and built so far has a certain amount of compromised safety.

I thought your precious Model 70 was the Holy Grail of rifle safeties. I've seen your work and you use them on Mausers and Remingtons.

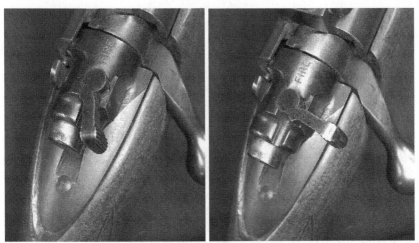

M70 Safety. Left: On safe. Right: Mid position, safe but with bolt unlocked.

I think the M70 is a great compromise and probably the best for the majority of hunters, but many shooters would rather have the safety lever on the right side, or a lever on the left or any variation of several methods. The rule of thumb is the safety should be 'natural' to use in a hunting gun and unnatural in a military small arm, but that rule has been bent so many times it's been lost.

Consider these safeties and how they operate:

M70 Safety on Mauser M98 (left) and Remington M722 (right)

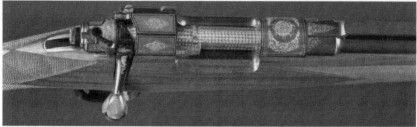

M70 Safety on custom Springfield. This is the American Custom Gunmaker's Guild #9 rifle.

Mausers use a rotary leaf at the rear of the bolt. It takes the whole hand to change from full safe to full fire. You can't pull the trigger when that hand is up on the bolt turning the safety.

Hoffman .375 with M98 Safety. Shown in mid position, on safe with bolt unlocked. Safe with bolt locked is 90° to the right, ready-to-fire is 90° to the left.

American and Russian rifles followed suit until the much faster and already described easy to get wrong lever on the trigger guard was adopted with the M-1 Garand. The Garand's lever is reminiscent of Browning's 'inside the trigger guard' safeties on the A-5. The P-14 and P-17 Enfield models used the British rotary safety on the right side of the rear tang.

Small Magazine Lee-Enfield (SMLE) Left: ON Safe. Right: Ready to fire.

You've been critical of the Remington 700 safety and it's on the right side like an Enfield, so what's wrong with it?

There is a very important difference that changes the military safety to one more suitable for a hunting rifle.

M700 Safety has short range of motion. Left: ON safe. Right: Ready to fire.

The range of motion was reduced for the hunting guns. The

military safeties are ON when they're horizontal and parallel to the bore line. That means a thumb, or more importantly the web of the hand, can't knock the safety to OFF under impact. The Remington rifles, except for the fine Model 725, have a safety that moves only about 25 degrees instead of 90. Instead of up and forward, the Remington and Remington style safeties start out about half 'OFF' and then go forward from there.

My safety is up on the tang like a shotgun. Is it any good?

Here's a great example of what the class is about. Where the safety is located has little to do with what it actually does.

Historically, shotgun safeties in double guns have been on the top tang. They're mostly blockers that keep the trigger from moving but some also block the sear. All such shotguns have direct-acting trigger systems. Bolt action rifles have override trigger systems.

How the manufacturer coupled a particular type of tang safety into their rifle determines how safe it is. One thing is for sure; a sliding safety can never have as much force available to apply the safety as a lever will have. Bolt action rifles have to have a lot of leverage to pull back and lock the cocking piece and firing pin. Consider the M-70 safety and the Remington 600/700 safeties. Both have about a 5 to 1 leverage advantage. A sliding safety is lucky to get 3 to 1 leverage and most are 1 to 1.

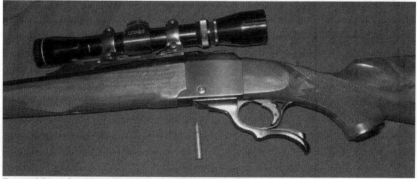

Ruger No. 1 in .22 K-Hornet with Canjar single-set trigger

There is one tang safety that perfectly locks hammer, sear and trigger so nothing moves, and the gun is actually safe. That is the Ruger Number One.

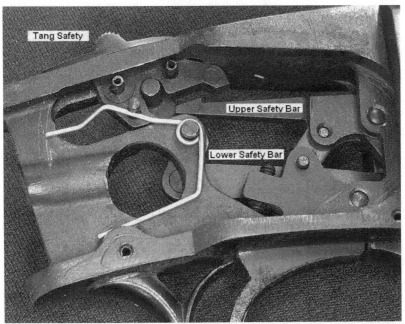

Ruger #1 Tang Safety System, shown OFF, ready to fire. Upper safety bar is linked to trigger and sear. Lower safety bar moves fore and aft, blocks hammer in forward position.

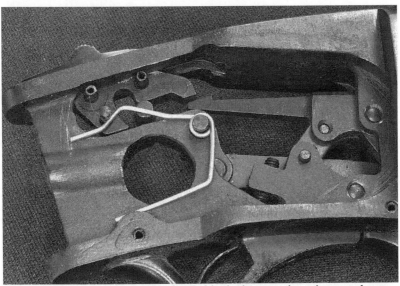

Ruger #1 ON safe. Upper safety bar is blocked preventing trigger and sear movement. Lower safety bar is in forward position blocking hammer. This gun cannot fire with the safety engaged, *by design.*

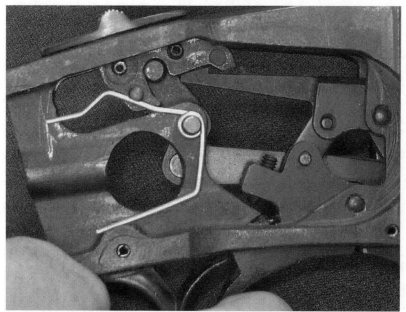

Ruger #1 in fired postion. Upper safety bar rotates up with trigger pull

There is another gun with a tang safety that is not a safety at all.
Nothing is locked, blocked or intercepted *by design*. The Nylon 66
is coming up.

Well, how in the world can anyone know how safe their safety is?

Safeties are rated as to how *positive* they are. Understanding
mechanics is an exercise in curiosity: Why does it do that? How
does it do that? And when does it do that, will usually answer
what *prevents* it from doing that, whatever 'that' might be when it
comes to the firing and safety group.

What we want to prevent, no matter what it takes, is the gun from
firing uncommanded. We know it's either a hammer or striker that
is going to hit, or cause to be hit, the *primer.* Protect the primer!
We can lock the hammer or striker, or block it or intercept it before
it gets to the primer. Or, we can do one or more in combination.

To be dependable and useable as a firearm it has to shoot when
told and not shoot until told. It seems simple enough until you
start looking at the possible results of spring energy being turned
loose at the wrong time.

John M. Browning started stacking up safeties in the Model 1911 .45 auto pistol so that it had about one of everything. I said 'about' one of everything. The 1911 is (was) not perfectly safe. There are several stories about General George Patton and his rise through the Army. He is one of the only people in history that had an AD with a 1911 in front of hundreds of witnesses. He hated them from that day onward and would not carry one. He carried the well known to be dangerous Colt Single Action instead. Go figure.

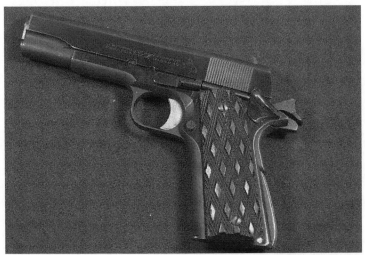

Colt M1911 Commercial made in 1957. Has a 1911 GI hammer and Giles match trigger. Barrel and bushing are new series 70 parts.

Colt M1911 grip safety.

The 1911 locks the hammer and sear together and disconnects the trigger. The firing pin is strongly inertial and is much shorter than the breech it goes through. The grip safety engages the trigger to the sear so that the gun is 'disconnected' if nobody is holding it firmly. There are other nuances that make it one of the most dependable pistols ever designed or manufactured.

You said it could fire, though. With all those safeties, how can it?

Great question and it makes a great teaching tool. Ask these questions of the gun: What keeps the firing pin from hitting the primer? Oops! The first question, if answered correctly, gives the answer you're looking for in this case. Before the Series 80 was introduced, the answer was 'nothing'.

M1911 series 80 began in 1983. Firing pin blocker protects primer unless trigger is pulled. It's totally safe to carry cocked and locked.

The next question should be: If nothing keeps the firing pin from the primer, how can it get enough energy to fire the primer? I see many hands go up, and you're right. Inertia from a dropped gun that lands flush on the muzzle will give (barely) enough energy to fire the gun if dropped from above ten feet or so. My question has always been, 'what happens then'? The combinations of energies intersecting at one patch of concrete might take a creative camera angle at a safe range to film, but it sure would be interesting to see that operation in super slow motion.

The Series 80 and later guns have a 'blocker' in the firing pin channel that is released by a trigger pull but not a dropped pistol.

The Series 80 added yet another safety to a kinetic gun. How many has your rifle got?

A general rule of thumb for safeties is: The closer to the primer the safety operates the more *inherent* safety it's likely to have. Firing pins are hard to block, lock or intercept on any gun but bolt action rifles. In other guns, whatever is closest to the firing pin usually gets locked or blocked. In descending order of distance from the firing pin are the hammer or striker, then the sear and then the trigger. When viewed from that direction, any gun that does not block, lock or intercept the hammer or striker must, by definition be less than safe *by design.*

Back to the two firearms design geniuses of the world for a minute because they set the stage for everything that came afterwards. Peter Paul Mauser and John Moses Browning designed guns by worst case scenarios. Both of them looked at their designs and asked very pointed questions of them. Questions like: What happens if this part is hit on a rock while the gun is upside down after falling ten feet? What happens if the soldier is upside down...will his rifle still function? Will the soldier be blinded if he shoots a rifle with mud in the bore? It is very clear both designers asked many thousands of questions of their designs and came to conclusions that are totally missing in modern firearms design. That is the key to understanding firearms safety.

That little gremlin Murphy constantly reminds us:

If it *can* happen, it *will*... and at the worst possible time.

Too many modern firearms are built under the premise: It won't happen often enough to cause trouble.

That suddenly makes some sense. Will you give some examples of those?

Of course, there are millions of them around. They can be identified by how the safeties operate, mainly. We see the Model 700 Remington-Walker locks and blocks the sear and firing pin but does not block the trigger. That causes a *lot* of trouble because if the trigger is manipulated during the time the safety is ON, the extra part inside the housing called the 'connector' can be displaced and FSR can occur when the safety is pushed to OFF. We've noted that many bolt action rifles operate the same way as the Walker but without the connector and without the failures, too. Their solid trigger telegraphs its position to the shooter and more reliably resets properly under the sear.

One solid trigger is always more reliable than a 'flexibly mounted' connector acting as a middleman in a dirty and violent environment.

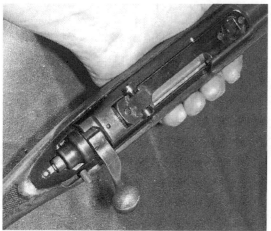

M700 with bolt handle in 'hunter safe' position

Some bolt actions, like Sako, Tikka and others have a sliding or rotating thumb safety. Some block the trigger and sear, which also blocks the striker. Some only block the sear and some block just the trigger. Many years ago I quit trying to imagine how the safety might or might not work so I lift the bolt handle. That blocks the striker with the bolt body and it's not going to fire no matter what sort of mechanical chain might be hidden out of sight. A lifted bolt handle means it's safe.

Bad safety designs have probably caused military deaths, too. When I was growing up, I heard several stories of Japanese soldiers shot while fumbling with the Arisaka's miserable bolt safety from my dad's friends, and there is a film clip of the battle of Okinawa that shows the frantic flinging of the right elbow as the Japanese tried to unlock his rifle, but he didn't make it in time.

Cops have been killed in shootouts where their duty gun is at fault, or their training in using it. The most noticeable are the old timers that grew up with a 1911 and P-35 and old Colt pocket model pistols, and then they get issued a service pistol with a 'reversed' safety. Many European pistols have a safety that flips UP to fire instead of down. I can testify, when the adrenaline squirts through your system and you're looking at a big hole with a bad guy behind it, your instincts for survival guide you. It's good when those instincts have been trained, practiced and thought about a *lot* before you really need it.

I know I have a lot of law enforcement in the audience and you'll recognize the 'planning for the worst' thinking that has to be a part of being ready for whatever happens. Nobody stands around and asks himself which way to run if the shooting starts. Most cops, like pilots, have already figured a way out of whatever emergency might come up long before it actually happens. Really good gun designers did precisely the same thing. They planned for the worst.

Why don't they now?

It costs too much money and nobody is watching. More importantly, nobody is being critical of anyone but the 'careless' shooter. Why bother? I think you'll agree there are no shortages of gun buyers and many buy according to price. It's easy to be controversial by pointing out that what a customer is actually paying for, is four dollars of steel and a dollar worth of sheet metal and plastic. I've always kind of enjoyed being controversial, so let's dive into this with safety in mind. First, a true story involving four dollars of steel and a buck's worth of sheet metal and plastic:

Indian Creek Nylon 66

Remington Nylon 66

The two brothers were rednecks at heart and it showed. One had been in a little trouble and couldn't carry a gun while hunting, but the other brother wanted to go small game hunting so brother #2 went along to look for arrowheads along a creek not far from the Mississippi River. They'd gotten there by truck to a friends house and then rode his borrowed ATV back through some fallow fields and pastures to near the creek bottom where #2 would generally parallel his brother as he hunted fence rows for rabbits and stands of hardwoods for squirrels. He had his Nylon 66 .22 auto rifle slung across his back with a make-do strap that was tied around the grip and the upper part of the forestock with lengths of parachute cord. They split up and were out of sight of each other for about an hour.

Brother #2 heard a shot up on the high ground and hoped they had a rabbit for lunch, but just a few minutes later he heard what he thought was a coyote whining, and thought maybe his brother had shot and wounded one so he went looking for it. What he found was his brother on his hands and knees, with the rifle laying just to his right, but the sling was still inside his hand on the ground. The bad part was the blood and brain matter that was splattering on the ground near that hand.

His brother was still on hands and knees and moaning softly when #2 started his long trip across the fields on foot, then ATV, to go use a telephone and call for help.

The information I received filled a banker's box with documents, but there were many medical papers I didn't have to read beyond calculating trajectories of the bullet and bits of bone that really did the damage, but didn't kill him. The rifle involved is one I was told by a Remington representative in gunsmith's school I shouldn't bother working on. "Just mail it back and we'll dump the guts and put in all new parts for about eight dollars." is what he told our Design and Function class. I had never bothered to do anything but that. I do NOT care to work on cheap guns so I avoid it. In this case, I had to be an expert on it.

The Nylon 66 was very highly touted at introduction. The new, coming wave of firearms design and materials had arrived fresh from Remington. They even had a guy shooting 2" wooden blocks until they stacked up in a pile over waist high 'without a single malfunction' with one of the things. It's no wonder. Nothing fits tight enough to gum up when it's dirty. They were right about the future, though.

Remington's Nylon 66 wooden block shooting demonstration

The first step was to see if the gun was at fault. There were no witnesses that could convey that information. The lawyers bought a half dozen Nylon 66s from pawnshops and gunshops up and down the river and sent me several to study. Eck!

The event first: From the hundreds of photographs (typically a scene has from 35 to 500 photos of it) I could see the ground cover was short corn stubble and new grass. There were no 'wait a minute' vines or brush and shin-tangle anywhere near high enough to pull the trigger. He was lying, by the time the ambulance got there, right in the same place. He'd simply collapsed. The pictures didn't show, but it was assumed he fell in the spot he was shot. The sling inside the hand placement was important. The gun had to have been slung over his right shoulder when it fired. The fired cartridge case was not recovered.

The bullet entered the skull two inches right of the occipital bone, the knot in the back of the human skull, and an inch above the ear canal level. It exited just right of center, high on the head. An exemplar rifle on the same sling rig slung on the back of a paralegal the same size and shape of the victim was videotaped from all angles and circumstances. It was clear the bullet path matched the wound. A thin dowel run down the bore and left sticking up two feet constantly hit the intern in the head as he walked.

Nylon 66/76/77 trigger demonstration fixture. Beginning with a few pivot holes drilled in an aluminum plate, it grew into an extremely valuable courtroom aid.

Then, we found an exemplar that would fire ON safe if it was twisted just right. By this time I'd drilled pivot holes in a plate of aluminum to match the rifle's "receiver" and learned the chittlins of the cheapest piece of junk I've ever looked inside of. Well, let me modify that. I took apart a toy alarm clock that was part of my sister's cooking set when she was about seven. I think it was maybe cheaper made, but it had the same sheet metal and plastic in it.

The Nylon 66 and its variants were made in several colors and finishes, but all are made from two halves of DuPont plastic glued together with model airplane cement. The barrel is simply stuck in a hole formed when the two halves were glued together and held in place by a yoke and set screw. It's the same process as gluing together the two halves of a model airplane fuselage and it uses the same glue.

The first of very many terrible decisions by BATF were made when Remington was allowed to call a U-shaped piece of thin sheet metal 'The Receiver' and so stamped it with a serial number.

Nylon 77 Apache version sold by K-Mart. The metal 'receiver' is a nonessential part. It can be removed and the rifle still fires.

<Lawyer #2 reveals himself as ATF when he asks>

How is that a mistake? It is the major metal part of the rifle.

I'll answer with another question. How can it be the 'receiver' if the gun shoots just fine without it?

Then what is the receiver in a Nylon 66?

The receiver is actually the stock. Its two parts are permanently attached into one 'receiver' that turns into stock on both ends.

What became uncommonly clear by assembling the gun where it could be seen was how tenuous the inherent safety is. Cheap guns have cheap ways. The M-3 'grease gun' of WW-II and Korea cost the Army about the same as a couple Jerry cans full of gas. The most expensive part was the magazine and it was more than half the total cost. *But*, an M-3 is locked and blocked in the cocked position. They are very much a kinetic gun but manage to be safe and cheap at the same time. The cheapest of the Savage, Mossberg, Marlin and other discount house .22 rifles were so much better designed than the Remington, it was striking.

It was strikingly evident to me, but the lawyer said he was still trying to figure out his cigar cutter. "Do the best you can" he said.

The Nylon 66 is a trapeze act of swinging bits of sheet metal that form an override trigger and the safety is nothing but a disconnector. There is *no* safety on a Nylon 66 worth the name. It just swings up the bar that connects the trigger to the sear. Nothing is blocked, locked, or intercepted. Would the same engineer take the chain off his bicycle to keep it from being stolen?

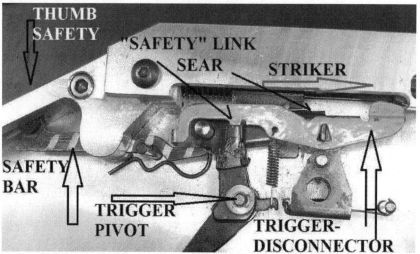

Nylon 66/76/77 trigger parts. Shown safety OFF, ready to fire.

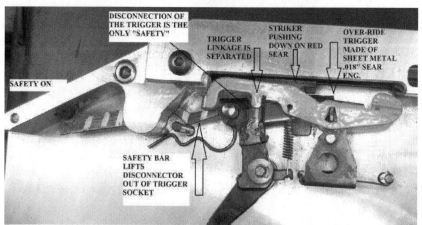

Nylon 66/76/77 trigger parts. Shown safety ON, trigger disconnected

That case took two years to go to trial in Federal Court. Remington had tried very hard to bleed a small law firm dry with the 'gamesmanship' that top lawyers play. Discovery materials came in banker's boxes and the Nylon stuff was in there, somewhere. Interns and paralegals were hired to sort it, but how can you explain what's important if it hasn't been seen yet? I was given a conference room with a long table to stack papers and scan and sort and sometimes examine with magnification because the "machine that prints from microfiche messed up somehow."

The case was tough and the testimony long, but I explained the total lack of anything that could be called a 'safety' although there was such a button up on the top tang portion.

Nylon 66/76/77 trigger in fired position.

I showed them how it could (easily) fire by bending or twisting and demonstrated it with the actual rifle on a sling and how that put bending and torsion to the entire gun. The victim was not in court. That would have been clearly inflammatory, but the jury deliberated and decided the bit of drugs the brothers had done the night before overrode any compensation the victim might receive from an accidental shooting the next day.

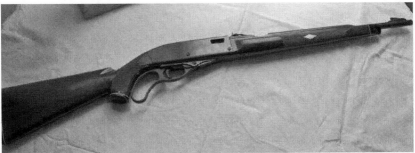

Nylon 76, lever action version.

That case toughened me up a lot. I wish I were free to say more.

It would be nice if you could tell us what happened.

I appreciate the new tone from the rear. Thank you.

From my point of view in the case, it was a slam dunk. There is no better example of a company bringing to market a gun, meant for beginners, that was clearly and demonstrably ill-conceived, ill-designed and with so many corners cut that there were none left to cut. It was a rifle designed to leave the plant with *no more than* $X invested. It was designed with molds and dies said to be good for a million rifles before replacement. They manufactured about 50,000 more than that and sold the completely worn out equipment to a company in Brazil. They showed back up under a different name in the discount stores for about a year. I would rather have a rattlesnake around my kids than trust a Nylon 66 except in tightly controlled conditions. They are the same by nature and all should be highly suspect.

I think you're being melodramatic .

I guess watching the testimony of a doctor telling how a bone chip wiped out part of your client's brain, because it deflected in a totally predictable manner when impacted by a .22 LR HP at a particular angle, does that to someone that loves guns and is affected by the pain of others when they aren't made right, *by design.*

I have a big shop and outlet stores as well as being a wholesaler. I used to carry these guns. I've heard my share of your 'Remington stories' and never really believed them. What strikes me right between the eyes is that Remington hasn't told me ANY of this. Why not?

I'm sure you know that question would be better answered by Remington. I don't know, but that has been a very large part of my curiosity also. It really makes no sense, unless you look at the economics of it. Then it makes perfect sense.

Many years ago I was in a lawyer's office going over letters of complaints. A paralegal said, "I just can't believe this." I suggested he call the Remington Service Center and ask about his

Walker triggered M700. It was recorded for use at trial, but I guess that case settled. Y'all can do the same thing. It's toll free and you can find out for yourself what the 'story of the day' is.

At least they learned their lesson, I guess.

Not at all. Remington has introduced several very dangerously designed rifles and shotguns since then. Who's complaining? They work three shifts as it is. The Ten Commandments in their various forms have convinced two generations that any gun that goes off is totally their fault and responsibility.

Remington created a pet store instead of a firearms manufacturing business. It was no longer their fault if the 'puppy' they sold grew up to bite somebody. Doing business is cheaper that way and others had to follow or go broke.

I thought you were going to finally talk about safeties and how they work.

I needed reminding. Where were we? Ah yes, lockers, blockers and interceptors. Let's short cut it a bit and get into more actual instances of them failing.

Just a quick review: The Mauser and the M70 safety work the same way but work ninety degrees different in direction.

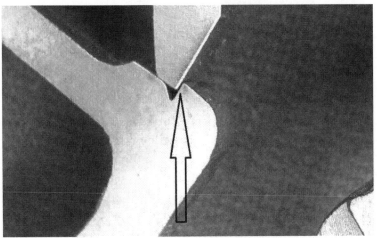

M70 Safety cams cocking piece away from sear, creating gap between trigger and sear contact surfaces.

Both cam the cocking piece, which is attached to the firing pin, rearward and off of and away from the sear. The sear is isolated from any pressure anywhere. Even though the rifles as designed have a direct acting trigger in the Mauser and an override in the Model 70, the safeties work the same in that cam action takes the energy of the mainspring and blocks it and isolates the sear.

Remington M30 safety lever operates in a different plane from the M70 but it does the same thing. It cams the cocking piece away from the sear. Shown ON safe.

Remington's Model 600/700 Walker triggers also have a cam action that locks the firing pin back. Remington uses the sear as part of the safety because it's caught between the safety cam and the cocking piece/stud. Remember that the sear takes the energy of the hammer or striker and transfers it to the trigger. In the Walker/XMP systems, the safety cam takes the energy away from the connector/trigger and the safety cam takes the load. It is an ingenious way to have a firing pin/striker blocking safety mounted to a removable trigger unit rather than the very expensive M70 shroud safety with a bolt lock.

I know you like the M70 trigger and safety, but my little brother had a fire on safety release with our dad's rifle.

Any override trigger can FSR if the trigger is displaced during the time the safety is ON. My point is that the M70 triggers are much less likely to become displaced because the parts are few, simple, and not contained in a trash trap. The *first* thing to check on any rifle said to have had a FSR is for any interference with the trigger motion. Glass bedding material or contamination can make a trigger sticky. Remingtons have a round receiver bottom and it's fairly easy to get one cocked to one side enough for the trigger to drag on the trigger guard. There is the well known case of Remington sending off a brand new M700 to a gun testing session for a national magazine and the trigger tip would drag on the trigger guard and cause an FSR every time! That got some attention I guarantee! The magazine reported it at the time and it was one of Remington's only embarrassments until about 2002.

Trigger return *must* be very positive. Don't back off on trigger pull springs more than the amount of friction present between parts. Let me emphasis this: If the trigger isn't under the sear when the safety is released, the gun *will* fire.

That seems to be a defect to me.

Here is where improvements in safe design affect your customer base in a BIG way. A pull of the trigger *while* releasing the safety results in the rifle firing from action of the safety. That is clearly a defect but....How about pulling the trigger while kicking a rock? If you're pulling the trigger, does it make a difference what else you're doing at the same time? Pulling the trigger shows your intent. Don't pull it if you aren't shooting something.

It would be easy enough to design a disconnector that would not allow a trigger being pulled at the same time the safety is being manipulated, but then the gun would have to be stored in the cocked position. There would be no way to 'follow down' and relax the mainspring. Some gun buyers won't stand for such factory interference with their preferences.

There are several things that are needed for the ultimate in bolt-action safety and some companies are sneaking up on them. The popularity of the Glockenclones has allowed rifle shooters to be at home with a center-leaf safety trigger. What in effect it is, is a two stage trigger. The center leaf is the first stage and the 'regular' trigger is the actual trigger pull. All these have the opportunity to be very good and safe triggers. The trend is also towards taking away some of the 'adjustability' to keep customers out of the triggers. I think that's a great idea. A trigger that could be preset to three weights by just changing a pivot pin would solve a lot of the experimentation by those that don't appreciate the pressures and stresses involved, and would be a great advancement.

Tom Butters is a proponent of a 'component reset' function added to the bolt or sear. In use it would, by motion of the bolt, reset the trigger under the sear before they came in contact. That follows the 'if it ain't right it don't work' design theory. All these ideas are valid and most are possible at some extra cost. Will the market bear it? I don't know.

Way back, it seems a month ago now, you mentioned an adjustable trigger was not good or not safe or something. Want to refresh that now that we might know what a trigger is?

Gladly. Let's use the M70 as an example because we can see it work. The M70 trigger is a good example of a fixed-dimension trigger. It is made to be right and messing with it makes it wrong.

M70 Trigger, 1953. Lines show sear engagement.

Notice that the amount of sear engagement is already determined by the depth of the sear step that's machined into the trigger. The sear engagement is designed for the steel and heat treatment used and designed to produce a trigger adjustable from about 4 to 8 pounds by spring pressure alone. The sear engagement cannot be changed without grinding away part of the trigger. Notice the faint change in color on the active end of the trigger. That's a heat-treat line. The triggers were probably held in a fixture and only the ends that needed extra strength and hardness were heat treated.

Obviously, if the customer has ground the engagement surfaces on either the sear or trigger, they have reduced the carefully engineered mechanism into something entirely different. Winchester can tell lawyers to go pound sand and usually get away with it.

It seems to me the balanced see- saw arrangements of the Sako style that Walker used would be better than the Winchester with a lot of trigger hanging down. Won't it shoot if it's bumped hard enough?

The Model 70 trigger is a lightweight affair made from very good steel. But you're right, one of its few shortcomings is the pivot point for the trigger.

The only identified weakness of the M70 trigger is the fact that most of the trigger's weight is below the pivot point. That means the trigger tends to pull itself if the butt hits the ground hard enough. Newtonian physics can supply the acceleration and mass and resulting force on the trigger.

It is said that a Model 70 has to have a certain velocity and hit exactly square to the pivot with the trigger at ninety degrees to have enough energy on impact to trip the trigger-sear connection. That velocity can be attained with a drop of about 18 feet, *if* the trigger is as factory set at 4 to 8 lbs. You can imagine how terribly unlucky a hunter would have to be to drop his rifle with the safety off, from that high or higher, on a solid rock, at precisely the correct angle and orientation to cause the rifle to fire. It is pretty obvious to anyone keeping track that should the rifle fire on impact it's likely to hit him dead between the eyes as he watches it fall, too. I've never heard of it happening, but in keeping with Browning and Mauser and Murphy: If it can, it will.

You mean you went through all that to say it doesn't happen?

Not yet. Consider this, though. I've seen two Model 70s dropped a long distance. One hit on the butt, but sheared the stock at the grip. Would it have had enough energy to fire if the wood stock had not have broken and absorbed some of it? What if it were a glass or plastic stock? I don't know that answer, but it could happen.

The point is in how far an investigation has to go to find the answer. It's amazing to me how many people look at guns by what caliber it is and nothing else. I have people regularly ask about their "30-06" or "I have a 12 gauge pump gun...."

This is a good time to point out how forced economics in the gun industry is a bad thing for all gun companies and especially their customers. We're all familiar with the phrase 'pre-'64' when it comes to Winchesters. That was the same year our coins went cheap, too. It was a watershed year for Winchester because it was either follow Remington and Savage down the path to making consumer goods instead of building durable goods, or continue to hemorrhage money. Remington had put tremendous pressure on Winchester by making and selling guns that still shot and almost looked as good, too. We're learning now how Remington gained that advantage.

M70 Triggers. Bottom: Pre-1964. Top: Later, investment casting

Winchester spent millions of scarce dollars to wreck their entire inventory of sporting guns. Going cheap meant (eventually) going broke, but they seem to have dodged most of the legal pitfalls that Remington created with their 'cheaper and more of them' marketing philosophy. Was Murphy just not looking?

We went over the only likely failure of an unaltered Model 70 Winchester trigger and why it's possible by design to fire the rifle with a drop on the butt. Almost all the weight of the trigger is suspended below it's pivot point and that makes it susceptible to a drop which 'pulls' the trigger by action of inertia on the trigger hanging down. The calculated drop distance with a properly set pre-64 trigger is about 18 feet minimum to make this happen. It's obvious to most that the further away an uncontrolled firing takes place from soft humans the better. It decreases the likely hood of somebody being hit. (Twenty miles is about right for me.)

Well, what happens when the marketing and manufacturing arms of one of America's most prestigious gun manufacturers take control over design safety parameters? *Or,* did the engineers not learn what I did in about the fifth grade about Sir Issac and his understanding of inertia? I think it was about then I read about the Gouchos throwing bolos to catch cattle instead of lariats, and we did have two calves to practice on.... Those things *hurt!*

The pre-64 Winchester M70 trigger is 16% lighter in weight than the later investment cast trigger, with a wider shoe to give a better feel.

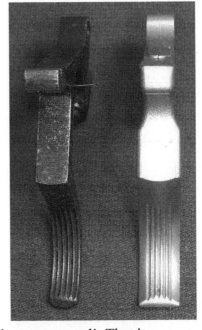

By fairly simple calculations we see that the 18 feet up the imaginary tree stand that it would take to make the pre-'64 trigger fail has suddenly become a limb or two lower. That is not the heart of the problem, though. By adopting an inferior material, that in this case didn't fully fill the mold, the amount of natural trigger-sear overlap has been degraded by approximately 80%! The trigger pull without a return spring is less than one pound! That is a factory made, factory specification compliant trigger that came from a brand new gun that suddenly changed from a four pound pull to a 1.8lb trigger pull. It could fire from a knee high drop with no problem at all. It failed the SAMMI drop test in three orientations. It didn't hurt anybody, though. As we've said, a certain amount of precision...

I think we all can see the train of thought that created a very dangerous trigger. Somebody at Winchester heard that rifle shooters liked the Remington wide and grooved trigger 'shoe' area that contacts the trigger finger better than Winchester's sharp and narrow trigger. As area increases the perceived force it takes to pull the trigger is decreased substantially, and a better 'feeling' trigger can be had without altering the weight of the pull. Target shooters have used trigger shoes from Flaig's and Ace for generations. I wonder who forgot to tell shooters why they're such a *bad* idea on non-target guns? A wider trigger has to be thinner by design so the weight distribution is not changed. It's simple mechanics! Who forgot to tell the gun designers?

Sir, I have three rifles with that same trigger in them. Nobody told me they might be dangerous.

I just did. Will you pass it on, please?

I see an adjusting screw on those M70 triggers, what is that?

That screw stops the trigger after the sear has disengaged. That is the OT screw in a Winchester. The spring around it is the trigger return spring and the two little nuts determine how much strength the return spring has. It should be at least half the entire pull. Mauser taught us that with the commercial trigger in his military actions.

Ok, I think we got this nailed down back here. And we have a collective question.

Good. Let's have it.

You made a big deal about how far a Walker trigger moves during firing and even called them out as liars about how the trigger moved at firing. You said the entire patent was a lie because it did not eliminate trigger overtravel as advertised.

I'll plead guilty to all that as long as you stipulate a nominal movement between sear and trigger to be .020 engagement and .010" OT for a total movement at the disconnect point of .030 inch.

Now you're getting complicated again. You said the Model 70 has a trigger overtravel screw. So, how much does each trigger move?

Great question and it makes a great point. The Model 70 trigger moves more than the Remington....*by design.*

You call it 'getting complicated' but just look at the difference in distance from the pivot point to the trigger finger piece. Both Remington (and most other) triggers have roughly the same .020" of engagement and the same .010" of overtravel. The portion of the trigger that contacts the sear on both rifles has to move the same distance to fire the rifle. But, the Remington trigger is much shorter and the pivot is in the middle, not up at the upper end. That means the Remington trigger moves the same amount on both ends like a teeter totter. The shooter feels .030" of trigger travel in his finger tip.

The Model 70 trigger is more like a wheel barrow. The sear hook portion is between the 'handle' where your trigger finger is, and the pivot point up top where the wheel would be on our imaginary wheel barrow. You have to 'lift higher' on the handles to move the center the same .030" as Remington and the others. That means a Model 70 trigger is not as *short* as the others. Motion at the finger piece is more like .050", but it's certainly crisp and clean. In the hunting fields it is a safe override trigger.

Most investigations are not nearly as simple as the .41 Ruger or H&R shotgun that shot the girl in Missouri. Some of these defects are rare and stay very well hidden until somebody goes looking for what is wrong about a gun that discharged, and not looking for an excuse for that discharge. To find a fault you must know why it was *designed* as it is seen in the gun. It is painful to see those designs determined by how much they cost instead of how 'safe' they are.

Did you completely forget about my 'adjustable trigger' question or did I just somehow miss it?

Well, now that you mention it..... Look again at the M70 trigger and sear. The geometry is set by the machine that makes them and any adjustments to the sear engagements are detrimental in one way or another. Let's just be clear, though. Natural wear of the parts improves the trigger pull. It's hard not to try to speed that process up some and many 'smiths do. *Don't* stone it, just a little 320 or finer lapping compound will take away the same amount of roughness from the parts as 200 rounds of shooting in about 20 pulls. Be sure to clean by brushing with solvent. A spray can of anything *will not* remove lapping compound.

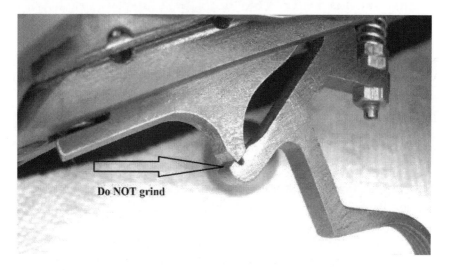

Do NOT grind

An adjustable trigger allows much more leeway in making parts. They just need to fit in the housing and pivot. The screws will set the critical dimensions......and then you put a drop of glue on the screws and say "our bad, you shouldn't touch those after all."

I was hoping you were going to talk about the safety on my 9mm that scares me every time I put it on because it make the hammer fall!!

Ah yes! Those are called 'de-cockers'. They scare me too. Here's a tip: Put the safety on while the slide is locked to the rear before loading the pistol. When the slide goes forward, the disconnector trips the safety and the hammer 'follows down' the slide. They don't look quite as scary that way.

But are they safe? I've got a .380 Walther that scares me every time.

It is no longer good enough to give caliber and maker, either. What I 'see' in my mind as a DA Walther is likely to be totally different than what you own or any gun shop now stocks. Guns change and what was steel is likely to be something lighter and nonmagnetic now. In my memory of the great Walther pocket pistols, the de-cocker was perfectly fine. What now comes in a Walther box is unlikely to be recognizable as belonging there and without examining it, we can't know for sure.

An old Walther PPK's safety will take about 200 foot pounds of impact energy before it breaks. The hammer is not going to do that even if dropped out of an airplane. It's safe enough to trust in your pocket. Besides that, the only time the safety is used is when the hammer is already cocked. *Don't* carry it that way. Hammer down, safe OFF is the way it's designed to be carried. The passive firing pin block is disabled when the trigger is pulled to cock it and fire double action.

I have a Model 700 rifle that doesn't always cock. Is that a bad trigger?

Yes sir! It is certainly out of adjustment at least. Anytime you have a gun that does not securely cock and remain that way it is unduly dangerous.

It has a great trigger pull, though. I hate to mess with it.

I understand, but you're at risk for common failures such as Follow Down, Fire on Bolt Close, Fire on Bolt Open, Jar Off and FSR.

You mean just that one little symptom could mean all those?

Now we're making headway!

An override trigger depends on a very small overlap to give the best pull, but the engagement has to be *enough* or those hard, rather brittle corners on trigger and sear start chipping and flaking

and degrading due to excess pressures. Anytime you notice a
difference in trigger pull, stop right there and find out why. The
importance of a consistent pull cannot be overstated. If the pull
varies more than 10%, something is wrong. Find out what that
might be. Sometimes a yo-yo trigger is traced back to a 'self
adjusting' connector. More often the accumulated gunk flushed
into the trigger over time is affecting how the trigger resets. It
could be just breaking things so it can unexpectedly scare you very
badly sometime in the future.

*I like button safeties on the trigger guard. I grew up with them and
can't get used to anything else. Which one is the best?*

Cross-bolt safeties are rated entirely on what they actually do.
Very generally speaking, if the button is forward of the trigger, it
locks the sear, hammer and trigger. If it's behind the trigger it only
blocks the trigger and *maybe* the sear. If the sear is locked the
hammer is too. It's important to know which is which.

I'll not try to go into every lever, switch, button or slide safety, but
all of them should lock or block the important parts of the fire
control group.....*by design.*

15. The Jain Rifle

Firearms safety depends on good design and the correct materials and the entire thing properly assembled, adjusted, and tested, to have a good chance of not shooting without (good) intention. From the cases referenced so far, the investigations showed the facts and they were observable and believable. What happens when 'it just goes off' and the reason is not apparent? Intermittent failures are tougher to explain to the mechanic and for the mechanic.

It's rare to have any firearms case where you say, "Let me show you a failure." It happens, but seldom. Most are what look like a 'freak accident' at the very worst time possible, but it's very important to know exactly what was happening when the gun fired. It was not just sitting there. Something 'triggered' the failure and that most times will lead to why it was set up to fail to start with. Broken parts within a gun provide the proverbial blood trail a blind man can follow.

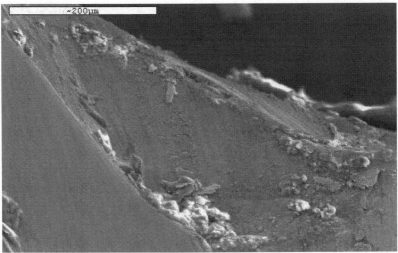

Damage trail caused by E-clip movement against safety plate, Knight MML muzzleloader. 75X magnification in SEM.

Sometimes no parts are broken, but they're scarred in such a way the point of failure can be found. The investigator *must* be sure of the facts of the mechanism as well as the law, and to do that, every tool at his disposal must be used. Sherlock's magnifier is no longer good enough.

After more than fifty years examining guns, it was only in the last twenty years of firearms examinations involved in litigation that the value of analytical examination became as important as 'just looking at it' to see if it works properly.

You tend to lean a little hard on us firearms examiners. Can you justify it?

I hope it's very clear that I'm trying to get out information so you and every shooter KNOWS what they're dealing with. It does no good for the shooters or the trade for a gunsmith to hand a gun back and say, "It can't fire the way you said" unless he knows that to be the case. When it comes to testimony in court that determines someone's freedom, the whole situation changes. I'm just trying to underline the importance of actually knowing how a gun works so you can figure out how it failed. You have to believe the only talking witnesses first, but the gun itself should be interrogated by someone that can 'see' inside by way of study of an exemplar gun and ask every question of the mechanism that a good lawyer would ask of a witness. Good guns have airtight alibis. Bad guns that are not asked the right questions are terrible witnesses.

Kendrick in Tennessee was convicted of murder and spent 19 years behind bars even though the rifle that killed his wife fired and shot a cop in the foot less than two hours later. The cop did not pull the trigger. Kendrick *said* he didn't either!

Casey, in Washington State is still behind bars because his wife died of a shot to the upper leg by a Remington Model 7400 rifle just like Kendrick's. The testimony in the Casey trial is painfully misinformed on the part of the firearms examiners. So much so, even NBC pushed for a new trial, but under Washington law, he's stuck. There are no more appeals even though his case and a civil case that I testified in the same year in Alabama were eerily similar.

I knew nothing of the Kendrick trial or the Casey trial even though I was in at least two depositions with Remington attorneys during that same time period. Did they not know of the two murder trials involving the same make and model and caliber Remington rifle as we were taking testimony about in civil cases? I don't know. They seem to know of every other case before I do. It seems unlikely that no defense attorney thought to ask Remington if there were reported failures in those guns, but it's possible. The list of failures known to Remington is a long one, but not near as long as the list of lazy lawyers.

I can't believe there are that many. I've never heard of one....the bad guns I mean. I believe the part about the lawyers.

I'll repeat the prior theory that analytical people usually start out at "It can't fire without the trigger being pulled." That, as we've seen, is not true at all, *by design.* If the first guy on the scene believes guns are infallible, who is he going to blame?

Then the problem is convincing the jury that something remotely possible actually did happen, and when it happened, the result was a hurt to somebody even though they've been warned all their lives to be careful! That is a stack of marbles hard to balance, but when a guy is disabled, a life altered or entirely taken away, what else can you do but very carefully try to place that first 'marble' so it can't wiggle.

That first marble is the *facts* of the case. The gun *did* shoot. Somebody *did* get shot. The second marble has to be very well balanced. The second marble is *how* did it happen and *why*? Usually a cop tells the 'how' because he investigated a crime. In civil cases, the firearms guy tells the jury *why* it happened the way it did. The defense tries to convince the jury it is too rare an event to ever happen and the plaintiff's lawyer tries to show the jury why it's not only possible, but probable and not only that but the maker was negligent in ignoring some rule, regulation or standard. That's a simplification likely to raise a blood pressure or two, but roughly that's the job they do.

Well how rare is it?

I thought you'd never ask!

It was one time calculated by a guy qualified to testify to it, that one of the nearly 30 million Remington Common Fire Controls would fail about as often as a family of four happens, all with the same birthdays. It sounds great and I'm sure that convinces a lot of people that guns don't shoot all that often by mistake, and I'm no expert on birthdays, but I know of more than 300 failures of the RCFC. I only know a handful of double birthdays and they're in families with twins. No family of four that I know of share the same cake.

I still never heard of even one and I've been around them on ranges and in cop shops for YEARS!

You get a free book. That's why it was written. I think the fact that this information is *not* known is why we still have too many firearms accidents. Not to mention victims of bad firearms designs still sitting in prison. *That* is a miscarriage of justice. We also have millions of customers that would handle their guns differently if they knew the safety was that in name only.

Why hasn't Remington gone to the court in Washington and shown them what's going on?

Thank you, ma'am. That would solve the problems but it would bring economic disaster to the company. How can you right the record without getting knocked out with the first mailbox full of lawsuits?

I've seen attacks on you saying you're trying to put Remington out of business. From what I've heard so far I'd say that's so.

I sympathize with your position. I hear numbers of dollars that sounds more like Congress talking than lawyers and wonder how in the world a company can keep paying and paying lawyers and still make the same product, sometimes cheapened even further, and just sit and smile and deny there is a problem. I'm not a businessman or a lawyer and the interactions of them and with me are on a totally different plane. There are answers hidden deep in 'the secrets': they can afford it. It's much cheaper to keep the production line going with new products than convert them to repair lines.

Are Remington's the only guns causing trouble?

No, unfortunately not. There are failures of others and some are extremely hard to figure out. Not only that, but the defense lawyers are so convinced they're defending a good product, they fight longer and harder and sometimes even dirtier than normal. Some seem to actually think they're right!

Beretta A-390 Autoloader

Two cases come to mind and they both demonstrate the point. First is the story of a duck hunter, sportsman, and farmer that mixed the three together quite well. He farmed rice. It was the first day of dove season and he was going to take his young son hunting at the noon opening. Their shotguns were already in the four door truck but he still had his Beretta auto loaded with steel #2 for early teal. One side of the truck was parked in the mud, so he opened the passenger side rear door to see the shotgun looking at his crotch. When he touched it, it shot him. He sat down hard and told his son to go get a towel and called his own ambulance. He was conscious and talking on the way to the hospital and his memory was still burning bright. He said, "I didn't move it but to just lift the barrel about an inch."

While he was on his way to the hospital with really bad injuries, his wife had enlisted one of the numerous close family members that had immediately gathered to, "Please unload those guns before the sheriff gets here."

The brother in law that took on the job decided not to mess with the gun still pointing towards the yard, except from behind it, so he got in the mud hole and opened the driver's side rear door and said he saw the gun, a high-dollar Beretta auto, lying on the floorboard among other outdoor gear. The right side of the gun was facing up and an empty shotshell was stuck in the ejection port. He held the pistol grip with his left hand and pulled the empty from the shot gun. When the empty came loose, he saw a loaded round slurp into the chamber. He pulled that out with the bolt by pulling back on the handle just like you would an A-5 or 1100. He put that loaded shell in the pocket with the empty and then, just to be sure, operated the operating handle two or three more times and no more shells came out. He reported all this to the sheriff's sergeant that showed up shortly thereafter and handed over the empty and the loaded shell.

The deputy decided not to do battle with the mud hole but warned the seven people watching to clear a way because he was going to recover the gun from the truck.

He sounds as melodramatic as you do!

Right on time!

The deputy opened the rear door and carefully grabbed the shotgun by the barrel, making sure it wasn't pointing dangerously, and carefully brought it out until he could stand the butt on the running board. He was holding the barrel with his left hand and with his right he opened the bolt and let it slam. Then he opened it again and let it slam, and BOOM! The shotgun fired a round right next to his head. It made a powerful impression on everybody watching!

Analysis of that shooting took quite some time and even more time to write it in a form a lawyer could really get his teeth into. It was a 26 page report that explained how that shotgun did not fail twice, but it had to have failed three times in seven tries. In an all day deposition, I explained it to Beretta attorneys and a contingent of Italian engineers and their assistants and translators, but in the end they determined I must be right, because the explanation is the only one that fits all the evidence and we don't have to invent new physics to do it. It's all right there to see.

But, you didn't have to explain that to a jury, did you?

Thankfully, I was spared that. It would have been very difficult to go through the cycle of failure in that gun, almost as hard as the one that came after it. But by that time we had a secret weapon.

The Jain Rifle

The weather was cold and windy and few leaves were left in the Wisconsin deer woods when the lone hunter prepared to go to his tree stand for a quick hunt after work and before dark. He carried a small section of thin foam pad to sit on and a muzzleloading rifle he'd won as a door prize. It was a Knight MML, straight pull, that used percussion caps and saboted pistol bullets instead of round balls.

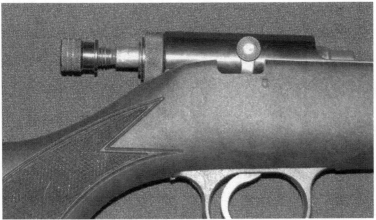

Knight MML Muzzleloader. Shown cocked, ready to fire.

He had very carefully read the instruction book and loaded the rifle the night before, but left it uncapped until he got to the field that windy cold afternoon. He drove past a friend's house and up a trail leading to a relay tower but pulled off on a grassy area near the fence line he'd follow to his stand. He capped the rifle with the secondary screw-type blocking safety ON. Then he put the side safety ON that is part of the Timney-design trigger installed at the factory. Then the positive safety was released leaving the trigger safety engaged. By training and being careful, he pointed the gun up and squeezed the trigger twice to be *sure* it was safe.

After just a few steps, he realized that to be ready for the deer that were likely feeding before the oncoming storm, he'd better stash the little foam pad in the game pocket of his coat. That pocket opening was on the right side of the coat, so he carefully lowered the gun so the butt was resting on the ground and then held the muzzle with his right hand as he stuffed the pad in the game pocket. His elbow was over the muzzle when the gun fired. The bullet exited near the shoulder.

Most trials have 'the rule' in effect. Witnesses don't hear other witnesses testify. In the case of experts it's sometimes different but we still spend many days prowling the halls of courthouses ready to trot to the witness stand when called. In the above case, I heard both sides and the judge's instructions.

It had been more than three years and plane trips to Texas, Michigan, California, Minnesota and four times to Wisconsin just to get to that courthouse. It was a brutal case made more so by the defense swapping lawyers in mid stream which caused me two depositions. Then the defense decided the damage they saw in Detroit from (mostly their) testing was caused by persons unknown on our side and that delayed everything for another year and another deposition concerning spoliation. It was bogus on its face but it cost cubic dollars to postpone, delay, and nitpick. Meanwhile, the man with the crippled arm was no longer able to do his job or his primary responsibility of taking care of his disabled wife. She was home in bed when the bullet nearly tore his arm off.

His testimony before the large jury was powerful beyond belief. He told the jury in a steady voice how he first just sat and bled and wondered how in the world it could have happened but he knew he had to find help if he had any chance of living. He was bleeding badly and the pain would not allow anything but trying to find help. Every house was dark in the gathering dusk as he sped down a secondary road, then another. At one point he realized he had lost too much blood and left the road on a curve but with his arm bones grating and increasing pain, he backed out of the ditch and got going again. The next intersection was a state highway. With flashers already going he pulled right in the middle of the highway and passed out lying on the yellow line. Somebody stopped and tightened his belt he'd put on as a tourniquet and a man he knew faded into view once and he told him where the house key was so he could tell his wife he was hurt as the ambulance crew fought to stabilize him for transport. She was told he probably wouldn't make it to the hospital but he did, then another hospital and then months of pain, traction, amputations of fingers and more pain.

The Knight override trigger, a poor copy of a Timney. Note E-clips used as thrust washers.

The victim hired a lawyer and the lawyer hired an engineer with a gun background, my friend Tom Butters in Texas. Then Tom suggested getting me on board due to my study of the override trigger designs and experience with them. I got pictures of the rifle taken out of the plastic stock and recognized the Timney trigger. I've been using them for nearly 50 years, but the lawyer for the defense said it wasn't a Timney.

My first advice to lawyers when a case is likely is buy exemplars, lots of exemplars, if they're available. With this rifle, they were available used or new and cheap, too.

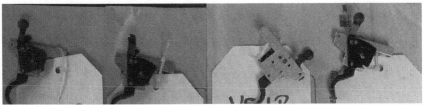

Knight triggers sorted and labeled

I think he bought a dozen and sent me a couple whole rifles and a handful of triggers. The first eight triggers I looked at were poor copies of a Timney. Every feature that we would normally recognize as a Timney trigger was there, but they all had very recognizable differences between them! Two had been made in Korea. They were the best of the bunch!

The first rifle examination was scheduled with experts, engineers, lawyers and assistants to meet in a conference room and photograph, manipulate and video tape the subject gun. From this exam would be taken the trigger pull amounts and any other test agreed to by prior, written protocol. I suggested we zap it in the NSI machine just across the state line a day early. That way Tom and I could have a leg up on the examination. With any luck we could see a defect in the X-ray before the other side saw it in person.

At first glance, in the darkened laboratory of NSI, at the slowly turning rifle in X-ray vision, we'd just wasted 100 miles of travel and a couple grand worth of CT electrons for nothing. It was what we expected to see. It was a Timney-design, override trigger with a thumb safety on the side that blocked the trigger movement with a plunger that operated off the safety plate. The trigger was made by design to work on the Model 1895 Mauser, which is the cock on closing daddy to the much more advanced model 1898. We had a hundred miles back to Wisconsin to talk about what we'd failed to see....an obvious defect or broken part or other causation. We needed at least one to win the case under Wisconsin law.

The next day was physical examination day and I had a mental list of several things I wanted to look at and listen and feel for. The one thing I notice more than any other in the physical examination phase is what others are searching for. In this case, two engineers and an 'expert through experience' like me were looking at the rifle one at a time and the lawyers and the rest of us were looking on.

When it came my time to examine the gun I was in full mystery mode. I had just observed a partial failure of the safety when an engineer tested it, but I could not reproduce it or detect any sign of what I'd just clearly seen. There's no way to call time out to discuss it, either. Keep going and make mental notes....like whose camera probably caught the failure. Hopefully somebody's did. There are usually multiple video cameras running as well as quite a lot of photography going on. (I've seen an engineer take 36 closeup exposures of the shipping label of a gun under examination.) In this case it was the defense videographer that got a close up of the hitch in operation that was a major clue in figuring out the most complicated, multifaceted failure I've ever been faced with.

Knight trigger, very poorly made trigger-sear edges

My first deposition (there's rarely more than one) was in San Antonio, TX. I was scheduled as the second deposition for the day. Tom Butters was first to be deposed and as always was a perfect combination of facts, figures, observations, useful references and enough qualifiers to assure we weren't going to be made a fool of. The trigger had not yet even been taken apart and the defense wanted definite answers before we looked inside. Lawyer's poker!

During Tom's deposition I'd felt that dreaded 'long tooth' that

portends an abscessed molar that had just been repaired. By the
lunch break, I felt like a nail was being driven into my left eye
socket from below. I called my dentist and he called in a pain
killer, but depositions don't wait. It was my turn at three o'clock
and I did my best to go through the multitude of possibilities and
scenarios and answer hundreds of questions, but by nine that
evening I would have testified to the composition of the moon if I
could just please get out of there and get some relief. The defense
argued for more time but 'my guy' finally told the defense attorney
we were leaving and if the defense wanted to follow through on the
threat of continuing the deposition the next morning, so be it. I
was supposed to be on a jet liner at eight the next morning and I
planned on being on it, but lawyers take advantage of weakness
when they can, and I was sure enough low that night.

My hero lawyer got us a cab and that took us to an all night
Walgreens about $30 dollars fare from the River Walk Hotel and
site of the day's battles Of course my dentist didn't use the same
name as on my driver's license, so the clerk was not going to give a
handful of 'forget it' pills and antibiotics to the wrong guy. I asked
my employer for some help in being understood. One easy
application of industrial strength, out of town lawyer had the
pharmacy supervisor taking over from the gum popper, and
thanking us for our business. We got back to the River Walk to
wash down some pain meds with a margarita too heavy to pick up
with one hand, and slurp a dozen no-need-to-chew raw oysters that
kept me from starving.

The defense lawyer didn't follow through with his threat to hold
me over in Texas the next morning but he did insist on a second
deposition at a time and place to be determined. Six hours wasn't
enough and the lawyers were changing seats anyhow. The new
guy had more questions.

The flight from San Antonio to Salt Lake was done with a raw
oyster and two handed River Walk Margarita hangover lurking
near by. By the time I was across the mountains to my podunk
airport and ready to drive 60 miles home, the pain from the
toothache was gone but there seemed to be too many cotton balls
in my life. On landing in the turboprop and the familiar taxi back
to the terminal, I thought my inventory of normalcy was going

pretty good until the plane wheeled into the parking spot, and there, standing on the tarmac, was Elvis and a leggy dancing girl that was already a foot taller than Elvis trying to hold a four foot tall Ostrich plume hat on her head in a semi gale force wind.

I was still hoping it was an apparition when the big jet with a casino's name across the side came into view and the camera crew shooting a commercial for direct flights to Vegas was visible. *Then* it made some sense, and it sure enough made an impression!

You must really hate those defense attorneys.

Oh no, not at all! I respect them tremendously. They have a tough job and I understand what it is and admire it. All of them are super bright, competitive, and sharp. Their energy level is about double mine on a good day.

And they've been through years of college to learn how to show you a fool in front of a jury. Doesn't that bother you just a little?

No, I'll talk about guns to anybody. The personal jabs and attempts to confuse me are opportunities to explain more about the mechanism we're there to talk about. I don't keep score and I sure don't worry about conflicting testimony. The trigger is right there. Unless it has changed, my story is the same. The danger is the lawyer that doesn't know what to ask in direct testimony so you can't get the important points across to the jury, but that very seldom happens. Lawyers are extraordinarily fast to learn what they have to, to win their case. Dealing with attorneys is a lot like dealing with our own back row. Some are a little caustic and snarly, but most like to learn something new.

In firearms cases, even when the defect in the gun can be shown, the results depend mostly on the one holding the gun when it fired. Juries are fair, if given a chance, and are not confused. It becomes the defense's job to confuse them as much as possible. If the best witness is straight with the jury and clean enough to be totally believed, the rest of the trial is just setting it up for his story to be told. That telling took a week in Wisconsin.

That case took three years for trial preparation with depositions, deadlines, and stacks of papers from examinations in engineering labs and metallurgy labs in Los Angeles and Detroit, and stacks of DVDs of photos and videos of interviews, testimony and research. It takes a law office with lots of good help to organize such a battle. It looks a lot like a trail drive with briefcases, roller boxes and file cabinets being herded from the office to the courthouse every morning and evening by paralegals, interns and lawyers, too.

Experts and other witnesses were scheduled and rescheduled around times of travel and availability. Doctors, nurses, game wardens, EMTs, surgeons, and physical therapists were mixed in with monetary loss experts and job related testimony. My testimony was to be straight through with direct in the morning and cross that afternoon. They never turn out that way.

The first use of a secret weapon is always nice, if it works. Ours was a computer simulation of the trigger operating normally and with several different points failing. We could see by computer each motion of the parts and where they interfered or clashed. Those were circled in red and close ups provided so we could 'zoom in' on the defect. I'd seen 'cartoon' clips of the Walker produced by Remington, but this was different. This was *the* trigger in animated form and shown on the screen about four feet wide.

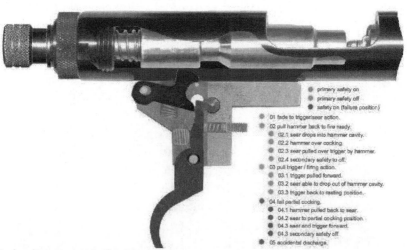

Mechanism at rest, in fired state.

The process of making the video simulation is to photograph each part separately and then use those photos to create motion by a 're-photo' in a new location.

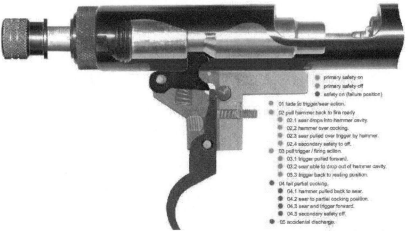

Short-cocked, trigger not reset under sear. Sear is barely supported. Trigger is jammed against safety plunger.

It's much like how cartoons are made but the computer allows all sorts of options to the results. We couldn't photograph the actual parts until much later in the process but we had the NSI files that gave us slices of cross sections of the trigger and all its pieces.

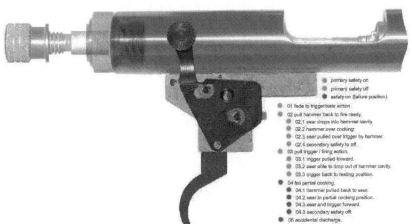

A train of mechanical actions that can end in tragedy, but it only happens intermittently.

Each part could be taken from those CT files and the simulation assembled so the entire thing could be seen in X-ray view at any point in operation. It was quite well done with control buttons to click with a mouse to watch the safety lever move from fire to safe in 3D or X-ray view. Without it, the case could not have been won, I don't think.

It took the defense totally by surprise but of course they had a lot of questions, too. Each question of the animation was an opportunity to drill home that this was *the* trigger, and point to the subject rifle on the exhibits table. This is not a cartoon.

These are the actual parts put in motion around their pivot points. When parts clash it can be seen and circled in red. For a very rushed job that took hundreds of emails and phone calls to get exactly right, the 'secret weapon' turned out just right.

Are you going to explain this case?

I don't think I can without two days and a video screen. A shortened version will have to do.

<...a big sigh all over the room>

It was clear by the discovery documents from the company that made the rifle that they had no clue about gun design but they had a price point in mind for the rifle and it was about half of the competition's offerings. There was a big market ready to tap. All they had to do was take an idea for a cheap rifle to market and try to keep up with demand. It worked great. The reports were excellent, accuracy was excellent and the wholesale price was just about what a Timney trigger cost in a retail store.

Obviously it was not going to be possible to keep the cost of stock and barrel and that trigger and sell it for the same price as just the trigger. Cost had to be reduced drastically. Besides that, Timney couldn't keep up with the demand and was unwilling to cut quality to give a better price. They turned to an alternative manufacturer and even experimented with Asian suppliers. They cut the cost of the triggers to less than a third of the Timneys and sold nearly a million of them installed in rifles to unsuspecting customers.

What's wrong with them? My kids and I have them.

It is a 'zip gun' that demands, but does not have, precision parts in it.

You claim a zip gun has to be precision made?

Not the gun, but the trigger. It is an override trigger. A certain amount of precision has to be there and... *precision costs money* (from the crowd.)

I've got a couple of them. They out shoot all my other blackpowder rifles. How can they not be precision-made? They shoot great!

The way they're made makes them accurate. Anybody with an automatic lathe can make every part on it but the stock and trigger in about fourteen minutes, starting from bar stock and a rifled barrel blank. The stock is cast plastic and the trigger was a very imprecise copy of a trigger that depends on quality and precision to make it work right. *The design* demands it.

Why didn't they hire somebody that knew how to make triggers?

They did. He knew a lot about how to make them, but not *why* they're made that way. He made some wrong assumptions and very few analyses of why they had so many problems. At one point in my testimony, I was asked to read a stack of memos from company engineers and QC people and the trigger maker and the customer complaint department. They were sketches and calculations and measurements from pulled samples and speculations as to why failures were happening, and triggers they just tested as 'good' had suddenly gone 'bad'. At the end of a dozen or more memos with questions about specific parts of each, I was asked what that meant to me as a gunsmith and firearms expert.

I said, "It shows three engineers over a three year period trying to find a solution that any competent gunsmith should be able to identify and repair in less than thirty minutes." It was truly that simple to see from a mechanics point of view and the reaction in the jury box said they saw it too.

I'm proud that I finally 'saw' a flopping Walker!

Progress back there! Congratulations. Is it understanding or did I finally just wear you down?

Both, I think.

Back to the muzzleloader in Wisconsin, I called it a 'zip gun' a while ago. That is the design designation. It is as close to a rubber band and piece of pipe as you want to get from a firing standpoint. The straight pull rifles *are* accurate and they *are* dependable, especially using 209 primers, but they have limitations. The method of cocking the gun is straight pull back on a knurled knob until you hear the zip gun click of the sear rising. (It brings back teenaged memories. If I'd had a lathe I wouldn't have lived through puberty.) That's the first step in figuring the cause of the accident. Since the cock is a straight pull, there is no 'how far does it have to go to fully cock' indicator. The click only means the sear rose. It says nothing at all about how *high* it rose or what might have caused it to not rise enough.

Hold on a minute now, you said that trigger was made for a '95 Mauser?

Yes it was, but that is a bolt action. The rotation of the bolt assures the cocking piece and sear are at a correct distance to allow full capture. You have to draw the bolt way back past the sear to load a Mauser.

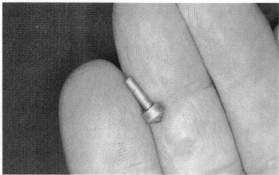

The safety plunger.

The Knight MML just has a knob to pull on. Nothing at all to tell it how far is far enough to properly cock it. Cold fingers with gloves on can cock it, but just barely. One of the engineers in the first examination had trouble cocking the gun. The mainspring is strong.

The striker's radiused edge caught the sear just about .008 too short on that Wisconsin afternoon. That 'short stroke' during the only way to cock the gun changed the path of energy from the striker to the rear upper corner of the sear and set up a path of energy that pushed the trigger forward and very nearly from under the sear. That dislocation of the trigger forward interfered with the action of the plunger style trigger block safety. The safety keeps the trigger from going forward, but it was already forward some and was sticking in the recess the safety plunger should occupy.

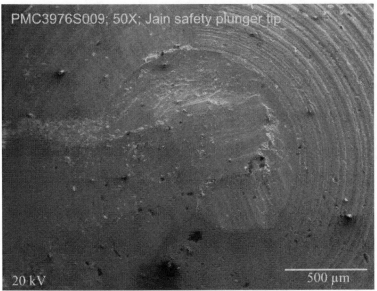

PMC3976S009; 50X; Jain safety plunger tip

20 kV   500 µm

This is the conical tip of the safety plunger at 50X SEM.

The safety plunger was not made correctly and had a radius on the active corner instead of a corner. That meant the safety plunger was wedged in its hole and it didn't go all the way in as it should. The actual safety lever was poorly attached to the side of the trigger and when the safety was applied by pulling it to the rear, the lever sprung outwards and back enough to make it seem like it was engaged, but was actually short of engagement and perched on a steep slope by friction and spring pressure.

The entire train of trigger-safety interaction had become a stack of marbles with 20 lbs of pressure on top. It all fell at the wrong instant, of course. Murphy is that way. Had he taken one more step or waited another second to start stuffing the seating pad, well, that's a lot of 'ifs'. Reality prevails. He was very badly shot by a gun that took itself OFF safety and pulled its own trigger seconds after passing a test of both.

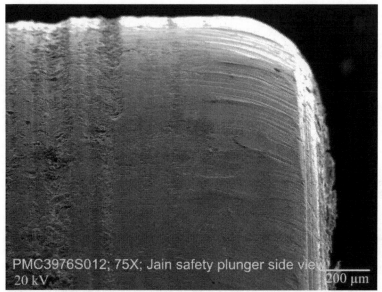

Safety plunger side view at 75X showing 'energy tracks' and radius on active corner. SEM.

I'm not sure I believe you can possibly know all this. How do you know all that happened?

Mechanical motion, especially if under unusual force, leaves evidence. When metal rubs on metal it leaves marks.

When those marks show movements that are in odd directions or under pressures not normal to the mechanism, it is an indication of failure. They are 'energy tracks'.

Under the scanning electron microscope in Los Angeles, the puzzle of the partial 'hitch' at the first exam was seen as explainable evidence in swirled lines of force across the improper corner of the safety plunger, and much of my theory of failure was confirmed through that one observation.

Technology is wonderful. The first rule of looking at anything is making sure you can see it. Here's a bet I'll make with the room. Get a flashlight and a 30X geologist's hand lens and look at the crown on your best rifle. You don't know it needs lapping until you *really* look at it, and I'll bet everybody here will want it done.

M700 Muzzle. Magnified 20X.

Here's a Model 700 with about a hundred rounds through it at 20X. The bright blue streaks are copper. The chunks missing out of the edge of the crown are accuracy wreckers.

The gun in Wisconsin was looked at by magnifying glass, CT scans, microscopes of digital and optical types, and the scanning electron microscope with atomic absorption metallurgical capabilities. Everything used to examine it, and every bit of evidence collected, pointed to multiple failures of several things at once.

Under Wisconsin law, a causation has to be shown, not 'the' causation. We had a bunch of them but it was like a Rube Goldberg contraption that didn't just jump track and stop working. This one jumped track and took a different route! The defense said it couldn't happen. But I could explain every motion. It took another route according to the laws of physics.

I took a plane home the morning the jury went to deliberate and expected a call by the time I got home. It didn't come. The next day it was the same thing. That's almost always bad news for the case.

On Friday the lawyer called and said the jury was still out and had asked the judge to come back on Monday. *What?* These 15 people had gone through two weeks of trial and four days of deliberation and they want to come back? That made both sides extremely nervous. One side had more than a quarter million dollars of the firm's money invested in three years of work and it could just all go away at any minute. The defense had outspent the plaintiff by three to one and the insurance company paying the bills had already been hit with a 3 million dollar judgment in Louisiana. Was this about to be another one? On Sunday the lawyers made a deal that would pay the plaintiff right then instead of dragging out a big verdict in years of appeals. It would pay all the bills, too.

It aggravated the judge to go through such a long process for it to settle the day before the jury was due to continue deliberation. She nearly killed the deal, but in the end agreed to meet with the jury and explain the sides had settled. She also passed along an invitation to a meeting at the plaintiff's lawyer's office to have refreshments and to meet the plaintiff's team and decompress and tell, from their perspective, how the trial went.

The jury met with the lawyer?

It's not allowed in some courts or states, but where it is, it's a very valuable tool. Some lawyers have a form with maybe a hundred multiple choice questions, others just have a group conversation and decompression. Bloody Marys and Mimosas are sometimes the 'paralegals' at such things and keep up conversation levels. In this case, the report from the jurors was heartbreaking to an attorney that makes his money on awards and the big ones can take a firm through slim times. The jurors said the case was ours. They were stuck on how much *more* than what was asked to award. The settlement was less than asking, for sure. As is often the case with law suits and guns though, there was an 'uncertainty'. It took 11 of 14 jurors in our favor to win. Only ten went to the office get together. The jurors thought at least one of the others were on board with the extra award, but nobody knows for sure. He could have gotten nothing.

It seems sometimes life is like that *by design.*

I think those guns are still sold, aren't they?

The last I checked they were. Nobody is stopping them. They've evidently acquired new insurance and will continue until their luck runs out. Their catalog shows pink and blue small sizes for the kids.

That seems a bad way to do business to me.

Me too. Why risk the life of your customers unnecessarily when other designs are better and cheaper? It seems so counter productive.

The fact is, you don't have to be an engineer to design a gun, but unless you are a gun designer, firmly rooted in firearms history, you shouldn't claim to be a gun designer even though you are an engineer. To attempt to put it in engineer's language, you shouldn't assume to understand the forces and stresses induced by the gun and the ammunition without much further study in that particular specialty.

Mechanics make things better. Engineers make things cheaper. Guns are plenty cheap enough already, *by design.*

16. Pumps, Autos and Trigger Systems

I've had feedback today that probably means I should call up a statistician to really bore everybody, but since I don't have one I'll have to do. Statistics are data collected by somebody and then arranged into a meaningful form by somebody else. The resulting charts and graphs and papers tell us what's going on around us that we can't see. When it comes to a gun that fired without a trigger pull, that data is subject to many forces and influences beyond what the gun tells us.

Firearms accidents are *bad* news. I'm hesitant every time I see a story about one to read it. Partly because it's always bad news but mostly because it's so likely to be so uninformed, inaccurate or incomplete to make the whole exercise one of frustration. It is my firm belief there is no class of ignorance so damaging as the ignorance of *reporters*. I consider myself a teacher of sorts. That's what the job of an expert is when the jury gets involved, but the first job is to educate the lawyer that's going to handle the case. It's been my experience that lawyers are extremely fast to learn and get the basics of the design and understand the failure. Otherwise he can't question the other side hard enough and pointed enough to get him backed into a corner. That is the goal on both sides. Paint the other side into a 'corner' from which the only escape is to admit a faulty conclusion in previous testimony or wrong conclusion on this one.

Reporters seem to look at all news from a totally different perspective.

I gave testimony in a murder trial one time as to how the Remington Common Fire Control (RCFC) is capable of firing from debris in one or more of five places *and* it could fire with the safety ON. Those five critical places were told to the court and pointed out using the gun that killed the guy and demonstrated on the stand by releasing the hammer without a pull of the trigger.

I know that case. Wasn't he guilty?

I think the jury said he was and they heard all the testimony. I didn't. I just testify to the facts of the gun involved. It's not my job to determine guilt or innocence, just gun facts and once in a while an opinion.

Remington Common Fire Control. Left: Hammer and Sear hung up point-to-point. Right: Cutaway showing gap that forms at heel of sear each cycle. Debris can collect there and prevent compete hammer-sear engagement. The drain hole was added to help keep that area as clean as possible.

After my testimony I was excused by the court and started to head home, but several reporters stopped me and were asking the same questions I'd just answered under oath. Reporters are an unusual occurrence with me and I was kind of enjoying being able to further the explanation, when one young guy from somewhere, I didn't get his affiliation, stuck a recorder in my face and said, "Don't you think you just made a fool of yourself? Everybody knows you can't shoot a gun without pulling the trigger."

I had six hours of desert Interstate to get home and cruise control on the rental car. You can't believe how many brilliant responses to the reporter I came up with on that drive home, but none of them presented themselves at the moment. I was just flabbergasted and said, "I'm sure glad you're not on the jury." I still wonder what he wrote or reported when he got back home. Whatever it was had little likelihood of being the truth.

I was being escorted by a Federal Marshal to a courtroom in Little Rock with a stack of guns as exhibits. On the elevator he asked if I could talk about the case. I assured him I could and told him of the case of an 1100 shotgun that fell from its perch and fired when it was caught by the fore end and hurt a guy and told him how. He just 'went off' on a rant about stupid people around guns and how they shouldn't be allowed to have one if they didn't have any more sense than to pull the trigger and then try to blame it on the gun, and declared the entire trial in Federal Court as nothing but a lying greedy, good for nothing ambulance chaser's exercise in holding up big business, and by implication those experts that worked for them were too. It was an epic four floor 'and your horse too' rant.

Remington M1100 12ga American Classic model

The elevator door opened and the victim was standing there ready to go down. His left arm was a mottled looking appendage that hung straight down and was two inches shorter than the right. When the Marshal saw who it was his demeanor changed so fast and so dramatically I can only imagine what he thought. He was in the courtroom when I testified and demonstrated how the gun can fail five ways. He left the courtroom with true confusion showing. All those people he'd believed all his life... what else did they get wrong?

Sir, I'm back here in the back row. I'm hoping you're going to tell how the lawyer caught them in a lie and they lied about the lie and then proved it a lie by lying again, and the judge said something about "write a check and get out of my courtroom."

I wasn't there and so I can't say, but that lawyer just passed away last month. He was one of the good guys that saw the fault, zeroed in on it, and showed the jury the defendants *knew* they were at fault. As it happened, the judge took it away from the jury due to some legal wreck after I'd gone home.

It IS hard to believe.

It sure is! But, I fear we're thinking of different failures. You're thinking it's hard to believe a gun can fire ON safe without the trigger being pulled, right? I'm talking about it's hard to believe a major arms company would continue to lie about and deny the existence of those defects in those firearms. They're still being made today.

You haven't convinced a bunch of us there's a defect, yet.

I realize that and beg your indulgence while I attempt to explain it.

Maybe tie all this in with pump and auto triggers before long?

Thank you! I'll do that too.

Pump action and semi-autos are almost always hammer fired, but there are exceptions. We'll be talking about the hammer guns that make up the vast majority of such sporting guns. What catches the hammer when you operate the slide on a Model 37 Ithaca pump?

The sear!

Ithaca M37, Hammer in cocked position. Sear is forward end of trigger.

The sear is the forward end of the trigger. You just pulled the trigger. Is it still pulled?

It better not be or it'll shoot again!

It sure will, but what held the hammer back long enough for the bolt to get back forward and chamber the new round? Why didn't the hammer just ride the bolt forward in a 'follow down' and not fire the gun? It has to have a *snap* to it.

The disconnector?

Good answer! The disconnector, for those that don't know, is any part that keeps the gun from shooting when it's not locked and completely closed.

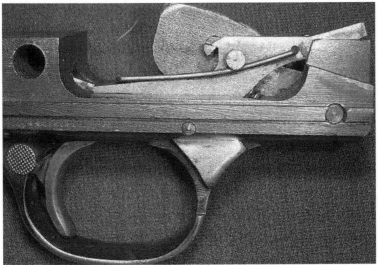

Ithaca M37. Disconnector holds hammer when bolt is open.

Sometimes it's as simple as the hammer not being able to reach the firing pin. Sometimes, like with the Number One Ruger, it seems like it would fire, but it won't. There are interferences inside to prevent it. On most of the pump guns, the disconnector is just a simple hook affair that holds the hammer back until the bolt gets all the way forward. You can see it in the Ithaca. When the disconnector falls off the action bar, the gun *will shoot* if the trigger is pulled. The same happens in the Model 12 and many more pump guns, but not all of them.

That sounds mighty dangerous to me! It shoots every time you pump it?

Only if the trigger is pulled. It is hard for new shooters to believe how difficult it is to *keep* the trigger pulled. It's actually pretty hard to do unless you concentrate. The recoil of a 12 gauge tends to un-pull the trigger at every shot. It's that pesky Newton thing again.

My 870 won't do that. Doesn't that make it safer?

Not really. In reality, it makes it much more dangerous.

<There is a general insurrection in the back row.>

I was taught in gunsmith's school to name all the parts of the RCFC whose name was totally unknown at that time, and what made them operate and what was likely to break and how to determine and repair all the various failures that can come from one of the most popular families of firearms on the planet. If a gun made by Remington has two dimple-ended pins showing through a big slab-sided receiver, it has the RCFC which was designed by Lexie Ray Crittenden about 1947 for the brand new Model 11-48 semi-auto shotgun. That shotgun was the Browning A-5, long-recoil design made by Remington's new processes and machinery, and extremely cheaply.

The brand new cost of the 11-48 was approximately half of the Remington Model 11 which is the A-5 made the way FN-Browning made them, from forged and milled and heat treated and fitted parts. But the Model 11 was a seriously degraded form of the A-5 already. Economy trumped good workmanship and complicated machining. The Model 11 service life is less than half an A-5, but from arms length, many people can't tell them apart.

Remington M11 12 ga. riot gun.

Shortly after the Model 11-48 came out and was a great hit with shooters, a pump gun was born from much the same design. The entire trigger group was the same! The Model 870 became the largest selling pump gun of all time just a few years after introduction.

How do you get a pump and an auto to use the same trigger group?

GREAT question! You know guns, I can tell! Let me catch the others up to speed first, then that question can be answered.

John Browning was not the first designer to invent a gun that would reload itself so all the shooter had to do was keep it fed and pull the trigger. Browning started with falling block single shots, progressed to lever actions and pump actions, and then invented the first *gas operated* semi-automatic by putting a gas plate and linkage on an old Winchester Model 1873 lever gun. He had noticed the grass waving from muzzle blast on the range and decided to use that energy to operate a gun. The first was a paddle arrangement. At each shot the escaping gas hit the metal plate with a hole in the middle for the bullet to get past. The gas knocked the plate out of the way. The plate was hooked to the linkage to the lever and Shazam! The thing would reload itself. That same linkage system was used on a machine gun a little later on that became known as the 'tater digger' because the linkage would dig a hole in the ground and throw dirt in the shooter's eyes if it was set too low.

Guns that operate themselves pose some interesting problems in the trigger group. A shotgun that shoots five shells with nothing but five trigger pulls was a duck hunter's dream (no plugs in 1905, guys.) But that same shotgun that shot all five shells with *one* trigger pull was really dangerous to be around! Remember the story of the Winchester Model 11 that would do that regular enough for somebody to notice it and figure out why.

Ah, sir, could you pause right there for just a minute? I think you just said a profundity and it shouldn't go to waste .

I did?

Would you like to state what the profundity might be, sir?

It seems clear to me the difference in these situations is by how much is known of the problems. Didn't they immediately recall the Winchester Model 11? How about the case of the misfiring spear

*gun in Key West not too long ago? Didn't they recall all of those
because just one went off in a shop, but nobody got hurt? Isn't
publicity the key?*

Winchester M11. Production ceased in 1925.

I wish I'd said that! You nailed it. If people know a product is bad,
they should speak up to save others from danger. Would
everybody agree to that?

**Not necessarily. You can't bankrupt a company for an honest
mistake.**

Bingo. Can we talk about honest mistakes when it comes to
triggers for a bit?

Would you say it a responsible business practice to build a gun that
will last at least 5,000 shots in every major part but the trigger? It
only lasts 500 or so and then becomes rounded, broken and
downright dangerous. Most just suddenly won't hold the sear up
and they follow down but don't shoot. The owners take them to a
local gunshop and for a hundred bucks plus labor walk away with a
rifle with 4,500 rounds still left in it. It'll need a quiver of barrels
and maybe a stock or two, but the simple, cheapened Mauser
Model 98 made in Yugoslavia and marked as Mark X Mauser is
that tough and durable and well heat treated enough to fire ten
times that many rounds. Some FNs have been tested in Venezuela
to 30,000 rounds with the original barrels! Is putting a cheap
trigger in an otherwise good rifle an 'honest mistake' or a
marketing decision?

How can it be a marketing decision?

On average, a big game rifle shoots 20 rounds a year, one box of
shells. So on average, a cheap trigger will last twenty five years.
It has to be worn out but not the maker's fault by then, right? So
why spend an extra $50 on a good trigger?

I can see his point, don't you?

Of course I do. That's a business decision just like tubeless tire valve stems.

You do have a talent for jumping track.

I was at the tire store with my dad watching the guy install new tires on our '59 Olds. He put three tires on without changing the valve stems. My dad asked him about it and we were told they lasted longer than the car, don't worry about it. Now I wonder who cheapened that product? Or did they find out valve stems were a 'weak link' that did occasionally fail prematurely. Surely the expense of replacing them was worth the additional safety and the customer ate the additional cost without knowing why. Does anyone deny that was a good business decision?

Then, I wonder if maybe triggers are like tires and valve stems. What comes on the car is OK, but if you want more performance, switch to tires better suited and since it's handy and a small cost for the added safety, use new valve stems, too. But, that leaves the question of triggers that don't 'wear out' like tires, they just fail to maintain their security....*by design*, at any time. What to do about those?

It is a stretched analogy, but as long as we're talking rubber I guess it's ok. If you were notified that one percent of two million tires manufactured were likely to blow out each year and the tires had a hundred year life span, would you buy them? How about used ones? If the company had carefully groomed an 'infallible' reputation to justify reduced cost, would it be a good business decision to just hide the one percent number and blame lawyers for bringing the subject up? How much of a role would customer loyalty play in that decision? The tires could have been under inflated or altered or badly repaired to cause the blow-outs, right? Why confess to bad tires when business is so good? The instructions say don't trust them, *caveat emptor* applies, right? Be careful!

Would you like to apply that same analogy to airplanes? How

about tie rod ends?

I'm seeing the light. Thank you.

Analogies can many times tell a better story than pictures.

While we're talking about triggers and guns and how long they last, how about trap and skeet guns?

Now we're getting somewhere. Somebody just introduced 'intended use', and it's a good subject. If we can we hold off on the auto versus pump actions just a minute....

If a gun is designed for a million rounds, should it have a million round trigger in it?

Fat chance of any trigger lasting THAT long!

They do. I've owned several skeet guns from the old Missildine School at Sea Island, Georgia. Fred Missildine sold Browning Superposed skeet and trap guns with the rental sheets showing a million rounds shot through them and his standard price was half whatever wholesale was at the time. They all had loose ribs and some had the locking block replaced and the ones not yet replaced needed it, but sears and hammers were never worn to the point of needing work but they sure were shiny!

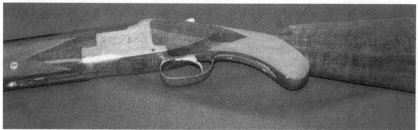

Browning Superposed, 1953 Pigeon Grade

John Browning had a near instinctive awareness of forces, stresses, steels and heat treatment. With an 8th grade education, it must have been instinctive. Even without three years of algebra he hit the perfect balance of pivots versus loads and wear versus impact. It is very rare to have to repair a Superposed Browning unless the rib comes unsoldered.

The old Black Diamond trap and skeet Model 12 Winchesters lasted longer than any other repeater of the day. The trigger would eventually wear too short and the action bar lock would become hard to operate, but all it takes is a hammer to peen the trigger about .005 longer and re-stoned to the proper shape and it's good to go another fifty to a hundred thousand rounds. Even the headspace is adjustable and the takedown feature is too on a Model 12.

The Remington pump competition guns of the day, the Model 29 and Model 31, were Loomis designed but were not well heat treated or fitted. Just like the Remington .22s of the day, they failed early and often while the Winchester built, Browning patent .22s and the T.C Johnson designed Model 12 continue to shoot and look good long after the Remingtons have worn completely out. Browning designs call for good materials and heat treatment. Remington was never willing to put that much into them and sold by cost instead of quality. Is that beginning to sound familiar?

It is said among lathe dealers there are no more destructive agents on earth to machine tools than students and convicts. Very few cheap lathes are worth buying after being exposed to either for very long, but the high quality machines not only survive, but still have a lot of life left in them. The same could be said of guns when it comes to competition shooters and shooting galleries. The difference between quality of materials, heat treat and finish was plain to see in competition and gallery guns in a very short time. Individual guns vary too much in use and care to judge.

It is safe to say that most competition guns will last longer than a similar hunting model *by design*. But, they also require more servicing and a better environment to work in, just like a race car or fine musical instrument. At the same time, it has to be realized that a different view of 'safety' is often seen in competition guns. Historically, target guns didn't even have safeties. In fact, many makers would supply guns without a safety on it, if enough were ordered. The original Winchester Model '03 was made for gallery use and had no safety at all.

In some guns it's possible to determine what it was designed for by how it was made. I looked at a fine Purdy double 12 ga. in Oxford

England while working with a past student trying to take advantage of the low pound to dollar rates of about 1986. From a distance I thought it was a very rare reinforced frame Purdey goose gun. Those are particularly desirable in America because they're made for much higher powered shot shells preferred by American hunters. This was before the ridiculous steel shot regulations that pretty much killed duck hunting in this country with good shotguns, so I risked the wrath of the snooty Englishman and asked to handle the gun. It was priced at just over double what I'd just paid for a used SUV back home and if it was a goose Purdy it would be worth twice what I paid in the shop in Oxford even after the hassle of buying a gun over there for sale over here. It was a live pigeon gun. It had no safety anywhere and had not been made with one. The reinforced frame and hidden rising bite third fastener showed it was made for heavy loads and a whole lot of them. Such a gun can be shot long after lesser guns are off the face, rattling hulks, but to sell a hunting gun without a safety would not be a good business decision in this country.

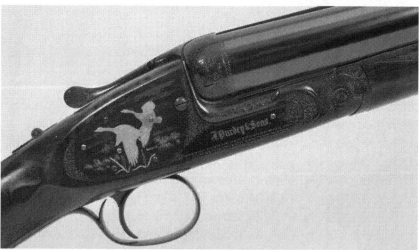

Purdey and Sons goose gun.

Did you run off the rails again or did I take a nap?

I plead guilty. Where were we before going to England to buy guns? Does anybody remember?

Something about pumps and autos being different, I think.

Good! As I was saying, automatics give trouble in how they're triggered. John M. Browning, in his infinite genius in all things gun related, came up with an outstanding solution that is still used today in many hammer-fired guns, the double-hook trigger-sear.

Browning A-5 Double Hook. Hammer is held by front hook, ready to fire.

The double-hook has two sears in a fork arrangement. The forward hook is offset vertically from the rearward hook. The hammer has two sear notches, one front and one back.

Browning A-5 Double Hook. Rear hook catches and holds hammer with trigger pulled. Releasing trigger transfers hammer back to the front hook.

At each cycle, the hammer is held by the rear hook until the trigger is released, which allows the hammer to slip off the rear hook and be caught by the front hook and be ready to fire again. It works the same as the 'escapement' in watch movements.

Let's think like Browning and Mauser for a minute, what can go wrong with the double-hook? How do you make it safe? I know that was a complicated question to work out on the fly and that wasn't the intention. Let's cut to the chase and compare for a minute the most simple of trigger mechanisms, also invented by Browning, that is easy to make safe. JMB was much too bright not to solve all the problems in both mechanisms so they had *equal safety, by design.* He did, too.

Ithaca M37 at full cock. Safety plunger blocks shoe end of trigger.

Remember the Ithaca M37 pump gun? Here's a picture of the firing system. It has two main parts, their pivots and their springs, and a cross bar safety that locks it all together when it's ON safe. Nothing *can* move, no matter what happens, unless something pushed the crossbar safety to the other side which unlocks the mechanism so that it can fire. Notice the hammer *can* rotate further to the rear. Nothing prevents that from happening. That means the bolt can override the hammer while the safety is ON.

Both these trigger groups are 'stack of steel' safety systems. The triggers and hammers are locked together until the cross bar safety moves. That is perfect for a pump, but it won't work on an automatic.

I'm not seeing the problem I guess. Can you explain it?

I'll sure try.

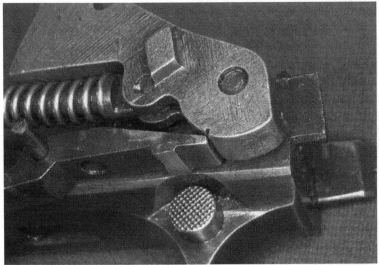

Winchester M12 at full cock. Safety plunger blocks sear end of trigger.

To have a positive safety that locks or blocks the hammer or striker from moving the safety must lock those parts together as we see above.

If we use the M-12/M-37 system in a semi-auto gun, the gun will fire every time the bolt closes if the trigger is pulled. That excitement is too much for most people, especially with a shotgun, so the firing system uses a 'disconnector' that keeps the trigger from operating the hammer as the bolt locks up. The Browning double-hook trigger does exactly that. If the trigger is still pulled when the bolt cycles, the hammer is caught by the rear hook. As the trigger is released, the rear hook releases and the hammer control is transferred to the front hook. The gun fires when the trigger is pulled again. I wonder if JM Browning saw a clock movement when he invented that.

Browning's first safety on the A-5 was a slide in the front portion of the trigger guard. Later, the safety was changed to a crossbar type located behind the trigger. Both safeties lock the trigger and sear from moving.

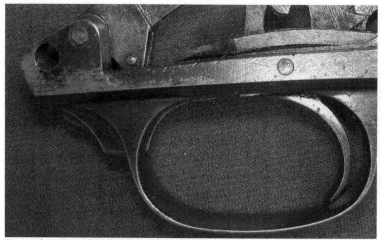

Browning A-5 sliding leaf safety in front of trigger guard.

Excuse me just a minute, how can it lock the hammer? Won't something break if the bolt is pulled back with all those parts all locked together?

Very perceptive. If the bolt is pulled back to unload the gun, something has to either break or the safety has to be taken OFF to unload it. With the pump systems above, the bolt pushes the hammer down further and overrides it so there is a gap between the sear and the hammer notch. When the bolt goes back forward the trigger and safety and hammer are still locked together and can't fire.

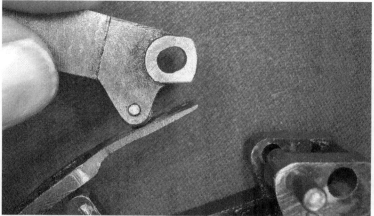

Browning A5, oblong hole in trigger. Avoids collisions.

In 1898 when the first A-5 was completed, John Browning knew it was a bad idea to have to take the safety off to make the gun safe(er) by unloading it so he figured a way to put some 'slack' in the hammer so the bolt would override it while ON safe and the gun remained locked up in the trigger system while the action is operated to unload it. The hammer pivot hole is oblong.

Look at the pains he went through to make sure the hammer was friction free even without lube by putting a roller where the hammer contacts the mainspring.

Most US military rifles have used much this same double-hook trigger system since before WW-II.

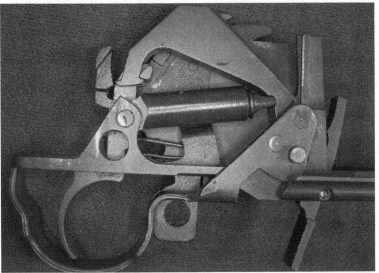

Garand/BM62 Double Hook Trigger in ready to fire position. Hammer is held by front hook.

The flexible double-hook designs have the hammer pivoted on a round hole but the rear hook of the sear is spring loaded to allow the hammer to engage while the trigger is pulled or the safety is ON. Compare the parts needed to make a pump-action trigger system and the parts of the original A-5. The extra machining steps and materials show why autos were more expensive to build.

'More expensive' was not acceptable to Remington after WW-II. They solved the problem of pump and autos having different systems by deciding not to lock the hammer or the sear, only the trigger.

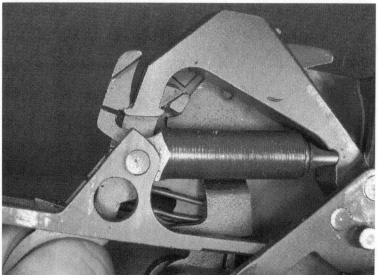

Garand/BM62 Double Hook Trigger in disconnected 'fired' position.
Hammer is held by rear hook until trigger is released.

They called it a safety but it is too far removed from the critical
point of failure to lock or block anything important.
The RCFC safety keeps YOU from firing the gun. The gun is free
to do whatever it pleases, whenever it pleases... *by design.*

17. Common Fire Controls

Somebody handed me a nice looking neck collar with a little black box on the back, but I refused to put on. I'll do better.

In 1970, I think, I saw the lead stuck in a Model 1100 hammer that caused a scarily lightened trigger pull. Mechanics *have* to have a good memory of such things or they lose money by searching for what has already been found. I knew a gunsmith one time that said the only way to make money was to clean every gun before you repair it. He had a point. Anybody can replace an 1100 extractor with a pocket knife in three minutes. That's why you don't 'repair while they wait'. A mechanic sells his expertise and experience. A good memory is the tool he uses to make sense of the evidence.

Just a friendly reminder...

Thank you! When I got a call from a lawyer in Little Rock with a case involving a Model 1100 Remington shotgun, I told him I knew they could fire without a trigger pull and do it while on safety too, but I'd never heard of it happening. I did that day.

Remington M1100. The Remington Common Fire Control is identified by 2 dimpled pins thru a slab-sided receiver.

The duck hunter was young and so were his partners. They stood thigh deep in the Pin Oaks of Arkansas shooting ducks on the Mississippi Flyway. The morning had been pretty good and it was time to pick up dekes and ducks and head home. He had a mallard down on the other side of the slightly deeper than his waders channel, and another party had a boat and offered to retrieve his duck for him. The footing in that direction was uncertain so he stood his shotgun on a stub of limb sticking out of a nearby tree trunk that was just above water level in the flooded woods and

©H.J. (Jack) Belk 2014

leaned the barrel against another (weaker) limb further up the tree. It seemed stable enough to leave it, so he waded on out to point out where he'd last seen the duck.

One of his hunting buddies moved up behind him just in time to see the twig give way that was holding up the shotgun barrel. The gun was tipping forward and would be in the water if he didn't catch it. He caught it ahead of the receiver around the forend and barrel with his right hand. The barrel was almost horizontal when it fired. The edge of the vent rib cut his hand from the recoil. The complete load of duck shot hit the owner of the shotgun in the back of the left, upper arm. There wasn't much to save, but they did.

The gun was recovered with the safety ON. Nobody said they put it on, but nobody said they *saw* it on at the time of the discharge, either. The owner said he put it ON before it was propped in the tree. The guy holding the gun was positive of his actions and very sure of exactly when the gun fired. He also confirmed there were no other twigs, brush or limbs that could have pulled the trigger.

The gun fired. Somebody was hit. Why? I told the lawyer that I'd seen a failure and knew of at least one way it could have happened and had even thought for many years the gun needed another safety and had one in mind. He offered to pay me to make one and I did.

Can you say why it needs another safety?

Good point. I sure will.

Remember when we talked about lockers, blockers and interceptors? We also talked about how safeties have to lock or block or intercept the firing pin or whatever drives the firing pin, or the sear and trigger, so the gun *can not* fire with the safety engaged. That's one of the rules that determine the 'safety' of a safety. This is where the pump-auto lesson applies. How do you make a safety that locks the sear or hammer and still allows that big old bolt to come flying back to re-cock the hammer each time?

Whoa now! I'm lost in the question and the reason for it. Explain, please.

I can explain but just understand there are literally dozens of pumps and autos so I'm using just a few to make a point. Look at your own gun to answer the questions I did in the RCFC to see if your gun is safe or not.

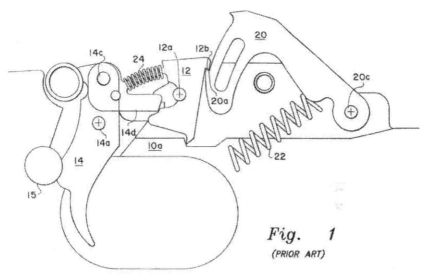

The Remington Common Fire Control. Safety (15) blocks Trigger (14), but Sear (12) is free to move independently.

First let's look at 'safe behavior' of the shooter and the gun. Guns are meant to be instinctive to use and not everybody is perfectly perfect, so *by design* certain things are done. Nobody rents a trap gun with a release trigger in it to *anybody!*

What's a release trigger?

Don't get him started.

Don't get him off track.

Thanks, ladies. Short and sweet: a release trigger is a system said to be a cure for a flinch. The theory is...

Ut oh...

You can't flinch and affect your aim if your trigger finger is going the other way.

WHAT?!

He said trap shooters. They're strange.

A release trigger is ready to shoot after you pull it. Turn it loose and it makes the big noise.

No wonder the sod is torn up in front of their firing lines! How do you 'unset' it?

I don't know. I don't base jump either.

To the distressed trap shooter I notice in the third row, it's all in fun. Golfers try to solve a bad swing with expensive, ugly, and unconventional clubs and so do competition shooters. Can't be a bad aim or slow reflexes, huh? Gunsmiths tend to specialize in trap shooters and I'm going to just shut up now.

Great idea. RCFC, maybe? Did you just call my trap gun a 'club'?

I'm with Abe Lincoln, if you're going to call for a duel, I choose horse turds at ten yards.

The RCFC safety *only* blocks the trigger. The firing pin is hanging out the end of the bolt. The hammer is compressing the strongest spring in the gun and is held back and away from the firing pin by a little bitty hook of hardened steel called the *sear*.

Remember the Browning double-hook and the Ithaca M37 and Winchester M12 sears? They were a part of and solid to, the trigger. When the trigger moved, the sear moved and the only way for the sear to move was for the trigger to move, too. It makes perfect sense to lock the trigger, which locks the sear, which is already holding and is now locking the hammer or striker. One part locks three more, a solid stack of steel. The RCFC has a sear that is pivoted in a cast aluminum housing. The trigger is a separate part entirely.

You make it sound so…important.

It is the key to understanding the RCFC just like the 'connector' is the key to the Walker.

RCFC Cutaway, M7400

The separate sear design allows a tremendous amount of latitude and interchangeability of parts between multiple guns, pump and semi-auto, shotguns and rifles, and that means many tens of millions of dollars in savings to the manufacturer.

There's just one problem.

You got more problems than that!

Nobody wants to believe it until they can 'see' it for themselves and I can't generate that much curiosity for somebody else. You have to help me.

The first real information I got on the RCFC was from the case in Arkansas. Once I saw the records of failures and complaints and how common it was to have a failure, it became clear whatever design change I could figure out to make them safe could be worth some money! That's something I'd never been much good at thinking about previously, so the incentive was strong to get it right. There was a lawyer about to present a case before a Federal Court, and if I could show the jury the gun was not only dangerous, but there was a simple and cheap fix that could have been done to prevent it, it would be a really good case and maybe

I'd make a buck on my idea. The lawyer was positive of it.

I already had the general parameters of the working principal, but to actually make it in steel and have it work is another matter. Out of lockers, blockers and interceptors, nothing in the RCFC locks or blocks anything but the trigger. Push the button and the trigger won't move. Safe? Not hardly, and several have paid for it with their lives. The simple motion of the cross bolt safety is not enough movement to transfer a locker or blocker to another part and it doesn't. The trigger is blocked from the shooter pulling it, but the sear is free to move with nothing but the spring pushing on the upper end from behind. If the sear can move, the hammer is not locked or blocked by anything.

My idea was to catch the hammer if the trigger didn't tell it to fall.

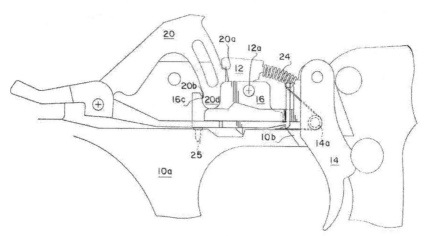

Belk-Butters Intercept Safety (BBIS) Interceptor (16) catches hammer (20) if sear (12) fails to hold for any reason. Interceptor moves forward when trigger is pulled and is held in the clear by finger pressure on the trigger.

It was an 'interceptor' safety, that operated from trigger motion *and* position, that was made in metal and taken by hand to the Remington plant in Ilion, NY, to be examined, photographed, measured, studied and manipulated by their engineers, as lawyers and I looked on. Of course Remington thought the lawyer had hired me to make him a safety instead of me making the lawyer a prototype of my safety because he paid me to.

Is there really a difference?

Just enough to argue about, for about 18 months. One of the many talents I lack is to be able to draw something and have it 'legible'. I see too many acknowledgments from too many ex students, but we know it to be true. I also needed help with engineering springs and metallurgical consultations as well as a kindred spirit that knows mechanics and how they apply to guns as no other. Tom Butters was working the same case and when I mentioned an interceptor on the hammer unless the trigger was pulled, he was on board for engineering support and ideas as well as money to apply for a patent. The international patent search showed the only thing close was for a side hammer shotgun in Europe. Our invention could be made for less that five bucks and the original cast trigger housings could be altered and retrofitted with the new parts.

So, you forced Remington to buy your patent and became a jillionaire, but the check bounced and now you're trying to get even with a book??

Cynics are always the best critics and without critics nothing gets done. Look at Washington, D.C.

Remington was offered use of the design. Nobody ever tried to 'sell' it to them. That might have been an assumption on their part, but it is in testimony: My goal is to make guns safer...

Well excuse me, but this is not teaching me a thing about this trigger.

I'm sure glad I didn't put on that collar you handed me.

The RCFC can fire without the trigger being pulled *and* it can fire with the manual safety engaged. It would be *safer* to use if it had a 'passive safety' that operated only by the trigger. That historically correct and common sense *design change* would have prevented the accident in the Pin Oaks. I offered that design change to the judge, jury and Remington. We can talk about it further if you like.

I was walking through a big flea market in Denver one afternoon... yes ma'am, it's about the trigger... and saw a stall full of old auto parts. They were in plastic bread flats and labeled by make and model and sometimes other information. I'm drawn to mechanical things and was rummaging through a bunch of stuff and saw something that looked familiar. There was the 'trigger and sear' of an RCFC in a stamped metal housing marked "40s Chevy door latch $100."

I didn't have a hundred bucks to spend on a door latch and sure didn't need one, but the design stuck with me. Years later, here I am being paid by an attorney to figure out how his client got shot and I'm seeing a door latch? It was interesting that LR Crittenden worked for General Motors as a design engineer and then at Remington in 1947, and there's a trigger that looks like a car door lock! They work the same way, too. The 'trigger' is the push button on an old car door and some medicine cabinets. That button pushes on a 'sear' that unhooks the door. The door swinging open is the 'hammer' falling.

What happens when something interferes with the sear? It makes no difference what the button or trigger is doing, what actually latches the hammer or door is inside. You can't affect it except to bang on it and hope it pops loose. Guns pose more danger than that, and in the Remington Common Fire Control, the safety only locks the button so it won't push as a car door latch, or pull as a trigger. The sear only has its return spring to make sure it does its job, but that job takes place in a very dirty environment.

It's about time you mentioned the role of dirt in these failures.

I'm encouraged that you recognize failures. There is progress in the back row and I thank you.

"Normal and expected use" means that guns are almost always some degree of dirty, depending on the perception and expectations of the observer.

<Even I'm impressed with that.>

Obviously a surgeon is not going to declare your gun clean enough to prop in the corner while he stirs your chittlins no matter what you do with brushes, rags and the man's only real cologne, Hoppe's

Number Nine.

A man's only real cologne along side some of the finest gun oil ever made.

By the same token, some shooters think if you can still recognize its heritage, it must be clean enough. No kidding - and this is in depositions somewhere - I found a shirt button in an RCFC one time. The important part of that is that it was finally washed out. I didn't see it, until the weed seeds, leaf litter and coagulated lubricants were flushed out with solvent, then a button fell out.

I'm really glad I'm not wearing that shock collar about now because we gotta talk about dirt, lubrication and gun safety for about that long...

<...holding up two joints of a finger>

Every handyman knows that if parts move when they shouldn't they need duct tape and if parts that should move don't, apply WD-40. That's just the way things seem to work sometimes. When WD-40 first came out it had a crude gun drawn among the outboard motors and fishing reels and lawnmower parts as part of the advertising. WD-40 is a drug to guns. That is not good. What happens is this.

All gun oils eventually dry out and become semi-hard. A little lint sticks while still 'juicy' and becomes reinforcement for the varnish that is dried oil. We can see that old, brown varnish in many guns. It used to be common to disassemble the gun, wash it in solvent, dry the parts, then wipe with just enough oil to change the color of the clean steel from gray to darker. That has all changed. One innocent squirt of America's favorite cure-all, WD-40, will slick that dude up like an old man with a young date. Guns that used to be hard to operate suddenly become easy to operate just like magic. "Hose her down and let the excess drain away" became a 'cleaning regimen' for way too many shooters.

RCFC from M1100. Typical caked-on crud and loose debris.

WD-40 is a powerful solvent that melts old varnish but it contains a very gummy residual wax. The solvent evaporates away and leaves the wax and the old varnish on the surface. That wax seems to be the most effective air filter on earth. WD-40 will gather and hold way more 'transient solids' from the air than other solvents or lubricants I've tried. It becomes a lint trap in guns and the resulting gummy residue makes guns very hard to operate, but just one squirt of WD loosens it right up! Of course that squirt of relief washes, blows and re-deposits the existing dirt and debris into new corners to become gooey deposits of mostly black *'gunk'*. As long as the gun has a WD fix every now and then, it'll work, but its becoming dirtier, faster than it should. Cops learned the hard way not to use WD-40 on duty guns. It's a very invasive solvent that deadens primers in the best of ammunition, sometimes in less than 24 hours. The world's best telescopic sights will be invaded and degraded by WD-40.

So, you just said you'd seen a Remington trigger so dirty that it hid a shirt button but it didn't shoot anybody did it?

No, it didn't that I'm aware of. The question shouldn't be "did it?" It should be "why didn't it?" There is nothing stopping it from an uncontrolled shooting at any time. It is only luck and careful gun handling that keeps the trigger safe and reliable. The Model 870 that removed a cop's thumb on the range had been shot 4 times since its last cleaning.

Did I miss an hour somewhere? How do they fail and what difference does it make if it looks like a door latch?

The independent sear depends entirely on its return spring to properly hold the hammer. There is a 'recapture angle' on the hammer and sear that adds to its security. These are not override triggers at all, and a long rough pull can be expected.

Mine has been worked on and it's great! Mine is in a rifle that I love.

Would you let me know what you do with that trigger at the end of the lesson, please? The problem with the RCFC arises when the sear can not return to its proper place. In that sense it is just like the connector in the Walker. It is an introduced complication that creates an uncertainty within the mechanism.

You're wasting time and this is ridiculous speculation.

Left: M1100 with drain hole for debris. Right: Early M11-48 without hole.

Would you answer a question for me? This bugged me for years and I finally found out. What is that hole for in front of the trigger and inside the trigger guard in the RCFC? Anybody know?

I think it has to be there to cast that part.

I think it's an assembly hole that some fixture indexes on.

Could it be for trigger adjustment?

How about just to bug you?

Have you seen one without it? The first three or four years, the RCFC was made without that hole in it.

Let's look at the RCFC diagram again.

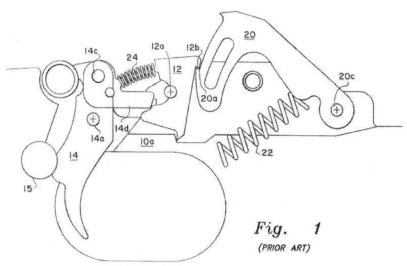

Fig. 1
(PRIOR ART)

RCFC Hammer (20) Sear (12) Two-piece Trigger (14 and 14d) and Safety (15)

When you strip the trigger group down to just parts that affect firing and safety of the gun, we find a hammer, a sear, and a two piece trigger. The sear controls the hammer, but the safety only controls the trigger. It has to be the sear that is faulty and turns loose without command. Why?

The first thing we notice is a pocket deep in the trigger housing that has the bottom half of the sear in it. In fact, it is that pocket that acts as a stop surface for the sear.

The sear is pivoted above that pocket so each time the sear rocks back and forth, it's packing any debris that falls into the pocket like a tucker stuffs mortar in masonry joints. Anything solid enough to be caught there and stay there naturally affects the critical sear-hammer notch overlap which is above that pivot point. The sear overlap is usually .025 inch. The lightest shot usually used in this country is #9 and they are three times that amount.

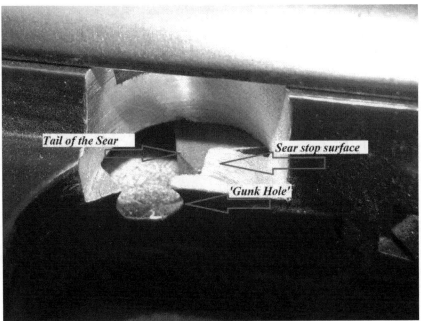

RCFC Cutaway showing tail of sear and sear stop surface

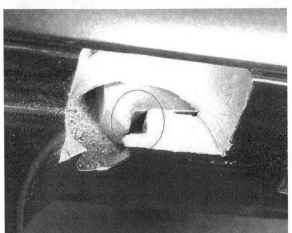

RCFC Sear Gap on cocking. Debris in the gap can prevent Full sear engagement with the hammer.

So, *you admit a stray bird shot can't do it?*

Not a whole one, but that wasn't a whole shot that came out of the

Coonbottom skeet gun, either.

Where'd the other part of that one go? Would you like to inventory the debris that is flushed out of a well used RCFC and sort by size to see what can cause a malfunction? We're just talking about that one location. There is a hole at the bottom of that pocket now to let debris drain on through.

Did that stop the accidents?

Not at all. The 'gunk hole' as it's known, certainly must have helped a lot, but that's just one troublesome spot.

RCFC Hammer-Sear full engagement and hung up point-to-point. Note 'recapture' angle.

The sear rides in a slot cast in the trigger housing. Sometimes the slots are machined, sometimes not. Sometimes the trigger group is sprayed with an epoxy-like paint for the black color. The over-spray from this operation can reduce the side clearance on the sear so that as it scrubs back and forth, a ball of epoxy can hang the sear in a less than fully recaptured position.

As I pointed out in the section on Kendrick's case in Tennessee, the RCFC has a recapture angle to the sear and hammer. That means if the sear is hung up point-to-point on the hammer, when the gun is moved, touched, jiggled or bumped, those points attempt to recapture to safe, but they're not always successful.

That's when people get scared, hurt or killed. One guy lost his arm in Arkansas, the next case was in South Texas where a man lost his life. It is the un-certainty of what is going to happen that makes it defective *by design,* but if the hooks are changed and there is nothing stopping the hammer should that tiny connection fail it, is *defective by gunsmith.*

Defective by Gunsmith. Recapture angle is gone.

There are other less likely spots that the right debris at exactly the right time of the right consistency, hardness and durability, could cause the sear to not correctly catch and hold the hammer, but it is the lower pocket, the hammer hook, and the sides of the sear where the greatest risks lie, *by design.*

What happened to your invention?

It was patented and offered to Remington and at one time Mossberg, I think. Remington's engineers took five samples for their test. The mechanism supplied was one representation of the operating principal. The Belk-Butters Intercept Safety catches the hammer and prevents the gun from firing should the trigger not be pulled and held to the rear. The BBIS was said to 'operate as designed' by the Remington engineers, but there is always a price to pay when dealing with some companies. We had requested that the examination of the BBIS prototypes be video taped by Remington to save me a trip to New York. They did that, but there was no audio to it. I had to hire a lip reader to reproduce what they said about it. It was worth knowing the difference between what was spoken and what was written, though. Behind the scenes there are respectful people that whispered in our ears, "Remington only makes what they invent in-house." If it had been their idea, I really think it would be different.

Aren't they working on that?

They seem to always be working on a lot of things. The question is if that effort is to make safer guns, or cheaper guns? Nobody is watching but the lawyers, but somebody has to get shot before they get involved.

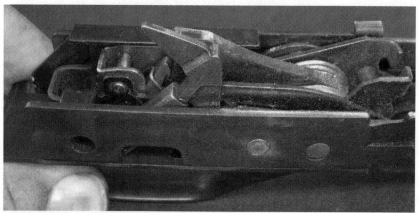

Winchester Common Fire Control from M1300 pumpgun. The M1400 autoloader has same parts in a different carrier. The 150, 170, and 190 rimfires share a smaller version. The flimsy, poorly made parts wear quickly.

Don't guns get evaluated and reviewed by the magazines as they come out?

That is where I think the basic breakdown has been in communications between the gun manufacturers and their customers. So many times the guns get lost in the marketing. The Nylon 66 was a prime example in my impressionable youth. I'd seen them on the shelf for several years and read all about them in a wide variety of gun magazines. I don't even care for a plastic comb. To make a gun out of it was just some Yankee marketing scheme to me at the time. Nobody I knew wanted one in the house. The gun writers were diplomatic in saying "tastes may differ but you can't deny Remington has come up with the look of the future." I just about gagged.

We've been through the Indian Creek case where the gun shot the guy in the back of the head while being carried by a strap. I also mentioned the Winchester 1300 that killed the kid in Arizona when a chintzy plastic bushing broke inside the trigger, probably when the kid jumped a ditch. Jumping ditches while dove hunting is one of those 'normal and expected' things to happen to a shotgun.

I don't think you've said all you wanted about the gun writer's responsibility.

You're right about not saying all I wanted, but that's probably enough.

My son read all the magazines. He lived them. He had his heroes, too.

I was fortunate to start out my 'gun guy' education with a collection of old magazines. My dad knew a guy that had stacks of American Rifleman magazines from 1921 to about 1962. I read the new outdoor magazines in the barber shop and the county agents office during 4H meetings. My dad would pick up anything that looked interesting and when others were begging their moms for the latest issue of Mad magazine or comic books, I was getting gun diagrams from the patent office. I became an NRA member for the first of many times in about 1962. I had to give back those stacks of magazines to my dad's friend when I went in the Army but my library still has most of them obtained from other places. Old American Rifleman's are like National Geographic's. They're very hard to throw away when they have good information in them. When you read gun reports from General Hatcher and Colonel Whelen first, the later reports are like watching a third grade school play. If you don't know anybody in it, it's pretty bad!

I've been very fortunate to be around quite a few gun writers and there's not a one I don't like and one in particular I think is the best ever. Most I'd rate as comical. That's not the slam it seems to be if you can just see the side of the elephant I'm staring at by training, avocation, personal passion and employment. I'm not marveling over his size, color, smell, glossy eyelashes or monster toenails. I'm looking at the *design* and how it affects safety because ultimately it will be *safety* and not politicians that affect our gun use and ownership.

You seem determined to make that happen.

You hit a nerve and introduced a good subject. Let's discuss responsibilities and obligations in the next chapter.

18. Responsibilities and the X-Mark Pro

There has been considerable criticism of your role in big cases against gun companies.

I didn't design their product. I didn't make it or market it. I sure have sold some, though. I'm not the 'causation' of their expenditure. I'm just the hired help pointing out mistakes made by people that should know better.

How can you say 'you' know better?

Because I know guns and they, judging by the guns they make, don't. It's just that simple. Many people get the impression a gun company is a collection of people that really know, understand and love guns. That's true at some places. Dakota was started by associates of mine in the ACGG, and Don Allen and Pete Grisel most certainly know guns and how they should be made. There are others with fine products made by people who care.

Yeah, but look at the prices!

That's what we've been talking about. Economy always plays a role, but the M-3 Greasegun and cheap .22s have shown that safety does not have to be compromised, but a certain amount of precision has to be present for a gun to be safe. And, all together now....precision costs money.

But you're still making guns much more expensive and complicated and all that writing on the side is just obnoxious.

Let me tell you about a deposition in a case several years ago that may shed some light on how the companies try to 'solve' problems.

It was clear Remington had a problem with the Walker trigger and the company was about to be sold to a new outfit that indicated they wanted to start anew with a new trigger. Alternatives to the Walker had been discussed for 60 years, but this time it looked to be happening. Part of my job was to read the depositions of three engineers hired to design a new trigger and look at the gallon zip lock bag full of triggers, prototypes, and parts they'd generated.

Tom Butters and I sorted the triggers first into a 'won't work' and 'might work' pile. At the end of the examination of more than a dozen prototypes, there was only one in the 'might work' pile.

I testified later that day that Remington would have been better served to hire a gunsmith, something they don't have, to walk across the street to the Remington museum and pick out a trigger they've already made. They wasted hundreds of thousands of dollars on trigger designs that had no chance of working in the idea stage, much less in actual steel. The fact is, they won't spend as much as is needed to build a really good trigger, and a really 'safe' trigger seems to be just out of their economic reach. The best triggers belong to somebody else and we sure can't have two alike, even though every bolt action rifle in WW-I had a Mauser trigger in it. It was the best so everybody used it.

What about the X Mark Pro?

The XMP is the trigger the Walker design would have been in 1947 had Mike Walker had his way, with one exception. Walker was a believer, right up until he passed away at 101 years old, of forged and heat treated steels in trigger parts. I'm with him. Again, economy has entered the picture and it's easy to see why. The XMP trigger design and features could have been taken from about five depositions between Tom Butters and me. Almost every thing we testified to be desirable in an override trigger was done in the XMP trigger.

One common impediment to total acceptance that Tom and I agree on, along with Walker: MIM (Mold Injected Metal) should not be the material used for the XMP trigger. It is already a failure.

I have three of them and they're fine.

They do not have the numerous faults of the Walker. There is no connector, the trigger body has bearing lumps that assures it is centered in the housing but offers very little friction even when dirty. The safety positively and with force, reseats the trigger in the unlikely event the dual return springs don't push it back into position. The trigger, sear, cocking piece and firing pin are all locked together while it's on safe. Nothing moves.

Remington has, I think wisely, gone to two trigger return springs. They hid one up in the mechanism in the usual spot and put another one accessible to the shooter to give him something to play with. It doesn't seem to be working. I see people fiddling with dimensions that increase fragility many times over trying to get performance above its intended *design*. That is a continuing problem, too.

Defective by Gunsmith

It is a common joke among gunsmiths that we've never had a customer come in with a gun in a grocery bag that HE took apart. It's always, "my son decided he was going to clean this gun" or, "I bought this at a garage sale and wonder if you can get it (back) together." The same thing happens when 'tuning' a rifle goes wrong. I've seen override triggers with the back of the sear ground and polished. No idea why except "it should be slick, right?" Experiments with bedding and scope mounting and handloading designed to make a gun better sometimes make it unsafe instead. Some people are just mechanically inclined enough to be dangerous.

I received an XMP trigger in the mail from a state I've only been to once and don't know anybody in it, I didn't think. It had a note with it: "Said to be dangerous. What gives?" Don't you just love a mystery!

The trigger had excess sealant on the front and signs that it had been disassembled. The XMP uses two fasteners that don't care for being disturbed and good luck finding replacements. There was no sear with the trigger. At first glance, I thought it was a badly broken XMP trigger. The active, rear corner of the trigger where the sear rest was *gone!* On further review under the microscope it was clear the trigger had suffered an untimely meeting with a hammer mechanic. It was defective by a very bad 'gunsmith'. Nearly a month after it mysteriously showed up in the mail, I got a phone call from an acquaintance that had moved to a strange place without me knowing about it. He asked about the trigger his neighbor gave him. Right!

Now, I'm really hoping that after this marathon session of talking about override triggers, everyone here sees there is a real problem with this trigger.

 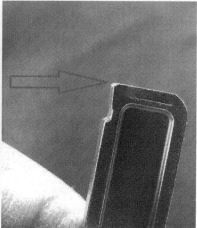

This is NOT how you adjust a trigger!!!

Note the dark vertical line near the bottom. That is a notch that seems to be where the sear was hanging on. Somebody want to say "skid angle?"

I used a Walker sear (same dimensions but different in looks) to show the normal overlap of sear and trigger and how it might have failed. I hope you got the sarcasm in 'might'. *This* is a deadly mistake by somebody not at all familiar with how the trigger operates.

This plainly shows that the rear of the trigger has been ground on and not at all that well, either! This is an example of trying to 'stone' or 'polish' a gun part by hand, too. This is a totally ruined XMP trigger that is in no way Remington's fault. Or is it?

Remington recalled the XMP because it had 'too much sealant' in it or on it. Most of the XMPs do have two different sealants in them or on them. One is red and one is black. I don't know which one Remington refers to, but neither is going to affect the trigger in a manner deserving of a factory recall as long as auto parts stores have solvents. What the recall does do is get shooters curious, especially those that don't want to send their rifle off by brown truck and maybe not see it again until after hunting season. Many shooters will try to fix the problem themselves. There is a 'neighbor' in Ohio that he thought would just 'work over' his XMP and save him sending it in. It's my understanding the trigger wouldn't hold after he got it back together so he bought an aftermarket trigger that uses the factory sear and gave this one away. I advised the 'neighbor' that sent it to me to please tell his neighbor to not mess with any more guns.

So, you think Remington is at fault for some idiot grinding the corner off his trigger?

Remington has no legal exposure whatsoever. I'm referring to the claim of excess sealant. As we can plainly see here there is sealant galore slobbered all over the front of the trigger. What you can't see is a rubberized type of sealant that is dark in color in the safety block. I certainly understand Remington not wanting customers messing with the safety block screw.

If the safety block screw is adjusted wrong the XMP trigger has no advantage over any other....or it doesn't work at all. It *has* to be right or it's wrong. It's best not to mess with them at all.

The exposure to Remington is greatly reduced in a recall unless people take advantage of it. Then it costs them money. I wonder how many people have cleaned the red goop off their XMP thinking they saved themselves a lot of bother? Did they repair anything? Did they hurt anything? Probably 'no' on both counts.

Why is that red goop on there, anyhow?

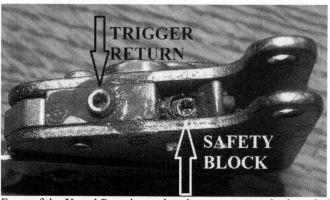

Front of the XmarkPro trigger showing two screws, both sealed but with different goop.

It seems the red sealant is the replacement for the old amber colored glue that Remington has sealed Walker triggers with for many years. As mentioned elsewhere, the first 'sealing' of the M721 triggers was by staking the screws so it really took some effort to get them to turn at all. Then the clear to slightly yellowish material was applied that for many years was said to have a radioisotope in it so Remington could tell if it was original or not. After 20 years of joint examinations with Remington's experts, I can say for sure I still don't know if the old story about the tracking isotope is true or not, but there has never been a question of what is original and what sealant is replaced. It's very easy to see the difference. The red stuff is new. I have a theory but no actual knowledge of why it was used so liberally but I do have an opinion I'm willing to share.

Notice the trigger pull screws are backed way out in both locations. The front screw was backed out by the factory and sealed with red stuff. The screw in the trigger was probably backed out to remove the trigger and was not readjusted, or the adjustment didn't work.

What ever the reason for the bottom screw being displaced as it is, it is the top screw in the front of the housing that is showing a lot of thread compared with other Remington M700 triggers. It was sealed with two threads out of the housing by somebody at the factory.

It has been my limited experience with XMP triggers that the older triggers without the trigger shoe adjustment screw have the top screw flush with the housing. This leads me to believe that when the change from the single to the double trigger return spring was made, Remington saved a penny or so and retained the old, stronger springs by simply turning the adjustment screw out like they were adjusting the trigger too light. The additional spring down at the top of the trigger shoe makes up the difference in energy the trigger needs to return correctly, and give the correct trigger pull. That red goop must be pretty cheap for such a cheap outfit to use so much of it.

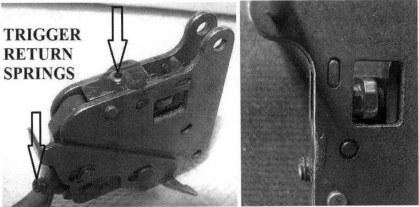

XMP Trigger. Note how far 'out' the return spring adjustments are.

Now, as to why Remington wants them back in the factory is beyond me. Send a handful of new, weaker springs for that top location to each gunsmith Brownell's has an address for and let them replace it or hand them out to people that own an small allen wrench set. Most shooters do. Or, is there something else we haven't figured out yet?

Why have two trigger return springs and make both of them adjustable?

This is an attempt to get shooters to quit messing with triggers when they don't understand the limitations of those triggers. It is a little late for that! Remington introduced the shooter-adjustable trigger on a hunting rifle in the USA and gave instructions how to adjust the trigger in the owner's manual. Then Remington, without fanfare or promotion of any kind at all, gave us 'lawyer triggers' which taught even the most dense of gun mechanics that all they had to do to correct them was to adjust the *one* screw in the entire mechanism that shouldn't be messed with. The sear overlap onto the trigger-connector is the *most* important and critical for safety adjustment in the entire gun, but in order to use a 'lawyer trigger' as made by Remington in the early '80s that critical dimension had to be reduced by the shooter/gunsmith. It is fair to say not many of those trigger adjusters knew how important the overlap dimension is to the security of the rifle.

SEAR ADJUSTMENT
SCREW–FACTORY
SEALED

The screw in the rear of almost all override triggers is the sear engagement screw. *Don't* fool with it unless you know the limitations!

Is it any wonder shooters are confused today? It's just icing on that cake of misinformation that those same confused people hear about 'bad triggers' or 'bad safeties' and have no clue who to believe, what to believe or whether to believe anything at all.

There is a conflict between safety and economy when nobody is keeping track of what is actually *right* in the product. When the entire 'recall' or 'advisory' process is voluntary, and nobody is watching the 'repairs' that knows what is needed to repair the fault that is present in the gun, we get Model 600s with coined safety cams.

Who do you trust?

I strongly believe a gun company should be responsible for *their part* in the safety of every firearm they build. That goes from concept to print, to prototypes and production. They built a firearm from materials that could have been tractor parts and lumber had they not made a firearm from it. There are certain things a firearm should do, like look good enough to sell and shoot good enough to sell even better. (That's the only explanation for buying an ugly gun I can think of, and still not a good enough reason for me.)

A gun is a special product and one that carries a lot of responsibilities. Life and death is as serious as it gets. There are some things a gun should never do. Shoot without a trigger pull and being capable of shooting while ON safe are two of them. That portion of *safety* belongs entirely to its creator for as long as that gun lives as it was born. When people like me come along and change a perfectly good military Mauser safety into a safety that works like a Model 70 Winchester, only then does it become my responsibility and not Mauser's.

So, you think somebody with a Stearman biplane should insist the company come back to life and make his plane safe enough to carry passengers?

That analogy is a tad extreme don't you think? I have a pre-1905 commercial Mauser action that is the heart of a really nice old German sporting rifle made by J.P. Sauer. Why you might ask does pre1905 make any difference? Until the change of '05, the Mauser firing pin was prone to breakage and the design of the front end allowed the gun to fire with the bolt open if the pin broke. The new firing pin has a blade on the front that only fits in the slot in the bolt when the bolt is closed.

Notice the narrow gas slots in the pre-1905 bolt body. The bladed firing pin has to have a wider gas slot for machining space.

Now, as a shooter and a gun collector I have a choice to make. Should I update this rifle to a post 1905 firing pin? That would mean the entire bolt body would have to be changed, along with the cocking piece.

No, I'll be more careful with it. Dry firing is what causes the firing pins to break, so I certainly won't do that. Besides, I'm pretty sure Mr. Mauser is dead now and his company no longer has parts. Do you notice the point to all this? The fault of the pre-1905 Model 98 Mausers is well known. It's rare to find an early action except for the commercial Mauser Werkes actions that were used as a basis for fine commercial rifles. The military arsenals refurbished infantry rifles with updated bolts and firing pins immediately. Civilians were taught to never dry fire guns. Most forgot which ones are damaged by it but it's safe to say "don't dry fire!"

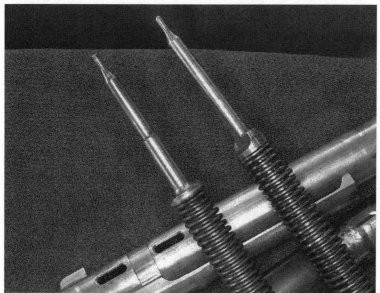

Pre-1905 Mauser M98 firing pin (left). No safety blade.

That means that beautiful color case hardening that is still bright and nice after a hundred years has to be replaced by something bright or blued?

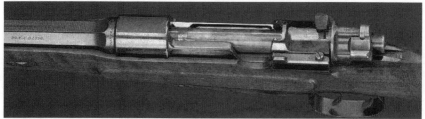

Pre-1905 Mauser commercial action, J.P. Sauer German sporting rifle

Education is the key. Knowing what is more dangerous than normal is like avoiding the fence with the bad dog behind it. The real secret to education is that it *be correct*. To have a correct and complete education in how guns are failing we need investigators that are actually looking for the basis of customer complaints, not just operating the gun a few times and saying "I don't see anything, but I'll give you a new trigger." That gets people killed and is *not* good for the gun business.

Tom Butters and I have for years discussed the 'ideal trigger' for a hunting rifle. The XMP is not it. The XMP is extremely well built and the design is mostly sound, but it's not as safe as it should be. Not only has Remington used a material unsuited for a trigger, but they also made a simple engineering error that could make it even worse.

Sir, I'm a PE and you're beginning to bother me a little bit. For a guy that never even had geometry in school you seem almost anxious to criticize the work done by people trained with years of study to do just exactly that job!

Thank you, sir. For those that don't know, a PE is a Professional Engineer. They take on the obligation to do right in the world and look for problems instead of excuses for them. Did I get that right?

It'll do for now. I'm not shy about speaking up.

Good. I have seen, but can't photograph without damaging the trigger, damage to the sear engagement surface by flaking away at the corner until the surface is reduced by about 10%. Given the fact that the load applied on the very last contact area as the parts separate is infinitely large, would that explain the flaking damage and conchoidal fractures? I see confirmation from the PE in the back.

There is a tremendous amount of wear and tear taking place on that corner in ALL triggers. Why is the one I have damaged?

I suspect it is because the material lacks internal cohesion due to its very nature.

Me too. It's hard plated and that plating failed first and then the MIM trigger body was next to chip away. Would you call that an engineering mistake even though the trigger has not yet totally failed in its duty to hold up the sear, but the effective surface is reduced?

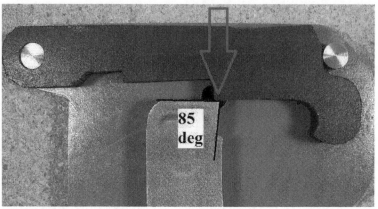

XMP Model. Arrow points to sear overlap area.

I can't see an alternative answer to that but, 'yes'. I can see where they thought it would work. The sear is MIM, isn't it?

The sear has been MIM since 1966 but, I've never seen breaking damage on a sear corner. I've seen plenty of cheap triggers made of other materials that fail in that way from excess hardness on too sharp a corner, but in the case of the XMP trigger, it seems to get progressively worse as the trigger is used. I'm wondering if some are failing already. The most used XMP trigger I know of had less than 400 rounds through it, so had been pulled maybe a total of 500 times. It was a wreck, but the guy couldn't afford to change it and said it was for target only so it should do even if it does fail. That trigger is still in a rifle and being used.

Let me call your attention to another engineering mistake in the XMP trigger body. See the acute angle on that critical corner? That is also a defect.

Now you did it and I can prove it. You sir are wrong. That angle has to be there to clear the sear when it drops. Did you forget the Remington sear is 'backwards' and pivoted at the front? That angle has to be there so the sear corner can clear the back of the trigger.

Class... have you ever had the perfect cast with a well tied fly settle just exactly right and the biggest trout in the pool sucks it down? Let's set the hook and reel him in gently. There is a great lesson to be learned here.

Let's go all the way back to the Walker patent's original language. Page 4 Sect. 4 lines 40-45 "...the connector starts to clear the edge of the sear step. <u>At this point the trigger stops...</u>"

Is it possible to stop the trigger at the point the sear falls off the trigger? Not as long as a finger is pulling it and Sir Isaac's laws still apply. The trigger *will* move until it hits the overtravel screw. Not only did Sir Newton firmly establish the laws of that motion, we can easily see it by simply looking at a trigger being pulled.

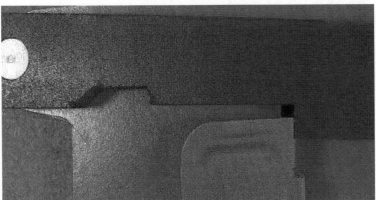

This picture shows the engineers properly calculated an event that can't happen.

The .008 to .010 inches of overtravel that is correct for all override triggers is far enough for the corner of the sear to have already cleared a SQUARE trigger rear corner. That 85 degree angle not only weakens the critical rear corner of the trigger, but it also is *not necessary to the design.*

Is that also an engineering mistake?

Yes sir, I believe it is. I didn't think of that.

Well, please correct me if I'm wrong, but wouldn't an engineer recognize the fact the trigger does certainly move after the sear disengages when it's pointed out to him?

Of course he would... Unless he was hired not to, I guess. I see

your point.

Actually the acute angle of the XMP trigger has not been brought up as a 'defect' to Remington beyond casual conversations. I was taught not as an engineer, but as a mechanic that the strongest edge has the most metal under it that it can have and still operate. We've seen how the connector has the reverse angle of the XMP because it is supposed to fly forward *by design.* It worries me that engineers that don't know guns are continuing to design them. This issue of how the trigger moves during the firing of override triggers has been known for at least 35 years and it just seems unconscionable they haven't learned anything yet.

XMP model showing square searing corner with clearance.

The XMP will work just fine with a ninety degree corner and .010" overtravel. Less than ninety degrees is a *defect in design* and it has shown itself to be a factor in XMP triggers failing too soon.

So, you say the XMP is no good and the Walker is dangerous and there are copies of Timneys coming from Korea, and triggers break and firing pins are sometimes too long... are you trying to scare people away from guns?

Not at *all!* I just want more people to know what they're dealing with. There is a vast number of shooters in this country that couldn't tell you what *model* gun he has in the closet and uses every year or so. He might know it's a Winchester pump and could recognize 'Model 12' if you mention it. He has no clue how it works, just that it does. That is the reality we're dealing with in the gun business. I do feel if that same mythical guy with the Model 12 in the closet reads Joe D. Blowem's gun defense article in the latest gun rag magazine and Joe says you should never leave the hammer cocked on a shotgun. So the M12 owner confuses the action bar lock and the trigger, and he kills the cat. He should be able to get some answers from *somebody* he can trust. It might save his marriage to convince his wife the gun went off with the safety ON, but we know it couldn't happen that way.

Reality may be a bitch, but it sure is durable.

19. Other Guns and Issues

Sir, I'm really interested in target shooting and my triggers are really light. Now I'm worried. The XMP doesn't have a connector, so isn't it just as safe as say, a Jewel or Shilen or Kenyon? They have two pound triggers.

Remember the importance of geometry, metallurgy, heat treatment, fit, finish, and alignment. A really good trigger is the ultimate in predictability that takes you by surprise. A modern gun manufacturer cannot produce a really good trigger for what they want to spend, but sometimes they get one just right.

I use Remington-Walker housings and sears as the foundations for very good, custom triggers with bronze bushings and lapped surfaces, but I spend a lot of time sorting through housings to find one with all the holes drilled square and straightening up minor mistakes and making sure it's actually the way it HAS to be to be a really good trigger. Everything has to be square, straight, smooth and right.

Of course you can buy a very light pull trigger from Remington. It is the 40X, 2 ounce trigger.

<...maybe not now>

Two ounces is too light!

Yes it is, for anything but on a range or varmint field, but you can put a heavier spring in them, you know. You didn't?

What's a two ounce trigger, anyway?

It's a set trigger. Any dummy knows that!

A set trigger can easily have a two ounce pull but that doesn't make it a two ounce trigger. Remington made this one very similar to the homemade bench rest triggers Walker and his shooting partners came up with. It has an extra lever between the sear and the connector. It further divides the energy to the top of the trigger by using a 'wheelbarrow' leverage system.

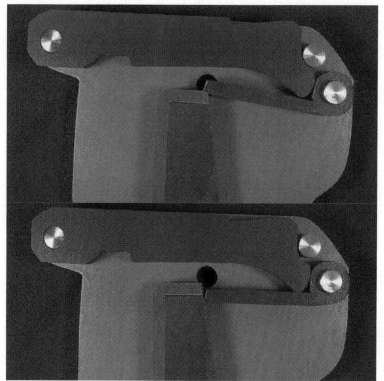

Two-Lever '2 oz' override trigger model cocked (top) and fired

Are you trying to dodge the original discussion on costing us money through your work?

Not at all, just back filling questions.

Here are the facts. The major gun manufactures are machine shops making parts that happen to be assembled into a firearm. There are exceptions to that of course, but the major market is for guns on a budget. Post WW-II, the competitive makers had to cut quality in order to reduce costs to stay competitive. Have you priced pre-'64 Winchesters lately? What about the '65 models?

Remington and to a lesser extent Savage, won the battle of the economical hunting rifle and it was a major one. Both those makers redesigned for economy. They make everything as round as they can so lathes and automatic screw machines can be used extensively. For every part possible, stamp it from sheet metal or cast it from white alloy or plastic. Save money! The difference between prewar guns and post war guns is much like the difference between farm tractors and automobiles. Before the war, many auto parts were machined in a way to last generations, as most tractors still are. After the war many car parts were stamped from sheet metal. They didn't last as long and bad parts had to be replaced rather than repaired.

Winchesters weren't designed to be made cheaply and were very unsuitable to be changed. The best indicator of the post '64 decline of Winchester was the commemorative Model 94s with sheet metal followers. JM Browning would be appalled. The guns were to be forged, milled, heat treated and hand fitted, *by design.* To change materials was a major disaster that eventually bankrupted Winchester. The new owners looked at Pre '64 prices and decided to improve quality to save the name. They had become a national firearms joke.

So, what's the difference, then? Why pick on Remington?

I'm not 'picking on' anybody. I answer the questions I'm asked. I haven't been called by a lawyer representing a client that was shot by a Savage, Winchester, CZ, Sako, Tikka, Ruger or Browning.

Could it be they don't fail as much? Or is it education? Maybe there are thousands of failures that nobody, not even the lawyers have heard of. Could it be Remington shooters are just more careless? The entirely anecdotal 'Remington Story' phenomenon, where anytime five or more shooters get together, somebody knows of a Remington failure, is a good indication of where the truth lies. I can't just lay out thousands of pages of proof of what I'm saying because I gave my word not to, but that doesn't change the fact that they *are* there!

Aren't any of the other companies doing the same thing?

That is suspiciously lawyer-like. Let's be specific about what 'same things' are, first. Can I assume you mean making guns with a visible and demonstrable defect that could kill somebody? Yes. No doubt about it.

Name them then!

The better way is to have you bring me the example you want me to assess. Guns change all the time. A general statement of one model that is dangerous has to be in historical context and not current manufacture. You have to look critically at anything and everything and then be willing to look some more if all the evidence doesn't clearly point in the same direction. Be objective, not protective. Just because you spent nearly two grand on a new gun by a maker with a two hundred year old name and reputation does NOT mean you're buying anything but what you see in front of you. If you open up your new acquisition and find a nylon sear, thin sheet metal parts and torsion springs like a clothes pins, don't say I didn't warn you. I could name it, but why bother. Just look at what you're paying for what you're getting. There are some guns today whose price tag would be too high to pay for the machine that built it!

So, we're supposed to sit here and just take your word that a bunch of guns are, or could be dangerous?

Just so we're clear, guns are dangerous *by design*. But, that is exactly what we bought, just like a guy buying an airplane. The only way to keep it safe is not to fly it. Guns are perfectly safe if not loaded. Both are pretty useless unless used as designed and intended. My complaint is that customers are not informed about faults that could kill them. That third leg of liability is 'Fail to Warn'. Wouldn't you think if a plane had a history of blowing a plug and puking the oil out while in flight it would warrant a little publicity?

One example, that still has had no publicity that I know of and so people just don't know about it, has a real legal twist to it. Many here have owned, do own or would like to own a TC Contender. Locally, Steve Herrett made a good living out of making grips for them and even invented a line of Contender-friendly cartridges. The .30 Herrett is still a favorite on Silhouette ranges.

There were a series of incidents with eerie similarities that got the attention of some lawyers, and about eight Federal Court cases were eventually tried or dismissed in a span of ten years or more. They were before my time. Only two of the accidents were witnessed, but all were shots to the center of the chest while the victim was bending over. Every one of the guns was carried in one particular shoulder holster that was made for the gun. All were fatal.

The Thompson-Center Contender system allows multiple barrel and stock combinations. The passive safety can be defeated by dropping.

The TC Contender has an internal safety that is released by action of the hammer. It was clear the gun was landing precisely on the butt in such a way the internal safety would have to be disengaged and then the gun would rotate so that the hammer hit the rock being moved or whatever it impacted. The maker of the guns denied it could happen that way and built a test stand to duplicate the events in every variable. In each case brought against the gun, the defense showed the test fixture in action and the gun being pretty much destroyed by repeated tests that failed to fire the gun.

Then, in the late afternoon before yet another trial was to begin in Texas, a courier showed up at the plaintiff's office with a VCR tape. The tape was of the FIRST test of the TC Contender on the complicated fixture that made it land just right. It FIRED! Then there was a discussion (on the tape!) of how to falsify the test because clearly that was not going to work for the defense. It was heard off camera a suggestion to just remove the firing pin. They did and then repeated the test many times to really show the jury it could NOT fail the way the plaintiffs claimed.

That constituted a fraud on the Federal Courts and that is something dear old Uncle gets real touchy about. There's not even a limit on time when a lawyer is safe from the wrath of a defrauded judge. It goes on forever. It was clear the conspirators seen and heard on the tape were out of the gun business for good.

You might have just stepped in it.

Yes sir, but do you have a TC Contender? Would you carry it in the shoulder holster that was made for it? Should those that do have them, know there is one particular way it can fall that disengages the internal safety so that contact on the hammer will fire it? Shouldn't they know? Who is going to tell them? When?

Given what I've heard here today, who in the world would understand it?

It is important for the gunsmiths to understand it. Many times it is the local gun mechanic that gets the call: "Hey, a guy just got shot dead in the chest with his own pistol with nobody within a mile of him. You ever heard of such a thing?" The gunsmith is assumed to be the authority. I know of two men that have spent a combined 40 years in prison because nobody in their cases knew of the prior history of the mechanisms under inspection. Under those conditions, it's easy to answer incorrectly under oath. I've seen it happen in multiple cases and it's heartbreaking to read the trial transcript of a lawyer asking questions of an expert that really makes a difference... and the highly trained tool and firearms examiner spouts total untruths that he could have avoided had he understood just what it was he was attempting to do. Too many times they have no clue how the gun works, what the testimony is about, or have any idea how to start looking.

Sometimes, the survivors are not at all curious about why or how the gun failed. Some won't even listen!

I sure don't see why somebody would just refuse to listen?

Several years ago on a lake less than 20 miles from me and just before Christmas, the brother of a county official was killed while ice fishing when a pistol he was carrying shot him in the chest. It sure sounded like a TC Contender had claimed another victim. I called the sheriff's office and left a message, but got no call back. A month later I tried again: Nothing. Then I saw somebody that knew the victim's brother and told him the story to relay. I heard back that it was none of my business, which was true. As far as I know he's still ignorant of the probable facts of the case. His brother was carrying the pistol hoping to get a shot at a coyote. Maybe it was a Remington XP-100 with the Walker trigger in it. They kill people by accident, too.

Some people just don't want to know. And, of course if they don't want to know, they sure don't want to pass critical information on to others and become teachers, either. I still wonder who inherited that gun and do they also hope to see a coyote... or did they just sell it.

What is the solution? What I've heard sure concerns me.

There's not just one solution. It's a complicated problem with multiple solutions. Education has to be first.

What are you going to do, sentence people to listen to you?

Now there's an idea! I guess repeat offenders have to listen to Al Gore talk about pruning petunias.

I'm becoming a convert. Does that mean I can come and sit up front?

I would much rather you stay back there and help the others through the maze. I see you back there in animated conversations and hope you're gathering all your objections. We're about to get serious.

Education has to start with an *admission*. Not an admission of 'guilt' or 'responsibility' or even economic liability. Just tell the facts so shooters will know the *truth*. "Some of our guns have defects that could kill you or others" and then an explanation of the defects. A target shooter probably won't care. It doesn't apply to him. The vast majority are just hunters and shooters and people that enjoy guns.

So, you think if Remington put out a press release saying, 'Oops, our bad, 30 million bad guns so sad.' and it would be all over? That's naive!

It seems to me a better way would be for Remington to gather together the gun writers at one of the great outdoor clubs they use to sell their guns, and explain the situation to them instead. The factory service stations, jobbers, wholesalers and dealers should get packets of information *that is factual,* with fliers for customers to read at home. Walker triggers should have a *good* replacement available at no cost to the rifle owner. Nobody should have to give their personal information or the serial number of their gun to get their rifles fixed, either.

RCFC owners, including cops, should know the safety is only there to keep the *person* from shooting it, not the gun. It *can* shoot anytime. We have to take what is not common knowledge and make it commonly known.

What's the deal about not giving information. My gunsmith takes information on my other stuff, why not this?

The goal is *safety.* The goal is to change as many parts as possible so the shooting sports are as safe as possible. That can't be done with complications.

How do you know? Just tell them it's dangerous and send them in.

Ruger has been doing that since 1973 and more than half the affected guns have not been returned for the upgrade. I tell a lot of people that and it's a 'so what?' response. That's up to the people, right? Yes it is, but why not make it easy to be safe and not hard?

I'm not following that. Sorry.

I know at least one of those dark figures on the back row could explain it better than me. Anybody back there want to tell him why you still have an Old Model Blackhawk without the trigger transfer bar upgrade in it?

Would I have to talk in those stupid black letters?

No, I'll darken the first word and indent it so people know it's you without the thick accent. Tell your story and I'm pretty sure there will be comments. I know you.

> **I have** a .357 Blackhawk my brother bought just before he went to Vietnam. He only shot it six times and the next day he shipped out for a year. The two of us cleaned it together that night and put it back in the box and he told me to take care of it and we'd shoot it together when he got back. I was 14 at the time. He got killed over there and I'm still waiting to shoot it.

Excuse me sir....please! That is heartbreaking but I know all about the Ruger thing and they don't hurt the gun, you can't even see the upgrade. All the original parts are sent back and they sure don't tell anybody else about it.

> **Are** you as sure about that as I was about Remington triggers before I met this guy?

> **Who** says NSA or some other alphabet agency hasn't installed a bug that downloads that information as it comes in the door? How about some 'Plumber bunch' shows up late one evening and steals the information? What happens if somebody steals the gun from the mail? The mail, UPS and FedX guys know there are dozens of nice guns a day going in and out of there. Snag one going in to be fixed and by the time it's missed it'll be snuggled up with those Fast and Furious guns down in the cartel's warehouse across the border.

> **Why** should I risk everything for an upgrade I'm not going to ever use. My brother is not coming back to shoot it with me and I'm not going to shoot it without him. I consider it a family heirloom but it has no real collector's value.

> **Also,** just in case you think my objection is only risking an heirloom, I have a half dozen other old Model Ruger's that I shoot quite regularly. They won't get 'repaired' for exactly

the same reasons as above. I load five and the hammer is on an empty chamber. Thanks to our speaker, I don't risk my great trigger by putting it on half cock, either. Call me paranoid or whatever you want, but once a gun goes to my house it stays there and it's nobody's business but mine.

I think that summed it up quite well!

I join in the applause.

So, when are you going to tell us your ideas? How do you get the word out? How do you change 200 years of history and what you called semi-instinctive use of a firearm? Do you think suddenly it'll be common knowledge that some guns are more dangerous than normal and get people to follow different rules just because of what I must say you've shown pretty convincingly to me is the reality of gun designs?

Education has to be offered to every gunsmith, hunter safety instructor, NRA instructor, camp counselor and scout leader. The teaching of guns has to include the failures. Otherwise 'be careful' doesn't carry the same weight.

What do you do about the weekend gun trader that has a whole bunch of affected guns? He's stuck with a reduction in value, isn't he?

That affects everyone equally. Right now, Model 700s are being devalued on the used market if they have a factory trigger. The goal should be to get a premium for a rifle with a good trigger.

So, you want to just scrap the Ten Commandments of GS and blame it all on the guns?

The TCGS is right dead on the money in its goal of firearms safety but they're written as a release of liability, not as education for shooters. Rewrite them so the Ten Commandments you want shooters to learn and remember are the same. Right now there are at least three versions.

So, you don't think personal responsibility plays a role in these

accidents.

You bring up a very good point. I've seen jury members that were strict believers in, "If you're holding it, it's *your fault*." Most of the time those jury members wouldn't award a dime if the president of the gun company demonstrated the defect on the witness stand. That is their position, period.

Courts don't care much for analogies. You're supposed to be able to say what's needed without comparison to something not in evidence, but this is my 'courtroom' and I'm making the rules so a short story will work for illustration purposes.

I bought a brand new SUV as a sales truck many years ago. It was the first new vehicle I'd had in 30 years and felt good to be in something dependable. My sales area covered six states and my accounts were remote mines, construction projects and mills of various sorts. The first week I had it, the thing failed to start at a remote phone booth up on the Yankee Fork of the Salmon. Since cell phones were still way in the future, it was fortuitous I was stranded where I was, near the phone with crackers and cold drinks. The dealer sent a mechanic from Boise which took 4 hours and he needed a wrecker which took six more hours and I missed two days of sales calls while the dealer said nothing was wrong with it. The mechanic turned the key and it started when it came off the wrecker hook. I had lights but no starter rotation at all just hours before and the mechanic saw it broken. How can there be nothing wrong with it? Do Japanese trucks heal themselves?

The dealer sent me on my way with no further looking. The following week it broke down in the last town in the lower 48 without telephones. The Yellowpine General store had a two way radio that could talk to whatever Arnold Aviation bush plane might be flying. Then the pilot could relay a phone call of sorts. That finally happened the next morning. They said they'd send a mechanic. I told them to be sure he was driving a wrecker. He should have been there by late afternoon... but he wasn't. The next morning I found out the wrecker had blown an engine on the hill out of Horseshoe Bend and they were towing it back to Boise that day. "We'll come get you tomorrow."

Needless to say, I had another sales truck within an hour of getting back to town three days later!! I made them take it back because it was not *dependable*. I had lost trust in something that should have been predictably good enough for my purpose. It wasn't. For those curious, it was a nut inside the flywheel housing. Sometimes it would land just right to lock up the flywheel. It took them a good while to find it.

Is there a point?

Maybe a dull point, we'll see.

Trust in a mechanism has to be earned. Gun companies are no different. We have the big ones that have been around forever and we trust them to give us a good product. Their old calendars stress that: Meeting a bear on a snowy cliff-side trail with his trusty Remington Model 8...or Winchester Model '94, or Marlin Model '95 or Savage Model '99. They all used the same theme time after time to reinforce *dependability* of their product. Gun companies still like to send the message: *We can save your life.* Pick up a home defense oriented magazine and read the ads. The bears are a little different and the snowy trail around the mountain cliff is now your bedroom hall with a shadow at the end. The message is the same: Trust us.

Well, what do you do when not only do you see an utter disregard for that trust, but an active campaign to perpetuate the trust while continuing to literally put people, a sport, and a way of life at risk?

What did you do?

I marveled at what I didn't know and tried to catch up. I agonized over answering really tough questions, and not just from opposing attorneys that took me by surprise. It was the questions I had of my role in it all that were tough. I dearly love guns. They are my life. What happens when the lie can no longer be supported? What happens if a concentrated, social effort, like no smoking and anti SUV sentiments, were to be applied to guns? It was looking very serious in the mid '90s when it seemed every effort of the government seemed to be, "For the children."

During that time, I was hired by a lawyer in Madison, Wisconsin to investigate a shooting. He represented the insurance of somebody. I'm still not sure who, but I went up there and surveyed a home rifle range. Its' not quite like mine with a five mile buffer around it and most of that buffer is visible. He had trees on his range in Wisconsin. There were lots of 4 to 6 inch hardwoods on a steep sided hill with a paved county road running parallel to the range and steeply down hill from it. He could get 200 yards range but the trees in the narrow gap had a lot of damage from bullet strikes.

Two young men were headed to a golf course on a paved county road on a Saturday morning. The passenger had his elbow out the window and they were talking about something. They'd only been driving a mile from home when a bullet came through the windshield and broke the passenger's right upper arm. He nearly bled to death, but survived with nerve damage to his dominant arm. It was a major injury.

The question was not just 'did that guy's bullet break the man's arm'? I was hired to find that answer and it was easy! There were bullets in the rain gutter of a barn 300 yards further down range from where the guy was shot. A lot of bullets had been going that way. One hit somebody and it caused a serious injury and a public firestorm. The bigger and much more troubling question was whether the county was going to outlaw centerfire rifles to be used for hunting within two miles of any road that carried a school bus. The lawyer and I went to the sheriff's office to chat with the guys.

Cops are the same all over and once part of the fraternity of 'sanitation workers', the language is the same, but that cold afternoon was hilarious with a clash of accents but common stories. I had just testified in a county commission meeting about shooting along the Snake River canyon rims and the situation in Wisconsin and Idaho were strikingly similar. In both cases, an accidental shooting brought a kneejerk, "get them away from here!" reaction. I told the deputies that were writing a follow up report that education is really the key. In Twin Falls County, it was the posting of simple notices at ammo dealers reminding shooters to not shoot anything but 'varmint' bullets with a backstop rock behind the target and no rimfires within 300 yards of the canyon rim. In Wisconsin, just tell hunters their stand has to be situated so they're shooting away from the road.

You're right about a dull point, anyway.

Surprise! We're not even there yet.

Not too long after the Wisconsin tragedy, somebody dropped an XP-100 out of a tree stand and it killed him. The long and odd linkages that connect that Walker trigger to the actual trigger meant it was pretty much meant to fail sooner or later. The engineers got to work that one more than me. Then a kid had an FSR on a deer stand in Kansas and scared him so bad he fell out of the tree and broke an arm, and then a rumor of a guy in California or maybe Arizona that shot a tan pickup truck going slow on a woods road and blamed it on an FSR. Well, weren't you going to shoot it anyway? You were aiming at it and then took the safety off, right?

All those together set my teeth on edge thinking about what mischief could be gathered up against hunting close to where other people are. It's a matter of *trust*. Not so much trust in our guns, but in our neighbor's guns, too. Most states now have 'short range' deer hunts to limit high powered rifles. What happens when the limit is two miles from a house or two miles from a school bus route. What then?

My favorite deer stand as a kid was about 80 yards from a very rural, all black church. That old, unpainted frame building was turned into a massive, thumping, hallelujah hall with stomping and hootin' and praising and dinner on the grounds all day on Sundays. I parked my jeep near their road that led into the church and some would holler 'good mawnin!' at me sitting huddled on a big oak limb watching the gas line right of way for deer and turkeys just out of their sight. They didn't mind. They didn't even mind when my first 'custom' rifle, an old .303 Jungle Carbine would gather up some venison with a big boom during their singing 'n shouts.

There was the strangest thing, too.

I killed a fork-horned buck on the gas line before church started one morning and had just gotten the deer back to the jeep whole. Florida deer don't spoil on the first bounce like western deer do and we seldom field dressed them in the woods. It was a small deer but they weren't easy to carry for a scrawny kid and I was blowing and leaning on my jeep when the pastor came by in his charcoal and pink '57 Mercury wearing the shiniest black suit of clothes I've ever seen in my life. I thought it was patent leather at first, but he said it was shark skin. It was *not* camouflaged. Anyhow, at that time in the south there was a certain deference by the rural folks to anyone white. The preacher stopped his car and came out with his Cadillac suit shining in the early Sunday sunshine and hemmed and hawed a little and talked about the weather and kept glancing back down the road.

Then, he asked me very politely to wait on one of the brethren if I would, please, because his wife was sick and needed a deer spleen and brain if I'd be so kind as give 'em up? I was 16 years old and that just about did me in. A what? He said they'd take up a collection for me. I guess he thought I was playing for getting paid. No way! I was just trying to figure out how to help him out without messing up that black & chrome suit... and where do I find the spleen? It was several minutes before a certain young man came by and stared bug-eyed at the deer. He was right back on the run when the preacher told him I was waiting on him.

He had on what my dad called 'ice cream britches', real lightweight, cool, wrinkled looking stuff the color of a slice of lime. I told him he could have whatever he needed just tell me when I got to it. He said, "Naw suh! I'll do it if you don' mind." and jerked a hawk-bill linoleum knife out of his rear pocket like a rattlesnake striking. It was open and in the middle of my deer before I could get out of the way. I've never seen the likes of it before or since, either. He field dressed that deer wearing a white dress shirt and bright lime pants without getting a drop of blood on either and he did it so fast all I could do was marvel. He worked at a packing house one time, he said.

It was only eight years later the same guy had neon red eyes in the dark corner of a juke joint after 'field dressing' somebody he had a beef with. He recognized me and went along peacefully. He said his wife got well, too.

Is that the point?

Have you ever heard of a Kukri fighting knife? It has a wavy edge and it takes a while to get to the point. We need to be able to trust our guns. It won't be too long before a great weakness on our side of the argument will be used against us.

Sure, with your help!

The weakness is there. At least 30 million of them from just from one company, but that is the vast majority of the known 'bad' guns. That's reality and reality is sometimes a real bitch, but it sure is durable. We try to wish or pray it away or pretend reality isn't there, but it still is. We have a *real* problem and it's time to face it, fix it and then defend our decision to do so. It is time for *responsibility* so we don't lose the trust of those that will never understand what we see in firearms. They don't have the interest and so we are a mystery. But we are an even bigger mystery if we defend the wrong thing.

You say this is rare to have a gun fail, yet you say there are 30 million of them that will. Could you explain that?

Many years ago the National Shooting Sports Foundation put out a study that could be right. The biggest members of the NSSF are the largest ammo makers in the country too, and they should know. The study claimed the average use of a firearm in the U.S. Was a box of ammunition per year. That would mean 50 rounds for pistol and rimfire, 25 for shotguns and 20 for centerfire rifles. I'm not sure I buy it, but that's what the manufacturers published. If we take 7 million Walker triggers times an average of 20 rounds a year with an expected life of 100 years, there are many, many millions of chances for something to go terribly wrong. The minutes of a meeting of the safety committee at Remington said about 1% of the Walkers made up until that time, about two million of them, would fail each year. There was even talk of a recall but they decided to risk the twenty thousand accidents a year and hope they didn't hurt anybody. Now, there are about seven million Walkers, but some are 'safer' than others by improvement of the *features* but not by basic *design*.

The RCFC numbers are somewhere around 25 million in use and

on average, are said to be shot 25 rounds a year. The fact is, a Remington gun is more likely to wear out, become lost in a house fire, or sunk in a river and *never* fail, than to fire without the shooter's control. The point though is, it *could* fail the first time it's shot. Remember the young man squirrel hunting? He never got the chance to wear out his new shotgun, but I saw a skeet shooter take the barrel off an 1100 and throw the rest of it in a trash barrel because "It was wore out."

But, the TCGS says don't trust the safety or mechanics because they break.

That brings us back to 'fail safe'. A gun that fails should fail *to* shoot, not shoot uncontrolled by a person. If a part breaks and the gun fires, it means the trigger mechanism wasn't properly designed. The old model Ruger Blackhawk's design was changed to prevent a broken part from being the causation of a shooting. Being a firearm, every part on it should break or wear out before the safety of the gun is compromised.

I don't see how the manufactures can come up with that many ways to make guns safe.

They can't as long as the 'we are the one' attitude continues and everybody has to have something different because patents and feelings and company pride is hurt if a good idea is copied. The patent laws are not friendly to safety features. Many companies defend patents that I see as patently stupid, and some companies spend millions on parsing words to an extent absolutely amazing to behold.

It sounds you're blaming Winchester for not sharing the Model 70 trigger with the world?

'Blaming'? No. I'm not sure I wouldn't sit in a tree stand and ambush the one trying to steal the Model 70 trigger if it was my idea. That is also human nature. I blame the cheapskates that wouldn't pay to use it. I'm also pointing out the facts as they stare us in the face: We're too cheap to buy good guns because nobody is forcing guns to be good and nobody is telling us when they're bad. That is a sad state of affairs!

Oh, so you want a 'proof house' like Europe to force guns to a certain standard?

That won't work either. SAAMI is doing a good job on standards and we don't need another layer of bureaucrats fingering our guns.

What then?

Self regulation and communications. Shooters need to *know* what guns to *particularly* watch out for. There needs to be a clearing house of information that keeps track of who has had what problem.

Isn't that the level of bureaucrats you're not in favor of?

You could be right. The government sure can't be near it.

If you walk into the truck shops and gold mills of the big mines or any big business, the bulletin board is full of safety warnings with crude drawings of how somebody got killed or injured on the job. It helped me be careful! Just like the old Ohio Safety films that showed the real gore of car wrecks in the eighth grade made me think when going too fast. Not think enough to make me stop, maybe, but at least think about it. At least I knew the possibilities. I could assess my own risk. Shooters should have that same *choice*.

What would be the first one you'd say was most dangerous to shoot?

A lawyer question again from the back row? Good!

I was told before my first deposition to always hear the whole question before starting to form an answer. That's a good example of a sneaky question.

I can only speak for what I've heard or know of to be true. The first ones that scare me enough to *not* shoot them would be the Vulcan .50 BMG and the Lorcin 9mm pistol. Both those guns can kill or hurt you bad by shooting them.

Why not Remington? You've been square on top of them and criticizing everything they make for what seems like a week.

I know of not one single, solitary Remington that is 'dangerous to shoot'. They had some terrible shotgun barrels one time, but I assume those have been bent double and hammered flat by now because they were blowing people's fingers off.

No? Those barrels weren't recalled? Oh yeah, they paid people a few bucks for them but didn't take them back. That won't save any fingers, but maybe that wasn't the intention. Well, I can't use any absolutes, then. I'd be cautious around all their shotguns until I figured out what barrels were made from high sulfur steel that caused the sides to blow out of some of them. Otherwise, Remington's are certainly safe to shoot..... Wait a minute, now. There was another cheap plastic .22 auto, the Model 597 that blinded people, too. Then I heard of another model I haven't seen yet... maybe we need a clearing house for me! I don't know what problems might be out there lying in wait.

Well, what's those other two you named? I've never heard of them.

The Vulcan was somebody's idea of an easy to make monster gun that is great fun to shoot, but a tad impractical and scary to the masses. It shoots the .50 BMG round.

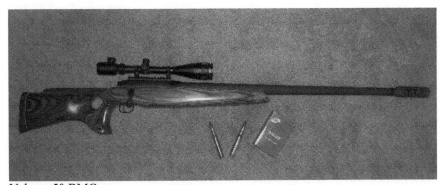

Vulcan .50 BMG

The 'engineering' errors would have resulted in the death penalty in China. The Vulcan uses a rotary breach bolt with interrupted threads to make it a turn to lock and unlock breeching system, but the threads are vee form threads like you'd find on a hardware store bolt. With very little shooting, excessive headspace develops and then the breech bolt blows out of the action and it does vast amounts of damage to the guy's head behind it. It was *designed to fail* very quickly, and it does. Great machinists don't necessarily know how a gun should be made. Some engineers have the same problem.

The Lorcin pistol and its clones like the Talon are made from the cheapest of alloys and have a stress riser in the ejection port that has failed in as few as nine rounds. It breaks the slide half in two through the ejection port. The rear half usually impacts the shooter just below the right eye. I haven't heard of any deaths from it, but I would imagine it installs a flinch that's very hard to get rid of. I don't want to aim one of them if it's loaded.

So, what do you do about it? You can't have people patrolling retailers warning about dangerous guns.

You encourage, through customer pressure, the manufacturers to speak up! Don't hide behind their Constitutional exceptions just for a profit. *Responsibility* goes both ways. Remember that guns are designed and manufactured to work. That's dependability. They should never fail to work but sometimes they do.

They should never fail to be secure, *by design.*

After several hours of some kind of hearing in Federal Court, and listening to the totally ridiculous argument that since the Model 600 trigger was different than a Model 700 trigger because they only use one part in common, the plaintiff could not use instances of failure in one to show the common defect in the other, I was frustrated with lawyers of all stripes. *Both* are Walker triggers. It makes no difference what they look like! But many times the judge goes along with totally ridiculous arguments that further muddy up the record of mechanical facts.

I told the lawyer that night after shuffling more stacks of documents that Remington seemed to think they owned a pet store instead of a gun company. They seemed to think guns are puppies and some grow up to be mean. It wasn't their fault of course. Upbringing, environment, treatment and such would affect that more than where the puppy came from. No way could they be at fault, especially since they told those people to be careful. All puppies have teeth...

Guns are sometimes unduly dangerous because somebody decided to risk other people's lives and health for additional profit, by either deleting a safety feature, or just not having enough experience with firearms to know that what they were deleting was very important. People's lives depend on it. When the inevitable happens and somebody is killed or maimed, and they are sued for the bad design, they deny the design is at fault. Then, historically, they raise the price to cover the additional insurance. And raise production to put more mistakes out on the street, and we pay for it. If a customer asked what the deal is with the bad publicity and TV programs that show the same familiar failure actually happening, they are lied to and misdirected without discussing the mechanical facts seen in the mechanism.

Then Remington has the gall to blame their customers for being careless with a gun they know has a 60 year history of failure. Who but a feckless corporation would instruct an employee to tell a grieving mother her dead son was the imperfect one instead of their gun. It's the same gun that the same company had to drill a hole in to make it less likely to fail, but it's still dangerous *by design*.

 And then the heart breaker is that the customers of the maker of demonstrably faulty guns will defend them at all cost and without any knowledge beyond what they hear from others... that don't know the facts, either. It should be past time that people start looking at the jobs guns are *designed* to do and to offer a correction if they don't, but most of all offer an explanation so your customers know.

The Walker Explanation was published several years ago. That has stood the test of peer review and has had plenty of time for critical review. It's in the record. Remington knows for sure how the Walker trigger works and how it fails and how to fix it. Yet, the continuing focus has been on discrediting the messengers without confirming or acknowledging the defects.

Of course not, that would open them up to every plaintiff's lawyer that wanted a piece of the pie. It would be 'Big Tobacco' all over again. Once a company admits fault, their tender parts are exposed and bankruptcy usually follows.

Let's talk about that some in the next chapter.

20. The Liability Tripod

The tripod of liability is defective design, defect in materials or workmanship, and failure to warn of a defect.

Defects in a product don't necessarily mean it's dangerous of course. Sometimes a product just doesn't work and it's not worth fixing. Defects that affect the safety, health and well being of the customer and those around him are much more serious.

In many guns, not just Remington's by any stretch, there are one or more dangerous conditions that are not addressed correctly or sufficiently to maintain the degree of safety that *should be* present in firearms. Remember the analogy that works best with guns also applies to airplanes. Both can injure or kill the operator, people around him and people miles from where the failure occurs. Guns in the class of firearms referred to in the early chapters as 'cocked' or 'kinetic' while loaded, are just like a plane flying above the ground. Gravity and springs acting like gravity are always working to bring them both to parity.

Walther PPS (left) and PPK (right)

Who says what is acceptable?

We do! The shooting public, the people on the ranges and in the old gravel pits plinking and having fun, the guy on the hunt of a lifetime with horses and tents and guides and yellow Aspens, with a taxidermist on retainer, and the kids in the barn lot shooting rats and in the woodlots shooting rabbits and squirrels. Who says we have to accept mediocrity, especially at the prices being charged? Do the guns above look like equal value to you? Both wear the same name and both are DA pistols but they were born 10 years apart.

I don't see where prices are out of range for what we get.

Compare a $300 hydraulic pump with a $600 rifle or shotgun, both made in the USA, and both made just last week. Look at the machining and the tolerances, the fits, the finishes and the materials. Do you see the pricing structure is reversed when you compare actual values? The hydraulic pump is easily worth double the plastic, sheet metal and aluminum, rattling collection of mismatched parts that make up a new pump shotgun. What do you think would happen if that hydraulic pump stuck a part of itself in an operator's chest? Would those machines and people using those valves be warned, or does the company hope just that one failed and maybe if it fails again nobody will get hurt. Sure, their own tests showed the defect, and a bunch of customers said they lost that one part. Can the maker of the hydraulic part bet on an injury not happening again? Will they?

We shooters have been told to be careful. We've been told that it's impossible for a shooting accident to occur if we follow the Ten Commandments. Isn't it also impossible to obey the Ten Commandments of Gun Safety as written? Go through them one by one and see what the lawyers have done to us. How much of a stretch is it to believe that a company just denies the failures occur. Thousands of letters of complaint and notification of failures say exactly that, "Unable to duplicate customer's complaint." It is striking to read stacks and stacks of official response letters that all say essentially, "We never heard of such a thing." Those letters of ignorance of product malfunctions in basic safety spans many years and answer exactly the same specific complaints over and over again as having no knowledge of it happening... You must have pulled the trigger. You didn't actually see what you think you saw. No way! We can't duplicate it, therefore you, the customer are wrong.

That makes no sense to me. Sorry.

You're not alone. Why not look for what caused the failure and believe the customer that observed it? I know Remington engineers. They are *not* that dumb!

Let's look at the market situation after WW-II. There weren't many hunting rifles around and those being made were being sold as fast as they could leave the factory. The economics of the situation said to take a chance. Sell the guns then worry about it later. Nobody was watching anyway. The guns shot great! All the magazine articles said so.

Remington knew in early 1947 the Walker trigger was defective because Walker told them so and yet they continue to this day to lie about a mechanical fact that can be explained. We've done it here today.

Why not just recall the bad triggers and be done?

The great outdoor writer, Robert Ruark, describer of the Mau Mau uprising in E. Africa used an old African proverb as the basis of a book, "If a man does away with his traditional way of living and throws away his good customs, he had better first make certain that he has something of value to replace them."

Recalls are something very rare in firearms. Legally, they can't be recalled as a mandatory thing, but many times it is a legal decision that dictates the terms of a notification or alert. The first question concerning the Remington Common Fire Controls and Walker rifle triggers should be: What are you going to replace them with and how? I wouldn't want the XMP as currently manufactured. There are many shooters that know the Walker is defective and believe the XMP is the safer alternative. Now, the factory says the 'good' trigger is 'bad' and the 'bad' trigger is ignored.

In fact, Remington has recalled the XMP voluntarily as we discussed in a previous chapter. They say the recall concerns a defect in workmanship. Let's take that at face value and accept the 'excess sealant' reason given. Does that mean the sealant is out of specifications? Is there too little or too much? What effect does it have on the trigger? How is that different than the epoxy paint overspray on the RCFCs? They haven't been recalled or anything said about them and the numbers are many times greater than the XMP triggers in use. Was it the labor force that screwed up or the engineers? Nobody seems curious enough to ask. We've all seen the YouTube 'proof' of failures in XMP triggers but none are credible as shown. What is offered as *proof* is only *evidence* of an extremely dangerous rifle. No effort has been made to determine *why* they fail. I 'm still trying to buy a bad one to find out why it fails for myself. I can well understand how an XMP trigger fails as shown online, but the adjustments can't remain sealed when doing it.

Defects in materials and workmanship include the materials specified in construction. If a company saves money with cheap steel, as Remington did in the big batch of shotgun barrels made of dangerously high sulfur steels, but then decided to use it anyway, the lawyers are sure to come calling when the sides start blowing out of the shotguns. It is a testament of the corporate lawyer's expertise and effectiveness that very few people know the truth about those barrels. Many Remington gun owners got a check instead of a new barrel, but the check wasn't enough to buy a new barrel. Let's assume for a minute you are part of a really good family and got a new Remington Model 870 for Christmas, and somebody must have told somebody because you get a letter about a bad barrel and an offer to receive a small check to just forget about it. You know lawyers and details... Hey! Free shotgun and a check for twenty bucks, too? Good deal...until it blows off a few fingers! The fine print has the details of course. Any lawyer can point to the page and paragraph that explains what money you've already received for your fingers. Tough luck! How about if you loan it to your best friend? Are you going to send him a check for about twenty bucks and not require he replace the barrel?

In the Winchester shotgun case in Arizona, it was a part listed in the catalog as costing $2.30 but it had the same amount of plastic as a ball point pen costing a dime. We didn't find out what kind of plastic the gun part was made of. Was it the plastic the blueprint called for? Or, something that cost a tenth of a cent less but becomes brittle in the presence of hydrocarbons like gun oil? I presume a check was written and that information was buried forever. Not even those that sent in their warranty card got new parts or notification of a bad one. Economics took the drivers seat and the case went away.

The bigger question is always *why*? The same company that took back the Model 11 and told their customers the Model 100 was unsafe to shoot doesn't say a word about a part breaking that causes an uncontrolled discharge in a shotgun? Why not? Could it be that nobody is watching? Maybe it's cheaper to just take the chance. You've already been told to be careful. Don't point a gun at anything you don't want shot.

Defects in parts are not the big problem. H&R had a quantity of firing pins too long for the M58 shotguns. Nobody knows how many bad firing pins were installed but you can bet there have been very few replaced. Some of those guns can fire if the butt hits the ground too hard. We have to accept they are out there and put that on our gunsmith's list of things to check during a 'Clean, Oil, and Safety Check' which is a major part of any gun repair shop's business. Changing a firing pin is a three minute job on those guns. It takes no disassembly to do and a two dollar part. It certainly should be done in the guns that need it. I'll bet every customer that sees the problem and understands why it's important to change firing pins will spring for the ten bucks or so that makes it one of the few profitable jobs in the shop. Isn't that just like changing valves stems when changing tires?

In the case of Winchester not being able to come up with a replacement firing pin for the Model 100 and declaring them as 'unsafe to use' instead, that situation was taken care of when an aftermarket company came up with a better firing pin that 'fixed' the guns. Unfortunately, there are not replacement barrels for the bad Remingtons unless you want another Remington. Who do you trust?

Defective design is what this book is about and hopefully by now everyone here has as sense of how far and wide defective designs have spread and how hard it will be to un-ring the bell we've heard all our lives... Guns don't kill people, people kill people. The seemingly immaculate reputation of guns only shooting by pulling the trigger is so instilled in our very being by education and well meaning instructions it will be a generation or more before 'Remington stories' will be believed and confirmed by investigations. Until then, it is up to us, the mechanics and the interested to spread the word.

Last week, two young teenaged boys were killed by a pistol in Utah. The pistol was one of four stolen from the kinfolks of another boy that was part of the group. They were 'playing' with the guns when one fired and killed one of the boys. As the others ran for help, the boy holding the gun when it 'just went off' shot himself. I won't name the gun, but it advertises a light DA pull. That is a 'defect in design' for the next hundred years that we'll have to live with.

Will the '15 pound rule' be recognized as valid for safety? That 'genie' is too big for the bottle because everybody shoots better in DA mode with a light trigger pull. Nobody asked why it wasn't done with the P-38 75 years ago. They think somebody is a genius for inventing such a gun and never think about how easy it is just to change the rules. Nobody is watching. When a gun shoots accurately it gets a good reputation no matter how 'bad' the safety features may be.

Design defects as we see in the Walker and the RCFC and the Mossberg 500 plastic series and the Vulcan .50 and Lorcin pistol problems should be publicized enough to let the public know you can *not* sling around some guns as seen in the movies (and real life among the idiots.) Guns are *not* to be trusted until you know they deserve it. *Look* at it really close. Murphy hides in strange places.

Is there anything not clear so far about the first two legs of liability?

I'm still not clear where the X-Mark Pro trigger falls in all this.

Me neither. Remington says there's excess sealant and it's easy to see many triggers have been slobbered over with it. That is a defect in workmanship if the amount of sealant was called out in the print and some triggers have too much. Is it safety related?

I think the sealant reason is bogus. I have personally seen XMP triggers that are broken as a direct result of bad material *in the trigger piece*. Remington has to know they are failing prematurely, but since they've told nearly a million shooters the triggers need attention from the factory, that could mean they have fulfilled the 'warning' part of the tripod, but count on very few guns being returned. If so, they saved themselves a whole bunch of money and waved off the lawyers, too.

I'm not sure I follow that reasoning. Could you clarify?

Product liability law says the company has to warn the customer of an unsafe condition in their product. Remember the toasters in the Ozarks? If a toaster is going to start spitting sparks and setting houses on fire just by trying to toast bread, those toasters have to be traced down and the customer's notified. We see it in toys and appliances and car seats and all sorts of things, but not with guns. Seriously, no one is watching!

A toaster is unlikely to be passed down from father to son to grandson, and all three of them treasure it beyond just utility. Guns are much like pocket watches and baby dishes. They're more often worth way beyond their commercial value in sentiment. That has changed some due to the serious decline in quality of guns, and the multigenerational guns are mostly gone now, unless you spend big bucks on an old one. The reality is that just like cheap toasters, guns sometimes hurt people and they have many more chances to do so because they live so long.

You say customers aren't notified of dangerous guns. Why not?

First is the issue of warranty cards included with every new gun. I've never sent one in, which on its own seems like the worst in anecdotal evidence because I don't buy new guns, but let me add something to that. I have never, in fifty years of gun trading, ever run across a gun being traded back in to me that had the warranty card missing. The warranty card has always been more of a collector thing than a useable tool for the gun owner. The long and short of warranty cards is that gun customers usually don't want to advertise what they have to *any*body. The difficulty in getting the news out to new gun customers is considerable. To 'recall' used guns by records of any kind is impossible unless you make slaves out of the keepers of the records. I know of one shop with more than 200,000 gun sales records. Who pays the clerks to sort out the bad ones and contact the owners?

That leaves only the popular press and word of mouth to spread the word. Can we look at history as an example of how that has worked out? We've come right back to coined safety cams, lawyer triggers and "the lawyers are picking on us!" as possible 'solutions' to unduly dangerous guns. I think it's clear the dangerous *designs* have to be addressed so that shooters understand what is being talked about, otherwise ignorance will eventually erode our position in the minds of shooters. Right now, we can not trust the gun companies to do what is right. We cannot afford to lose the trust of the public as shooters because we defend the indefensible, either. We *must* educate ourselves and depend on spreading good information to defend what we love.

What kind of 'warnings' should be forthcoming?

That's a great question. Who do we trust to give a warning? Who might understand all the legalese likely to be a part of such a warning? If instruction manuals are any indication of what a warning will be, not many will bother to read it. It will be what is said in response to any recall or advisory that will determine how effective it is. The gun writers will read the warnings and report the reasons for them, or they will (again) protect the advertisers and declare the people that use guns as being responsible for what the factory did wrong. Some people just don't want to know. It is a shame that it is those people, the people that would rather not confront the truth that write what the rest of us learn from. The process of delivering information through the popular press took a dive after the War, too.

I'm still unclear on the XMP thing. I think that is the #1 issue in the gun world that has people choosing sides and setting up their defenses. I'll ask you the question... Who should we believe?

You have to believe in your self or choose an advocate, one or the other. We can look at the design of the XMP and we see the safety, *by design,* resets the trigger to the proper position under the sear every time it's applied if the triggers return springs should fail. So, how can it FSR?

You're the expert. How?

If the safety block is properly adjusted so the trigger actually is pushed back to the proper position, and the trigger and sear have the proper overlap and geometry, *and* the critical rear corner of the trigger that supports the sear is not broken, we can conclude FSR didn't happen as a *defect* in the trigger.

I don't see that. The rifle clearly fires in the video.

Yes it does. That is a fact we have to live with and account for. What made it fire? It fired when the safety was pushed forward, right? Doesn't that mean the safety cam was supporting the sear? That means the trigger wasn't under the sear where it was supposed to be. The fact also that the gun doesn't always FSR means the trigger is *sometimes* under the sear and *sometimes* not. Those facts in evidence point to an uncertainty in a mechanism designed to be certain. That means there could be a mistake in materials or workmanship that is to blame. We're just following the process of deduction.

Now, look at the trigger and sear. Are they broken? If not, the only answer left in the trigger assembly is in the adjustments of it. If it's not in the adjustments, it has to be in the gun instead of the trigger mechanism. It's reality. The gun fired. There IS a reason for it. Find it!

I can predict what that YouTube trigger will look like when it's examined. It's typical of 'gunsmiths' that have no clue what the screws do, but they must be there to 'adjust' something so they twist and find out. To duplicate the failure seen on YouTube, the sear screw would have to be turned in so much that the sear and trigger have only point to point contact. The trigger would be *too* light that way, so the return springs would be compressed more by turning their screws inward. That sometimes makes a very nice 3 lb trigger, but the safety won't work! But, there's that screw kind of hidden in the front recess. Turn it out until the safety works and, SHAZAM!, an unbelievably crisp, light pull on a trigger the factory says should be 4#. Some even charge money to do that!

Ah, sir. How else do you adjust a trigger?

First of all, we go back to Mr. Mauser's 'rule of thumb', half friction, half spring. The above trigger will trip at less than an ounce if the return springs are totally relaxed. The amount of friction is likely to change as the corner of the trigger continues to flake off, too. The trigger is *un*predictable, exactly as shown in the video and it is just as dangerous as some of the 'sniper rifles' in many police departments.

Is there a way to determine what you say is true without taking the gun apart and looking at it?

The critical dimension is between the trigger corner and the sear step. The rifle's stock has to be removed to see it. That critical overlap will have been adjusted much less than the specified .018' to .025" to reproduce the failure we see on the internet. Of course that overlap may have been reduced by breakage of the trigger, too. You cannot take the XMP trigger apart without wrecking two fasteners so the geometry and surface conditions can't be easily seen.

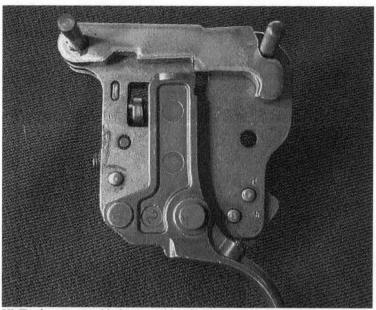

XMP trigger assembled on outside of housing with Walker sear

Here's one in profile arranged on the outside of the housing to see the trigger-sear relationship. This is seen with a Walker sear.

I see that angle you talked about.

This trigger was thrown away because the corner was showing degradation of the surfaces and the customer decided not to trust a Remington trigger.

It looks to me like this a good place to just resurface the trigger. It's not that bad and it should sharpen right up.

Ask yourself why did it fail the first time? If a trigger breaks it's too brittle, if it bends it's too soft. You're not going to improve MIM material no matter what you do to it. What happens when the whole corner breaks as the safety is flipped OFF and the load of the firing pin is put on the top of the trigger? How much of a bump can the cocking piece withstand if the trigger is prone to brittleness and breaking off? If the engineers paid to figure out what material to use in a trigger failed in their assignment, do you think it's a good idea to adjust it so that it takes more stress? I don't. Besides that, by taking some material off the top of the trigger you set up bad geometry. The sear has to go further down to reach the trigger. That puts additional pressure on the very front lip of the sear. Also, you have to consider what happens 'upstream' when geometries are changed. How much area does the cocking piece have in contact with the sear? There's not much to begin with. Don't reduce it by altering the trigger! That would make it dangerously defective by gunsmith.

The X-Mark Pro trigger design is a very good one, but a certain amount of precision has to be present. In this case it's not the machining and grinding of precision shapes and geometries that's important. That is done in MIM parts by forming the trigger in precision molds, but if the material can't take the forces and wear required of it, all the precise measurements make little difference. If the trigger fails, the rifle fails and it *fires* without control of the shooter. That makes it a defective rifle by definition and design, but that hasn't been determined by a jury.

Yet.

What do you mean, YET? You mean after a company totally redesigns a trigger you say is faulty and makes nearly a million of them, you come along and say it's still bad and they'll be sued for it?

The design is good, but the rifle is dangerous *if* the trigger is made of bad material. Just because it hasn't been held responsible eight years after introduction for a failure doesn't mean it won't fail. It will. There is nothing to prevent it, *by design.*

So, you hold them responsible for a piece of steel breaking?

Of course I do. The law does too. It's not like buying a tree from a nursery and a limb breaks off in a wind. Trees are that way. Some are weak and some are strong and neither you nor the nurseryman can tell the difference. Guns aren't that way. They are made from 'scratch' using mill certified metals which are then processed into gun parts. Many parts are farmed out to subcontractors and they're delivered sometimes by the drum full. If the material is 'bad' it is most certainly the fault of the maker the same as if you bought a tire with inferior rubber or an ax that shattered while chopping wood.

Well, you say the XMP is a good design, yet you say it can fail. How do you reconcile those differences?

The XMP is a good design. It's not a perfect design. First off, any override trigger will fire on safety release if the trigger is being held as the safety is released.

Whoa now! You've been calling FSR a most dangerous event and the gun's fault all this time. You can't change now.

It's clear the design failures are still not well understood. Let's go back and fill in more background and then add some details.

Nothing is changing when I say most rifles will FSR if the trigger is pulled when the safety is switched to OFF. FSR is a very dangerous condition that can be readily created by just moving the trigger out of the way before removing the safety. What prevents FSR if the shooter is pulling the trigger and taking the safety off at the same time? The answer is nothing in most guns. That is the way they operate and it's analogous to flooring the accelerator and then shifting into gear.

So, why not fix it? Is it that complicated? My truck won't let me shift into gear unless the brake pedal is depressed. Isn't it the same thing?

Complicated? Not particularly, but many shooters just will not tolerate a disconnector or interlock. The disconnector will not allow the relaxation of the main spring for storage. Most shooters don't want to store a gun 'under tension' so they relieve that compression by pulling the trigger and closing the bolt at the same time and creating a 'follow down'. Then the rifle is at rest. Shotguns can use 'snap caps' or simply a fired empty to allow them to be relaxed in storage.

"Same thing" would mean an interlock switch or mechanism that demands the trigger not be pulled *as* the safety is released. That feature has been suggested for decades, but they're still rare. A trigger system that would allow a follow down by design but prevent FSR seems to be a good idea.

I always follow down my bolt action rifle, but I've seen a lot of people store bolt actions with the bolt open and that means the mainspring is compressed.

Relaxing springs results in guns lasting much longer so I do it, too. *But,* watch out for the Walker triggers under those conditions.

Now what?

When a Walker trigger is stored with the firing pin 'down' and the springs relaxed, the connector is not being held against the trigger body. The sear holds the connector slightly forward.

The gun is unloaded and in storage. Who cares?

You better care because long term storage hardens oil and allows WD-40 to turn to semi-glue. On the first few operations of the gun, it could very well fire on bolt opening, fire on bolt closing, or fire on safety release. They are especially dangerous after storage for that reason.

The 'storage failures' are more common on the stamped housing triggers and the double sear triggers.

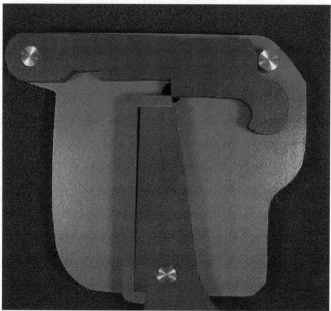

Connector position when rifle is stored with firing pin down. It's the same after a failed trick test. The difference is that after the trick test the gun is still cocked. It will fire when the safety is moved to OFF. After storage with springs relaxed, failures usually come soon after reactivation.

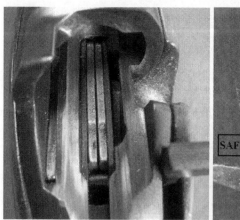

Early Double-Sear Walker

The what?

The first Walker triggers had two stamped metal sears side by side. All the model 721 and 722 rifles have this trigger. Economy was the goal and they already knew how to stamp out steel good enough for sears. One side is the sear and the other side is the safety. That means these particular Walker's only have half the sear engagement of a later M700. 'Half' means about .001 of a square inch and the contact patch is only on one side of the connector. The picture below shows the difference in (normal) connector wear at the sear contact patch.

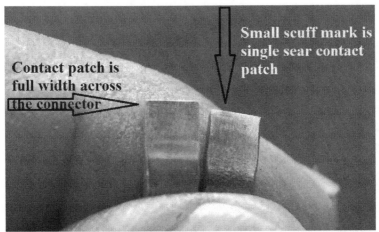

The eccentric forces on the top of the connector with half the contact area makes the two-piece-sear Walker trigger more hazardous than later single-piece sears

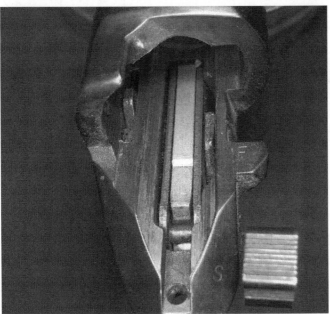

Single-piece MIM sear in a Model 600 Remington.

I'd still like to hear more about the XMP trigger. I've got one and

like it.

The X-Mark Pro incorporates the features Walker wanted for the trigger in 1947. He saw the weakness of the connector becoming displaced and designed a system working off the safety plate to assure replacement of the trigger when the safety is applied.

Of course that leaves the problem of shots between safety applications. Fire on Bolt Close, FBC, has always been a problem and it is worse if the bolt is operated fast and with lots of energy...like when the big buck needs another shot. Since the connector is separate from the trigger, any sort of recapture mechanism would be complicated because it would have to gather the connector and the trigger together and replace them under the sear on each cycle. That is a lot of linkage to keep dependable.

I need some clarifications of what you're talking about, please.

Of course, back to basic operations of the override trigger. There are two levers, one vertical 'trigger' pivoted in the middle and a horizontal 'sear' that is pivoted on one end. The trigger props up the sear but only a very thin part of their corners overlap.

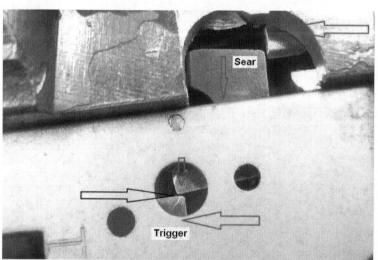

Simple Sako design showing lines of movement at contact patch (black arrow.)

In the Walker, there are *two* parts displaced when the trigger is pulled, the trigger and the connector. The trigger return spring pushes both parts back under the sear at each shot. Tom Butters has suggested a 'reset' or 'recapture' function that mechanically replaces the trigger under the sear instead of relying on just one or two return springs. You notice the XMP trigger has two trigger return springs and a mechanical reset on the safety which does positively reset the trigger as the safety is applied if the return springs should fail.

I can't think of a trigger that operates with a reset but it sure seems like a good idea.

It is a good idea and there have been some target triggers built that way, but usually on small bore rifles with frightfully light, multi lever triggers. The extra linkages and the need to link the bolt position with the trigger add enough hardware to affect accuracy, but I feel there are ways around it. The bottom line with any trigger system is *predictability*. It seems a contradiction, but the shooter should be surprised by the shot but never unpleasantly so. The key to accuracy is in trigger squeeze and a rifle that takes you by surprise means you were concentrating on the sights just perfectly. But a gun should *never* shoot without intention.

I think the XMP is a good trigger design. Remington incorporated Walker's original ideas and I recognize features deemed desirable by Tom Butters and myself and expressed in numerous depositions. That's not bragging about our prowess in trigger design as much as it is Remington finally showing some common sense and adopting features known for many years to be beneficial.

The features pointed out by Tom and me, like locator bosses to avoid tight places in the housing and positive reset of the trigger using additional leverage from the safety plate, should have been there to start with, had they been more concerned about how triggers are supposed to work to be safe instead of worried about every penny of manufacturing cost.

We can see with a cheap, cast Winchester trigger, economy is NOT the answer unless a company decides to put their customers *and the customer's neighbors* at risk of death. Winchester made great triggers for 25 years and then forgot how?

I've pointed out the mistake in geometry in the trigger angle of the

XMP trigger and have noted the MIM material has a very long history of protestations by engineers and advice to *not* use that formed metal for such an important part.

M70 cast trigger

Remington did it anyway, and now, after making nearly a million guns incorporating the 'safer' XMP design, I see signs that the triggers are breaking in use, presumably from bad material. The recall is for excess sealant that sure looks scary enough to be recallable, but is the real reason bad material or too much sealant? Is this considered a 'warning' under the law? I'm still not a lawyer. I don't know. One thing is plain though, you've been warned not to use an XMP trigger. If it fails without having been sent back to the factory, can you sue them? I kind of doubt it.

So, has Remington inoculated themselves against further law suits even though they have to know by now these triggers only last about 500 pulls before changing to the point of needing to be readjusted for more weight as the corner breaks off? If you return your rifle as part of the recall, what trigger goes back in it? Your trigger that hasn't yet started breaking, or a new 500 round trigger if it has? Should owners of these triggers be told how to detect when breakages are happening? Or, is it better to tell the customer his trigger needs to be cleaned? Does that cleaning take something that can't be bought at the auto parts store?

Who do you trust?

What should they replace the XMP with?

I predict the XMP actual trigger will be replaced with a trigger piece that is still MIM, its' too complicated to make otherwise, but it will have a hardened insert in the critical corner as the active searing surface. That is done by Browning and those triggers have given no trouble that I've heard of. I think Remington would be better served to adopt a center-leaf, two stage trigger much like is used on current Savage and Marlin rifles. If it's a good design, pay for the use of it!!

Wouldn't you be critical of a trigger that's glued together?

I sure would! A trigger should be approximately as hard and as tough as a power saw blade and any hardware store has those with carbide inserts soldered on. Expense can't be an argument, either. Some of the blades with 30 teeth are ten bucks, retail. Of course, carbide wouldn't be the material used, but the process is the same. Ask Browning, they've done it on the BBR for years.

Whatever the trigger design, it should be drop-in retrofittable and done in your local shop with same day return. The money involved in that sort of repair would break Remington Arms as it's now constituted. The blame for that would have to be placed squarely on the company that perpetuated the fraud on the public and then covered it up long enough to spin off the gun company and stick the future owners of it with nearly a billion dollars in liability. The law would have to change for that to happen, *or* the company would have to come clean with their customers. That part is up to them... and you.

I think the evidence is very clear and long lasting: DuPont used the exemptions of the U.S. Constitution's Second Amendment to cheapen Remington guns to the point of being dangerous, and then denied fault and liability when that proved to be exactly true. DuPont and their successors have spent millions of dollars and decades covering up one of the largest frauds perpetuated on the American people. Not only has their business model placed millions upon millions of hazardous guns in the market place for generations to come, but the secrecy that has surrounded the problem for decades has been made much worse by the willingness of the company to continue the cover-up despite the clear evidence of their failure. Is it any wonder there are problems in selling such a company? Who would trust them?

The sad fact is, once it was proven by Remington that a company didn't have to admit a mechanical failure had occurred no matter how many people told you it did, some other gun companies followed suit. Why not? There's more profit that way. They just deny any accident and tell the court that since it can't be reproduced at will in the laboratory it must be impossible. At the same time, your customers are already on edge because politicians without Constitutional knowledge have threatened to take away by law an inanimate object by blaming the object for committing evil. Of course those customers are going to defend the makers of their guns no matter how cheap, chintzy, dangerous and ill-made those firearms may be! It is a gun and must be defended from the tyranny of those that don't understand basic self defense. That strategy for dodging liability has worked with some success for more than sixty years.

The company's economics practically dictated that their customers would be getting shot by faulty guns. They were given time and again a chance to improve the product but didn't follow through even though discharges without trigger pulls were known of and understood to be in need of correction. Of course that business model used in the manufacture of a deadly instrument is unconscionable, but let's go a step further. What happens when your non-shooting neighbors find out your guns are unsafe. *Your* guns don't depend on a trigger signal from you to shoot. *Your* guns can shoot anytime they feel like it.

There are places you can't smoke in your own home because others might smell it. Let's not turn over our gun rights to those kinds of people. Self regulation and communications with a healthy dose of education should prevent that adverse reaction from happening, but we can never predict what event might get the wrong people involved. I'm in favor of cleaning our own house and let the chips fall where they may. There is no good reason for any gun owner to defend a gun that wasn't made to be basically as safe as historically possible or defend the company that made it. That means DA revolvers *must be* inert. There can be no DA revolvers suddenly show up on the market that can fire if dropped. That problem was solved in 1898 by a pair of bicycle mechanics. To introduce a DA revolver that is less than totally inert now would be irresponsible, but it *is* legal. Yes, it is legal to build a gun with less than the 'normal' amount of safety inherent to it. It's been done for years.

What do we do when a shiny little self defense revolver with a recently purchased major brand name on it impresses the hell out of multiple gun writers before we find out they aren't inert? That scenario has happened several times before and we've seen the results. "Our Man in Africa, David Omney" was the Winchester spokesman during the 1964 self immolation of the company. I often wonder if he threw up between commercials. They must have paid him a LOT of money to say the things he said. Or, he could have been just stone ignorant!

Sir, I know you're on a roll but could you talk about defense guns and how to store them?

Home defense and personal defensive guns play a special role in American lives and deserve their own chapter. It's next.

21. Defense and Defensive Guns

There are very few ex law men that don't have a gun within arms reach most of the time. I see by the smiles in the audience it's true here too. Several people have asked me why ex LEOs always seem to carry a gun and all I can say is, "Once you see with your own eyes what the *lack* of a gun does, it's easy to decide to never be a victim... and also, because we can't throw a rock 1200 feet per second."

The way of nature is to fight or flee, and since I don't run as fast as a bad guy's bullets, I have my own means of defense. I assume everybody else does too. In 47 years of near constant carry, I've been glad twice and sad once I had a pistol in my pocket. If anybody is keeping score, that's a two to one margin in favor of always having a gun handy.

I'd just started a traveling sales job that took me to some pretty rough places. I had a lady construction worker jump in the truck to escape a bear one time and barely escaped fight night at the Owl Club in Salmon, Idaho. Part of my job was hanging out with miners, loggers, cowboys, steel mill workers and welders. Most of those guys drink beer, shoot pool and fight for entertainment, but that wasn't why I was carrying. I know those folks and the bear had a gun of his own under the seat but it wasn't needed.

C.G. Haenel .25 ACP, made on Schmeisser's patent.

My carry gun was an old, ragged, worn shiny Schmeisser .25 auto

©H.J. (Jack) Belk 2014

(actually made by Haenel) that was brought back as a war relic from Germany. It was small, compact and dangerous to carry loaded. I had the magazine full but a dry chamber in a vest pocket when I called on the slot shop of a monster casino in downtown Reno one winter morning. The door was at the end of a long, sloping alleyway that dead-ended at a truck bay door. To the left, in that corner was the entry door to the maintenance shops that I called on selling specialty welding supplies. I'd set up the appointment early so I could buy the guys donuts before work. It was 6:50AM and chilly but not cold.

The guy was typical of the homeless, but younger and taller and had a bright pink scar on his chocolate colored chin. He asked me for a dollar. He didn't get it but when I was half way down the alley he came in behind me. It wasn't really dark, but it was dim enough to suddenly get that surge of dry mouth and beating heart just like when it's *really* a deer that same time of morning. This was the real deal. My heart told me so.

CZ M1945 .25 ACP. Safe to carry fully loaded, *by design*

I don't run, I don't even walk fast when I'm nervous about something or somebody. I'd rather fight than run, but I will walk away any chance I get. That morning, he was walking the same pace I was and the door was supposed to be open at the end. I had an out and I had a gun in my right pocket but it needed the slide operated before it was any good at all. That takes two hands and I'd really like to have a spare hand to defend myself with instead of using the extra hand just to get in action. I had a thick catalog book in my left hand with a bunch of give-a-way pens, notebooks, key chains and demonstration welding rods for the casino guys stuffed inside the cover. My plan was to throw the book at him and hope to shoot him in the confusion... but the door is coming up and it's supposed to be open.

It was locked. Murphy was on duty I guess. My heart told me I'd better get ready, he was coming on after glancing back up the narrow alley. I tapped the bottom of the door with my foot and it sounded like a bass drum in the concrete alley. The guy was now maybe ten feet and slowed down and stopped and said, "F--- dat dolla' gimme ever'thang, I gotta knife."

Ten feet is too close to any sort of knife and too far to throw a book full of sales crap. All I could do was talk to him really seriously. I begged him to show me the knife so I could shoot his black ass plumb full of big holes...."come on ass hole, let me see that knife. Give me an excuse to kill you right here because I *want* to." It was said with a certain amount of sincerity, too. It took a couple of applications, assuring him of certain death, but he backed off and then started running when the door opened behind me.

CZ M1945. Simple is almost always better.

I captured a kidnapper as a deputy and went through my share of dark businesses responding to silent alarms. I've seen the inside of a big pistol pointed at me and survived the misfire of an old single barrel shotgun, but that morning in Reno taught me a LOT about defense guns. I traded that Schmeisser that same day for a safe to carry DA pistol.

I'll bet it's bigger than a pipsqueak .25 too!

No, same thing, just *better by design.* Defense guns are a lot like binoculars. You're much more likely to have a small gun with you when you need it than one unhandy to have around. Casinos don't allow guns no way no how.

If you need a gun, nobody is going to blame you for having it. If you don't need a gun, nobody should ever know you had it. I hope I'm smart enough to not try to fight bigger guns if there's an option, but if there's no option, I'd rather have a tiny gun in my hand than a big one out in the truck or at home because it makes a big lump on my side. One thing for sure, a pocket auto unsafe to carry loaded is not safe enough to carry at all.

As a deputy, we had to have a gun on our person any time and anywhere the sheriff might show up. If he caught you unarmed you were gone. I like to fish in cut-off jeans and a tee shirt so I learned to make do with a little gun. Just to prove a point, I qualified on the PPC course which required shots out to sixty yards with a Budischowsky DA .25 auto.

Budischowsky TP70 .25 ACP

My first recommendation for a defense gun is a quality, double-action revolver. The laser sights in the grips are an added bonus that does not detract from the gun if the batteries are dead. It'll shoot just fine without the laser.

A DA revolver is the ultimate in 'inert' guns. There are no springs compressed anywhere. It is a lump of iron with from five to ten little capsules of energy ready to do battle with the bad guys at just a pull of the trigger. If one shot doesn't work for some reason, pull the trigger again. One handed, either hand, no safeties to remember and no processes to go through to shoot it, just pull the trigger.

S&W DA's, bottom to top: 4" J-frame .22LR M34 kit gun , 3" K-frame .357 M13, and a custom 3" N-frame .41 Mag.

About 1975, I was asked to dispose of a gun for a widow. It had belonged to an old man that had just died and his wife was determined to "get RID of it." She wouldn't sell it, not even to a deputy. It was a very early Forehand and Wadsworth, .32 rimfire long. It held five rounds and they were collector's items. The gun had seen too many sweaty hands and Florida humidity to be a collector's gun but it still shot just fine.

Florida's disposal law says guns will be dumped in at least 20 feet of ocean water and out of sight of land. The Gulf of Mexico qualified. The first fishing trip in the spring usually saw a box of cheap handguns gathered from juke joints and fights and just picked up on the street if somebody got nervous enough at uniformed presence to get rid of it. Nobody ever would claim one so we put them in a box and first trip out we'd shoot them at sea gulls or coots and when the ammo ran out we threw it away. In today's world of law enforcement, it would take three full time employees to document the 'cases' we never made because common sense supplied a much better solution than the law. If a gun is the problem, throw it in the ocean.

Old fashioned inert defense guns, a J.P. Sauer fluid steel barreled double gun with hammer block safety, and a river-salvaged single action Ruger .357, now .41 Mag., one of the author's favorites.

Many people like the modern, light weight, light pull automatics. I understand you like them even though I'll never completely understand why. We've covered those pretty well. An auto takes some maintenance to keep it ready. Magazine springs can relax in about 50 years. They'll still shoot a couple or maybe more, but then quit. You should be suspicious of any magazine that's been loaded for twenty years or more. They are not dependable. Aftermarket magazines have a terrible reputation, too. *Always* have a factory original magazine in a defense auto. Presumably, the factory made the magazine to work correctly. The aftermarket magazine maker hopes to make a profit on duplicating rare magazines. Seldom are they as good as OEM.

All autos are ammo sensitive. Many will shoot almost everything you might feed it, but without trying it first, be very suspicious. The more unusual the bullet is, the more careful you should be. Automatics are not fit for defense without a good bit of 'experience' first. Shoot it slow and fast, gripped tight and as loose as you can without dropping it. Test it with the ammo you'd like to shoot but accept the ammo the gun likes best instead. The gun should have plenty of experience with *that* ammo before it's trusted.

Single action revolvers are good home defense guns in the sense they're inert until you cock them. Like an auto, they take some getting used to and most people cringe at having to reload one in the middle of the bad times. The old Westerns had it right...just shoot until the film runs out. Real life is not nearly so kind.

This is a good place to remind folks how to *un*-cock an exposed hammer gun like the single action referred to above. Many discharges are traced down to trying to let the hammer down without firing. There is a trick to it that is anti-Hollywood... which is to say it's sensible.

Remember the finger spring! When de-cocking exposed hammers, take your finger spring away from the trigger as soon as you can. Hold the hammer firmly, release the full cock, and immediately take your finger off the trigger and concentrate on letting the hammer down easy into the first available place. That will be the loading notch for single actions and the half-cock or safety notch on most others. Believe me, having a hammer slip and breaking the end on the trigger is better than turning loose a bullet, no matter which way it goes. If you have doubts you can hold onto the hammer, then block it with a finger or the other thumb between hammer and frame. Jam a finger down close to the frame near the hammer and then pull the trigger. It might pinch, but it won't shoot. Release the trigger as soon as possible and that activates the passive blocker safety feature. *Don't* let the primer be hit!

Shotguns are becoming a favorite tool for home defense. I see several nods around the room. Nobody is snooping on us so let me see a show of hands that have a shotgun with ammo handy for home defense, please... Good, more than half! Now, how many are pumps? How many are not a pump? That's what I thought, all pumps. Now I understand the furrowed brows during the RCFC talks. And, that explains the pained look when I told of Tom Butter's case of the little toddler breaking the Mossberg 500 trigger guard, too. Accidents take on a different meaning when your own guns are involved. Just to tune up that Mossberg story a little, we found the plastic ears that hold the trigger housing in place will break if you dropped it just right, too. Then the gun could fire anytime it liked. The safety linkage no longer works. Of course almost all JM Browning designed repeaters have trigger housings that use that same 'fork' arrangement to hold the front end in place, but those are steel 'ears', not plastic.

Shotguns are special and take special considerations. The only true inert shotguns have external hammers. As noted in two cases involving external hammered shotguns, both were defective and not safe from impact. The popularity of Cowboy Action Shooting has brought a new influx of hammered shotguns to the marketplace, but most are imported from places known for torturing metal into crude tools of one kind or another. Sometimes the victims are shotguns. Pump-action shotguns are a better choice at this point.

Ithaca M37

All pumps should be stored with an empty chamber and the hammer should be down, or in the fired position. The mainspring is uncompressed but the magazine spring is under load. I suggest loading one short of capacity in the magazine and have extra ammo handy. By shortening the compression of the magazine tube spring you lengthen its life about three times. It's worth the one shell sacrifice for greater reliability.

The safety position should be OFF unless that makes you uncomfortable. There are shotguns that fire as the action is closed if the trigger is pulled. How nervous are you going to be? How much time do you have? It will feel like it takes minutes to pump the gun no matter how fast you do it. Your heart will tell you how slow you are, too. You will recognize those 'running in quicksand' nightmares when the time comes to do battle. The hammer is in the 'fired' position which means the pump handle is 'loose' and can be pumped without manipulating the action bar lock button. The sound of a pump shotgun getting ready for battle is the last thing a lot of bad guys hear. Not because they got shot but because they left!

Now, let me set up a scenario for you that is true and see how well prepared you are.

There was a bump in the night but she was not really asleep anyhow. The sheriff's deputy had served the restraining order on him that afternoon and she knew he'd be furious... more so than usual. She had no where to go, only the trailer back in the woods and two small kids asleep in the next room. She had heard a couple of trucks go by and then she maybe dosed off just a little, and then the bump... but the creaking of the floor and slight shifting of the trailer said he'd come for her. It had to be him! Her heart was thundering and she was shaking as she leaned over and grabbed the shotgun by the barrel and drew it across the bed....he tried the door but it was locked. It was also a mid '60s mobile home. When his foot came through the flimsy door he got hung up and tripped because he was drunk. The first blast of bird shot cut a ragged hole through the door at chest level but he was knee high at the time.

The next shot left a pattern in the back window of his pickup truck as he left the yard. I wrote the report on the incident and put him in jail for violating the order later that night. I had the option of arresting her for reckless endangerment from the second shot. The spacing of the shots was wide enough apart to show a jury she missed him when she had cause, but then followed him to finish the job. That's more like attempted murder in the second degree if an aggressive prosecutor wanted to push it. I'd seen an 870 in the corner and assumed that's what she'd shot at him with, but it wasn't. She didn't know how to work the pump gun. She had a 20 gauge single shot with a shell in it but had to go into a hunting vest in a closet to find the second shell to shoot! I showed her how to load and shoot the pump gun in case he came back, but he kissed a tree rather hard one night not long after that so she didn't have to shoot him after all.

A single mom, remote house, with an angry ex known to be abusive and she had *one* #8 birdshot to do battle with him! He would have killed her though, had it not been for that first 'warning' shot. Some things cut right through the fog of whiskey. Chest high meant she tried to kill him and he knew it. The memory of a gunshot burns deep when it's aimed at you, too.

I've got an 870 in the corner full of double aughts. I'm ready!

I'm not sure of your living arrangements but I've seen 00 buck shot penetrate four mobile home walls. A military 30-06 bullet made it through nine. Are you sure you need that much firepower? The one thing you don't want is collateral damage. There is a story of a 9mm Calico that shot a kid and his mom in the next house over coming up.

Never underestimate the power of a bullet or the reach of Murphy to be mischievous or injurious to something or someone you love. Everybody knows a .22 short can't hurt much. We shoot them indoors into piles of magazines, no problem. But one guy let the hammer slip on a tiny North American Arms revolver, like the one in Alaska, and it went through a basement ceiling, through the main floor and just barely clipped the edge of a half inch hole in a steel plate that was the frame holding up a hundred gallon aquarium. The bullet barely clipped the hole so that it ricocheted into the aquarium bottom of course. *One* 36 grain indoor short flooded a room and left flopping fish all over the floor.

One time I had occasion to help a lady out of a real jamb. Her ex had left for her a booby trap, pure and simple. She'd felt something odd about the dresser drawer and carefully uncovered a fully loaded and cocked single action, .357 magnum revolver with the barrel pointing straight out the front.....right where she would have been standing had she gone fumbling in the drawer without noticing something odd. Both her kids were in the room with her and the gun was pointed across their escape route. I told her to put them in the tiled shower and then get a pencil and answer some questions while she was looking at the gun.

It was an old model Ruger Blackhawk on full cock. Remember the finger spring? I had her stick the pencil between the hammer and the frame down low, turn the gun in a safer direction then pull the trigger and immediately release it. That took some earnest conversation, but she finally did it. The hammer hung up in the loading notch, as designed. At that point I had her turn it away from the path to the door so the kids would quit screaming and I could hear what she was saying again...this was all by long distance phone call. Then, I stepped her through opening the loading gate and had her just pull the entire cylinder out of the gun. It was inert for sure now. The cops came to write a report and noted the "gun was broken and not fire-able". They *did* change it though when I called and offered an affidavit to counter his false assertions (and hammer him for making it.) Cops should at least listen to the best witness before writing down an obviously ignorant claim. If he didn't know better he should have asked somebody.

Defense guns should be what you are comfortable with. In the middle of a panic is not the time to be reading instruction manuals.....

Excuse me, I'd just like a blank pistol or something to scare them away with.

Then that's what you should have. Bad guys stay scared about an hour and then they're bad guys again....unless they're hurt really bad or dead. Nobody can put the grit in someone that's needed to fight back. Sometimes threats to kids will get a woman to fight, but unless she's so inclined to start with she's unlikely to be prepared for it. I saw that a lot as a deputy. Peaceful, serene women beaten, stabbed, raped and some murdered. When it came their time all they could do is scratch and scream but they always knew they were at risk.

The concealed weapons classes are full of such victims that have decided once is enough and even more students that believe 'never is better'. The bad guy installed the grit. The next guy is in for a hard time. I'm glad to see armed citizen responses getting more publicity. In decades past, the only time you read of a citizen fighting back was in The Armed Citizen section of the American Rifleman magazines. Publicity works very well in an ordinarily uninformed population. Some hyperbole sometimes helps. When a habitual thief was caught half in and half out of a citizen's kitchen window and had used a large knife to split the screen and still had it in his hand, the home owner shot him in the face with a shotgun. The word 'on the street' about the results brought a very marked decline in residential burglaries for many months. Nothing was in the news about the damage, but it sure got around in a hurry. (Some are probably wondering how so many could know so soon.)

What do you think of lights mounted on shotguns?

I love them. The Picatinny rail has opened up an entire universe of clamp-on accessories and a really bright light is confusing to the bad guy and illuminates the target quite well. Or it lights his way to the door should he decide not to stick around. Show them where the hole is going to be and let them make a fast decision.

It was either my mom or her sister that shot the long johns on the clothesline one breezy night when they were home alone and really *knew* somebody was out there, but he wouldn't go away. They both told the story but both denied being the shooter! A good flashlight would have been handy then. Taking time to light a lantern and exposing yourself is not a good idea. A cautious person with suspicions of bad doings around his place is well prepared with a shotgun attached to the flashlight. Just don't confuse the switches.

I want one gun that will never leave my side. What would it be?

The answer is as varied as the audience. What is perfect for one is poison for another. The everyday use of it would be a variable that is near infinite.

There was a time I shot a .41 Mag. more than any other caliber and it was on the truck seat beside me at all times. That was the hard winter of '78-'79 when it was common to see deer and elk hung up in fences and stuck in snow banks with broken legs from being hit by traffic. I shot eleven deer in one trip from town to home one time. Other times I've spent a week with nothing but a two shot High Standard Derringer or little S&W Kit Gun somewhere in my backpack.

I knew a lady bartender that sold fighting juice to loggers and cat fishermen and was always complaining about the chair flinging fights that tore her place apart about bimonthly. She kept a Colt Junior .25 auto in her rather ample front bumper assembly. I never saw her draw it but I understand it was something to behold. There were more than a dozen holes in the ceiling above the bar from her calling the place back to order. She finally shot a guy right in the chest but his cigarettes caught the bullet. The fighting tapered off considerably after that, though. Never try to predict what a bullet may do, either.

My advice for an everyday gun is to look for *inert quality* in a caliber that encourages you to shoot it. Forget the $40 a box super wonder bullets guaranteed to go down range but with a lot of other advertised features greatly inferred but not assured. Keep it simple.

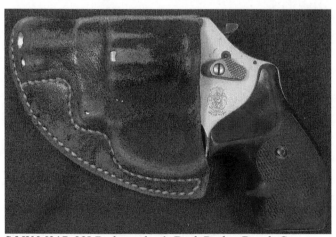

S&W M317 .22LR, the author's Back Pocket Ranch Gun

I like a .22 lightweight revolver with fixed sights and very short barrel. It's not concealed in my hip pocket but I don't care. I'm four pistol shots from the nearest neighbor and my dogs consider the pocket .22 just right for the occasional rattler and more common pack rat, skunk or other varmint that shows a need for killing. The town gun is much smaller and easier to carry. The truck gun is big enough for injured cattle, horses or game. The truck rifle is just right for 250 yard coyotes and the shotgun next to the door for woodpeckers and magpies is a modified choke M59 Winchester, but I leave it unloaded with an open bolt. There are no 'kinetic' guns with a round in the chamber. In fact, I follow the old African hunter tradition of standing a loaded round in the muzzles to keep the insects and dust out. My defense guns are out in the open, loaded and unlocked, though. I lose keys pretty regular but never a gun.

S&W M317, first 2 loaded for snakes

Build confidence in whatever you carry. Cycle old ammo out and new ammo in once in a while in anything you're going to trust. If it fails you once, you'll have some hard choices to make. If it's an auto, try different ammo, if it's a revolver, trade it. You can't doubt the tool that is there specifically to save your life. That's why life rings on boats are solid foam and not full of air. Dependability is first, always. Never give Murphy a chance. He'll damn sure take it.

High Standard had a batch of riot guns that failed to feed because the magazine tube was too long and the line of shotshells too heavy. On the first shot, they were likely to spew three or four loaded rounds out the bottom but fail to load one in the chamber. Sometimes a seven shot shotgun only shot twice. In about 1969 a Brazilian company known for really crude guns sold the Snake Eye. It was a .410 single shot pistol but stamped on the barrel '.45

Colt and Shot'. They didn't get away with it for long, but the ones that went into use nearly all blew the bottom of the folded sheet metal barrel out. You should never be scared of your own gun. It's hard not to be when you're missing fingers because of it. It's natural to be scared after being scarred.

Sir, I'm on a fixed income and the prices I see for even what you call the 'plastic automatics' are just totally ridiculous. I can't afford a good gun and my neighborhood has changed a LOT in the last 40 years. I NEED a gun!

The gun market at the end of 2014 is as crazy as I've seen it since Winchester took a dive in '64. 'Guns' will sell no matter the quality, no matter the price, no matter how ugly, ill-made or cheap looking. The shame of it is, it takes a very educated and discerning eye to tell them apart. I tend to be aligned philosophically with my Grand Dad who automatically went backward in time until he found a tool that he knew worked and was comfortable with. He could limb a downed tree with an ax while the cousins were still trying to start the chain saw. When a friend asked my recommendations for a pocket pistol I skipped all the plastics and suggested an old Interarms PPK/s. When a lady asked me about a purse gun, I found her an old M37 Airweight Chief's Special for less than $300.

Smith & Wesson M65 .357 Mag, internet sale for under $200

I'd take that one!

$300 S&Ws are available. Some for less than $200 are for sale. Returned cop guns are sometimes $189 for a SS .357. I have one.

Check the side plate screws for *any* damage. If it's there, pass on that one and choose another. If the sides of the hammer and trigger are polished, pass on that one too. It's been my experience, that any S&W that's been 'tuned' has a one in a thousand chance of being 'improved' in any way. The chances are 999 to 1 it's been screwed up. Pass on those no matter how impressed the owner is with it. I'll not name that one-in-a-thousand exception because I still want one.

S&W M65, side plate removed.

It is a fact that some 'plastic pistols' are good enough to carry and trustworthy enough to own. Since I'm a slave to what I write, I'll not be making any recommendations unless I'm looking at its innards first. Guns change from day to day sometimes and what was a great gun last month could be nothing but junk today. I just saw my first 'modern' S&W defense handgun... I'd rather pick out a really... nice... round... rock.

You seem to be overly opinionated.

I am, but I still have my choice of defense guns and mine don't have plastic parts. Period. Buy whatever *you* like and can afford. My point is price is *not* a determination of quality. Today's market is ample proof of that.

The M65 shown here is totally inert and cannot fire with less than 16.3 pounds of applied and maintained pressure on the trigger. It cost one quarter the amount of the PPS pictured below.

New generation Walther/S&W model PPS

That one removed a body part when the owner sat down with it in the waist band of his pants. It takes 8.1 pounds of applied force. Which gun would you rather own?

I didn't hear the mental comments in the audience but I know what you thought "I like automatics better so I'll take the Walther."

That is the difference of opinion that makes poor land sell and ugly women find a husband.

There are people that like sports cars and private jets, too. I'd rather have a good pick-up and an ATV and both happen to be cheaper, but my needs are much different than the guy craving a shiny, fast thing and a plane to go to Paris. It really all boils down to 'need' and 'want' and 'price'. I tend to look at materials, workmanship and design much more than flash and features.

I think you just hung yourself on your own petard. Wouldn't you agree the sports car and jet plane will have better materials, workmanship and design than your pickup truck and quad buggy?

I would certainly agree to that, but the utility and cost of the bubble car and the jet means they were never in direct alignment with my needs and wants to start with. Let's lift the hood and take off the trim and *really* look at each product in comparison with others of the same utility, and then compare that with asking price. You'll have to call experts in trucks, cars and airplanes first because I don't have a clue. I'm a gun guy. If you want to debate the attributes and advantages of thermal polymers versus heat treated steel in firearms applications, then we have a contest where individual tastes come into play along with experience and knowledge and some skill in telling guns apart and how they interact with their parts. When I know certain steel parts cause trouble by loosening, bending, wearing or breaking, and then see the same part made of plastic, I already know the result of the substitution and will not contribute money to the experiment.

Gun designs have always been my passion. I'm 'interested' in a lot of things and tend to study my interest a little more than some seem to do. I enjoy scenery, especially mountains, but I haven't 'gone away' as one lady friend described my minutes long stare at a cliff, I'm inventorying stratigraphic features of the cliff so I can look up the geologic map that applies to that area and find out exactly what that formation is as soon as I get home. I'll be disappointed if I'm wrong in my amateur assessment, but I'll readily accept a better explanation. It's the same with guns. I can sit and stare at a drawing or a gun and at the end of it, I know that gun and most likely what will fail first and be the hardest to repair. I welcome any further information anybody may have about it, too.

Hunter Matte finish, M870

To one knowledgeable in how guns are built, from concept to steel, and has done it several times and knows what it takes to fit, finish, and figure out how it all works together, it is painful to see the shortcuts and how they've been folded into our thinking about firearms. What's called 'hunter matte finish' is actually sand blasting without at least two intermediary polishing steps first.

You can bet that saved a *lot* of time and money at the factory. So, why did the price go up? The old LAPD Model 37 Ithaca cost more because it was Parkerized and had open sights, but the metal was fit and finished especially for Parkerizing. It took extra steps, extra time and cost extra money. All that figures, but paying four times more for much less is not my idea of a bargain. I don't pay candy bar prices for coconuts... especially if they might be poisonous.

Are we still talking about home defense?

Yes ma'am! All I need is reminding once an hour or so. You have a question?

I sympathize with the gentleman in row two that said his neighborhood had declined. Ours has too. My husband is disabled, my son lives a hundred miles away but had a 'FSR' (I'm amazed I know what that is now!) with a Remington Model 700 but couldn't make the meeting so I've been recording it for him because you've been over my head since just after "good morning." I'm not so much confused as I am in awe that there is so much know about a GUN! But now that we're talking about a gun around the house I have specific questions to ask if I may:

I'm a small lady that may be gray but I'm sure not going to take any crap from any punk that breaks into our house. My husband no longer has the strength or mental capability to fight back. We're sitting ducks and we're surrounded by feral beings that have no respect at all for anybody. We hear gun shots and sirens and bull horns... A ninety year old lady was raped last year just two streets over... I'm going to buy a gun TODAY and learn to shoot it well enough to kill the SOB that thinks I'm an easy target. What should it be and what do I need to know?

On this very spot, in the year 2014, this entire gun discussion comes down to this one very important question and all the nuances and innuendo buried in it. Right here is where the rubber meets the road. Is there traction or is there not? I predict a lot of spinning, squealing and smoking before traction finally wins out, but we'll see.

Ma'am, I'm going to answer your question in the least controversial way I possibly can, but no matter what I answer it'll be subject to extensive debate because my answer won't be just about what gun to buy, it'll be about more about the process than the product.

I'll start with a rhetorical question. Who do you trust?

You say your son shoots but you haven't asked him about a home defense gun. You said during a break you'd been to three gun stores and had to doubt what you heard from the salesmen there. I confirmed it as mostly useless information. The local cop said he'd be back in touch, but he didn't say what pay period that might be because it's been two weeks with no word from him, yet.

What do you trust? Are the magazine articles telling the truth? How about the internet? The Vice President even had a suggestion. Should you trust politicians? How about the sane ones?

"The perfect gun for the masses" said Senator Palmoil, chairman of the design committee.

Who *can* you trust? What *do* you trust? How much trust do you place in a product that is as deadly and as dangerous as it gets, but is a mystery inside?

When it comes to self defense, you can only trust yourself. It is up to you to find the information yourself and determine what is exactly right for exactly who is going to be protected. Read the magazines, watch the guys that post their ideas on the internet listen to all sides of the story and determine which guns you want to try out. *Then* go to a range with the list and see how many of those they have on hand. Resist the urge if told "you might want to try this one because it's an improvement over that thing (we don't have) on your list."

Deal with them just like a car lot and don't test drive anything until you've finished your first list. That first list of three to six guns will, more than likely, contain the gun you eventually buy. Most gun stores don't have ranges attached for try-outs, so check with the local CCW teachers and hunter safety instructors and the police and sheriff's departments. We had a lady come into the shift change room one night and ask to shoot a machine gun because she always wanted to. We accommodated her until she shot up all the ammo she brought with her and set up an appointment for the next week for the Thompson. Several deputies taught people to shoot well enough to protect themselves, and we all helped citizens with their guns if asked.

I haven't forgotten that you said you wanted a gun *today.*

'Today' means you want an interim gun for protection when you walk in the door later tonight and you don't have time to practice, read manuals or insert batteries for the sights. You want something that will hold its value because you might want something else once you do your research, and you don't want to have any trouble trading it or selling it later. You're worried about your safety now and you're more likely to spend the money now rather than later. We never want to risk having a refrigerator or car to find out we have extra money to spend, and we'll sure spend it! Apprentice Murphy's maybe?

My advice would be to buy a used S&W M36 Chief's Special with unmarred side plate screws and five rounds of ammunition. You may want to try the double action pull with no ammo in it (and the cylinder has to be closed to do it) just to see what 17 pounds of pull feels like. When you're ready, load it with all five cartridges, close the cylinder and it is at your command entirely. Pulling the trigger fires it and not pulling the trigger means it's just a pretty special 'rock' in your arsenal.

If my past experience holds true, you'll put that gun in a handy but hidden place and it'll stay there until somebody else moves it. Practice comes under the same heading as exercise, jogging and going on a diet. Good intentions are time sensitive and usually get delayed. Don't worry about it, the gun is inert but ready anytime you are.

There are other equally well qualified guns other than the Chief, and there are at least nine variations of that one model, but the size, shape, operation, quality and dependability are the same or close enough. My definition of 'quality' is that you can buy it retail, use it for 20 years with ordinary care, and still sell it at a profit. I sold my Dad a brand new Model 36 Chief Special just as discussed above for $86.50 plus tax in 1969. The manager of the shop let me throw in a box of ammo because he was my dad and should get a break somehow. That gun is worth three to five times that now and it won't get any cheaper. At the present rate of use and care, it has hundreds of years of life left in it.

Quality guns seldom cost too much, but sometimes you can buy them too early.

That brings up my question, how do you store and protect a defense gun but have it ready to use at the same time?

That depends entirely on your specific situation. You won't lay a Glock on a nightstand with kids around because even a fifteen month old can (and did) shoot one. By the same token, you don't keep a gun near the alarm clock or your cell phone or stuffed under the pillow, either. Guns only need energy to shoot. A sleep walker is plenty strong enough to pull a trigger. At least one guy thought he was answering the phone when he shot half his eyebrow off. I met a guy as a deputy that kept a cocked and locked 1911A1 under a cocked but unlocked mouse trap. He said he was bad about dreaming he needed a gun and that reminded him he was still asleep. I don't think I'd want to live near him when his conscience and subconscience compared notes with Murphy.

Trigger locks are fine for those that think they have time and the nerves it takes to line up a key with a keyhole in the dark. I don't. Lock boxes are the same way but biometric locks means quicker access without compromising security....if the battery doesn't go dead or a mouse pees on the sensor. For many, just a dresser drawer or nightstand or headboard is just fine. They can be stolen from there and those with nosy kids should find another place, but hidden and handy is usually the protocol.

I'm a little unconventional, but I like a leash in some cases. Several times I've installed a ring on the butt of a revolver for a simple loop of high tensile SS cable to be looped into and clamped in place. The other end is padlocked to part of the house. There is enough slack for the owner to fight from the bed but not enough slack for the bad guy to get it to the pawn shop. Don't loop the cable through the trigger guard unless you want the guy trying to steal it to possibly shoot himself. Finger springs don't apply if the force is held long enough on the trigger for the hammer to fall.

I thought you said this would be controversial.

If you didn't get the point maybe I skirted too much around in the white without poking the yolk. Unscrambling an egg is as difficult as un-ringing a bell and I've been cautious. Remember, the ones that most need to know are the least likely to listen. I asked "Who do you trust? What do you trust? How much trust can you place in the gun business?"

In 1944 in an arsenal in Yugoslavia, a tiny rind of steel was deleted from Paul Mauser's Model 98 design. Without it, hot gases from a ruptured case are free to blow back to the rear and spew out right into the shooter's eye.

Within weeks, in Czechoslovakia, the bolt guide rail was deleted, too. The expense and materials needed for a milled magazine box assembly and floorplate had been deleted earlier, but that wasn't safety related as much. Did the soldiers know? Some found out that slave labor had scared them by sabotaging the heat treat process, but the *design* of the Mauser means it can be shot several times with no heat treatment at all. The German troops were surprised their gun blew the bottom out and smoked like it was on fire, but it didn't hurt him because the design was strong enough, but admire the courage of the slaves working in armament factories for the Nazis, though. The simple, 'Please remember your friends the Czechs' and 'Don't forget your friends the Slavs' notes inserted into Nazi bomb and artillery fuses that made them duds were read by GIs and appreciated.

M98 comparison. Left: FN corrupted the M98 in 1949 with the easier-to-machine 'double cut' design which defeats the greatest attribute of the M98. Right: Older and safer C-Ring design of Paul Mauser. No safety glasses needed.

Who do you trust? The largest arms maker in the world is FN in Belgium. Shortly after WW-II, FN took over where Mauser Werkes left off and began making contract Mausers for many countries. In 1949 a very major change was made to those guns. The entire Mauser gas handling system, the part of the Model 98 that made it famous was essentially gutted by the simple expedient of redesigning one section of the receiver to allow a broach through access. That one machining step saved a tremendous amount of trouble and money and I can find no record of any country protesting the wrecking of the rifle they were buying. Since the Model 98 has several redundant features that also guard against injury of the shooter, nobody seems to have noticed.

In China, when one of the massive bronze cannons exploded and wiped out the gun crew, the chief cannon caster was cast into the next cannon. I'm sure competition for the job was still strong, but

hold on a second now.....somewhere there has to be enough
responsibility to ensure *trust* and the Chinese solution seems
extreme even for the most rabidly responsible among us. I'm not a
metallurgist and can't judge what fluxing a retort full of bronze
with a scrawny supervisor might do, but it seems to me it either
worked very well or they would have eventually run out of
prospects for the job. Can we say Chinese cannon blowups were
rare? I wonder what they did to the guy that let the powder get
wet. I still wonder who has the guts to be a dictator's dentist?

Did your track turn without you again?

Sorry. Personal punishment for bad designs or even bad guesses is
not the answer, but somehow the gun business needs to get back on
track. It's going to take the education of those that already are or
think they are educated. Mechanical devices are not mysterious
things hidden from view. They're only complicated by what we
see.

 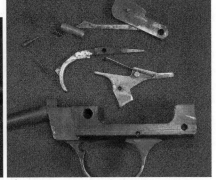

Ithaca M37 trigger, complete and stripped

*Right! That's the problem. A bunch of that is just a wad of metal
that can't be seen.*

Sometimes you can reassemble the innards on the outside using the
pivot pins and holes. Some guns resist that cheat really well,
though. Good luck with a Savage 99! You can almost always strip
the excess parts away to get to the triggering part of it.

There has been, since roughly 1950, a concentration on the wrong
features of firearms by the manufacturers, the gun writers, the
gunsmiths and the barber shop experts that read all the magazines

and therefore must have all the answers. Guns aren't about *looks* at the sacrifice of safety. Guns should never be about *price* over the basic rules of *safety*. Guns are different by design and some are harder to make than others. Expect prices to reflect materials and quality and *nothing* else. I'll use an old gun to make a point:

In the '70s, Weatherby had the market cornered on flashy rifles that looked better than they shot, but people with money bought them two to one over the better at the time Ruger 77 that was about 20% the cost. Weatherby became famous for the imported MkV and later the Vanguard. Roy Weatherby was an arms importer much like Charles Daly and Browning USA. Weatherby specified the guns and the manufacturer supplied them. Of course cost for the importer is always a factor. That's why Mark Vs are marked as made in Germany and Japan. Cost is always a factor in quality, but sometimes politics and labor unions and a wide variety of factor affect import prices. When Charles Daly changed from Sauer in Prussia to Miruku in Japan as the supplier of his shotguns, at least the cost came down with the quality of the guns. Sometimes it goes the other way.

One of Weatherby's imports was an over and under shotgun with a coin finished receiver and glossy finished walnut stock. Sitting on a gun rack, they were fine looking pieces and all that engraving sparkled in the sun. They cost as much as a Browning Superposed and since it was a Weatherby, it should, according to fans of the brand. One of my customers in Tallahassee bought one to shoot skeet with. It was his dream gun and he had turned down my deals on used Browning Grade I skeet guns at half the price and new ones at the same price, but he had to have the Weatherby and ordered it from another shop....thank Goodness for that! It lasted about two cases of shells and then the trigger would pull all the way back....hard...and then fire when you bumped it....sometimes. The other shop didn't have a repairman so I got paid to look at it, even though it was still under warranty.

From the proofs and the engraving, done it seemed with kitchen utensils, it was made in Spain. No part was even filed smooth. The hammers were 'finished' by bench grinder. No part had any heat treatment at all. The 'problem' was very easy to see: the tails of the sears were dead soft and had bent upward so the sear end almost disengaged from the hammers but not quite. It left the lower barrel on a point to rounded point like two ball bearings stacked up and waiting for a vibration. The hammer faces were mushroomed from hitting the firing pins, the top break lever spring was at about half strength and the entire thing was already loose in the hinge. I told Weatherby's warranty people it was only good for decoration or a decoy anchor. I suggested the latter. I've never seen another one of those shotguns and maybe I just used a bad prototype as an example, but it does illustrate the point. You can paint a road apple red, but its' still a road apple. For those in the city, road apples are planted by horses and tend to be sour.

In the last three weeks, I've bought the first three gun magazines since I went in the Army. I've been given some because my work was inside them or an article I wrote was published. Of course the antiques in the doctor's office are always entertaining, but I spent green dollars on research this time to get a cross-section of the 'gun world' as it is right now. That's not enough for a scientific sample so I got a Gun Annual, a Cabela's Fall Edition and Midway's sale brochure to round out a fair sample. I went to a couple internet advice sites but my stomach is just not that strong, yet. The old adage about the only thing being wrong with the world is that 'the competent are full of doubts and the incompetent are cocksure' applies to the World Wide Web. Of course there are some real jewels there, too.

Nowhere in my magazine and catalog research have I found the same information as I've written here. There are no discussions of accidents, though I know of several in the past year that should be exposed. There are no articles on marksmanship, only how to hit people-looking targets with black guns. I figure my research cost me about a dollar a minute. That's too much for my blood.

Years ago there was a late night AM radio guy that had voice inflections and timing to make the most insane things seem important. When a guy called in and said he'd looked at the moon and he could see a structure up there just like the Astrodome, the host replied in a very serious voice that he had *never* heard *any* scientist say there wasn't.

Stupidity is fun when watching monkeys play but it seems

somehow cruel to use somebody's ignorance as radio entertainment. The host of that program was making about nine times my salary for just being able to drag out such a conversation for more than one sentence. I couldn't do that job.

To hear a TV reporter ask a hurricane expert which way the wind is going to come from grated on my nerves so bad I gave away my last TV. No way should someone be required to act that stupid just for money. Have the hurricane guy tell the folks about hurricanes and they can see for themselves which way the wind blows and why. Don't dumb yourself down to ask a stupid question just for a paycheck.

Not long ago I was asked by a lawyer to look at a YouTube video of a gun failure. The only reason I got to the very end is because I was being paid to watch it. It was stupid cubed and then smothered in ignorance. It was painfully ignorant. What the lawyer considered proof wasn't even good evidence! The fact that the guy in the video had no clue how to proceed and no idea what was causing the failure was a large part of getting this book to market. From all the research I've done, it's needed.

Didn't you just say you spent just a few minutes in 'research'?

I sure did. What would you do if you opened the new National Geographic and find it had a map of a flat earth? I went to the magazine with the scary looking pistol with a flashlight down the barrel. They say plastic is better than steel because it won't rust and some nut called a hideous piece of black plastic "elegant". Why not balsa wood painted purple? It's rust proof for sure. I'm sure you could glue some glitter on it to make it elegant.

Then there's the 'rifle' with the tractor fuel funnel scope with four knobs, three internal colors and a battery and a reticule at home in a submarine periscope. It had a fluted barrel, adjustable bipod, a black plastic accessories rack and web gear strapped to it fit for a parachutist... and then the pistols that look like the box a pistol should come in. There are plastic film camo finishes and skeletonized aluminum and carbon fiber 'stocks' and enough Pictatinny gadgets to break a gunshop trying to stock them all. It seems the quality gun manufacturers are under too much economic stress to advertise. All it takes to bring out a new product is a CNC machine shop and a plastics contract. Nobody is watching but the lawyers and somebody (sober and straight) has to get accidentally shot first. That still seems a bad way to do business to me, but I understand the pressures on the gun companies, too. Politicians are on one side, zealots on another, investors on another side next to the mandatory points of performance and price, appearance and then insurance. Back in the corner rubbing hands and grinning are lawyers and Murphy waiting on an opening.

1922 Colt Officer's Model

The facts are durable. There are dangerously defective guns in use and for sale on the market that will probably last another hundred years at the present rate of use. I'm talking about the guns we generally think of as quality guns according to the rule stated earlier. Only the crudest of imported junk guns the press dubbed as 'Saturday Night Specials' and the very economical .22s and shotguns that were sold by discount stores under their names but made by Savage-Stevens, Marlin, Mossberg and others will not today show a profit from their purchase price, but it's good to be able to ignore inflation. Those cheap guns are gradually melting down into parts bins and dusty drums of gun 'long parts'. I have several boxes of guns not quality enough to fix and not safe enough to sell.

The quality guns last longer, are passed down to the next generation and remain in the marketplace for several more generations. Not long ago I bought a 1922 vintage Colt Officer's Model that had been carried so long the grips were worn smooth, but it hadn't been shot as much as the new pistol a friend bought in July. I had to pay ten times 1922 retail for it and consider it a real bargain.

This gun only shoots when the trigger is pulled. It has internal safeties that operate from the trigger. The hammer is blocked from the firing pin. It cannot fire in its safe position. It is 'inert.' Firing from gravity is blocked. It is one of the many millions of 'safe guns' that are not showing their age.

How about the millions of guns that are *not* that safe, *by design?* They are just as durable, just not as safe.

22. Wrap-Up, Q&A Preview

We all have our favorites of most everything and tend to defend them like a wild dog does her pups. It's just human nature, nobody is at 'fault' and nobody can be to blame. My Granddad used to say, "Difference of opinion is what makes poor land sell and allows ugly women to get married." I put that in quotes because he passed away in 1966 and never heard of a feminist or political correctness or any of the other small insanities that have brought us to this place in history where the truth cannot be heard if it might hurt somebody's feelings. He was born in 1886 and would be totally, completely, and irretrievably lost in our world of today when 'stream of thought' speech gets you looked at close and sometimes arrested, like the kid that took the bite out of a pop up toast 'em and it looked like a pistol so he got arrested in school. *That* is the sort of nonsense that would have been judged totally insane by him and even me, in my early lifetime. And it wasn't all that much earlier, either!

I was a deputy to a very strong, Constitutional sheriff. He insisted we do things right. In fact it is entertaining to put today's news into yesterday's world and play out the scenario. The kid with the blueberry breakfast pistol is an example. Had a principal told me to arrest a student for violating a 'no gun' policy in school for gnawing on a pop tart I would have petitioned the Court for a sanity hearing.

I traded pistols in school in the seventh grade. My 'bestest buddy' and I traded ammunition daily in grades one through six. I did a show and tell in the third grade on a .50 BMG round I found at the beach. I was a gun nut by then and most of my teachers didn't mind.

Don't our so called educators have the common sense to see creativity? How about the human trait of mimic? Wouldn't a better response be, "Don't point that! Eat it before the barrel falls off." And if you're really a screaming meemie type, you could look real stern when you said it. Arrest a seven year old? Absolute insanity! Where are the adults?

Education is the key. It shouldn't be punishment.

Human nature is reflected quite well in our firearms. They are, as the eggheads say, part of our nature. Of course, eggheads already have sex on the brain and they think everybody else is similarly afflicted. One of my customers and boss for a while was a dentist that was small in stature and had a mannerism that belied his history and his hobbies. He was an ex-Navy carrier pilot and an elephant hunter. He told one nosy blue-hair carrying a sign outside the Clearwater gun show, "No ma'am, I need a big gun to shoot big animals very dead with."

Some people will not look, listen, or try to reason why somebody else thinks of something different than they do and some go over-board trying to comply with each new thought or theory. When talking guns, it's amazing how many times someone that knows what I do in regards to firearms design tries to preempt any possible criticism of their gun. I had a guy try to really impress me with his only loading four rounds in a five shot Chief's Special. He made it known right from the start he was much smarter than most and he *knew* it could shoot if he dropped it.

Do you think I should have corrected him and told him he had his gun confused with an old model Ruger? Not me. I told him that was always a good idea when you weren't sure and he was happy to have the compliment. Education doesn't have to hurt. I used that particular example because that guy has passed away and can't be embarrassed by it now.

I've been accused of being a firearms busybody and critical of just about everything I see. To avoid that, I don't go to many gun shows anymore. What do you do when you see a guy reaching for wads of bills while lusting for a Vulcan .50? I'm seriously asking that question of everyone. I can't buy every dangerous gun I see and I can't carry around a soap box and preach, either.

At a gunshow in Denver many years before I started testifying, I saw a man and a young son looking at .22 rifles. I love to watch people watching guns and they were a study. They were looking for something really cheap. I thought the kid wanted the gun more than his dad, but his dad was going along if it was cheap enough. They fondled every old Mossberg and Savage and beat up old

Coey in the show and then seemed to settle on the one gun there that was likely to blind the kid in both eyes and it could do it on the very first shot. They had seemed to decide on a Stevens Crackshot with a $60 price tag on it. It was worn out and the chances of it catching the rim of a modern .22LR between the extractor and barrel was very real. On closing the lever the gun fires out of battery and the brass fragments fan out in a pattern nearly assured of blowing out one or more eyes. I didn't know the dealer, but at least I had sixty bucks so I went over and told the dealer I was about to screw up his sale and here's the money up front, and then explained to the man and his kid how it was dangerous and helped them buy a Winchester Model 69-A for just a few bucks more.

Education is sometimes expensive, but how would I feel if that kid, that wanted to learn to shoot, was blinded by a bad gun? How would you feel, now that you know? Nobody wants to be part of something bad. I know people in the defense industry and they're proud of making the tools of war. They do a good job because it's a good job to do. Would it be the same if they were asked to make suicide belts?

We have an innate morality that prevents us from standing by while someone else gets hurt, though the videos posted on the internet of exactly that is not only puzzling but very troubling. Most of us have the Good Samaritan reflex that contributes to the safety of us all.

Firearms and their owners need warnings that aren't plastered all over the gun. Information, education and awareness are needed, otherwise we risk losing what we have the perfect right to have.

We will try to trip you up bad in the Q&A, but for now I speak for several that think you've made your case. There are some holdouts, of course, but those that have businesses that depend on guns that won't shoot our customers rely totally on what is said in the popular media and the rumors we hear sometimes and it's pretty obvious we're not getting the right information or good information. How do we get it?

Correct, accurate, responsible information should be in your email or mailbox or smart phone, in digest form, of every failure reported that seems to have credibility, from every firearms manufacturer on a regular basis. With the web of interconnectivity between people, businesses, trade organizations and hobby groups available today, it should be easy. Law enforcement has to help with make, models and serials in every report. "Dropped rifle and it shot him." was in a game warden report one time and I thought he should have been fired for incompetence. How can a biologist not have basic powers of observation? Details are extremely important. Any forensics investigation involves basic information and for generations firearms accident reports have not had that information included.

Who remembers Taps Tips and It Happened This Way every month in the sports magazines? That would be a good place to try educating the generation coming up still wanting to know how to zero a rifle and field dress the results, but as we've already heard, Ruger has tried to educate the public about the dangers of the old model single actions for the last 40 years, but less than half have taken advantage of it. There are some that will *not* send their gun in to be fixed.

If people don't know to look for these defects, or how to look for them, how can you expect to have enough investigators to handle the load?

The investigators are already in place. They are only lacking one thing. Just one detail would completely change the entire way we do gun business. They need to know what has already happened. There would be a period of angst and agony as the popular notion that guns only shoot when somebody pulls the trigger is absolutely and provably shown wrong. Guns *do* kill people and they all have to be pointed somewhere all the time.

There is no safe direction to point an unsafe gun. And some guns are unsafe *by design*. That will cause some debate, for sure.

And that will bring you publicity and give the politicians the perfect reason to try again to outlaw them all.

I'm getting impressed with the back row. Your questions and comments are as important as the answers.

I'm wondering how anybody could doubt any of it so far. I assume you didn't draw something backwards or just tell an outright lie to us. How can you tell 'people' about a problem without telling the problem to the people?

Better yet, ask him what he has to gain by it.

I have no dog in the fight. I don't make triggers except for special guns for special customers and I'm not asking for any work. I have plenty. I've testified in a couple dozen cases. I'm a slave to what I said because the Court writes it down. The other side has months to read, watch, analyze and rebut what I said before trial. It is a sword fight where only one side has a sword at a time. It can get pretty bloody if you're short on facts. I've not yet gotten a scratch.

When a lawyer asks if the trigger you're holding while being video taped is 'defective' or not, for the record, it is important to know the real and correct answer because the next hundred pages of testimony will center on that answer. It very well could be that millions of somebody's dollars are on the line, too. If it's not right and really right, you could end up in the woman's restroom of the Federal court house when the juror ladies that just laughed at your incorrect answers on the witness stand need to *go*.

I've told every lawyer I've worked with my 'order of dread'. I'd rather be killed than hurt really bad, and I'd rather be hurt real bad than embarrassed on the witness stand. One impeachment is usually the end of a career. I prefer to keep working because somebody needs to be able to tell the mechanical truth and to do that takes a certain amount of education.

To educate the public, without scaring them or calling attention to something we'd rather handle quickly and quietly, will take some finesse by the people that know and love guns.

Several years ago I was on a big pheasant hunt in the midwest where my group of guys was invited to a farm to hunt with a family. We were standing around the farmyard introducing ourselves and watching out for impending possible dog fights when I saw three teenage boys load up their shotguns, put the safeties on, and stuffed them into soft cases laying on the floor of an SUV. We had a small but intense class on gun safety that concentrated on 'what ifs', and when I 'shot' one of the boy's Model 870 with my thumbnail after having him put the safety ON, it made an impression. I asked them to pass the word on to their other hunting partners and let them know there is *never* anything inside the car that needs shot so don't put it at risk.

Their rather macho display is the kind of "I'm sure 'nuff ready now!" activity that is passed on from person to person and family to family like a virus. Sometimes you find a family like I did in Nebraska one time that didn't think anybody could take the safety OFF, and still have time to shoot a rooster, so didn't use them at all....Sometimes one person just can't educate the world. I've never been so nervous in all my life!

It's time to wrap it up. Questions and answers are next. I'm impressed by the questions that have poured forth so far. The bad ones didn't get written down so the ones in the book are the ones that I felt needed answering first. I've received feedback during the breaks and other questions have popped up that didn't quite fit the discussion at the time, so they've been saved for last. My case is the mechanism itself. I give voice to whatever actual mechanism we want to talk about. If I haven't seen one, bring one. We'll do a 'Jim Johnson' on it together and figure it out. I'm not an engineer and will defer to those with that distinction in the audience, but please have the calculations done or quickly explainable so we don't get hung up. This has been a long session and I'm ready to hear the applause and go home.

Fat chance of that.

Well, I could go to Denny's and shake the ketchup bottle with the lid off again. I got applause for that.

I'd like a self-moderated debate that gives all sides a chance to state their case in about a minute.

I really appreciate the back row sticking around. I realize it must be like Chinese opera on a motel Muzak to some of you here, but now it's your turn. Please be civil and reasoned in your questions and statements. There are victims among us that absolutely know the dreadful truth. They're waiting on you to see and accept that truth, acknowledge their pain, and then *teach it* to others so nobody else has to suffer like they have. You've been very vocal and sometimes effective in swaying public opinion while really not being in possession of all the facts at the time. Please, either have the facts or defer to someone that does.

Ah, teacher. Did you forget this loaded rifle aimed at the bowling ball back here?

Thanks for reminding me! What is the very first thing you do with *any* loaded gun when you want to make it safe? We've learned that 'activity' leads to failure, so the first thing is to mentally trace where the bullet will go if the gun fires when you touch it. Remember the rice farmer? Remember the booby trap Ruger in the dresser drawer? Make sure the bullet path is clear before the gun is even touched. That applies to *all* kinetic guns, which a single action revolver certainly is when the hammer is cocked.

As for the rifle in the back of the room aimed at the bowling ball, they were just imaginary teaching aids. You can relax now.

I welcome any question you may have. If I don't know the answer, I'll try to figure out how to find it.

To the gun guys in the back, here's your chance.

This is mechanics. It's what we do.

Have you ever wondered what they call the medical student who graduates last in his class? They call him 'Doctor'.

Let's see how good a mechanic you are.

Questions and Answers

I appreciate being called on first.

My boys and I have always owned Remington shotguns. My dad started with the Model 11 and bought me an 870, 20 ga. When I was eleven years old. I did the same for my boys as well as two nephews and a neighbor kid. We have always been safe hunters and we have NEVER had a single problem with any of them. We've always cleaned them the best we could and I couldn't ask for a better shotgun. Now you say they not only can fail, but they do! You even say the safety is no good.

My question, sir, is what do I do now? Now that I know they can fail, how can I in good conscience continue using those guns?

You become an even better teacher of firearms safety because you know the truth. Pass that on to the next generation or two and let's try our best to stop putting economy ahead of common sense. *Insist* on good guns and insist on good information. Ask Remington what their plans for the safety of your guns are. If you agree with me that a gun that can fire without the trigger being pulled *and* can fire with the manual safety ON is a defective gun, then you were sold a defective product and they should tell you about it and figure out a way to fix it.

Now that you know of the defect, you will be more careful when you load those guns. Don't you think if the defects were better known, we would have fewer accidents? I've challenged shooters for many years to try to consider the possible consequences of one of the 'kinetic' guns loaded for 24 hours straight. Some ranchers will say, "Mine is that way 24-7/365. What's the big deal?"

The big deal is a toddler sitting with his mom in the parking lot of a grocery with a 'kinetic' Mossberg M500 on a gun rack in the back window. On safe, of course, but that makes no difference when the little boy pulls himself up to look out the window and breaks the weak plastic ears that hold the trigger mechanism in place. It killed the guy walking by.

Keep them unloaded until you're going to use the gun. Have it pointed safely when you do load it. Some guns can fire while on safe. Kinetic guns should be left Unloaded in storage and disconnected while carrying.

Teach yourself and your young hunters to always have the safety ON until the barrel is catching up with the game he's about to shoot, and *always* 'break the action' when around other people. Those with semi-autos should unload out of range of others. It's easy to see you're in the right crowd when six guys come together at the end of a pheasant drive and all have come within about 20 yards of each other and a big rooster flushes square in the middle of that space...and nobody has a loaded gun. That is the way it should be

Guns react to energy inputs. Opening, closing, bumps, knocks, drops and jars are all prime times for tenuous engagements to slip and the gun to fire. Use particular care during activity. A youngster was killed when his buddy jumped a ditch. A golfer lost a thumb when he dropped a shotgun. A young man lost his life when a cheap pistol fell from a holster.

I hope you've learned that guns that are storing their energy, the 'kinetic' guns that want to shoot but can't, should be locked, blocked or intercepted to positively prevent an uncontrolled discharge. You have to find out or figure out what locks, blocks or intercepts. In the Remington Common Fire Control, the answer is absolutely nothing. We can clearly see that by simply looking at it.

Did that answer it?

Not really. We're already careful and I was taught exactly as you describe. I want to know how to fix the damned things!

There is no 'fix' for the mechanism that would satisfy John M. Browning without starting over from scratch. Pumps and autos take different triggers. To make them 'common' with other models takes a *compromise in design.* It has killed people and injured many. The misunderstanding of the mechanism by firearms examiners has incarcerated two men 'that I know of' unjustly.

<The back row is antsy and they have a spokesman.>

We are convinced the big reason you say the RCFC is somehow dangerous is because you and Butters own a patent of a safety that 'fixes it'. You're just mad Remington didn't bite and pay you off.

You're referring to the BBIS or Belk-Butters Intercept Safety. It was never represented as a product for sale. It was an idea that could be retrofitted into existing trigger groups. Our idea was to have an option of a safety that goes right in your gun, but you don't have to send the gun in to have it installed. Just change the part that falls out when the two dimpled pins are removed. That would make it simple, economical and more likely to be done by the customer than something complicated that risks the whole gun.

The practical *design* was an interceptor safety. Nobody *ever* said it was the safety the RCFC should have. It's nothing but a practical and economical fix that could be supplied to shooters like the man down front. The BBIS looks the way it does because I used the machines that I had available. Of course there are better ways to do the same thing, but I needed something to show the jury. Theory is not enough for them to understand... I'm sure some here can now agree with that.

I see your question and will save us time. The interceptor only works *after* the trigger has failed. That is very rare, but it *does* happen. The interceptor safety is a rope attached to the horse that is jerked on when the barn door closes behind him and keeps him from running totally away. There are a bunch of BBIS units on competition guns and hunting guns as 'test subjects. None have failed to operate or caused any problems, but it's not ready for prime time in the current configuration.

But, you told Remington if they bought it, you'd retire. They showed you saying that under oath somewhere.

What would you say if you washed and waxed your car and detailed it real nice and somebody offered you ten times Blue Book for it? Nice car! Lots of work, but it was just done for your satisfaction and to prove a point. Suddenly you're asked if somebody wrote a check for about $25million you wouldn't go do something besides talk to lawyers?! Damn right I'd retire. Then I'd write more books, train a new generation of gunsmiths, cops, mechanics, writers, teachers and shooters and go somewhere and hunt something with rifles I've built and would enjoy using them more. My job is not as an expert witness except by the court's definition. I don't have a company that investigates accidents and advertises in magazines lawyers read. In fact, I've never advertised anywhere. I do the job because I enjoy it and charge the lawyers for the days of my life they interfere with.

Where'd you come up with that figure of $25 million?

I was told by the lawyer I was working for when the BBIS was being examined and patented that it was customary to receive roughly a dollar per application if the patent is licensed. He said it was a basic figure to work from given the cost of retrofitting. I told him anyone offering a check for half that was subject to paper cuts as it was jerked from his hand. It became a standing joke among us.

You know that feeling you get when the Power Ball gets to $300 million or so and you think about what it would mean if you won it? I'm seeing everybody nod. Now, think of the feeling you get when you realize you're not going to buy a ticket, so it ain't happening. I'm a gun guy, not a money guy. I'm still trying to think of a better, simpler, more economical but absolutely safe way to redesign every dangerous gun I've ever seen... and I'm not finished! There are a lot more ideas to put into steel and points to prove. Nobody is standing still in this matter. Or, at least I hope they aren't!

Since I've got more of my minute left... I was happy to be paid to make the prototypes. I was even happier to be paid to escort those prototypes to New York and be deposed for an upcoming trial. I traveled to Little Rock and to S. Texas for trials and sat on the witness stand and defended the BBIS theory, and Tom Butters demonstrated how the BBIS worked and how it would have prevented the accidents involved. We were told early on that Remington only built what they invented. Great! Get after it. What are they waiting for? The purpose of the BBIS was to improve the safety of Remington's common fire control and *others that use similar systems.* It was shown as proof-of-concept and accepted as that.

That brings my question, please. What are the gun companies doing to fix the problem of unsafe designs?

The short answer is 'nothing much'. I would imagine there are new models somewhere on a drawing board, but I don't know if they follow basic safety guidelines or not. Historically speaking, it'll have more plastic, less work, less quality and a higher advertising budget. That sells a lot of guns these days. I would like to believe all the gun companies would do all they can to assure their products are safe. It will only take a couple more hits to the insurance industry to make them just quit writing policies for guns. That will put most small makers out of business, unless they have a gun like S&W, Colt DA, Ruger, and a multitude of others. If the design can be understood to be *safe,* the victim of a shooting suffered another kind of accident. Sooner or later there will have to be a firearms underwriter's laboratory that actually examines guns for their potential. Put them under a bright light and interrogate it like the terrorist it can be. Interrogate it until Murphy is exposed and either eliminated or be made perfectly known to the world. Murphy's hiding places should be shown to gun owners and buyers and sellers.

To reiterate, guns should fire only by someone pulling the trigger as an act of defense, sport, or being a crook in some way or other. "The gun did it" should never, ever be a consideration, but we know now it has to be considered. When the gun does it, the insurance company pays, sometimes millions.

You said yourself, reality is durable and I agree with you, but you also say there're 30 million or so suspect guns. You can't stuff the genie back in the bottle. What do you do?

That's why the world needs critical thinkers and lookers and people with experience telling the others the life lessons and hard earned knowledge that most courts keep secret. People that know guns should know how to identify a dangerous one. No one should take just the word of anybody when you consider gun design, and that includes mine. Look at the mechanism and think like John M

Browning, Paul Mauser, Georg Luger, Carl Walther and the other pioneers that knew their guns had to be safe or they couldn't sell them. At the time the great advances were being made in firearms it was because the whole world was either at war or planning on going to war soon. Safe guns are very important to the infantry.

Sporting guns are usually cheapened copies of those military designs. Why cheapened, you ask? Because when arms companies sell to governments the price reflects the very best they can do....and get away with. Deer hunters are not going to spend that much money unless it looks expensive, and that drives the price up even further. It becomes a matter of who do you trust and how much you want to spend.

I suggest a lot of very expensive guns are paying insurance premiums with an increasing amount of money. Shouldn't insurance be cheaper for a safe product? Safe drivers get a break, how about safe gun companies? I don't know. I'm asking them.

Sir, my brother was killed by a thousand dollar gun and somebody told me it was 'common knowledge' they shot people by accident, but I can't find anybody that knows of his case. It was in Alaska and he bled to death after getting shot in the leg by his own gun. Can you tell me anything about it?

I think so. I know of it. The gun was a .454 caliber Casull revolver and one of the best made guns on earth but it has one flaw that cost your brother and some others great grief. It'll happen again, too, but Alaska keeps pretty well informed on gun problems and the world of the Casull revolvers is still pretty small and well informed. The word is trickling out, just not yet in complete form.

The big Casull revolvers have a safety that operates off the hammer. It's a single-action revolver and that certainly makes sense. With the hammer down, the firing pin is blocked from access by any energy. At a certain point, fairly early in the motion of the hammer, that safety system is disengaged and a trigger transfer bar system rises into place to make the gun safe until it reaches full cock and a finger pulls the trigger. So the first safety is part of the hammer motion and the last part operates off motion of the trigger.

It was found in testing that there is about a .020" gap between those two safeties that is just far enough into the hammer motion as to supply just enough energy to fire the cartridge. That means, an event you can't duplicate by thumb because of the 'finger spring' being present, *can* happen if the hammer snags on something just exactly 'wrong' and causes a discharge without a trigger pull. One fired from a rain slicker being removed, several have happened while ducking through bear tunnels and brush. I've seen a loaded round with a seriously dented primer that did not fire. It was taken from a guide's 'bear gun'. It showed the defect but he didn't suffer from it. Luck plays a very large part, no matter what you call it.

Those thong keepers over the hammer and full flap holsters are important and Alaskans and others that carry the Casulls have that pretty much understood, but probably don't know exactly why.

So, you're saying brush happened to hit that magic twenty thousandths of an inch as a hunter ducked under it?

Yes it did. At first, it was thought the hammer was pulled to full cock and then somehow the trigger got pulled, but some expensive holsters were cut apart to assure the trigger was in no way involved, that left as the only answer the .020" gap fairly early in the hammer motion.

John Taylor, the old English elephant hunter that wrote several books of his daring exploits, tells of the gun bearers in Africa that commonly carry a rifle by the barrel with the center part of rifle balanced on a shoulder, finding hammer guns cocked and of course both barrels pointed at the boss's head as they go through the brush. It was enough of a problem that the better makers put locking hammer safeties on dangerous game rifles.

Sir, I'm a reporter and need facts and figures. How many people have been hurt or killed by what kinds of guns. It seems easy to me to see what guns are dangerous by what guns are on the reports. Somebody should have charts and graphs just like the Uniform Crime Report does.

Nobody knows for sure. There have never been standardized questions on the various accident reports that give consistent information. For many jurisdictions, spanning decades, accident reports only listed the caliber and sometimes one other identifying factor like 30-30 carbine or 30-06 pump. We can surmise a Winchester or Marlin was the 30-30 but the only 30-06 pump around is a Remington with a RCFC in it. That accident is not listed as 'Remington' though it has to be. There are thousands of such reports in state archives that can never be properly inventoried. The numerous 'Remington Stories' indicates there are very few 'Winchester stories' to tell.

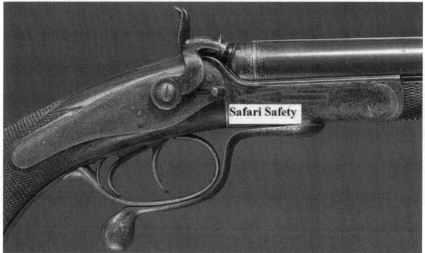

MacNaughton double-gun with Locking Hammer or 'Safari' Safety

Where is the NRA in all this mess?

That is a question I can't answer, but is probably available from the NRA. I've been a member many times because you have to buy your way into their big show every year, but I'm not actively involved. I would hope they would accept information from factual sources as valuable to the cause, but advertising money from full page ads can't help but have a tempering effect on their response. Maybe if more members that have had mechanical failures would remind them of their obligation to shooters, it would be different. The old Dope Bag column in the American Rifleman was my favorite until suddenly advertising dollars sponsored it. The column changed to the point of being useless. They used to talk about 'heart beat and respiration'. Now it's eyelashes and toenail polish.

You've skipped all over the place and mentioned several times variations that are more dangerous than others. Is there a time line and some way of telling what trigger you have?

You didn't mention what gun we were talking about, so let me generalize the answer.

There are many reasons why a gun is changed to another variation. Minor parts are almost always changed in some way that seems inconsequential. If these small variations are studied closely they almost always fall into one of three categories:

Dependability... The first generations of some guns show weakness in design or material that makes them break too often. Remington's Model 1100 extractors broke, early Ruger Number Ones had a bad forend hanger attaching point.

Safety... Many times a small change is to correct a defect. I suspect the H&R M58 that shot the girl in the gut was a gun that was almost immediately changed to a shorter firing pin. The Howa/Vanguard bolt sleeve is a great example. In the case of Remington's Walker trigger, there is a progressive move to more safety with every change. The early, stamped and folded housing, dual sear Walkers are very dangerous. Each change improved the reliability of the trigger, but the connector remained the same and that, as we've seen, is the root of the failures in the Walker trigger. While accidents might have become more rare, they were just as deadly. One is too many.

Economy... This has changed dramatically since WW-II and even more so through the antigun government administrations. A bad political climate almost always causes a cheapening of guns. The greatest driver of poor quality is the desire for economy in mechanisms that *must* have a certain amount of precision, and we all know that precision costs money.

Looks... Many times this is just collateral damage to the other three. Sometimes it's to fill a niche market. Commemoratives fit that category. In many guns built to be 'collector's items' right off the shelf, the overall quality says they really weren't expected to be used and I would imagine the majority of them are still in boxes somewhere waiting for the price to go up. The real quality guns built at the same time are already way up.

Rifle styling goes in waves by continents, it seems. Most American sporting guns followed the 'thin, trim, balanced' European model until Roy Weatherby and Tom Shellhammer and some others created the 'California' style. Thankfully the well formed Ruger line of rifles designed by Leonard Brownell stopped the gaudy-with-corners look by the mid '80s and even Remington offered 'oil finished' stocks and well done matte finishes. Now, the Europeans are copying Weatherby and their guns are ugly and ours (were) getting better.

If you use car styling as a rough analogy, we're in the early '70s as far as quality but the late '50s tail fins are now in Europe. And then the car companies made clown cars.

The various firearms models and variations of those models many times occupy an entire book. Stuart Otteson has written about bolt action rifle design and excellent books on trigger mechanisms. Frank DeHaas Senior and Junior have books that describe trigger mechanisms as well. Information is power and I highly recommend them all.

How many more stories of gun failures have you got that you didn't talk about?

A few, but they are either redundant or serve little purpose in this class. There is one that is extremely interesting just because of how it was so unusual and it involved a Remington Model 700 Walker trigger that probably acted just like it was supposed to, but the victim was shot in the head with a .270 Win. 150 grain R-P Power Point. The unusual part was that he was drinking a beer and smoking a cigarette when the first EMTs came on the scene.

The bullet was recovered and the entire event recreated on paper sufficient to realize the trigger had probably been pulled. Great photographs of the scene and the recovery of the bullet at the scene made it a matter of looking real close and doing some measuring and knowing how guns work and bullets look after impact with various objects, and it became clear what had happened.

If you're being obscure, mysterious and obtuse to keep us in suspense, it worked. Now please tell us how somebody was shot in the head with a .270 and the bullet was recovered and he lived through it. That bullet goes through 12 inches of deer every time!

It's still fun for me to get a rise out of the back row even though you've calmed down a lot since we started.

The gun was stored in a hard case on the floor of a lawn mower shed that was located so the entrance was under the wide eaves of the house. It was raining and the owner of the rifle was worried about it being out in the shed. He'd been hunting that day and thought it would be OK, but now he had his doubts. Just a minute later his dad heard the loud bang of a rifle firing behind the house and went out to inquire. His son was lying on the sidewalk between the house and mower shed. There was blood under his head and a terrible looking wound above the right ear. He ran back inside to call for help. While the 911 operator was going through their usual inane sounding conversation to one impatiently wanting assurance an ambulance is on the way, the wounded son came in the back door, went to the fridge and popped the top on a beer and lit up a cig. He was bleeding but not that bad. The pictures taken by the EMT shows bright skull bone showing in a ditch half inch wide about two inches long right up the side of his head. The police came and took photographs and found the bullet in the puddle of blood. Their excellent photos also showed a white powder in the blood.

I was sent the photos and the bullet and given access to the rifle, but didn't need it. I started picking up bullets that have hit various things when I was too young to hold my own rifle. My dad shot some out at the county road camp range and I'd dig through the sandy butts and take home a pound of pistol bullets to play with. Some had hit sand, some had hit wood and some had hit other bullets. I could tell those apart by the time I could read. The .270 bullet showed a bone smear on one side, a concrete or stucco wall on another and white paint from something made of wood on another portion of the bullet.

.270 bullet impact with Wood (left) and Stucco (right)

.270 bullet glancing impact with Bone

By knowing a .270 rifle has a one in ten twist in it, I could calculate from the pictures taken how far the bullet traveled from his head to the stucco wall to the eaves of the house. The lawyer had a private eye go out and run a tape on the house and found my guesses and reality to be within about 10% of each other. In ballistics investigations, that's pretty good! It was clear by the pictures taken at the scene before anything was disturbed, the trigger had probably been pulled by a sloppy nylon carrying strap with about a foot too much 'tail' to it. The tail end of the strap was tangled in the rifle and the case latch, and it was easy to see the interaction that probably happened when the guy reached in on hands and knees and pulled the rifle out of the case by the front of the carrying strap. That caused the rifle to rotate to the right that created the correct height and angle to ricochet a bullet built for Elk off his skull, rotate two and a third times before hitting a stucco wall, then deflecting about 35 degrees upward while rotating four and a half times, and then impacting the painted wood of the eaves.

There is lasting injury and no doubt the rifle shot him, but the lawyer looked at the facts, spent some money on the PI instead of sending me out there and accepted my interpretations of the case to be true enough to decide not to pursue it. The rifle had been put in a case loaded with the safety off? Then a guy picks it up from the front to drag it to him? And the first thing he thinks of is a beer? Those are the jobs that pay me nothing, but keep me working because they're so interesting to figure out.

I find it hard to believe it paid you nothing to figure that out.

I'll talk about guns to anybody as long as you don't waste my time. As a matter of fact, I probably rolled that case into several more that the attorney presented for examination. At some point, they totaled up to a day of time I'd rather be paid for than have for my own and I sent him a bill, but commonly my bills to lawyers are 50% or less of 'professional experts' that I'm often pitted against. I'm what is called an 'un-papered expert'. I'm not sure if that means I'm a mongrel among purebreds or that my 'diplomas' don't count because they aren't framed.

Plaintiff's attorneys tend to specialize and gather cases of a kind together so there is a short list of calls I get from the same lawyers with a possible case to look at. Rarely do they become sure 'nuff law suits with blizzards of paper and details to keep track of. Sometimes half a dozen 'possibles' come together at the same time and I'm hired to go to NSI and examine the guns and watch Remington's people examine it and document what we find. I charge money to leave home to work.

My goal is to eat regular but pay no taxes and make guns safer. Does it make sense, now?

Sir, early in the session I told you I had a Remington rifle with a RCFC in it. I didn't know what that was or what it meant or how badly my trigger is messed up until you explained it. The recapture angle that gives it extra security you talked about is totally gone. The gunsmith had stoned them flat and then, like you also said, when I looked under a magnifying glass, I could see everything was rounded and downright SCARY! What do I do now?

RCFC bad trigger job. Recapture angle is gone.

Please call Remington with your gun in front of you so you can answer any question that they have. Tell them somebody has worked on the hammer and sear and they're messed up. Tell them the trigger group is out of the rifle and suggest just sending the RCFC instead of the whole gun. It seems they're making an effort to help and that would be a good protocol to institute for people that find they have a bad trigger made worse. Just drop it in a small prepaid box and it comes back the same way.

I don't want to cause that little monster named 'Dread' to sit on your head at 3 AM and remind you of places that loaded gun was pointed and the safety was doing nothing but preventing *you* from shooting it. The rifle hammer and sear were free to fall off that slick, round surface anytime it pleased. How did Murphy overlook that?

<The pained look told me that bell won't be un-rung.>

I think I 'adjusted' some just like that because it was what the customer wanted. That's my business. What do I do now?

Yours is a rough road and one that I travel every day. All I can say is 'be true to your learnin' and never forget your place in the universe. I think that was my Granddaddy's way of saying, remember you're nothing but a speck and what you learn is only valuable if you use it. I admit I adjusted RCFC triggers, too. I can't go back and track them down and you probably can't either. Those triggers are an * asterisk on your conscience along with mine. I see nods all over the room. We're in a bind and it's not unlike what is facing the gun companies. How do they fess up without going belly up? We gunsmiths have a dozen or more 'bad' triggers made much worse to worry about. Most of us in the gun business are 'turnips' to lawyers and they know any blood extracted will be not worth their effort. Insurance is already nearly impossible to buy for gunsmithing activities. Some gun companies have 30 million or more defective guns in use. What do they do?

Obviously every gun is not going to be suddenly repaired, but if they can't be repaired, let's at least recognize them for what they are: *dangerous* to people and by extension, our way of life

I saw a particularly distasteful Hollywood actor slinging around a gun recognized to be unsafe after Hurricane Katrina and acting the tough guy. It's safe to add a coat of firearms ignorance to his already tree-ringed persona. He probably wouldn't listen to reason anyway, but in cases like that, a safe but accidental shooting might have woken him and the public up to the danger.

I still think you're hoping to get rich on somebody else's misery.

Most everybody here has tried their very best to make a deer out of a stump or bush in that time of morning you still can't see color. I did it as a kid until I was convinced it must be a deer. But, my heart said it wasn't. When the deer actually showed up my heart let me know it was a deer! No doubt about that!

Our 'hearts' are like that. In the middle of the BBIS 'fights' where Remington was accusing me of things I'd never even thought of, and at the same time, I was being told multi millions of dollars would be coming my way as soon as Remington realized it was a good idea to make the RCFC safer. I never made plans for any money. I don't count chickens, either. I'm not a gambler.

Anyhow, right about that time was the Elian Gonzales deportation fiasco in south Florida live on TV. I watched a fully militarized anonymous somebody carrying a riot length Model 870 with the slide closed and the barrel pointed on purpose straight at half a dozen terrified people as he jostled for position. With just about heart-stopping dread I saw him bang the buttstock several times on a big refrigerator.

In my heart of hearts, I was very relieved nobody got shot. So extremely relieved! I was also relieved when I really thought about it quite a bit later. I didn't mind at all that what would have been a nationally witnessed proof of the RCFC defect that would almost assure me of an avalanche of money, didn't happen. I'd rather have someone not get hurt and not even know about it, than more money than a circus dog can jump over.

For me to get a raise somebody has to get shot. I'd rather be broke. Think what you will, my heart tells me I'm in the right place in the universe.

In the mid '90s a lady and her son were shot with one bullet in a subdivision near where we lived in Reno. The news said it was accidental but the guy went to jail. I remember Belk and Butters from a news report and now I'd like to know what happened?

Memory tests are always fun.

The gun was a Calico 9mm 'ugly gun' that had jammed up on the range. The owner's buddy had borrowed it and stuck a badly reloaded round in the chamber. The trigger group was removed from the bottom and the odd, rotary magazine from the top of it. That way the remaining barrel and receiver couldn't fire by pulling the trigger. The trigger was totally gone from it.

I think it was days later, the owner of the gun got it from the closet to see what the problem was. He got a screwdriver and tried to unlock the stuck bolt. One of the parts he pulled on was the spring-loaded striker. He pulled it back and it slipped off the screwdriver blade and the gun fired. The bullet went through his house wall, a pine board fence between properties, through the adjacent house wall, through the chest of a one year old boy and lodged in his mother's leg as she had him propped up in bed playing patty cake with him. Thankfully the boy and his mom recovered.

The gun operated as it did because there was nothing to prevent it. It did not fire as part of 'normal and expected use'. The guy that owned the gun had some other problems other than being a very bad gunsmith and he was jailed for it.

How do you know that's what happened with that Calico gun?

If we take what we were told to be true and the magazine and trigger group were removed from the central receiver, the firing pin striker was the only part that would move from energy applied by a screwdriver blade and it could only be applied in one direction: towards the compressed, stored energy direction. When the screwdriver slipped, that energy was released and fired the gun. It was a simple 'follow the energy case' that took less than two hours to explain to the lawyer.

And you charged him to do it, too, right?

I've forgotten now. I'm a gun guy not an accountant. Tom and I were already in Reno for the American Custom Gunmaker's Guild show and we always combine trips if possible to save lawyer's money.

Sir, I'm retired now, but I'm reporting back. I know now some reports I did were 'incomplete' at the very best. Some might come back at 3 am and torture me. Firearms Exam and Tool Marks school never taught me any of this, but I can sure see it now. What can I do?

I worked as a county jailer for over a year before 'going on the road' as a criminal shift deputy. Every prisoner says he shouldn't really be locked up. Most can massage, turn, twist and knot the skinniest thread of bad logic into a hawser that should get them out. Most of the time it's either funny or just pitiful.

But, there are some who should *not* be there. There *are* innocent people doing the hardest time on earth. Their lives have been stolen because time cannot be bought, sold, bartered for, or replaced. The fact is, at least one man is doing life because a firearms examiner thought he knew enough to testify to the facts of the gun in question. He did not and may still not know to this day. I'll send him a book and hope he does the right thing.

But, you asked what to do about it…

I would approach the district attorney and see if you can explain where your doubts are and why. *Nobody* wants to admit they're wrong. Nobody wants to carry the burden of knowing they were wrong and continue to cover it up, either. Nobody with a conscience, anyway. Sometimes corporations forget about that part. A company can fire their 'conscience' and replace him with someone that knows no history. The problem is solved in the board room but they remain out in the field for generations.

I gave an example of changing testimony by gaining additional facts with the 'why does it have a connector?' testimony. As more information becomes available your opinions have to change. That is only sensible. When it comes to a man that lost his wife and his life to an accident involving the RCFC and is still hearing cell doors slam, it becomes imperative to let the new information be known. I would go to the highest ranking lawyer in my jurisdiction and let him deal with it. Call me if you need help.

Where are the tough questions from the back row?

Tough questions have been asked of us! Some still won't believe a word of it. I fear we're still split along 'responsibility lines'. It just seems so clear to some that guns are imperfect, we know that. Why make waves and risk it all?

I see your point, but that seems so 'selfish' somehow. Responsibility starts with the idea of accepting it. If you're a dealer selling unsafe guns, you're stuck square in the middle. If you knew it was unsafe, why did you sell it? Who's responsible for putting that dealer in that position?

Every maker of every firearm should take responsibility for their firearms from conception to use in the field. Every step along the way should be examined according to the risk to the public. We, as responsible gun owners and users should insist on a higher degree of engineering scrutiny of firearms design. We've all seen the pictures of dozens of blown up guns that circulate around the internet. Some of those are design related, many are human mistake related, but most are predictable materials failures by obstructions or overloads. Some of the design related failures are from somebody not knowing how much stress a gun part takes in operation. Some don't care.

You mean engineers don't care?

No ma'am. They're paid for a very specific task. Many times junior engineers are given one part and told to figure out how to make it cheap. Is that part of a charcoal grill, a can opener, or a gun? Some times they don't know. Professional Engineers, like Tom Butters, have a public obligation to warn of unduly dangerous conditions in their field of expertise.

It is the 'designer' of firearms that I have a beef with when they ignore history in search of profit. The straight-pull Knight muzzleloader is a good example. When production engineers, CNC machinists and marketing people get together, gun quality can take a dive while gaining converts and fans in the hunting fields and marketplace at the same time. The antigun sentiments of the pillow biters and city-centered whiners keep gun owners on the defensive so if somebody suggest their latest, most-accurate-ever purchase is somehow faulty and dangerous there could be a boycott of the magazine for subversive activities! So, bad engineering and cheap manufacturing kills somebody and the customers of the company won't believe it because theirs hasn't messed up, so it must be another antigun trick. Education stops right there. That has to change.

Sir, I am a mechanical engineer and during the period of this rather drawn out class, have already come up with solutions to the bolt action trigger problem and there is no good reason not to incorporate it.

Such an advancement in firearms safety would be extremely

valuable and any company that has it would automatically be the 'top dog'. But if you'd like to whisper it to the class, I'll try to explain why it hasn't already been done.

It can't be a mystery at all. By combining safety systems already in place, it's easy to make bolt action rifles as safe as your precious DA revolvers. Just put an inertial firing pin in the bolt and a transfer bar system in the trigger. Problem solved, rifles are now safe. Maybe I should design guns for a living. It seems easy.

Your ideas have been tried numerous times. They *do* make guns safer, but they make bolt action rifles shoot like slingshots flinging oval rocks.

Accuracy *relies* on three things and *depends* on many more. Straight, Square, and Solid has to be the foundation of accuracy. Then, the speed between the time the sear gets out of the way of the cocking stud and the ignition of the primer (the so called 'lock time',) bedding, barrel quality, crown, and many other factors work in concert to make a rifle accurate. Then, as we used to remind ourselves in gunsmith's school, "It could be the loose nut behind the trigger that causes the problems."

Inertial firing pins 'rattle' too much. Transfer systems add mechanical linkages to the firing process and complicate matters to the detriment of accuracy and dependability. The miserable performance of the very cute and practical Ruger 77 in .22 Hornet proved multi-piece firing pins are very bad for accuracy. Even set triggers are avoided because pure accuracy is degraded by the delay in lock time. A light trigger pull in varmint shooting and sports accuracy contests benefit more by a light trigger pull than the quick lock time, so the set triggers are becoming more popular.

I fully agree with you that bolt action rifles can be made more safe, but a gun company that spends the hundreds of thousands of dollars it takes to bring a new model to market that shoots in random directions *by design*, won't sell and your job is probably lost. I think you've made an illustration of what's been going on too much already. Just because it works safely doesn't solve the problem at all.

Shooters want a 'good trigger' and a 'bad trigger' sinks marketing ships. For gun safety to benefit, a newly designed 'safe' trigger has to be liked enough to be used. To be used by good shooters it has to be very crisp, short and almost light enough to be dangerous for the target shooters, and heavier for the hunters, BUT many guns are suitable for both. Somehow, rifle triggers have to become 'more certain'.

I've seen a dozen guys on the internet demonstrate an FSR with a XMP trigger. Can you explain them?

Not without examination. By design the trigger can't fail in that way unless out of adjustment or broken. As far as I know, no one has actually looked to find out. They act like its some kind of proof of something. It is, of course, it's proof of a *very* dangerous rifle but no investigation has been done whatsoever. Maybe we can change that.

OK, this seems a good place to examine a mechanism you call safe and dozens of people say they have failures. Where would you start the investigation with the XMP trigger?

This is a timely exercise in the Fall of 2014. The XMP trigger, by design, relocates the trigger to the proper position under the sear each time the safety is engaged. *If* the trigger has a fire-on-safety-release, FSR, what has to have happened?

The sear or the trigger must be broken, so the sear is only supported by the safety lever?

Exactly right, but keep going. Why didn't the rifle just 'follow down' when the bolt was closed? Notice the shooter on YouTube applies the safety when the bolt is open. That turns the safety lever into the trigger.

I have one that will FSR sometimes and neither the sear nor trigger is broken.

Then, the questions become numerous and the analytical mechanic asks them in rapid fire sequence. Some have to be seen and some have to be tested and some have to be figured out: What is the trigger pull? Is the trigger pull the same each time? Is there movement to the trigger besides what is preloaded by the return spring? What is the gap between the safety push bar, visible on the left side of the trigger, and the face of the trigger? Are the trigger and sear in alignment? What's the condition of the contact surfaces? How much sear engagement? Is it constant in trigger relocation? Are the seals broken? Are the pivots square? Is the cocking stud too short? Was the receiver bored true? Trying to figure it out without having it to look at is like trying to buy watermelons by long distance.

Obviously, it takes hands-on examination and application of a Mark One calibrated eyeball to figure out something that is happening outside its *design*. Many times, over an amber drink with a little ice, Tom Butters and I have marveled over the physical 'tests' of the opposing expert witnesses as they 'examine' a gun. When a gun mechanic examines a gun, it is by looks, feel, sounds and variations in pressures and motions that gives the mechanic a semi-visual 'picture' of what is occurring out of his vision. It is hard to see the opposition wrecking any chance of actually being able to point to the failure, but our job is to teach a jury, not the opposing experts how the gun operates and fails.

The ghost of Jim Johnson says, "Know what you're looking for first. Study the *design.*"

If the design is good, how can it fail? Aren't the design failures you've been talking about the critical part?

The design has been the focus of this effort because so many people don't appreciate the lack of design perfection in firearms. Materials and how and in what condition they're applied is just as important to the inherent safety of the design. We could be seeing a slow motion train wreck in the XMP if investigations show the material is not lasting long enough or is failing in very dangerous ways. I've seen and own XMP triggers that are showing damage from much less use than is normal, but it still takes a microscope to see it.

I've been trying to hammer home a very important point and the

XMP problems may demonstrate the importance of it. It takes a certain amount of precision to make a safe gun and precision costs money.

Precision must start with good materials. Good materials are expensive. Check any tool store for a wrench. Compare prices based on materials and workmanship. You usually get what you pay for in a product. Compare the materials and workmanship in a new gun to the tool store tools. Wouldn't you agree that too many guns look like the Indian copy of the Taiwanese imitation of the tool Japan stole the design for? Who remembers 'Crescent wrenches' made by Crescent?

Plastic was introduced by Remington as nylon buffers in the back of the old Model 11 and replaced the Bakelite of the earlier guns. Stampings, castings, formed metals and plastics of various sorts came into firearms, primarily by Remington at the end of World War Two. We see the results. Can we be surprised?

This should be a continuing dialog so we all can learn. Everybody here has had experiences with firearms I haven't even seen yet. If you see something wrong, speak up!

Guns are dangerous by nature, but can only be *safe by design.*

Sir, I'm dead center the back row and I came here today under considerable duress. I'm the firearms expert in my area and my customers believe me when I tell them about guns. I made a big deal of the anonymous emails and internet postings I sent when you were trying to help the Barbers. Some of my customers thought it was funny what I was doing to disrupt the conversation. I quit when somebody ratted me out, though.

I'm just like you. I was making pistols out of bicycle spokes and casting lead hand grenades and setting the woods on fire with homemade black powder before I could drive. I made rockets and haunted Sears and Roebucks for ten dollar Chilean '93 Mausers to experiment on and counted on Santa to bring me more little round BB packages than my five year old hands could carry. I also am fascinated, enthralled and enthused about guns of all kinds. I have to admit, you have more Army time and you obviously got more from one-armed Jim Johnson than I did. I tried for an hour to make a Colt rebound spring fit in the side lock shotgun he'd given me to learn. Up until today, I thought he just picked on me with the parts swapping thing. It just made me mad! Quite frankly, so have you over the years.

Today, as a shadowy silhouette, I apologize. I'll probably never have the courage to do it man to man and eye to eye, but I want you to know and the Barbers to know and all the people that have suffered that I was ignorant of the very facts I thought I knew so well, but now I see a level of firearms hidden from me before now. What can I do to help?

Well, you just helped me a *lot.* Thank you. Now for the rest of the folks that need to know; I don't expect a bunch of disciples to spread out and teach the facts, but it would be good if you bought your local Hunter Safety instructor a copy of this book. I figure gunsmiths and Hunter Safety instructors are just about equal in numbers. If somebody could make sure the Scout leaders and camp counselors and NRA ranges and CCW instructors all have a copy and somebody sends one to their favorite gun writer....the smoke should be cleared and the gun companies will be forced to fess up in less than ten years. I plan to see that happen, but we all know that those most needing to know are the least likely to listen.

Anything further?

I just want you to know I completely understood at least 5% of the words you uttered and might get to 50% by looking at the pictures real close, but my whole family shoots and hunts and reloads their own ammunition and trips over stacks of gun magazines that overflow the coffee table. They still talk about the time my son was caught shooting a cannon he'd made out in a lake where people were trying to fish and his daddy told him to throw away the gunpowder he'd made and the cannon was thrown in the river. Then the hollow tree he hid the gunpowder in got hit by lightning and would have burnt the whole place if the rain hadn't a put it out...but my question is this: When is volume two?

Thanks, Mom. Rest in peace knowing I probably got it out of my system the first time, and I'm sure the statutes of limitations have run out anyway.

November, 2014

10th COMMANDMENT
Learn the Mechanics and Handling Characteristics of Your Firearm.
Not all guns are alike. They have different mechanical characteristics
that dictate how you should carry and handle them. Anyone who plans to
use a firearm should first become totally familiar with the type of firearm it
is and the safe handling procedures for loading, unloading, carrying,
shooting and storing it.

Dedication

This book is for all the victims and their champions. It is time for
your stories to be told. May your sacrifices serve to warn others of
the dangers when the pursuit of profit (or just plain ignorance)
causes death and destruction.

Made in the USA
Columbia, SC
30 November 2021

50038097R00252